Political Economy and
Critical Engagement in South Africa

Political Economy and Critical Engagement in South Africa

Essays in Honour of Vishnu Padayachee

Edited by
Rajend Mesthrie,
Robert van Niekerk and
Imraan Valodia

UNIVERSITY OF KWAZULU-NATAL PRESS

Published in 2025 by University of KwaZulu-Natal Press
Private Bag X01
Scottsville, 3201
Pietermaritzburg
South Africa
Email: books@ukzn.ac.za
Website: www.uknpress.co.za

© University of KwaZulu-Natal 2025

All rights reserved. No part of this publication may be reproduced or transmitted in any form or by electrical or mechanical means, including information storage and retrieval systems, without prior permission in writing from the publishers.

ISBN: 978 1 86914 574 3
eISBN: 978 1 86914 575 0

Project manager: Sally Hines
Editor: Karen Press
Typesetter: Susan Elliott
Proofreader: Judith Shier
Indexer: Christopher Merrett
Cover designer: Marise Bauer, M Design
Front cover images: Vishnu Padayachee, featured in *Garden & Home* magazine, August 2000
Back cover image: View of Umkomaas River

This work is supported by the National Institute for the Humanities and Social Sciences

Print administration by DJE Print Solutions, Cape Town

Contents

Acknowledgements		ix
Acronyms and Abbreviations		xi
	Vishnu Padayachee: Themes and Perspectives *Rajend Mesthrie, Robert van Niekerk and Imraan Valodia*	1
1	Reflections on Intellectual Engagement in South Africa *Vishnu Padayachee*	16
2	The Significance of Umkomaas: Place, Time and Community in the Making of an Academic *Rajend Mesthrie*	25
3	Curiosity and Commitment: Vishnu Padayachee, Global Scholarship and Politics in Durban in the 1980s and 1990s *Robert Morrell*	42
4	The Measure of Mistrust: African Artisanal Gold Mining and the Geopolitics of the Barbarous Relic *Keith Breckenridge*	58
5	National Development and the Enlightenment Gaze: A Joint Project with Vishnu Padayachee *Bradley Bordiss*	76
6	The Richness of Development Measures in Post-Apartheid South Africa? *Dorrit Posel*	100
7	The Political Economy of Nationalism and Populism: South Africa, India and the United States *Gillian Hart*	109

8 The Economics of the Feasible in a Democratic South Africa: Anglo American and Economic Policy 125
   Gavin Keeton

9 An Unfinished Research Agenda on the South African Reserve Bank: Linking Academic Scholarship and Monetary Policy 134
   Jannie Rossouw

10 Heterodox Economics and Macroeconomic Policy-making: A Critical Review of Vishnu Padayachee's Contribution to Fiscal Policy 145
   Seeraj Mohamed

11 South African Capitalism: Conversations with Vishnu Padayachee 163
   John Keith Hart

12 Reflecting on Ideas, History and Institutions in South African Social Policy through the Prism of Vishnu Padayachee's Method 182
   Robert van Niekerk

13 Locating Vishnu as Engaged Political Economist: A Personal Journey 198
   Ben Fine

14 Accounting for Some Recent Deaths in South Africa: Zombie Economics Blues 217
   John Sender

15 Regional Integration as an Instrument of Industrialisation: Perspectives from South Africa 238
   Nicolette Cattaneo

16 The Engaged Intellectual, the State and Civil Society in the Post-Zuma Era: Lessons from the Eastern Cape 266
   Janet Cherry

17 'Exodus without a Map', 2: What Happened to the Durban Moment? 281
   Edward Webster

18 Race and Identity: The Revival of the Natal Indian Congress, 1971–74 293
   Goolam Vahed

19	The University of Durban-Westville: Transition to an Open University and Merger with the University of Natal (1990–2003) *Jairam Reddy*	312
20	Graduate and Research Outputs and Efficiency in South African Universities *Pundy Pillay*	328
21	Books, Bannings and Activism: Excerpts from an Interview with Omar Badsha *Rajend Mesthrie and Robert van Niekerk*	341
22	An Intellectual in a Time of Struggle: A Tribute to Vishnu Padayachee *Alec Erwin*	350
23	Vishnu Padayachee: An Economist's Tribute *Imraan Valodia*	358
24	The Most Special of Special Assistants: A Tribute to Vishnu Padayachee *Jairam Reddy*	369
25	Four Slips and a Gulley: Reflections on Cricket in Vishnu Padayachee's Life *Suresh Naidoo*	373
26	Vishnu Padayachee at Ike's: A BMW Life (Books, Meanders and Wine) *Joanne Rushby*	377

Notes on Contributors	381
Index	389

Acknowledgements

Thanks are due to family, friends and colleagues of Vishnu for supplying photographs and related materials, some of which are used in this book. Almost all photographs used were taken by them. The *African Guernica* painting by Dumile Feni is taken from E.J. de Jager, *Images of Man: Contemporary South African Black Art and Artists* (Alice: Fort Hare University Press, 1992). The National Heritage and Cultural Studies Centre at the University of Fort Hare is the custodian of this artwork.

Funding for the editing and the Symposium in Honour of Vishnu Padayachee ('Scholarship, the Intellectual and Fundamental Social Change', 20–22 July 2022, Wits Club) was provided by the School of Economics and Finance and the Southern Centre for Inequality Studies, University of the Witwatersrand, and a UCT Faculty Block Grant to Rajend Mesthrie. The Wits School of Governance supported flight and accommodation arrangements for some participants to attend the symposium. Fatima Sadan assisted the editors to arrange the symposium and supported the book project, too.

The publication of this book was supported by the National Institute for the Humanities and Social Sciences.

The editors are grateful to UKZN Press, and especially Sally Hines, for their collegial collaboration throughout the preparation of the manuscript. All authors have praised the astute copy-editing by Karen Press.

Acronyms and Abbreviations

ACCORD	African Centre for the Constructive Resolution of Disputes
ADB	African Development Bank
AEC	African Economic Community
AfCFTA	African Continental Free Trade Area
ANC	African National Congress
ARV	antiretroviral
AU	African Union
BC	Black Consciousness
BCM	Black Consciousness Movement
BLS	Botswana, Lesotho and eSwatini
BPC	Black People's Convention
CACM	Central American Common Market
CEO	chief executive officer
CHE	Council on Higher Education
CIA	Central Intelligence Agency
CMA	Common Monetary Area
CODESA	Convention for a Democratic South Africa
CODESRIA	Council for the Development of Social Science Research in Africa
COMESA	Common Market for Eastern and Southern Africa
COMSA	Combined Staff Association
CONSAS	Constellation of Southern African States
COP	Conference of the Parties
COSATU	Congress of South African Trade Unions

CS	caesarean section
CV	*curriculum vitae*
DA	Democratic Alliance
DBSA	Development Bank of South Africa
DEP	Department of Economic Planning
DHET	Department of Higher Education and Training
DRC	Democratic Republic of the Congo
DTI	Department of Trade and Industry
ECOWAS	Economic Community of West African States
EPA	Economic Partnership Agreement
ET	Economic Trends Group
EU	European Union
FINCE	Financial Institutions in the Natal Colonial Economy
FOSATU	Federation of South African Trade Unions
FRD	Foundation for Research Development
FTA	free trade area
GDP	gross domestic product
GEAR	Growth, Employment and Redistribution
GR	graduation rate
HIV/AIDS	human immunodeficiency virus/acquired immunodeficiency syndrome
IDC	Industrial Development Corporation
IEJ	Institute for Economic Justice
IFI	international financial institution
IFP	Inkatha Freedom Party
IIE	Institute of Industrial Education
IMF	International Monetary Fund
ISER	Institute for Social and Economic Research
ISI	import-substituting industrialisation
ISP	Industrial Strategy Project
JSE	Johannesburg Stock Exchange
LPA	Lagos Plan of Action
MERG	Macroeconomic Research Group

MPC	Monetary Policy Committee
NACTU	National Council of Trade Unions
NEC	National Executive Committee
NEDLAC	National Economic Development and Labour Council
NEPAD	New Partnership for Africa's Development
NGO	non-governmental organisation
NHI	National Health Insurance
NIC	Natal Indian Congress
NIPF	National Industrial Policy Framework
NP	National Party
NPR	National Population Register
NUMSA	National Union of Metalworkers of South Africa
NUSAS	National Union of South African Students
OAU	Organization of African Unity
OPEC	Organization of the Petroleum Exporting Countries
PAC	Pan Africanist Congress
PG	postgraduate
PTA	preferential trade area
PV	photovoltaic
PWC	post-Washington Consensus
RDP	Reconstruction and Development Programme
RDP BD	Reconstruction and Development Programme Base Document
RE	renewable energy
RISDP	Regional Indicative Strategic Development Plan
RVC	regional value chain
SACHED	South African Committee on Higher Education
SACP	South African Communist Party
SACTU	South African Congress of Trade Unions
SACU	Southern African Customs Union
SADC	Southern African Development Community

SADCC	Southern African Development Coordination Conference
SADESMO	South African Democratic Students Movement
SAICCOR	South African Industrial Cellular Corporation
SANCO	South African National Civics Organisation
SAPPI	South African Pulp and Paper Industries
SARB	South African Reserve Bank
SARS	South African Revenue Service
SASCO	South African Students Congress
SASO	South African Students Organisation
SCOF	Standing Committee on Finance
SDS	School of Development Studies
SOAS	School of Oriental and African Studies
SRC	Students' Representative Council
SSPP	Sustainable Settlement Pilot Project
TARP	Troubled Assets Relief Program
TBVC	Transkei, Bophuthatswana, Venda and Ciskei
TFTA	Tripartite Free Trade Area
TUT	Tshwane University of Technology
UDF	United Democratic Front
UDW	University of Durban-Westville
UG	undergraduate
UJ	University of Johannesburg
UK	United Kingdom
UKZN	University of KwaZulu-Natal
UL	University of Limpopo
UN	United Nations
UND	University of Natal (Durban)
UNECA	United Nations Economic Commission for Africa
UNISA	University of South Africa
UP	University of Pretoria
US	United States
VAT	value-added tax

VoC	Varieties of Capitalism
Wits	University of the Witwatersrand

Vishnu Padayachee
Themes and Perspectives

Rajend Mesthrie, Robert van Niekerk and Imraan Valodia

Vishnu Padayachee (31 May 1952–29 May 2021) was first and foremost an economist. He was also a scholar, intellectual, bibliophile, humanist and committed activist for social justice who stood out strikingly from his peers. As well as being a trained economist, he was also an autodidactic historian who developed sustained interests in local history, finance history, economic policy, economic development and the history of sport in South Africa. His knowledge of sport from an early age, above all of cricket, was phenomenal. He was a polymath who was widely considered to be of exceptional erudition and personal integrity. His intellectual influence on the critical, non-Stalinist 'left' political tradition was felt by the generations of academics and policy-makers he robustly engaged with, as well as by students fortunate to be mentored by him. Many of these students became influential scholars in their own right.

These traits are attested to in all the chapters of this book, from the opening three chapters that detail aspects of Vishnu's early life and career to the middle section of essays on economics and political economy, to the closing section of short personal tributes. The germ of this book lies in the special symposium, 'Scholarship, the Intellectual and Fundamental Social Change', held in honour of Vishnu at the University of the Witwatersrand (Wits) on 20–22 July 2022, where he had held a distinguished research professorship for seven years until his untimely passing in 2021. All the contributions to this book except one were first given as working papers at the symposium, which was a successful three-day event attracting a range of academics and family members. The exception is the first chapter, 'Reflections on Intellectual Engagement in South Africa', which we publish as a posthumous contribution from Vishnu, based on an essay he wrote in 2020 as part of a project that he had been undertaking with Eddie Webster and Robbie van Niekerk on the role of intellectuals and engaged scholars in three eras: the 1970s, the 1980s and the 1990s. The essay published in Chapter 1 was meant to initiate such a project and is in fact cited and discussed in Chapter 17 by Eddie Webster. It is included here as an overview of, and look-ahead to, many of the themes fleshed out by scholars in this book, all of whom had known and worked closely with Vishnu. It could equally have stood as a poignant closing chapter to the life and intellectual interests of a great scholar.

Several themes occur in the 26 essays that constitute this book, spanning the humanities, economics, politics, sport and activism in the apartheid and, especially, post-apartheid contexts of South Africa. Where the humanities are concerned, there is attention to (a) the significance of family, early education and place in shaping an intellectual trajectory; (b) the history and political transformation of the University of Durban-Westville (UDW) and the connections between it and the later merged, deracialised University of KwaZulu-Natal; and (c) the world of antiquarian books and book trading in Durban. In his chapter, 'The Significance of Umkomaas' (Chapter 2), Rajend Mesthrie presents a historical overview of the small town on the south coast of KwaZulu-Natal where Vishnu was born, brought up and educated. Umkomaas combined features of a small-town resort, an international rayon-factory hub, sugar cane plantations and rural life generally – all in reasonably close proximity to Durban. Mesthrie – a lifelong friend of Vishnu through high school, university and their lecturing and research careers – poses the question of how it was that a rural upbringing in a small town amidst the constraints of apartheid education could produce a scholar with the outstanding qualities referred to above. In answering this question, he traces influences on Vishnu of his family, school and local communities. Mesthrie's chapter stops at Vishnu's university days, but it is worth recording that he was the most renowned economics student of that era, and later a mentor to other important figures in South African academia like Imraan Valodia, Adam Habib and Lumkile Mondi. Chris Torr, a leading economist and former lecturer at UDW, wrote: 'If my memory serves me correctly, it was in 1974 that I first became involved with postgraduate teaching. And Vishnu was my first honours student.

While that is special, I would, of course, have remembered Vishnu had he been my 1 347th honours student.'[1]

Likewise, Chapter 3, 'Curiosity and Commitment', by Rob Morrell also begins with an account of 'place' and the early influences of Umkomaas, notably from the town's Italian community, which afforded slightly more cross-racial contact than was typical at the time of apartheid and repression. More broadly, the chapter deals with Vishnu's activities in terms of global scholarship and the local Durban politics of his times. On the basis of an interview in 2017, Morrell also highlights Vishnu's early career at UDW, as a lecturer in economics, researcher at the UDW Institute for Social and Economic Research (ISER), and member and secretary of the Academic Staff Association and later the Combined Staff Association. These bodies were crucially involved in transforming the campus, steering it away from the stranglehold of its apartheid beginnings and Afrikaner control. ISER hosted members of the very influential Economic Trends group. Vishnu's standing as an economist, lecturer, researcher and departmental administrator is emphasised in Chapter 23, 'Vishnu Padaychee: An Economist's Tribute', by his former student Imraan Valodia, himself a professor of economics and currently pro-vice chancellor at Wits.

The importance of place (this time of Durban) features strongly in other essays, amidst a focus on economics, education, opposition politics, trade unionism and intellectual life (in Chapters 3, 11, 13, 17, 18, 19, 21, and in all five tributes in Chapters 22–6).

Central to Vishnu's intellectual contribution was his astute academic leadership in the task of building an anti-apartheid academic project of the highest scholarly merit and progressive purpose, in the context of the South African political transition of the 1990s. Several chapters therefore, unsurprisingly, have a focus on higher education in relation to South African history, politics and the economics of transformation. Chapter 19, 'The University of Durban-Westville: Transition to an Open University and the Merger (1990–2003)' by Jairam Reddy, deals with the era of transformation at UDW, a university created under apartheid for Indian South Africans, seen through the eyes of its first post-apartheid rector and vice chancellor. At this university Vishnu Padayachee received his BComm, BComm (Hons) and MComm degrees in the 1970s and 1980s. The period was a very turbulent one for the university, resonating with the national anti-apartheid campaign and characterised by marches and boycotts. Reddy was appointed rector and vice chancellor in 1990, in the dramatically changed political circumstances exemplified by the unbanning of the African National Congress (ANC) and other political parties in 1990 and the subsequent release from prison of Nelson Mandela. In his chapter Reddy reflects on the significant transformative changes and challenges at the university, including the admission of greater numbers of black students, recruiting a progressive and better qualified staff, fundraising, and attention to increasing the postgraduate intake and research output. Vishnu, then a senior researcher at ISER, was seconded to the rector's office as special adviser for a period of three years. Chapter 24, 'The Most Special of Special Assistants', also by Jairam Reddy and originally written as an appendix to Chapter 19, was excerpted as a special tribute to Vishnu's role in that process (see also Chapter 3 by Robert Morrell). In Reddy's words, 'Vishnu's calm and sober judgement, his disarming style, his deep knowledge of the context of the university and its environs together with the fact that he was a young and rising star in academia provided enormous strength to the office of the rector.' Thus, Reddy refers to him as 'the most special of special assistants'.

Morrell's chapter also covers Vishnu's move from UDW to the historically 'white' and 'liberal' University of Natal (Durban [UND]) in 1995, where he eventually became head of the School of Development Studies. (After the passage of the Higher Education Act [No. 101 of 1997], UDW was merged with UND to become the University of KwaZulu-Natal in 2001.) The chapter highlights Vishnu's role, and that of his colleagues like the now late, highly influential historian Bill Freund, in in-depth, innovative, engaged and transformative scholarship focused on the Durban area. Those who were part of the School of Development Studies across all levels of the staff establishment remember Vishnu's intellectually innovative, rigorous but also deeply humane headship with fondness (see also Chapter 23 by Imraan Valodia). Judith Shier, for example, who was the website and information manager at the school, said: 'I worked under Vishnu at Development Studies. He was a marvellous head – and a model of how to be a good human being in a university institution, and the world.'[2] Dori Posel, later the Helen Suzman Chair and Distinguished Professor in the School of Economics and Finance at Wits, wrote: 'In addition to being a first-class academic, Vishnu was the most wonderful head of school – completely on the ball, efficient, fair, far-sighted and astute (qualities which were even more welcome after the reorganisation of the university in the 2000s).'[3] The reorganisation brought increasing managerialism, and a lack of transparency and debate as documented by Nithaya Chetty and Christopher Merrett (2014).

In the light (or perhaps Eskomian darkness) of the continuing economic crisis, Pundy Pillay's chapter, 'Graduate and Research Outputs and Efficiency in South African Universities' (Chapter 20), continues the focus on the theme of higher education, by analysing the efficiency of resource utilisation at universities. This was a matter of concern to Vishnu, who himself supervised more than fifty master's degree dissertations and a number of doctorates to completion. Pillay scrutinises the relationship between university funding, enrolments and graduate outputs in four South African universities. The data show that graduation rates, particularly at the undergraduate level, are exceptionally low across these institutions. He suggests that education policy-makers in South Africa need to focus urgently on how graduation rates can be raised. The context of increasing numbers of young people desiring access to universities amidst decreasing resources clearly demands this.

Academic engagement and the role of intellectuals in societal change is a theme that runs through most of the book; it is a topic on which Vishnu reflected and published extensively. Chapter 22, 'An Intellectual in a Time of Struggle' by Alec Erwin, is both a tribute and a short essay in its own right on South Africa's political struggles. Erwin was a lecturer in economics at the University of Natal from 1971 to 1976, a leader in the trade union movement, and the minister of trade and industry and of public enterprises in President Mandela's and President Mbeki's Cabinets. In his chapter, he reflects on the intricacies of and challenges to the role played by intellectuals in the South African democratic struggle. He considers Vishnu to have been an exemplary intellectual who played a full and richly constructive role in the transition to democracy. Erwin's assessment is that Vishnu's work with the rising trade union movement in the late 1970s and 1980s, and his inputs into the formulation of economic policy, were particularly important, as was his contribution to building the institutions of the new democracy.

A further link between intellectual engagement and political struggles can be found in Janet Cherry's critical reflection on 'The Engaged Intellectual, the State and Civil Society in the Post-Zuma Era' in Chapter

16. Cherry argues that while the development studies discipline was an ideal academic space in which to induct students into the process of exploring new forms of social and economic organisation, it was far from easy to translate ideas about development into practice. The chapter details two initiatives based on development studies programmes at Nelson Mandela University in the Eastern Cape province that show the difficulties of working across university academic spaces and state institutions in participatory action research. These initiatives concern the politics of land and sustainable informal settlements as well as of more formal townships. While striking a sombre cautionary note about political chicanery, power and violence, Cherry reflects on the still relevant role of the intellectual in searching for viable means of achieving sustainable development (see also Chapter 13 by Ben Fine).

Concluding the humanities strand running through the book is a focus on the book world of Durban. Chapter 21, 'Books, Bannings and Activism', is based on a portion of an interview with Omar Badsha by two of the editors of this book, Robert van Niekerk and Rajend Mesthrie. Badsha, an acclaimed photographer, artist, historian and political activist, was part of an active resistance group in Durban from the 1960s onwards. The full interview (in the editors' possession) provides a window into the underground world of resistance politics. Its opening sections were selected for inclusion in this book because of the details they provide concerning three significant mentors who influenced Vishnu in matters of books and politics: A.K.M. Docrat, Ike Mayet and Enver Motala. Badsha engagingly reflects on the role of literature, art and creativity in the struggle years, which the resistance group tried to utilise in seeking ways of earning a living while advancing the underground struggle.

Chapter 26, 'Vishnu Padayachee at Ike's', by bookshop owner Jo Rushby, is a tribute to Vishnu in relation to Ike's Books. Now a landmark of Durban 'left' cultural life, the bookshop's offerings combine an interest in struggle and activism, colonial history, political ephemera, collectibles and memorabilia. Vishnu joined the original owner, Ike Mayet, in running the bookshop in the 1980s. Rushby has run the enterprise in the new millennium, now as a proprietor herself. The subtitle of her chapter playfully points to the more debonair side of Vishnu's life, with his attachment to his BMW, good wine and meanders through the KwaZulu-Natal Midlands in search of collectible books and rarissima. Vishnu's role at Ike's was also acknowledged by prize-winning writer

J.M. Coetzee, a special guest at the formal opening of the bookshop in its new premises in 2001.

The political thread running through this companion to the life and work of Vishnu has already been highlighted. Politics as a theme receives explicit and dedicated treatment in two further chapters, which have a strong focus on the cultural and (de)racial politics in Durban between the 1960s and 1980s. Chapter 17 by sociologist Eddie Webster, 'Exodus without a Map, 2' revisits 'the Durban moment' to argue that resistance to apartheid took a decisive turn in Durban in the early 1970s. The Durban labour strikes forcibly placed class politics, as articulated in the black workers' movement, at the centre of the non-racial liberation movement, continuing into the early 1980s. Webster critically examines the argument put forward by some theorists that an embryonic political theory sensitive to class mobilisation and dynamics emerged at that time, which could have led to a more pro-poor and egalitarian post-apartheid developmental path. He considers the chapter to be a contribution to an unfinished conversation between Vishnu and himself on what happened to the Durban moment (touched on by Vishnu in the opening chapter of this book). Sadly, Webster himself passed away in 2024, before this book went to press. We are grateful to have one of the last essays of this profound intellectual and activist in this volume.

The theme of anti-apartheid politics, race and identity in Durban is explored further in Goolam Vahed's chapter on the revival of the Natal Indian Congress (NIC) in the early 1970s, 'Race and Identity' (Chapter 18). Black Consciousness (BC) activists criticised this move, believing that it undermined their attempts to overcome racial divides through building a movement that focused primarily on the politically oppressed under the system of apartheid and included Africans, coloureds and Indians. The subsequent arrest of BC leaders meant that the NIC, aligned to the United Democratic Front, was the pre-eminent anti-apartheid organisation among Indians in the 1980s. Paradoxically, the majority of Indians in KwaZulu-Natal voted for the former white ruling party when the country's first democratic election was held in 1994. Vahed raises the question of whether a unified black or non-racial political body would have led to a different outcome as far as the Indian vote was concerned.

The majority of the essays in this book, as expected, deal with economics and political economy. Among Vishnu's most significant and influential scholarly contributions was a careful dissection, as an economist, of the failure of the neoliberal paradigm to address the underlying structural inequalities of South Africa's racial capitalism. In the face of this failure, he was one of a group of like-minded scholars positing a considered, alternative redistributive economic development strategy based on the insights of heterodox, post-Keynesian economics. Some of these scholars formed part of the Macroeconomic Research Group (MERG), and the economics of transformation in South Africa and the report produced by MERG thus feature strongly in several chapters of this book. Appointed by the ANC under the auspices of Nelson Mandela in 1991, MERG was led by a steering committee that comprised representatives of the ANC, the Congress of South African Trade Unions (COSATU) and also the South African National Civics Organisation (SANCO), a civil society formation. The committee was chaired by the ANC Department of Economic Planning head Trevor Manuel. It comprised a core team of Vishnu Padayachee, Ben Fine and John Sender, led by Vella Pillay, with a number of researchers located primarily across the historically black universities also making contributions.

In a detailed report released in 1993, MERG envisioned a two-phase 'crowding-in' approach to South Africa's development. The first phase would be a state-led social and physical infrastructural investment programme focusing on housing, education, health and physical infrastructure investment as the growth drivers. This would be followed by a more sustainable growth phase that would see private sector investment kick in more forcefully as growth picked up (MERG 1993: Chapter 1).

On 3 December 1993, the MERG policy framework was presented to the public at the Rosebank Hotel in Johannesburg, where it was disavowed by Trevor Manuel as not representative of the economic policy thinking adopted by the ANC. This claim flew in the face of the original request from the ANC for the MERG team to prepare a comprehensive series of proposals for macro-economic reform. Moreover, the ANC had been kept abreast of developments within MERG.

The story of MERG is related in detail in *Shadow of Liberation* (Padayachee and Van Niekerk 2019). As Padayachee and Van Niekerk (2019: 103) argue,

> [what is] critical to understand is that the summary and neo-Stalinist dumping of MERG by sections of the ANC leadership meant that this created the momentum for agents in the ANC,

politics, business, civil society and the academy, to abandon independent and critical thought, and to fall behind a 'default' market friendly economic policy position. This could be summarised as 'there is no alternative', in the process paving a path (largely hatched in secret) that led in mid-1996 to the production of the Growth, Employment and Redistribution programme (GEAR) with the announcement that it was 'not negotiable'.

Despite all the controversy, the MERG report was later published by the Centre for Development Studies at the University of the Western Cape, as a book titled *Making Democracy Work: A Framework for Macroeconomic Policy in South Africa* (MERG 1993). In addition, forty-five research papers and reports were produced by the MERG research teams over two years, and dozens of young economists were trained.

Seeraj Mohamed writes on Vishnu Padayachee's contribution to economic thinking about fiscal policy in South Africa in Chapter 10, 'Heterodox Economics and Macro-Economic Policy-Making'. Mohamed, who is deputy director for economics at the South African Parliamentary Budget Office, writes that MERG presented a vision of how to address the legacy of unemployment, poverty and inequality resulting from colonialism and apartheid – a vision directed towards transformation of the South African economy. The success of economic policy, including macro-economic policy, would be measured by the extent to which there was progressive redistribution and increasing employment in a growing economy. Mohamed accepts that corruption, state capture and poor management in the public sector are major reasons for the poor state of the South African economy. However, equally causal in his account is the role of neoliberal ideology and its poor economic outcomes for the majority of citizens.

Drawing on what he describes as Vishnu's historicised method, Robert van Niekerk brings out an added comparative dimension in Chapter 12, 'Reflecting on Ideas, History and Institutions in South African Social Policy through the Prism of Vishnu Padayachee's Method', as he sets out and ponders on some of the historical and institutional lessons of the eras of the 1940s and the 1990s. Van Niekerk reflects on the continuities and discontinuties of current social policy initiatives with previous historical attempts at effecting redistributive social policy. Specifically, he critiques government policies on health, welfare and education aimed at comprehensively meeting the social needs of citizens. He points to inherent contradictions in the ruling party's attempts at implementing egalitarian social policy through governance institutions established during the apartheid era, and which were originally established to serve the racialised, exclusionary purposes of apartheid development policy. Van Niekerk further contrasts the equity-focused, redistributive economic underpinnings of MERG, as the core of a proposed future development strategy, with the government's choice to privilege economic stability and growth through the market, as a precondition for social development in the post-apartheid era.

In Chapter 11, 'South African Capitalism: Conversations with Vishnu Padayachee', John Keith Hart describes his personal relationship with Vishnu and locates him in his city, Durban, as someone who built new institutions and social networks. The chapter summarises approaches and findings presented in key joint publications that focus on South African development, from the 1860s onwards, in African and world economic history through the concept of 'national capitalism'. Hart sketches national capitalism's rise and fall at the global level and identifies its collapse in the 2020s as the cause of the current world crisis. His concluding remarks refer to South Africa's present problems, and to Vishnu's example as 'a beacon in the darkness'.

Parallel to the accounts by Mohamed and Hart, Ben Fine's chapter, 'Locating Vishnu as Engaged Political Economist' (Chapter 13), reflects upon the disastrous state of the post-apartheid economy, especially when assessed against its aspirations and potential. Fine argues that the fate of post-apartheid economics has been equally dismal, in sharp contrast to the apartheid period during which the nature of the apartheid economy was both closely examined and critically assessed from a variety of perspectives, deploying political economy analytical tools. Like Mohamed and Van Niekerk, Fine is critical of the neoliberal orthodoxies that now flourish in both policy and discursive worlds, leaving political economists with the need to compromise between being heard by the powers that be and retaining intellectual integrity. Like all the authors focused on economic policies in this book, Fine argues that Vishnu Padayachee addressed this challenge with considerable acumen, displaying the breadth and depth of his scholarly talents.

John Sender's chapter, 'Accounting for Some Recent Deaths in South Africa' (Chapter 14), deals with South Africa's health crises in terms of political economy. According to his analysis, the HIV/AIDS pandemic prefigured some of the policy responses, nationalistic posturing and xenophobia that resurfaced as a reaction to the Covid-19 pandemic. The chapter contrasts the differences between MERG's approach to policy issues and that of many economists currently discussing public expenditure on health (and other forms of state intervention required to introduce national health insurance). South African interventions during the pandemics were underpinned by the arguments of mainstream economists, who, Sender argues, had a malign influence on policies in the health and other sectors that still continues today. The National Health Insurance Act (No. 20 of 2023), signed into law by President Cyril Ramaphosa on 15 May 2024, sees the vigorous fanning of the flames of a moral panic about the tax consequences of a national health insurance scheme. Sender, contrarily, foresees the probability of lengthy implementation delays and new opportunities to water down the recently signed legislation.

Sender reminds us that criticism of these mainstream economists and an accurate prediction of the consequences of ignoring the costs and inefficiencies of private sector health provision were published in 1993 by MERG. However, even MERG failed to predict how rapidly alternative analyses and policies would be abandoned, or that orthodox arguments would so rarely be questioned by senior politicians. An attempt to address this conundrum can be found in Gavin Keeton's account in Chapter 8 of 'The Economics of the Feasible in a Democratic South Africa', with a focus on Anglo American Corporation policy. The corporation played an unusually important role in the post-1990 debate about appropriate economic policies for a democratic South Africa. It also played an important role in big business's controversial 1996 'Growth for All' policy recommendations. Keeton recounts that while the subsequent withdrawal of business from public policy engagement is regrettable, the adoption by the ANC of conservative fiscal policies was not influenced by business. It was driven by the ANC's fear of the debt trap inherited from apartheid, and a fear that failing to escape from this trap would place South Africa under the control of the International Monetary Fund and the World Bank.

The remaining essays on economics in the book deal with more specific topics related to Vishnu's interests outside MERG per se. Keith Breckenridge, in 'The Measure of Mistrust' (Chapter 4), considers Vishnu Padayachee as South Africa's most important Keynesian, a view refined in Chapter 13 by Ben Fine. Breckenridge also sees Vishnu as a serious opponent of the hard-money, gold standard doctrine that was supported by the economists associated with the mines. At the heart of the Keynesian argument (and of Vishnu's conflict over the fate of MERG) was trust in expert economists' capacities and intentions for managing aggregate demand. Breckenridge examines how gold has returned to the global economy as the financial instrument of those who do not – indeed, cannot – trust experts and institutions. The chapter explores the explosion of artisanal gold mining across the African continent, now probably the largest single industrial employer with more than ten million workers, in response to the global expansion of mistrust in the institutional custody of monetary assets.

In Chapter 5, 'National Development and the Enlightenment Gaze', Bradley Bordiss, a former master's and doctoral student of Vishnu's, cites their mutual interest in Keynesian economics as a driving force. The chapter applies insights from the history of economics to modern developments in Africa. Bordiss draws on the key elements of economic nationalist thought, from both the mercantilist writers and the post-Adam Smith neo-mercantilists, to mount a counter-Enlightenment defence of African nationalism as a political project. Finally, he considers how the tools discussed in his analysis apply to struggles against neo-imperialism in African countries.

Chapter 6, 'The Richness of Development Measures in South Africa?', by Dori Posel, is concerned with the status of quantitative micro-data in post-apartheid South Africa, focusing on the calibration of unemployment and employment, and on the measurement of income and the poverty rate. The chapter reflects on how disputes over data quality have deflected attention away from more policy-intensive discussions, a disquiet expressed by Vishnu (Padayachee 2006). It argues further that these debates have been important in helping to enrich the quality of indicators that inform the development discourse in the country.

In Chapter 7, 'The Political Economy of Nationalism and Populism', Gill Hart compares the political economy of populism and nationalism in South Africa, India and the US. Starting with Vishnu Padayachee's critique of the 'varieties of capitalism' literature, she outlines a global framework that resonates with his critique and alternative approach in three key ways. Firstly, it supports his insistence that, far from being exceptional, South Africa participates in and contributes to interconnected economic, political and social processes under way in other regions of the world – albeit in an extreme and specific form. Secondly, the chapter echoes Vishnu's attention to combining political economy with cultural politics and practices. This linking of heterodox economics and the humanities implies a refusal of methodological nationalism. Finally, the chapter endorses Vishnu's emphasis on 'the centrality of history and of the global dimension in any account of capitalist development', but always in conjunction with close attention to local specificity and dynamics.

Jannie Rossouw's contribution, 'An Unfinished Research Agenda on the South African Reserve Bank' (Chapter 9), foregrounds the link between academic scholarship and monetary policy. The chapter is informed by the shared interest in the South African Reserve Bank (SARB) of the author and Vishnu, who first met when Vishnu was appointed as a non-executive director of the SARB in 1996. Out of the resulting friendship came several very productive and mutually beneficial research collaborations. Rossouw and Padayachee were joint authors of wide-ranging publications pertaining to inflation and monetary policy. Their research showed that scant academic attention had been paid to the institutional support of monetary policy in central banks and their internal decision-making processes, to the Common Monetary Area, and to seigniorage emanating from currency. As Rossouw demonstrates, these remain fruitful areas for future research, though he laments that Vishnu's collaborative insights will be missed.

Niki Cattaneo's chapter, 'Regional Integration as an Instrument of Industrialisation' (Chapter 15), focuses on Southern African initiatives and obstacles they have encountered. Cattaneo argues that the evolution of regional integration policy on the African continent is connected to linkages between ideas and policy-making in the broader arena of political economy. She draws on the late Thandika Mkandawire's analysis of such linkages over three phases since the 1950s (a development planning phase, a neoliberal structural adjustment period and the 'post-Washington Consensus' phase), and on Vishnu Padayachee's scholarship on ideas, power and policy-making in the context of South Africa's democratic transition. Together these provide insightful complementary lenses through which Cattaneo considers a number of key questions concerning the continent's integration trajectory.

In Chapter 25, 'Four Slips and a Gulley', Vishnu's cousin, Suresh Naidoo, reflects on the major sporting love of Vishnu's life – cricket – despite being brought up in a town that had no playing fields for it. Vishnu's knowledge of the game was phenomenal. As recounted by his cousin, Satya Padayachee (in comments from the floor at the Wits symposium), he even practised doing radio cricket commentaries as a young boy and lost no chance to get his cousins – boys and girls – to join in a game at Lords or the Oval (his nicknames for the front and back yards of their adjoining properties). In his more mature years Vishnu was able to reflect on the history of cricket, as in the 2002 tome *Blacks in Whites: A Century of Cricket Struggles in KwaZulu-Natal*, co-authored with Ashwin Desai, Krish Reddy and Goolam Vahed (Desai et al. 2002). In a personal e-communication with Vishnu via Rajend Mesthrie, Nobel laureate J.M. Coetzee recounted how he had read the book 'lovingly'.[4] Vishnu was later a member of the committee that selected the selectors of the national cricket team. Naidoo takes up the theme of cricket and transformation in his tribute, and also pays fond homage to a young Vishnu as his sporting mentor in the 1970s and 1980s.

We cite an observation by J.M. Coetzee to close this introduction and serve as an epigraph to the chapters that follow:

> I remember Vishnu Padayachee most clearly from Ike's Bookshop in Durban, which he succeeded in turning into a lively centre for the exchange of ideas. In the course of time, he himself developed into an important figure on the South African intellectual landscape. But above all he was a generous soul. We are the poorer by losing him at such an early age.[5]

Notes
1. Personal communication with Rajend Mesthrie, email, 2 June 2021.
2. Personal communication with Rajend Mesthrie, email, 2 June 2021.
3. Personal communication with Rajend Mesthrie, email, 31 May 2021.
4. Personal communication with Rajend Mesthrie, email, date unknown.
5. Personal communication with Rajend Mesthrie, email, 30 May 2021.

References

Chetty, N. and C. Merrett. 2014. *The Struggle for the Soul of a South African University: The University of KwaZulu-Natal: Academic Freedom, Corporatisation and Transformation.* Pietermaritzburg: Natal Society Foundation.

Desai, A., V. Padayachee, K. Reddy and G. Vahed. 2002. *Blacks in Whites: A Century of Cricket Struggles in KwaZulu-Natal.* Pietermaritzburg: University of Natal Press.

MERG (Macroeconomic Research Group). 1993. *Making Democracy Work: A Framework for Macroeconomic Policy in South Africa.* Cape Town: Centre for Development Studies, University of the Western Cape.

Padayachee, V. (ed.). 2006. *The Development Decade? Economic and Social Change in South Africa, 1994–2004.* Cape Town: HSRC Press.

Padayachee, V. and R. van Niekerk. 2019. *Shadow of Liberation: Contestation and Compromise in the Economic and Social Policy of the African National Congress, 1943–1996.* Johannesburg: Wits University Press.

1

Reflections on Intellectual Engagement in South Africa

Vishnu Padayachee

I began teaching economics in 1977 as a junior lecturer in the Department of Economics at the University of Durban-Westville (UDW), a university set up under apartheid by the National Party and designed exclusively for South African students of Indian origin. The government did not anticipate that it would turn into a place of political activism and protest and of intellectual ferment. Many of the brightest minds who led the struggle against apartheid, and have gone on to represent the country in creative and novel ways in politics, economics and society in the early democratic era, had their apprenticeship there in the 1960s, 1970s and 1980s.

My early days as a lecturer were devoted to teaching foundational courses in macro- and microeconomics at undergraduate level. But in 1982 I was asked to teach a new course blandly titled 'South African Economic Problems' to third-year students. That was the beginning of my own intellectual enlightenment, which saw me move away from mainstream economics à la Paul Samuelson's neoclassical synthesis into the beautiful world of Marx and Keynes. I was forced to read up material on the political economy of South Africa. It was not a good time for young scholars trying to find their way into their careers. Many key texts and journals on the political economy of South Africa were banned. But there was a highly effective underground intellectual world where, with effort, you could find almost anything. I not only discovered Marx and voraciously read all of the first three volumes of *Das Kapital*, but found eye-opening articles by Harold Wolpe, Martin Legassick and others, members of the early 1970s generation of exiled Marxist South African scholars who had emerged to challenge the dominant liberal school of thought about race and class under colonialism and apartheid in South Africa. As I worked backwards from the literature of the early 1970s into the early post-war era, I found little that could be regarded as constituting the roots of this later radical tradition. I did find the monumental volume by Jack and Ray Simons (1969), but the book was for me somewhat turgid and caught in the grip and mould of Stalinist-Soviet thinking. It was an important book, but it strangely failed to break out of the mould of an essentially liberal interpretation of race and class in South Africa. Among Communist Party-aligned scholars, Ruth First was a brilliant revolutionary researcher and activist and I enjoyed reading her more open-minded arguments, which I found underground in the Penguin African Writers series. Her books on South African capitalism, but also on Libya and South West Africa, and especially her account with Jonathan Steele and Christabel Gurney of Western investment in apartheid South Africa (First, Steele and Gurney 1972) captivated me, and the third-year course that emerged at UDW included some readings by some of these scholars – Wolpe, Legassick, First and others of that era. My students soon joined me in my enthusiasm for these discoveries. The current dean of the Commerce, Law and Management Faculty at the University of the Witwatersrand (Wits), Imraan Valodia, was one of these eager students and he frequently recounts these engagements with me in the early 1980s.

What we enjoyed most, I believe, looking back, was the sense of freedom we had in our protected university world, despite the tight security that dominated our lives and work. Our intellectual work was essentially that of critique of the apartheid system, of 'racial capitalism' and the relationship between race and class in the making of modern South Africa. Those were exhilarating times of discovery and stealth. My senior colleagues, including the head of the Economics Department, Professor Louis Fourie, were quite liberal in their thinking and gave us the space to express ourselves, within limits of course. We took that space and moved beyond it too.

In 1985–86 I accepted a fellowship at the Paul Nitze School of Advanced International Studies at Johns Hopkins University in Washington DC. William Zartman asked me to teach a new course for them on the political economy of South Africa, and at last I was able to find all the material I needed. I constructed a course free of apartheid constraints that attracted some very bright students from all over the world.

Significantly, and it was the mid-1980s with South Africa in turmoil and under a state of emergency, I found myself thinking more and more about the future, about what South Africa's economy should look like after democracy. I gave a talk at a seminar at Humewood, the Baltimore main campus of Johns Hopkins University, where I reflected on South Africa after apartheid. Looking back, I was mostly wrong in my idealism and optimism (my thesis was that a progressive trade union movement would trump the excesses of a likely African nationalist project and usher in an era of social and economic justice). Who can blame me?

In October 1986 I travelled to York University in the UK to participate in the first of the 'post-economy' conferences, which saw liberal and progressive South African economists and social scientists engage with exiled African National Congress (ANC) activists from London and Lusaka to talk about the future South African economy. Among those present on the ANC side were Harold Wolpe, Rob Davies and Essop Pahad, all famous names. I met Alex Callinicos, the Socialist Workers Party activist, who in a famous exchange on the floor of the conference took on Pahad about some obscure point in Lenin's writings. I cannot recall the details, but it was wonderful to be there to witness this unplanned debate, something that would not have been possible at a conference inside South Africa at the time.

I was too young and naïve to make sense of what has come to be called 'the Durban moment' of the early 1970s – the rise of the working class in protest against capitalist barbarism on the factory floor, of worker organisation and political uprising. Or of the pioneering work around participatory democracy led by Rick Turner, back from his studies in France. But I was hugely privileged to learn about those momentous and revolutionary times when I moved into a flat in Silver Palm Road, Overport, in 1980, and after Enver Motala returned from the UK in 1981 having completed his MPhil in law at Warwick University under Sol Picciotto. Enver was one of the attorneys who, with Halton Cheadle and other young University of Natal law students, represented workers in the court cases that followed the worker uprising of 1973. Enver and his wife, Kulsum, attracted a whole range of new people into my life. I lived in flat 3, they lived in flat 4 above me. Ravi Joshi (tragically murdered in 2001), Alec Erwin and A.K.M. Docrat, as well as the great man of books, Ike Mayet, were regular visitors, and we played bridge every Friday night. Kulsum cooked for us some of the most delicious Cape Malay-inspired food in the world. We were lucky fellows.

My colleague Eddie Webster, whom I did not meet until about 1985 at Wits, was also in Durban in 1973–75, and picks up this story of the Durban moment from his angle [see Chapter 17 of this book – eds]. I met Eddie in the course of researching my first book, *Indian Workers and Trades Unions in Durban, 1930–1950*, published as a monograph in 1985 (Padayachee, Vawda and Tichman 1985).[1] I was in fact looking for Daryl Glaser and Raymond Suttner, and stumbled into Eddie's office to ask about them.

What does this personal narrative tell us of the trajectory of intellectual life in South Africa from the 1960s to now, the subject of my intended work with Eddie Webster?[2] It would not be right to generalise from my experiences, but I think it would be fair, looking back, to say that intellectual life in South Africa among anti-apartheid progressive scholars made a distinct shift from trenchant critique of 'racial capitalism' to policy work for the new democracy. From the late Mbeki years, especially because of the president's genocidal policies around HIV/AIDS and his enthusiastic embrace of neoliberalism, a certain degree of doubt began to colour our work – what were we hoping to achieve through our scholarship; in whose service were we working? That mood grew into one of utter and desperate despair under Zuma, and into deep confusion and outright anger as we emerged after Zuma into an era of debilitating and nihilistic factional politics within the ruling party.

In the early 1990s that shift from critique to policy work was first evident in the important book edited by Stephen Gelb titled *South Africa's Economic Crisis* (Gelb 1991), which arose from the work of the Economic Trends Research Group (ET) that began in 1986. The book represented a clear tension between the old world we knew best (critique) and the demands for more policy work (what is to be done?).

Some critics and organisations did not spare us for our approach. The Congress of South African Trade Unions (COSATU), and especially its metalworkers affiliate the National Union of Metalworkers of South Africa (NUMSA), were unrelenting in their criticism of our work and the book for failing to come up with a viable socialist alternative to South African capitalism. In a blistering polemic in the journal *Debate*, activists and public intellectuals Ashwin Desai and Heinrich Böhmke traced what they termed the current 'retreat' in the thinking and practice of the small group of progressive South African social scientists and economists from the mid-1980s (Desai and Böhmke 1997). The mainly white, male economists in the ET, they observed with approval, were initially closely allied to the non-racial trade union movement and distinguished themselves by being unafraid to criticise the tactics and strategies of the ANC-led liberation movement, when they felt this necessary. An anti-apartheid, 'Bohemian-style' sub-culture, they asserted, knit this exclusive group of intellectuals together. However, with the demise of apartheid, beginning around 1990, the 'bottom fell out of their market'. As the 'new government moved to the right', these critics contended, so the research work and theoretical disposition of progressive economists, 'moved in tandem' with it (Desai and Böhmke 1997: 30–1). Most of the ET, they contended, tossed their main weapon – critique – into the sea, and sought their political rehabilitation as the balance of power shifted to the ANC by quickly becoming consultants to the ANC, and then by providing academic rationalisation for the neoliberal economic philosophy of the new ANC-led government. 'Because this same set had so dominated left-thinking in South Africa, their betrayal has all but crushed a critique of the transition', they stated (Desai and Böhmke 1997: 32).

It is worth quoting here from my inaugural lecture given at the University of Natal in 1997, as it reflects my thinking then of what the future would hold for South African progressive intellectuals, especially in the field of political economy:

> I would contend that the exciting, albeit problematic era, in which university-based academics played an integral, often leading role, as policy advisors and experts to social, labour and political movements, and through which both academics and social movements' leaders learnt so much and pushed one another to the outer limits of their roles and responsibilities, may well have come to an end. It is increasingly as technocrats only that the government may turn to academics, and not only to progressive ones either. Perhaps those academics really serious about contributing to critical and effective policy debates and analysis may, like they did in an earlier period, find more socially useful roles to play in the civil society movements of post-apartheid South Africa.

It is instructive in this regard to take note of Radhika Desai's views on the role of progressive intellectuals in the current context, as set out in her article on think-tanks in Thatcherite Britain (Desai 1994). Conditions in post-Thatcherite Britain, she argues, demand a different role for intellectuals than that played by the Thatcherite think-tanks, or indeed by the Fabian socialist intellectuals in an earlier era. Her conclusion is one which the South African academic Left in general may want to consider in our new context:

> How exactly this [role] is played is still an open question. Gramsci, for one, attempted to envisage a role for an 'organic intellectual', yet the concept was always more programmatic than analytical. For the left today, an intellectual practice which could intersect with social forces, giving them shape and direction, seems distressingly unreal. In our contemporary over-institutionalized intellectual life, this remains nevertheless the real Gramscian imperative (Desai 1994: 64).

This kind of engagement would not, in the current South African context, necessarily imply disengaging from the structures of the state. The real issues in any such engagement within the state would revolve around how such relationships are fashioned (for example, is such participation dependent upon a prior unconditional commitment to political or organisational loyalty or not?); around the space which exists to force socially relevant issues into state debates; and around the way in which progressive academics relate in this very process to civil society movements committed to the broadening and deepening of development and democracy.

A dynamic engagement between South African academics, the new state and indeed the business community may well be sensible and beneficial to wider constituencies, and would also force universities to develop new and creative links within the new society, but I would argue that progressive academics in the new South Africa should resist the temptation to respond to the technological and developmental demands of the state and business in narrow and technicist ways, that is, in ways which run counter to the ethos and culture of university life, which is after all one of the few remaining sites for a critical and humanistic engagement with issues such as poverty, inequality, oppression, exploitation and democracy in contemporary society.

South Africa's transition to democracy and development is far from complete. That is one reason why I would maintain that the task of progressive economists, political economists and social scientists is to seek actively to rebuild relationships with modernising social movements in civil society, while at the same time, wherever possible, to exploit and expand the new spaces opened up at the level of the state by the triumph over apartheid oppression. In case this still sounds too vague, let me advance one possible, more specific task which could be taken on in this context. That would be to develop, debate and contest the theoretical frameworks, policy instruments and organisational forms needed to give effect to an approach to South Africa's reconstruction and development, which Michael Burawoy (1997: 16) has compellingly referred to as a 'state-led reconstitution from below'.

I would concede that a number of problems are beginning to emerge in regard to giving effect to the multipronged approach I have proposed. One is that the strategic and political vision, as well as the organisational capacity, of most civil society organisations, including the unions, have been badly affected by aspects of the transition. The capacity within, and indeed the willingness of, such organisations to relate to the academic community and absorb its ideas in dynamic interaction (as the unions did in the 1980s) have deteriorated. A second problem is a sense I have that the spaces for progressive engagement within the state are in fact closing up rapidly. The government has consolidated a new, highly loyal and pragmatic economic and technical elite, drawn in part from the former progressive economic community, but mainly from the rump of the old apartheid state machinery. Technical economic advice from academic economists may no longer be that important, and progressive ideas and critique from this quarter may not be well received or tolerated for much longer.

However, even if direct forms of engagement with the state and civil society organisations are ruled out for these or other reasons, there still remain challenging and important tasks for South Africa's progressive academics, including its economists, to busy themselves with in the post-apartheid era. These tasks, in John Bellamy Foster's words, could include moves

> to advance a politics of the truth; to avoid easy compromises; to address the immediate and long-term needs of the mass of the

population and of those who suffer the most severe forms of oppression; to search for the common ground of that oppression; to resist ideological claims that 'we are all in the same boat' in this society; to reject what Mills called the 'crackpot realism' that makes the status quo into a kind of inescapable second nature and closes off the future; to fight market fetishism. In short, to avoid making what Raymond Williams called 'long-term adjustments to short-term problems' (Foster 1990: 286).

As I look back to what I wrote in 1997, I can see how wrong I was even in my narrowing optimism. The South African intellectual landscape has collapsed to new lows, not because we are not talented enough or well enough trained in new world politics and economics, but because we have been overwhelmed by the desperately pathetic, factional politics led by the ANC. Our trenchant criticism of the 1960s to 1980s has gone, a distant memory which few practise in their work, and which the new democracy does not value.

Students through the #Fees Must Fall movement and related formations may be reviving Biko's work, as Barney Pityana argues (Pityana 2015), but they have little or no knowledge of anything else, certainly not of Turner or Wolpe, even Ruth First. We have become the 'old people' who matter no more. Perhaps that is right, and new ideas and new organisations may emerge from this ignorance or antipathy.

Notes

1. This book, which was reprinted in 1988, is now out of print.
2. This essay was sent in draft form to Robbie van Niekerk in 2021 and subjected to a light edit for this volume. Given its original title, which we have kept, and its concerns, the essay makes a fitting opening chapter to this book.

References

Burawoy, M. 1997. 'Neoliberal Pitfalls: South Africa through a Russian Lens'. Inaugural conference of the Harold Wolpe Memorial Trust on 'The Political Economy of Social Change in South Africa', University of the Western Cape, 1–2 April. http://burawoy.berkeley.edu/Southern%20Africa/Neoliberal%20Pitfalls.pdf.

Desai, A. and H. Böhmke. 1997. 'The Death of the Intellectual, the Birth of the Salesman'. *Debate* 3: 10–34.
Desai, R. 1994. 'Second-Hand Dealers in Ideas: Think-Tanks and Thatcherite Hegemony'. *New Left Review* 203 (Jan/Feb). https://newleftreview.org/issues/i203/articles/radhika-desai-second-hand-dealers-in-ideas-think-tanks-and-thatcherite-hegemony.
First, R., J. Steele and C. Gurney. 1972. *The South African Connection*. London: Temple Smith.
Foster, J.B. 1990. 'Liberal Practicality and the US Left'. In: *The Socialist Register 1990*, edited by R. Miliband, L. Panich and J. Saville. London: The Merlin Press.
Gelb, S. (ed.). 1991. *South Africa's Economic Crisis*. Cape Town: David Philip.
Padayachee, V., S. Vawda and P. Tichman. 1985. *Indian Workers and Trades Unions in Durban, 1930–1950*. Durban: Institute for Social and Economic Research, University of Durban-Westville.
Pityana, B. 2015. 'The Tip of the Iceberg'. *City Press*, 25 October.
Simons, H.J. and R.E. Simons. 1969. *Class and Colour in South Africa 1850–1950*. Harmondsworth: Penguin.

2

The Significance of Umkomaas
Place, Time and Community in the Making of an Academic

Rajend Mesthrie

In this essay I attempt to put into its early context the extraordinary life of Vishnu Padayachee (31 May 1952 – 29 May 2021) as academic, economist, activist, administrator, humanist, historian, bibliophile, art and antique collector, amateur architect, sportsman, sports lover, humorist and perhaps man-about-town. It is the very incongruity of being born and brought up in an unfashionable backwater, amidst the further segregated confines of South Africa's racial hierarchies, that demands such an enquiry. In the course of the essay, I will refer to my lifelong friend by his first name rather than his full name, Mahavishnu Srinivasan Padayachee.[1] His middle name was that of his paternal grandfather. Had he been born a generation earlier, Mahavishnu would have been known as M.S. Padayachee (and perhaps M.S. for short), but in the modern age of the 1960s he was 'Vishnu' to all, with his middle name not known outside the family.

Place

Umkomaas in the 1950s was a sedate one-horse town – metaphorically speaking. It did host a railway station, with services running one hour north to Durban and two hours south to Port Shepstone. Almost all Afrikaners in the 'village' (as the town was called) were employed by state organisations (the post office, police and railways), amidst a larger community of English-speaking residents, including retirees for whom the town provided an attractive setting. English names of early pioneers and sugar barons still grace the streets: McKenzie Street, Robinson Street, Reynolds Street and McLean Street, among others. Another Robinson

(Sir John), the first editor of the *Natal Mercury*, was a prominent advocate of colonial development south of the Umkomaas River (now officially known by its isiZulu name, Umkhomazi, though both river and town are still 'Umkomaas' to the Indian citizenry) in the 1860s. The town had a large Italian community and boasted an Italian restaurant and ravioli and pasta factory from the 1960s on. The Italians, too, were largely residentially segregated from other white residents in a pleasant section of the town called Saiccor Village, adjacent to Widenham, which I would now like to relabel the Friulian quarter. These were workers and families brought from a lesser-known part of northern Italy to start the South African Industrial Cellular Corporation (SAICCOR) factory in the 1950s. SAICCOR was a large, state-owned initiative producing rayon (cloth derived from wood, or more technically a synthetic textile fibre made from cellulose). In recent times SAICCOR has merged with the global forestry company SAPPI (South African Pulp and Paper Industries Ltd). Together they produce interminable smoke streams and pollutants that reach into the neighbouring areas once set aside for African and Indian occupation and still largely arranged in this manner.

Vishnu completed a short academic article on the economic history of Saiccor (Padayachee 2020). He was very enthusiastic about the project, having based it on community interviews in addition to economics research. The article draws parallels with other industrial towns in South Africa, with Umkomaas being described as 'a small but not insignificant manufacturing town ... [like] Sasolburg and Vanderbijlpark ... both company towns in the Transvaal associated with Sasol (synthetic oil from coal) and Iscor (steel) respectively' (2020: 128). In his essay in this volume (Chapter 3), Rob Morrell provides further insights into the Italian community and its influence on a young Vishnu, using an extended interview of 2017 with him.

The Zulu population resided on the periphery of Umkomaas, having been pushed out to areas like Magabeni, Dududu, Ilfracombe and further inland to places barely signposted, like Vulindlela. Also adjacent to Umkomaas was Amahlongwa, where the poet Masizi Kunene had been brought up and gone to school. This author of the epic poem *Emperor Shaka the Great*, who was later designated Poet Laureate of Africa by UNESCO, lived much of his life in exile in the United States. Likewise, Clansthal – with which Kunene also identified – was adjacent to Umkomaas, and famous for its lighthouse high up on a hill. That beacon was much needed to keep sailing ships away from the Aliwal Shoal. The shoal is a large sandstone reef considered one of the top ten scuba diving sites in the world, complete with corals, sponges and fish, and is not ignored by passing turtles, whales and sharks. Excitement for Umkomaas – apart from the sardine runs – came once in a while by way of a good shipwreck.

'*Umkhomazi*' in isiZulu means the place of the cow whales (Doke, Malcolm and Sikakana 1982: 557), perhaps more evocatively 'place of the great female blue whales'. The modern rendition of the place name in isiZulu orthography is *uMkhomazi*. There is an occasional spelling '*Umkomanzi*', but this is a false etymology, as the name is not connected with the waters (*amanzi*) as such.[2] Yet another official appellation of the area was Lower Umkomanzi for the district, as distinct from the Upper Umkomanzi River flowing past areas like Bulwer, Impendle and Richmond.

The reference to the whales is no mere legend: according to the recollections of now deceased residents, whales would even move up the river about three or four kilometres past Drift, just short of Gravesend, in the 1940s. There are three different pronunciations of this venerable name, rather symptomatic of earlier racial separations: the original *Mkhomázi* of isiZulu being changed to *Umkomaas* mainly among whites (with the first syllable rhyming with *book*) and Indians (for whom the first syllable rhymes with *rum*).

Colonial and later apartheid planning policies reserved the upper parts of the north bank of the river in Umkomaas, the province's third-largest river, to be part of Zululand. (This was contrary to the earlier wishes of Theophilus Shepstone – also known by his isiZulu name, Somtseu – who had plans to carve up the colony into consolidated Zulu areas, rather than piecemeal). This was, however, a part disjunctive from Zululand proper in the north-east of the colony, without the intervening city of Durban and other areas like Ilfracombe close to Umkomaas town. Under apartheid planning, the south bank of the river became reserved for whites along the coast and for Indians slightly further inland.

Initially known as North and South Barrow, Umkomaas was laid out as two townships by the colonial government (Osborn 1964), again showing the intransigence of the river as a divide. The word *barrow* means a hill or mound, and is related to words like *burg, berg* and *borough*. The name is commemorated in Barrow Street,[3] one of the main streets of Umkomaas today, which once housed the cinema (Robin Hood), bank (Barclays Dominion Colonial Overseas), hotel (Umkomaas) and restaurant (Italian).

From the *Area Annals* we learn that the hamlet of Umkomaas evolved as a settler node on the south bank of the river from the early 1860s (Warner *c.*1980). It was hoped that the sugar cane could be transported from inland along the river to the sea and thence to Durban by small steamer, instead of relying on unwieldy land transportation by wagon, which would take a week (Du Bois 2015: 35). This plan came to fruition, but only in a small way and for a short time (about ten years). The combination of strong winds and uneven ground at the would-be harbour led to more than one mishap, and shipping had been abandoned by 1883 (Du Bois 2015).

Travel was only secured after the building of the railway from 1897. After that a settlement 'that relied entirely on the sea and the river for its charm' (*Natal Mercury*, 11 November 1907, cited by Du Bois [2015: 35]) gradually turned into 'the Scarborough of Natal, the queen of watering places' (*Natal Mercury*, 20 January 1906, cited by Du Bois [2015: 35]). The colonial account rightly tells of the heroics of the pioneers in this area: for example, Reverend J.A. Butler, who was attacked by crocodiles while crossing the river on horseback in 1853, and of Georgina Reynolds, who took over as ferry keeper after the death of her husband (Du Bois 2015: 26, 32). Traversing the unbridged river was not for the faint-hearted: 'At the Umkomaas travellers had to offload their wagons, take them to pieces, send them across on a flimsy pont, then reassemble them on the other side' (Hocking 1992: 54). (A *pont* is a South African term for a flat-bottomed ferry worked on by cables or ropes.) Umkomaas Hill remained a stiff challenge for decades (Hocking 1992: 42). There is a drawing purported to be of an ox-wagon making its way up a clearly treacherous Umkomaas Hill in 1856 in Osborn's *Valiant Harvest* (1964: 152). Unfortunately, no source is given for the illustration, and it is likely that it is a generic picture of trekkers in South Africa and hence not relating specifically to Umkomaas or the 1950s.[4] Of course, the role of the labour force of Zulus, Indians and others such as the amaTonga migrant workers in construction, laying railway track and carrying out the small everyday tasks that made the settlement viable should not be downplayed.

Indians played a major role in what the *Natal Mercury* (10 June 1858) termed the 'southward extension of the cane enterprise' (cited by Du Bois [2015: 27]). By 1866 six thousand indentured labourers from India were working the land, mainly along the Natal coast. Africans and Indians worked together: at Canonby estate in Umkomaas in 1870 there were 60 Indian and 130 African workers (Osborn 1964: 304). Most Indians stayed on after their indenture contracts ended, and slowly took advantage of opportunities in the colony. For example, B.C. Rambachan, who laboured in the fields at Umzinto and Hull Valley, Umkomaas, later prospered as an ironmonger and wheelwright on account of the blacksmith skills of his *lohar* caste. He was eventually able to buy a large, thickly forested tract of hillside with some flats along the river at Gravesend. One descendant of indentured labourers, R.C. Naidoo, who was born in Durban in 1880, played a leading role in the history of Indians in Umkomaas. A school brochure describes him thus:

> He was the youngest, so they called him Chinayya ('little one'). Chinayya was brilliant at school and his friends called him 'Acharayya' which means 'professor'. He spoke Zulu, Telugu, Hindi and English fluently. His father died suddenly, when he was thirteen, leaving his family financially disadvantaged. His mother and the three boys moved into a small back rented room. To earn his school fees Chinayya took a newspaper round and delivered *The Natal Mercury* from house to house (Naidoo Memorial Primary School 2016).

Unable to take up an offer to study at the Inns of Court in London for lack of funds, R.C. Naidoo became an articled clerk in a law firm in Durban. He was advised by a Mr Jhavery, a shoe merchant and client, who acted as his sponsor to move to the south coast, where he purchased a store from Harvey and Greenacre at Roseneath in the early 1900s. He subsequently bought large tracts of land and encouraged smallholding farmers to earn an independent living in far-flung places within Umkomaas – at Fountain Head, Roseneath, Craigieburn, Crowder, Willow Glen and Amahlongwa. The family members set up shops in these areas and were able to act as founders and grantees (trustees in receipt of a grant) of schools in Fountain Head, Roseneath and Craigieburn. The Naidoo Memorial and Naidooville primary schools still carry the family name – the former referring to the founder, R.C. Naidoo, the latter to his sons S.P. and C.C. Naidoo, after whom the area was named. The Telugu community of present-day KwaZulu-Natal tends to be somewhat overshadowed by other communities, but it is worth remembering that the leading Indian family of Umkomaas (the R.C. Naidoos), with enormous standing since the early 1900s, were of Telugu descent.

Time

Vishnu's family were of indentured stock, his father's side arriving in 1888 and serving their indenture at the Reynold Brothers estate in Umzinto on the south coast.[5] The ships' lists give the names of Sreenivasa (spelling obscured in the document), a male of 30 years, and Thayamathi, a female of 19 years. They travelled as a married couple. On his mother's side Vishnu's family hailed from the Thanjavur district of the Madras Presidency (as it was then designated). Vishnu's mother, Mrs Mahalutchmee (Leila) Padayachee (née Moodley), was from Mayville, Durban, and aged 16 when she married R.N. Padayachee. She passed away in December 2022 at the age of 89, outliving her only son by 19 months. A member of the Moodley family was the founder of Pakco Pickles (the brand name is based on his first name, Pakkiri, and he was, in the fashion of the times, known to many as 'Pakco'). The Padayachee family lived in Sunny Brae, adjacent to Roseneath and more or less considered part of it. In this family it was Ramsamy Padayachee who became famous; he was later known as Father Padayachee. (His full name was Srinivasan Ramsamy Padayachee, showing the familiar Tamil pattern of father's name + one's personal name + title). Ramsamy was born in the colony of Natal in 1895, seven years after his parents had arrived from India. It is said that on his first trip to India as a young man he was so moved by the abject poverty in the villages that he took spiritual vows on his return to Umkomaas and sold many of his worldly possessions (to the dismay of some of his family) in order to send donations to India. In this process he became one of the founders of South Africa's Divine Life Society, originally founded in 1936 in Rishikesh. He is described on the society's website as a great devotee who had visited the Master, Swami Sivananda in India.[6] This organisation continues to unite spiritual concerns and religious links to India with community-based uplift projects, aimed – it must be stressed – at KwaZulu-Natal's Indian *and* African communities. At the family homestead, Father Padayachee built a prayer place which attracted devotees mainly from Durban and the south coast. There was a service every Sunday. Swami Sivananda of India directed a schoolteacher and new devotee, Srinivasan Sahajananda, originally from Estcourt, to take religious instruction in Umkomaas from Father Padayachee. Sahajananda travelled by train and bus to Umkomaas, and his arrival on their doorstep with a suitcase is still remembered by older family members. Vishnu's mother would have had to do the catering for such guests. Sahajananda became famous in the history of the Divine Life Society of South Africa, later taking the title Swami.

Vishnu would have imbibed some of these influences growing up, and he was close to his grandmother after Father Padayachee's death in 1971. As a child he spoke fluent Tamil with his grandparents, among whom he lived as the child of their eldest son. (On starting primary school, however, he completely switched to English, never speaking Tamil again, though he retained a good 'passive' or 'receptive' competence in it all his life). The four sons of Father Padayachee lived within one fairly large property, originally fifteen acres (six hectares) in size, in Sunny Brae. They built separate homes close to each other upon marriage, so that they benefited from an Indian joint family arrangement combined with a Western-style nuclear family autonomy. In this enclave there was a family temple that still stands today. Father Padayachee's meagre quarters became known within the family as the *mado* – the Tamil word for 'monastery' – but in this case a medium-sized room for religious contemplation. It was taken over after his passing by a teenage Vishnu, who used it as *his* retreat (filled with less unworldly books, sporting memorabilia, art and artefacts). We need look no further for the rudiments of the making of Ike's Books. Father Padayachee's grave remains visible in one corner of the yard of Vishnu's first home in Sunny Brae.

The *mado*, when I first visited it in early 1972, had a large glass bookcase with a stock of old books, inherited from uncles and older cousins (the grandfather had sold all his!). I remember a book from that first visit, on Casanova; it was called *Wild Life in Venice*, and was the only one I cared to borrow (but never quite finished). There were Ian Fleming thrillers and Agatha Christie mysteries. Copies of *Mad Magazine*, *Goon Show Scripts* and cricket magazines were on display. Vishnu had posters on the wall, mainly sport-related, including boxing. He would occasionally try his hand at painting. I cannot say if he was a good painter, but the very fact of a young person seriously attempting fine art at home in Umkomaas was remarkable. There were some old artefacts and ornaments around, from African and Indian cultures. The least attractive part of the *mado* to visitors was the shelf of lab bottles containing snakes preserved in formalin. To the relief of all, Vishnu's scientific turn did not last too long, though I have no doubt that under different circumstances he would have made a first-class scientist or medical researcher. He also wrote poetry – in a slim notebook, a teenager's poems kept at the *mado*.[7] I remember one incisive poem about a youthful distrust of liquor. It was a critique of those who averred that their true selves only appeared after a drink or two, and concluded with the only line that I can recall verbatim: 'Society needs men, not chameleons'. Though he might have later changed his mind about the qualities of intoxicating nectars, Vishnu's incisive wit was certainly present in that poem. Here is a poem titled 'He', which Vishnu wrote in memory of his grandfather in 1968:

He
Somewhere far below – or maybe above
The silent murmur of the breeze rose
Among the crackling leaves, and
In this, an archway, a stone
Lay bare, yet weathered and beaten;
I gazed, a long gaze, and lo! It changed
It was his face, old yes, very old
And here as I sat,
I remembered his formal stare,
A happy man, divine and gentle,
A dog sat at his feet bare and a stick
Stood propped to the wall,
I see now how we 'feared' him.
The tap, tap of a stick approaching
And our game shuffled up and away.
But was it fear? You could not fear him,
And yet ... Then the tap, tap of a stick –
I stiffened, subconsciously and then ...
The rustle of the breeze above
Awoke me ... It stopped
He was not there.
The stone was still bare.

Community

There is no record of missionary education for Indians in Umkomaas, though there was a Beulah Mission school for Zulu children, high up on a cliff in Fountain Head. Education thus came mainly at the initiative of the Indian community. In 1929 the Rambachan and other families, including the Someras and Bhimas, started the Umkomaas Drift Primary School close to the river, four miles (six-and-a-half kilomentres) upstream. (This was the primary school that well-known politician Narend Singh later attended). A few years later, after a long period of planning, the Umkomaas Government-Aided School was started in 1936, an initiative led by R.C. Naidoo. The land had been donated by descendants of the Rambachan family (the Ramphals and Mesthries), though family records about this are sketchy. Mrs R.C. Naidoo became manageress of the school in 1937 and encouraged attendance among Indian girls. Prior to apartheid rule some Zulu children attended as well. In 1945 the school and land were transferred to the Natal Provincial Administration, making it possible to attain 'government' status. The buildings to which Vishnu would have been accustomed as a child, from his first year of school in 1958, were fairly spacious and blended nicely with the rustic setting of Roseneath. The school grounds were ample, planted with *umdoni* (forest myrtle), fig and other trees, with the main school building boasting a cemented quadrangle – almost but not quite a courtyard. In years to come, as the school expanded, it lost some of this rural charm, with its prefabricated extensions and less inspiring brown, double-storey brick structures. But the original section retains much of its character till today. In a speech that he gave on the 80th anniversary of the school, on 27 February 2016, Vishnu paid homage to 'the institution that so deeply shaped my formative years and the values I have carried all my life' (Naidoo Memorial Primary School 2016). He particularly mentioned the trustees of the school, from the founder R.C. Naidoo and his son, C.S. Naidoo, to subsequent trustees like L. Singh, R.S. Padayachee ('Mayor'), S. Ramphal, R. Bhoora and, above all, Dr S. Somera. Of such people Vishnu said: 'Their generosity in terms of resources, time, energy and vision was the stuff of legends, and like the many other trustees of Indian schools all over Natal under segregation and apartheid, we owe them an enormous gratitude, one that cannot be easily captured in words'. Reference to the stuff of legends was no exaggeration. In that same brochure, Mrs V. Padayachie (so spelt, a paternal aunt of Vishnu) recalls the funeral of the founder of the school, R.C. Naidoo: 'The day that Mr. Naidoo passed on was very sad. The hearse was driven around the school before his burial.'

The primary school gradually expanded into a high school, with standard seven (grade nine) introduced in 1965, and so on incrementally until a first small batch of entrants sat their matriculation exams in 1968. Prior to that there was no high school in Umkomaas for any racial grouping within the small town. A few from the Indian community would travel to or board in neighbouring Durban to the north (studying mainly at Clairwood High or Sastri College) or Umzinto down south (at Umzinto High). Children of the white population were bussed to high schools in places like Kingsburgh or Amanzimtoti. Vishnu was in the second batch of matriculants of 1969 at Naidoo Memorial. He was the head boy that year, well-liked by students and staff alike. In my experience from joining the high school section in 1968, following him by two years, Vishnu already stood out for his good humour and poise – while still having an easy-going, common touch. In his later years Vishnu reflected, in that same speech of 27 February 2016: 'When I was at school our teachers were the rock stars, today they have faded from the things that matter to young people. We need to work hard to reverse this and restore the teaching profession to the honourable and noble status it once held'. The rock star status is perhaps a slight exaggeration, though at least one of his teachers proudly confided to us in 1968, 'in my younger days I was known as the Elvis Presley of Natal'.

Most primary school teachers of the time in fact played a role that was both pastoral and pedagogic. What they may have lacked by way of certification, they made up for with care for their children, diligence, good humour and tolerance – balanced by harsh words when necessary. They were responsible for prolonging and enhancing the strong community spirit going all the way back to the days of indenture. Sport played a major role in this. Vishnu was goalkeeper of his cohort, and my first ever sight of him was in goal for Naidoo Memorial in 1965, when I was still at the Fountain Head Primary School. (He was already a Spurs supporter – having been taken by his uncles from the city to see the 'Tottenham Hotspur versus an NFL XI' match at the Stamford Stadium in Durban in 1963.) Vishnu stood out as the only well-togged player on the field in Roseneath; all the other kids played barefoot. What struck me as novel was that when the ball went out into the cabbage patch immediately behind the goal, Vishnu would stand expectantly while one of his defenders hastened to collect it for him. At high school the teachers were thankful to Vishnu, who could act as impartial referee and even as coach to the boys' team when they took on the teachers in an occasional challenge match.

Sports days at primary school were a major event, since six Indian schools from the area came together competitively. There was certainly a pecking order here: Naidoo Memorial and Naidooville were the strongest in terms of numbers and prowess and were usually the host schools. Renishaw – based largely on the community of Indians still working and living on a sugar estate just south of Umkomaas – was also strong, while Umkomaas Drift was middling, having too small a community to threaten the big squads. The remaining two schools emanated from further inland, with its heavily forested and steep terrain – Fountain Head and M.M. Govender School of Ellingham. They usually came last, though not without providing the occasional surprise. One such surprise came when Fountain Head beat Naidoo Memorial in 1965 in the Cup Final of the senior teams, with a thunderous, barefooted, swerving free-kick by Vijay Mesthrie that went past a stunned, well-togged goalkeeper. 'I never saw the ball,' Vishnu good-naturedly told us a couple of years later, with a smile.

For those who came to know Vishnu well as an adult, it will be something of a surprise to learn that cricket was not played at Naidoo Memorial. In truth the sports facilities were basic, and there were almost no champions of cricket among the teachers (Mr Mehta, the maths teacher, being an honourable exception.) The football pitch was among the worst in the province, sloping at an angle of about 30 degrees, with large boulders impinging on the sidelines. On late January days one got blisters on bare feet from the heat of the ground.

Academically speaking, while the primary school teachers were organically in tune with the needs of their pupils, high school was a more challenging experience for all. Of the first batch of successful final-year pupils, no one gained a university exemption. The second-year cohort of matriculants fared slightly better. Vishnu Padayachee and Chundra Venketas were the first pupils of the school to qualify for university studies, and two or three others of this class of eighteen pupils went to a college or technikon. Some high school teachers were inspiring, but some were not. A few encouraged rote learning, with geography lessons especially comprising interminable sets of dictated notes, which could not have appealed to Vishnu much. In those first two years, the teachers of matric Latin, English and accounting were really good; the teachers of other subjects (mathematics, geography, biology) perhaps less so. No other subjects were on offer, though for recreation one had to take art or music once a week. Classes studiously avoided any mention of politics and the struggles of the black neighbours of the area. The school started to attract good teachers two or three years later, and built up a good reputation. In the year after Vishnu matriculated, a young Narend Singh was head boy, with me as head boy in the following year (1971). The head girls were Priscilla Moodley for the first two years, followed by Parvathy Naidoo in 1970 and Ambigay Naidu in 1971. Some teachers were influential beyond their subject expertise. From English master C. Jugnath, Vishnu would have learnt that teachers could be on friendly – even jovial – terms with students. From Mr Mehta he would have learnt that even accountants could have a sardonic sense of humour and know something about cricket.

To understand in retrospect why Vishnu stood out so in transcending the limits of time, place, school life and curricula, we would need to look at the other influences in his life. His social awareness, sense of charity and possibly commitment to development economics came mainly from the Father Padayachee line. Vishnu's dad, R.N. Padayachee, was a schoolteacher and later principal in a number of places, from Mooi River to Port Shepstone. He worked late hours to ensure the success of these schools and was committed to social and community work on weekends. Vishnu's mother, Leila Padayachee, was the anchor of this existence. Vishnu was connected with the R.C. Naidoo family via his aunt (on his father's side), who married C.S. Naidoo, the son of R.C. Naidoo. Vishnu's interest in commerce did not come from his grandfather or his mum and dad, who were avowedly non-materialistic. (Though Father Padayachee did run a shop that sold mainly fruit and vegetables on the family property alongside the main road at the top of Umkomaas Hill, catering to passing traffic, with the produce coming from the family farm.) More significantly, two of Vishnu's father's brothers ran larger and more successful general dealer stores on behalf of the Naidoos from the 1960s on. From them Vishnu imbibed a spirit of fairness, business ethics and service, not always present in his home province. The Roseneath

Store was run by his uncle, R.S. Padayachee, who was very much a community man, known fondly by all – including occasional visitors and customers from Magabeni – as 'Mayor'. The store was a lively centre for news and local gossip (without actually selling newspapers). Brij Maharaj, based on his short experience as a schoolteacher there, later described Umkomaas as the only place where news travelled faster than on the internet (Maharaj 2021). 'Mayor' ran a small postal service for the Roseneath area from within the shop – really a small box outside and a folder of letters under the counter; he could be relied upon to ensure that every letter found its intended recipient. Customers could enquire whether there were any letters for them; non-customers would be found by word of mouth in an area without street names, or indeed streets.

Further down the hill, across the river's drift, was the Drift Store, run by another uncle, R.V. Padayachee. The initial R. in the brothers' names stood for Ramsamy, their father's personal name, which was adopted by Tamil convention as their first name, equivalent originally to a Western surname. South African bureaucracy required a fixed surname at the end of an individual's name, and so the family adopted the caste name 'Padayachee' for this purpose. As a surname it is something of a South African speciality; in India it would be used – if at all – as a title for members of the *Padayachi* – a subgrouping of the *Vanniyar* (also known as *Palli* or trading) caste. Such caste matters became much less significant in South Africa, and more or less irrelevant from the 1960s onwards.

Being on the north bank of the river, the Drift Store had a largely Zulu clientele. It was adjacent to the defunct Drift Hotel, originally opened in the late 1850s as an accommodation house for those settlers and visitors making the perilous journey across the river. R.V. Padayachee spoke fluent isiZulu, English and Tamil. Adjacent to the store was a herbalist's shop; in the 1970s it was run by a young Indian named Siven, whose knowledge of spoken isiZulu and traditional Zulu medicines and cures was profound.

During university holidays Vishnu was tasked with designing and putting up Christmas decorations at the store, which he undertook with characteristic enthusiasm and careful planning, down to detailed sketches. He had learnt to play cricket and about the history of the game via an uncle (Vasa) on his mother's side, on visits to Durban or on the uncle's reciprocal visits to Umkomaas. As the only child of a dedicated schoolmaster, Vishnu must have pored over books and encyclopaedias covering history and general knowledge, while also taking in the lore and laws of cricket. His love of crossword puzzles was of his own making. In initially trying and failing to crack their code (in the daily crossword of the *Natal Mercury*), Vishnu relied on the vague advice proffered by his father that, from what he'd occasionally observed among teachers in the staff room, the answers were somehow hidden in the clues themselves. Initially Vishnu didn't have a great interest in popular music, despite the explosion of music in the 1960s. He acquired a taste for folk, folk rock, soft rock and baroque music during his late undergraduate years via me, though I failed to persuade him of the merits of hard rock – not even of the Mahavishnu Orchestra, which was a New York jazz-rock band of the 1970s.

Vishnu has sometimes been described (incorrectly) as more of a dapper English gentleman than an Indian *sahib*; but even if this is so, it could not have come from his immediate family. His Uncle Vasu of Drift Store had no pretensions to Englishdom, and he was quite rooted in the local Tamil and Indian culture, down to being an expert *thanni* card player. So where did the Englishness beyond that propagated at schools come from? I never ever discussed this with Vishnu but have since followed the trail to the R.C. Naidoo family, with some help from Vishnu's cousin Satya – more sister and companion than cousin. It is likely that this influence may have come upon a young Vishnu when he had to reside with his aunt for a period of about six months during his parents' itinerant years in Mooi River. The aunt, who was married to C.S. Naidoo, lived only a short distance up the road. While not ever flaunting their wealth (being more active in community development), the Naidoos *did* follow something of an upper-class lifestyle in their double-storey mansion in Roseneath. They had servants in the Victorian style, one for each kind of service (laundry, scullery, cooking), and a driver. They had – according to one visitor – the first morning cup of tea in bed and ate with forks and knives. All of these customs were alien to the rest of Umkomaas's Indian community. But one family member (Jana, son of C.S. Naidoo) cautions against exaggeration of the Englishness. As one who lived briefly in the UK and for a long time in Germany, Jana does not think that his own upbringing in Umkomaas was very 'English'. This is what Vishnu said in a speech on 30 October 2012, at the funeral of his cousin Tej Naidoo (son of C.S. Naidoo):

I knew Tej best in the 1960s and 1970s. For a time I lived at his parents' home... Then we shared a bedroom upstairs in Roseneath with mosquito nets mounted over the beds and the most beautiful linen and fabrics, and in the mornings we were served tea in bed by Mariamma or one of the other domestic servants. It was an altogether different world despite being in the middle of grand apartheid. It changed my life forever, that experience, and Tej was a central, yet unassuming part of it... (Padayachee 2012).

The Naidoo family conversed on a variety of topics and entertained important visitors. While not being involved in the political struggle, they nevertheless hosted individuals like activist Monty Naicker. H.I.E. Dhlomo, the writer and former editor of *Ilanga* newspaper, once rented quarters in an outbuilding, in a refreshingly non-racial arrangement for the Umkomaas of the times. When literary historian and critic Tim Couzens visited Umkomaas in the 1970s, following Dhlomo's trail – and perhaps manuscripts – he was immediately sent by 'Mayor' to a young undergraduate Vishnu for information. Another link with the English and global world was R.C. Naidoo's son, Dayanand. He went to university in Glasgow in 1936 and stayed on in the UK, later becoming dean of psychiatric medicine at the University of London. Vishnu noted with amusement how on a visit to London, Dayanand spoke to him fondly of his late father, whom he always referred to in a Dickensian kind of way as 'the Founder'. Vishnu considered Dayanand to be the 'most brilliant and the most eccentric man I have met' (Padayachee 2016). This polymath was researching the Silk Road in his retirement, which took him to India, Tibet and China. He is said to have become fluent in Chinese. Dayanand also had complete fluency in 'deep' isiZulu, which he was able to resurrect on his occasional return visits to Umkomaas. He died of altitude sickness in Tibet, with his ashes being scattered in the Brahmaputra River there. There is also a commemorative gravestone at his ancestral home in Roseneath, Umkomaas. The *Journal of Psychiatric Medicine* carried an obituary on Dayanand in 1992 (Gaind 1992).

Conclusion
Umkomaas remained with Vishnu all his life. Leaving it in 1970 to go to Salisbury Island for two years, to attend the University College for

Indians, must have been something of a wrench. Staying with family and family friends closer to the island and the Durban city centre in places like Isipingo and Reservoir Hills did not compare well with the free life in rural Umkomaas. By his third year, the college had relocated to Chiltern Hills to become the University of Durban-Westville. Vishnu and Chundra Venketas were instrumental in organising a lift club from Umkomaas that included Narend Singh, Nundgopaul (Ronny) Govender, Perisamy (Perry) Moodley and myself for the long daily trek to varsity. This was a return journey of three to four hours, depending not on traffic but on which part of Umkomaas you lived in. That world of university and 'UDW days' is worthy of another telling.

Acknowledgements

Thanks are due to family members, especially Satya Padayachee, Jana Naidoo and Suresh Naidoo, for their insights into Vishnu's life and for confirming and adding to some of my recollections. For other information on Umkomaas, I thank Narend Singh and Vidia Misthry. Nishi and Sonali Padayachee hosted me on a visit in 2022 and allowed me to peruse some of the materials referred to in this chapter. I also thank Catherine Burns and Judith Shier for passing on some important materials to me; my fellow editors for their insights and recollections; members of the 'Celebrating Vishnu' WhatsApp group, and all participants at the Vishnu Padayachee Symposium at Wits in July 2022. I also thank the National Research Foundation for a SARCHI Chair grant (No. 64805), which gave me the freedom to pursue this research.

Notes
1. In South Indian tradition his name would have been different, with the name of the village where he was born first, followed by his father's name (*Nadarajan*) and *Mahavishnu* coming last.
2. There were also occasional spellings like 'Umcomaas' in the early records.
3. Warner (c.1980) however mentions an official, Mr. Barrow, after whom this street could have been named. I have not been able to find any further details about this.
4. I thank historian Duncan du Bois for confirming this (personal communication, April 2022).
5. The key figures mentioned in this chapter, listed by their relationship to Vishnu, are: Paternal grandfather: Father Padayachee (Srinivasan Ramsamy Padayachee); Father: R.N. Padayachee (Nad); Paternal uncles: R.S. Padayachee (Satchie or

'Mayor'), R.V. Padayachee (Vasu); Uncles by marriage on his father's side: R.C. Naidoo ('the Founder'), his sons Dayanand Naidoo (the Dean of Medicine in London) and C.S. Naidoo (entrepreneur in Umkomaas); Mother: M. Padayachee (Leila).
6. See dls.org.za.
7. I have taken the liberty of citing one of the poems from that notebook, as it is an artistic recollection worthy of preservation, despite Vishnu's overall reticence about what he thought of as his juvenilia.

References

Doke, C., D.M. Malcolm and J.M.A. Sikakana. 1982. *English–Zulu Dictionary*. Johannesburg: Witwatersrand University Press.
Du Bois, D. 2015. 'A Sketch of Colonial Umkomaas'. *Natalia* 45: 26–38.
Gaind, R. 1992. 'Obituary: Dayanand Naidoo.' *Journal of Psychiatric Medicine* 16: 247–8.
Hocking, A. 1992. *Renishaw: The Story of Crookes Brothers*. Bethulie: Hollards.
Maharaj, B. 2021. 'Vishnu Padayachee, a Formidable and Enigmatic Intellectual'. *News24*, 9 June. https://www.news24.com/news24/opinions/columnists/guestcolumn/tribute-vishnu-padayachee-a-formidable-and-enigmatic-intellectual-20210609.
Naidoo Memorial Primary School. 2016. *Naidoo Memorial Primary School Anniversary Brochure 1936–2016*. Umkomaas. Includes a two-page spread of excerpts from a speech by Vishnu Padayachee. Full text in the author's possession.
Osborn, R.F. 1964. *Valiant Harvest: The Founding of the South African Sugar Industry, 1848–1926*. Durban: South African Sugar Association.
Padayachee, M. 2020. 'Comment: Short Notes on SAICCOR'. *Transformation* 103: 127–30.
Padayachee, V. 2012. 'Tribute to the Late Tej Naidoo, 30 October 2012'. Unpublished speech in the author's possession.
———. 2016. 'Speech on the Occasion of the 80th Anniversary of Naidoo Memorial School, 27 February 2016'. Text in the author's possession.
Warner, A. (ed.). n.d. *c.*1980. *Umkomaas: River of Whales: Area Annals 1828–1980*. Project of the Federation of Women's Institutes of Natal and East Griqualand (Umkomaas Women's Institute).

3

Curiosity and Commitment

Vishnu Padayachee, Global Scholarship and Politics in
Durban in the 1980s and 1990s

Robert Morrell

This chapter is based on an interview that I conducted with Vishnu Padayachee in 2017. I was interested in his life and career broadly speaking but was particularly keen to make sense of his interests in politics, universities and sport. I first met him in 1985, when I had just joined the Department of History at the University of Durban-Westville (UDW) and Vishnu had just moved from the Economics Department at UDW to the Institute for Social and Economic Research (ISER) headed by John Butler-Adam. The United Democratic Front (UDF) had been formed in the wake of protests against the tricameral parliamentary system being punted by the apartheid government, and in 1985 a limited state of emergency was declared, affecting primarily the Eastern Cape but having national reverberations.

In thinking about Vishnu's life, I reflect on the current moment in South Africa. We are in a time of questioning; much of the critical heat comes from the wave of protests unleashed from 2015 onwards by the #RhodesMustFall student movement, which was followed in 2016 by the #FeesMustFall movement. There were two major elements of this movement, which is now generally and generically referred to as Fallism. The first was the students' demand that universities should be decolonised, and the second was the demand that access to universities should be widened and enabled, and that the cost of such a process should be carried by the state.

Vishnu would have found himself in broad agreement with these demands. His work, as I shall show, demonstrated a lifelong commitment to social justice. He sought to make his research relevant to the project of national liberation and to communities on the wrong side of apartheid, as well as to addressing issues of class inequality. But he might have been distressed by the lack of historical appreciation among supporters of Fallism. In this chapter I show that the work of 'decolonisation' began long before 2015, and that the terrain of higher education and the process of knowledge production were transformed by the collective actions of a generation of scholars dating back to at least the sixth decade of the twentieth century.

My essay is influenced by a literature that has focused on the recent history of Durban by bringing into focus the lives of those who brought progressive energy to the city, and particularly to its universities. It includes a resurgence of interest in the life of Rick Turner (De Kadt 2017; MacQueen 2018) and the 'Durban moment' of 1973 (Hassim 2019; Morphet 1990; Webster, Chapter 17 in this volume), and in the lives of activists such as Pravin Gordhan, Pregs Govender, Jay Naidoo and Kumi Naidoo, who were active in the 1970s and beyond (Ancer and Whitfield 2021; Govender 2007; Naidoo 2010; Naidoo 2022). This reading sketches the contours of the period leading up to 1994. An apartheid system was still in place but facing increasing challenge. Racism and authoritarianism were experienced in many ways and places, in daily life and in heightened moments of confrontation. Yet opposition built steadily during this period, some of it located within the city's universities.

Vishnu's early life
It says a lot about Vishnu's curiosity and sense of place that he began our interview with a statement about being born in May 1952 and growing up in Umkomaas:

> It was a small town, racially segregated: a very odd combination of people that made up the town mainly because of the very strong influence of an Italian semi-skilled worker community that came to that area as semi-skilled and skilled workers to the SAICCOR factory [the South African Industrial Cellular Corporation] including the rayon factory. This was a joint venture between a British company Courtaulds and the South African IDC [Industrial Development Corporation] and with

> some formal contractual labour link to Italy, which is why these semi-skilled and skilled workers came to Umkomaas largely from the Milan [area] ... So as a boy I remember reading to try to master Italian; I knew a lot of swear words because we used to attend their football matches which was very strange – a small town and there was a kind of odd multinationalism about it.[1]

In this description we are immediately introduced to Vishnu as somebody who asks questions and seeks answers – about his local context and his place within it. He had a keen eye for social detail (more detail of Vishnu's experience of place in Umkomaas is provided by Rajend Mesthrie in Chapter 2 of this volume). He expands on this in the interview by discussing the social arrangements of the town and analysing the way segregation worked there. He notes that 'people of colour [were permitted] to attend the movie house when in fact most of these movie houses at the time were completely closed to people of colour'. Vishnu highlights this 'liberal' oddity in a small south coast town renowned for its conservatism, and he notes its hierarchical racial character: 'Indians could sit on these seats, discarded seats from the downstairs but at least they had backs. And Africans sat on the same level but on benches which had no backs and were not raised so if you were sitting two benches behind you could barely see the screen'. He notes not so much strict segregation but mingling, the manoeuvring between laws and norms.

> The football ground was similarly open in a sense; there was no separate entrances or separate seating – all the football teams were Inter and Juventus and so on, so they were all Italian made. Everything that happened was Italian, and not just in the football ground but the stalls selling food were not segregated interestingly but everything ... was sort of somewhere between Swiss German and Italian.

Vishnu went to Naidoo Memorial School, where he matriculated in 1969. Here too, he noticed both segregation and integration: 'Many of my teachers, or some of my teachers and many other teachers in the school were white'.[2] He grew up in a decade often described as the height of apartheid, and yet he recalls that his best friend in his primary school years was the isiZulu-speaking Milos Maseko.

This biographical introduction begins to explain why Vishnu was a supporter of non-racialism, the UDF and the African National Congress (ANC), and why he committed himself, throughout his life, to working for a new order in South Africa, a post-apartheid order that would be characterised by the ending of racism and the installation of processes of redress and social justice.

The UDW years
Vishnu attended UDW, where he did a BComm and then a BComm (Hons), which he finished in 1974. He then studied for an MComm, but soon began lecturing in the Economics Department at UDW and became a full-time staff member of the department in 1977, where he remained until the end of 1984 when he moved to ISER. During this period, he was also lecturing part-time for the Economics Department at the University of Natal (Durban [UND]), working with Mike McGrath and Gavin Maasdorp. This latter point is important because there was a geographical and hierarchical gap between UDW and UND. The respective institutions were racially distinct, one set up as a colonial institution for white students, the other as an apartheid institution for students classified as 'Indian'. UND, by dint of its age and resources, was considered to be the premier university in Durban. But Vishnu's life left him with no sense of inferiority. For some months, while he was still a school pupil, when his parents were living in Mooi River he had stayed with his aunt and uncle. They were a 'very anglicised family'. Another uncle, Dayanand Naidoo, 'had a house in England in a posh part of London'. Vishnu would later visit and stay with him. He was 'an amazing man. He spoke sixteen languages, retired as a military psychologist in the Saudi Arabian army and died all alone on the mountains in Tibet'.

From an early age, Vishnu felt part of a world much larger than Umkomaas and South Africa. He read prodigiously and found himself in the company of intellectuals who were friends of the family, including Dr Monty Naicker, president of the Natal Indian Congress (NIC) and the South African Indian Congress in the 1950s, who was placed under serial banning orders by the apartheid authorities until 1973. When he was older, he travelled beyond South Africa's borders, and continued to do so frequently throughout his life. He was energised by issues of social justice, and he put his efforts into worker education, initially with workers in the Chemical and Industrial Workers Union, together with Pat Horn. This work resulted in his first publication, a collaboration with Paul Tichman and Shahid Vawda (Padayachee, Vawda and Tichman 1985). It explored key themes that feature in many of his later works: the labour conditions experienced by Indian workers, radical ideas, and organisation to fight against discrimination and inequality. Vishnu spontaneously supported 'the underdog'. He was attracted to radical ideas partly because orthodox explanations of South African society that highlighted race but ignored social class failed to persuade him. And he believed in the importance of collective action.

Vishnu's interest in economic struggles had a concomitant focus in his dislike for sectarian, race-based politics: 'I grew up [that is, matured politically – RM] in a kind of Trotskyite world with Enver Motala and people like that who are also fiercely anti-nationalist; really concerned as socialists and people that are prosecuting a workers' struggle agenda'. He was attracted by the ANC's non-racialism while at the same time distrusting the politics of the NIC: 'I never joined the NIC . . . I never felt comfortable in a kind of ethnic political organisation.'

At the end of 1985, Vishnu headed off to the United States on a fellowship at the Paul Nitze School of Advanced International Studies at Johns Hopkins University, and he remained there until the middle of 1986. During this time, he recounts:

> I became a lot more politicised in the US; we were basically dealing with all these anti-apartheid movements. The Americans were, in the time that I was there, pushing through legislation that became that comprehensive Anti-Apartheid Act which basically set out the kind of sanctions framework. And there were lots of occasions on which I was invited by Mobil, by the state department . . . I [also] actually got to know some of the ANC people there.

As a result, he 'made a decision . . . to throw my lot in with the ANC. But I was also coming from a socialist background.'

On his return, he found that growing dissatisfaction with university management at UDW and a groundswell of national dissatisfaction with the apartheid regime were resulting in important campus developments. Student activism was on the rise, with the UDF, Azanian People's Organisation and Unity Movement all active on campus via student organisations. Students had been active in opposing the tricameral elections in 1984, and the campus was buzzing with political tension. Kumi Naidoo, who was a Students' Representative Council member in 1985 and 1986, remembers that 'every day there was a new social or political activity happening on campus, from someone being arrested to a new campaign being launched, or a strike taking place' (Naidoo 2022: 110). A particularly notable protest occurred in the wake of the assassination of the anti-apartheid lawyer Victoria Mxenge in Umlazi, by what was later discovered to be an apartheid hit squad. UDW students led a protest to the Durban City Hall on 2 August 1985 that resulted in a confrontation with police and multiple arrests (Naidoo 2022: 149–51). On 12 June 1986 a new state of emergency was announced that applied to the whole country. South Africa now entered 'an entirely new era of repression' (Green 2008: 217).

Insofar as UDW staff were concerned, there was a gap between a largely white management, headed by Vice Chancellor Jaap Greyling, a member of the secret Afrikaner nationalist body, the Broederbond, and both academic and non-academic staff. Management frequently refused to negotiate or even meet with the two existing organisations, the Staff Association and the Academic Staff Association. For example, they refused to recognise the rights of the staff associations to negotiate maternity leave (Morrell 1991: 67). In April 1986 frustration with the refusal of management to engage with the staff led to the beginning of a process in which the two staff associations agreed to amalgamate, resulting in the establishment of the Combined Staff Association (COMSA). By the end of the year, they had drawn up a constitution, which in 1987 was accepted and gave them official recognition on campus. Vishnu was a founding member of COMSA and part of its first executive. The executive included Alan Brimer, Vishnu Padayachee, Prem Naidoo, Kasturi Bhana, Surendra Bhana, Trish Gibbon, Jairam Reddy, Dasarath Chetty, Robert Morrell (secretary-treasurer), John Butler-Adam (chair) and Mala Singh.

COMSA as a whole was clearly aligned with the political direction of the UDF and rapidly found itself in conflict with UDW management. But the political terrain was shifting, and in the next few years, together with student activists and as a result of changes in the university's council, COMSA was able to engineer major developments. Professor Jairam Reddy, the deputy chair of COMSA, became vice chancellor in the middle of 1990, and Vishnu was shortly thereafter appointed as his adviser, moving into a key decision-making space (Morrell 1991). John Butler-Adam remembers that time well, and how COMSA changed the direction of the university: 'Vishnu was appointed by Jairam to the administration, and he brought Angina Parekh [an academic in the Psychology Department] in, and Angina brought Trish Gibbon [an academic in the English Department] in, and they were responsible for drawing up plans for the new structure of the university, academically' (Butler-Adam interview 2020). Both Gibbon and Parekh had been very active within COMSA, and this network ensured a takeover of the management by COMSA-aligned academics. Vishnu reflected on the political significance of these UDW engagements: 'I always felt not only that we were kind of contributing to something nationally ... but that we were not just part of it, we were in many ways the centre of it.'

The developments within staff politics had a complement in the concentration of high-level economic expertise within ISER, according to Vishnu: 'Steven Gelb, myself and Doug Hindson were the movers and shakers.' This group enjoyed close working relations with staff at UND, including Mike Morris and Dan Smit. 'So, when serious national meetings happened, they happened in Durban and at UWC.' When negotiations about the future of South Africa began, 'if you were thinking where the centre of alternative thinking about the economy was for the future – that's where it was [in Durban]'.

UDW was also central to the development of the Union of Democratic Staff Associations launched in 1989. Mala Singh (of the UDW Politics Department) was elected president and Mike Morris (of the UND School of Development Studies) became the secretary. Vishnu was a founding member.

Research, debates and knowledge production
By the time of his death, Vishnu's research excellence was widely acknowledged. He was Distinguished Professor and Derek Schrier and Cecily Cameron Chair in Development Economics in the School of Economic and Business Sciences at the University of the Witwatersrand. He was a member of the Johns Hopkins University Society of Scholars and an elected Fellow of the Association of Science of South Africa. He had received his PhD (supervised by Bill Freund in the Department of Economic History) from UND in 1989. In 2018 he was awarded an honorary doctorate by Rhodes University. He authored or edited nine

books and four special issues of accredited journals. He had written or co-authored thirty-seven book chapters and more than one hundred and ten articles in accredited and peer-reviewed academic journals.[3] He was particularly interested in banking and in trajectories of economic development. I shall return to these themes shortly, but for now I want briefly to describe the academic world of knowledge production as it was when I first encountered Vishnu in 1985.

I took up a position as lecturer in the UDW History Department in January 1985. It was headed then by Surendra Bhana, who, together with Joy Brain, had developed a line of research specialisation on 'Indians' in Natal. Surendra was working on questions of indenture while Joy was focusing on Catholicism. But the action in the discipline of history lay elsewhere. The rise of the new Left in Europe and the student uprising in Paris in 1968 seemed to propel radical scholarship. South African university students began to engage with a new revisionism. Frederick A. Johnstone's *Class, Race and Gold* (1976), which had been preceded by an influential article in *African Affairs* (Johnstone 1970), was very influential. It questioned the liberal thesis that economic integration would eventually end apartheid, and pointed out that capitalism enjoyed a comfortable relationship with apartheid. Colin Bundy's *Rise and Fall of the African Peasantry* (1988), the main thesis of which was first published as an article, 'The Emergence and Decline of a South African Peasantry' in *African Affairs* in 1972, showed how racial capitalism emerged by preventing African farmers from developing their enterprises and competing on open markets. Harold Wolpe (1972) and Martin Legassick (1974) showed how the homeland system and authoritarian government assisted capital accumulation. The orthodox national historiography pioneered by liberal historians half a century before was under attack, mostly by young, Marxist-inclined, foreign-trained scholars. In addition, following the lead of Basil Davidson, the precolonial history of Southern Africa was coming into focus. The growth of indigenous polities and their encounters with imperialism were bringing new detail to old debates and highlighting both indigenous political and military agency as well as aggressive and militaristic British imperialism (Bonner 1983; Guy 1982; Peires 1982).

Within the History Department when I joined, only one other staff member took the same interest in these debates as I did – Shireen Hassim. But the winds of change gusted through the corridors of L Block, and it was another colleague, church historian Mandy Goedhals, who defied the apartheid law that no images of Nelson Mandela could be reproduced when she set an undergraduate tutorial on Madiba (long before his release from prison). Studies in political economy at this point were de rigueur among revisionist scholars. Debates about the transition from feudalism to capitalism, the form of the state, forms of capital accumulation and the relationship of the metropole to the periphery dominated attention. Vishnu's own teaching reflected this trend. Imraan Valodia, a student of Vishnu's who later worked at UND's Trade Union Research Project, remembers:

> I would pop around to Vishnu's office and he used to give me stuff to read. The two things that I think had a big influence, he gave me one of Harold Wolpe's articles to read and Martin Legassick; and for the first time I think I started to understand in kind of class terms and look at the linkages between class and race. I had to write an economics essay on the homelands and so I started to read (Valodia interview 2018).

Against this backdrop Vishnu, Shahid Vawda and I formulated a research project in 1987 which we called FINCE (Financial Institutions in the Natal Colonial Economy). Eventually, although it took some time, the project produced two published pieces. The first showed how imperial capital contested for control of credit provision in the colony of Natal at the end of the nineteenth and early twentieth centuries, pitting the local Natal Bank against the London-based, imperial bank, Standard (Morrell, Padayachee and Vawda 1993). A second paper looked at distinctions among Indian traders – those who had arrived independently in Natal and were connected to Indian Ocean networks, and those who had exited indenture and were making their way towards economic independence by opening small shops. It analysed access to credit and focused particularly on the ability of Indian traders to work outside of the conventional banking system (Padayachee and Morrell 1991). Both of these papers were mindful of the social and economic complexities of colonial Natal and of the North–South inequalities that are a feature of geopolitics.

The potential of FINCE was damaged by my ejection from UDW at the end of 1988. My yearly contract that had previously been renewed without question was, in mid-December, summarily cancelled for the following year. It was difficult to avoid the suspicion that this was a political act to remove me from UDW because of my activities within COMSA.

Other factors were also influencing Vishnu's intellectual orientation. ISER was the centre of debates that increasingly focused on issues relating to South Africa's transition. Within South Africa the politics of ungovernability, which resulted in constant boycotts, protests, strikes and challenges to the apartheid regime, was putting great pressure on the government. Academics were involved in these developments both as opponents of apartheid and also as intellectuals to whom it fell to imagine a post-apartheid future. Vishnu recalled: 'Think of the people, you think of the type at ISER in 1986–'87, '88 with [Steve] Gelb and [Doug] Hindson and Tim [Quinlan] and Anne Vaughan and John Butler-Adam and Trevor Bell and so on. It was a fabulous place.' Issues of development began to dominate futurist thinking. Economists began to move from critique to a more engaged style of scholarship. In the case of Steve Gelb, for example, his important work with John Saul (Saul and Gelb 1986) which described the South African 'crisis' led logically to the formation of the Economic Trends Group (ET), founded in 1987 with eight members. By 1990 it had grown to twenty-one members. This group was constituted to respond to the request from the Congress of South African Trade Unions for an assessment of the impact of sanctions imposed in 1986 on the South African economy. The headquarters of the ET were based at ISER. In 1991 the thoughts of this group were published in an edited collection (Gelb 1991) and featured a number of chapters by Durban-based authors – Anthony Black, Steve Gelb, Doug Hindson, Mike Morris and Vishnu.

In 1995 Vishnu moved his location from UDW to the School of Development Studies at UND. He became head of the school and was renowned for being a skilful negotiator and team-builder. 'What Mike and I and Imraan [Valodia] and Julian [May] built – we created something fabulous.' Before long, the school was one of the most productive units in terms of postgraduate students and publications. Vishnu developed a research collaboration with Bill Freund, a professor of economic history at UND and supervisor of his PhD. They began to dig into local histories and together edited *(D)urban Vortex* (Freund and Padayachee 2002). This reflected Vishnu's lifelong association with and love of the city. The project also reflected his desire to contribute to a post-apartheid transition. Debates about knowledge production had begun to surface during the transition years. In January 1992 a symposium was held at UND on the 'Role of Research in Transforming South Africa'. On behalf of the organisers, Bill Freund and Mike Morris explained that 'our rationale in holding this symposium was that research in the social sciences in South Africa, both inside and outside the universities, has had a major effect on both the maintenance of apartheid and attempts to dismantle it' (Freund and Morris 1992: i). In the course of the symposium, the UND vice principal, Chris Cresswell, admitted that the challenge facing the university was to 'ensure that we make a valuable and a helpful contribution to the local community. It is through this latter activity that the university will become respected and acknowledged as a valuable asset and to which the whole community will be proud to be linked' (Cresswell 1992: 55). Vishnu was very mindful of this and was bringing his own expertise in the area of finance and banking into conjunction with the development challenges that lay before the country. Cities, he noted in the acknowledgements in *(D)urban Vortex*, 'were not just geographical concentrations of financial and industrial power, but were essentially about people, many engaged in constant struggles around work and livelihoods' (Freund and Padayachee 2002: vii).

Research dissemination and activism
Vishnu was mindful that research could be a more effective form of transformational power if attention was actively paid to its dissemination. This was one of the reasons why he gladly accepted the invitation to join the editorial board of *Transformation* in 1987 (having previously been an associate editor). His commitment to critical debate and worker struggles and his familiarity with the other editors facilitated a good working relationship, although he acknowledged that some of the editors 'were very wary about it [ANC nationalism]. So the journal I think was largely reflecting a kind of western-Marxist perspective'. After 1990, he became more active within the ANC:

> When the ANC was unbanned ... I was already working in many ways as a kind of young runner for the ANC. My house was a safe house for ANC activists ... we basically were the foot soldiers running around even in the time before the ANC was unbanned, distributing leaflets, speaking at secret meetings, and so on.

After the 1994 elections, in which the ANC obtained 62.65 per cent of the vote, he increasingly put his professional expertise at the service of the ANC, including accepting a position in April 1996 as a member of the board of directors of the South African Reserve Bank.

Reflecting back on this period from the vantage point of 2006, Vishnu described the 1990s as an 'exciting, albeit problematic era in which university-based academics had played an integral, often leading role, as policy advisers and experts to social, labour and political movements' (Padayachee 2006: ix). Referring to his 1997 inaugural lecture at UND (subsequently published in the *Review of African Political Economy* [Padayachee 1998]), he argued that

> progressive academics in the new South Africa . . . should resist the temptation to respond to the technological and developmental demands of the state and business in narrow technical ways – ways which run counter to the ethos and culture of university life, one of the few remaining sites of contemporary society for a critical and humanistic engagement with issues such as poverty, inequality, oppression, exploitation and democracy. Those academics serious about contributing to critical and effective policy debates and analysis, may, as they had done in our decade of liberation, find more socially useful roles to play within the emerging civil society movements of post-apartheid South Africa (Padayachee 2006: ix).

Conclusion: 2000 and beyond

Vishnu remained very involved in university, research and public affairs during the 2000s and indeed up until his death in 2021. For example, from August 2002 to June 2003 he served on the board of directors of Cricket South Africa. In 2004 he was elected for a two-year term by the academic staff as one of the founding members of the governing council of the then newly merged University of KwaZulu-Natal (UKZN).

By 2000, South Africa and its universities had changed dramatically from what they had been in 1980. Processes of knowledge-making had changed, and the very content of what was known had changed too. In the decades to come, the country and its higher education institutions would face new challenges. The democratisation of society and institutions would be challenged by new forms of managerialism and an audit culture in universities, and by a narrow nationalism that would emerge in the company of corruption within the ruling party, meaning that the hopes expressed in the Reconstruction and Development vision of the 1990s were not realised and, horrifyingly, social and economic inequalities would actually increase. The trade union movement would lose members and influence. Intellectually, there would be renewed interest in the position of the Global South and 'Southern Theory' would begin to shape knowledge debates.

Vishnu was well aware of the changing landscape and was aware too that transformation was not a linear process. After UDW and UND merged in 2004 to become UKZN, processes were initiated by the new vice chancellor, Malegapuru Makgoba, that produced division, centralisation and disillusionment (Chetty and Merrett 2014). Many academic staff members left the university, and with them gone, the golden age of development studies at UND ended. Vishnu said of these changes: 'I am still so angry about how it all ended . . . they destroyed the institutions that I spent my life building'.

But he remained committed both to contributing to government and to research. His last book was a combination of both of these imperatives, critically reflecting on the development of ANC economic policy and the role of intellectuals in this process and noting the disappointments of post-apartheid developments (Padayachee and Van Niekerk 2019). It is noticeable and relevant that Vishnu always understood himself as part of a community of 'progressive academics'. He consciously positioned himself in relation to fellow academics and to the ANC. As he said when I interviewed him, 'By 1990–91 my heart and soul and everything went into the ANC.'

What did it mean to be an activist scholar before 1994 and an activist scholar in the post-apartheid era? In an earlier period, under apartheid, Rick Turner had been synonymous with radical academia. He is credited with being an inspiration of the 'Durban moment' in 1973, when thousands of workers went on strike (Keniston 2017; Webster, Chapter 17 in this volume). He was assassinated on 8 January 1978 in Bellair, Durban, while confined to his home under an apartheid banning order. Raphael de Kadt describes Turner as 'exemplary in the conventional "academic" sense of a philosopher', but he emphasises that he was 'also a radical activist' (De Kadt 2017: vi). There is no doubt that Vishnu, too, was exemplary in the conventional 'academic' sense of an economist. In the post-apartheid period, being aligned with the ANC and therefore with the government, Vishnu could no longer (and did not) claim to be radical. He pursued his vision of activism through service, though he never lost his curiosity and his desire to gain a deeper understanding of the world around him.

Notes

1. Unless otherwise indicated, all quotes are taken from an interview between Robert Morrell and Vishnu Padayachee in Cape Town on 28 March 2017.
2. Eds: This appears to be a lapse in Vishnu's account. The only white teacher at the school in the 1960s and 1970s was a Mrs Rippon, a humanitarian who taught music on a part-time basis; all the other teachers were local Indian South Africans. Mrs Rippon owned the local Robin Hood Cinema mentioned in Chapter 2 of this volume.
3. I have calculated these figures from a *curriculum vitae* that Vishnu sent me at the end of 2017, and by using Google Scholar to 'count' his productive output from 2018 to the present.

References

Ancer, J. and C. Whitfield. 2021. *Joining the Dots: An Unauthorized Biography of Pravin Gordhan*. Johannesburg: Jonathan Ball.
Bonner, P. 1983. *Kings, Commoners and Concessionaires: The Evolution and Dissolution of the Nineteenth-century Swazi State*. Johannesburg: Ravan Press.
Bundy, C. 1972. 'The Emergence and Decline of a South African Peasantry'. *African Affairs* 71 (285): 369–88.
———. 1988. *The Rise and Fall of the South African Peasantry*. Oxford: James Currey.
Chetty, N. and C. Merrett. 2014. *The Struggle for the Soul of a South African University: The University of KwaZulu-Natal: Academic Freedom, Corporatisation and Transformation*. Pietermaritzburg: Natal Society Foundation.
Cresswell, C.F. 1992. 'Research in an Established South African University'. *Transformation* 18–19: 52–7.
De Kadt, R. 2017. 'Editorial'. *Theoria* 64 (151), Special issue: 'Turner and His Times': v–vii.
Freund, B. and M. Morris. 1992. 'Editorial Preface'. *Transformation* 18–19: i–ii.
Freund, B. and V. Padayachee (eds). 2002. *(D)urban Vortex: South African City in Transition*. Pietermaritzburg: University of Natal Press.
Gelb, S. (ed.). 1991. *South Africa's Economic Crisis*. Cape Town: David Philip.
Govender, P. 2007. *Love and Courage: A Story of Insubordination*. Johannesburg: Jacana Media.
Green, P. 2008. *Choice Not Fate: The Life and Times of Trevor Manuel*. Cape Town: Penguin.

Guy, J. 1982. *The Destruction of the Zulu Kingdom: The Civil War in Zululand, 1879–1884*. Johannesburg: Ravan Press.
Hassim, S. 2019. *Fatima Meer*. Cape Town: HSRC Press.
Johnstone, F.A. 1970. 'White Prosperity and White Supremacy in South Africa Today'. *African Affairs* 69 (275): 124–40.
———. 1976. *Class, Race and Gold: A Study of Class Relations and Racial Discrimination in South Africa*. London: Routledge.
Keniston, B. 2017. 'The Weight of Absence: Rick Turner and the End of the Durban Moment'. *Theoria* 64 (151): 20–8.
Legassick, M. 1974. 'South Africa: Capital Accumulation and Violence'. *Economy and Society* 3 (3): 253–91.
MacQueen, I.M. 2018. *Black Consciousness and Progressive Movements under Apartheid*. Pietermaritzburg: University of KwaZulu-Natal Press.
Morphet, T. 1990. '"Brushing History Against the Grain": Oppositional Discourse in South Africa'. *Theoria* 76: 89–99.
Morrell, R. 1991. 'Power and Politics at a Non-racial, Ethnic University: A Study of the University of Durban-Westville'. *Critical Arts* 5 (4): 49–77.
Morrell, R., V. Padayachee and S. Vawda. 1993. 'Banking, Credit and Capital in Colonial Natal'. In: *Local Supplies of Credit in the Third World 1750–1945*, edited by G. Austin and K. Sugihara. London: Macmillan and St Martin's Press.
Naidoo, J. 2010. *Fighting for Justice: A Lifetime of Political and Social Activism*. Cape Town: Pan Macmillan.
Naidoo, K. 2022. *Letters to My Mother*. Johannesburg: Jacana Media.
Padayachee, V. 1998. 'Progressive Academic Economists and the Challenge of Development in South Africa's Decade of Liberation'. *Review of African Political Economy* 25 (77): 431–50.
———. 2006. 'Foreword'. In: *Voices of Protest: Social Movements in Post-apartheid South Africa*, edited by R. Ballard, A. Habib and I. Valodia. Pietermaritzburg: University of KwaZulu-Natal Press.
Padayachee, V. and R. Morrell. 1991. 'Indian Merchants and Dukawallahs in the Natal Economy, *c*.1875–1914'. *Journal of Southern African Studies* 17 (1): 71–102.
Padayachee, V., S. Vawda and P. Tichman. 1985. *Indian Workers and Trades Unions in Durban, 1930–1950*. Durban: Institute for Social and Economic Research, University of Durban-Westville.
Padayachee, V. and R. van Niekerk. 2019. *Shadow of Liberation: Contestation and Compromise in the Economic and Social Policy of the African National Congress, 1943–1996*. Johannesburg: Wits University Press.
Peires, J.B. 1982. *The House of Phalo: A History of the Xhosa People in the Days of Their Independence*. Johannesburg: Ravan Press.
Saul, J. and S. Gelb. 1986. *The Crisis in South Africa*. New York: Monthly Review Press.
Wolpe, H. 1972. 'Capitalism and Cheap Labour-power in South Africa: From Segregation to Apartheid'. *Economy and Society* 1 (4): 425–56.

Interviews
John Butler-Adam, virtual, 17 February 2020.
Vishnu Padayachee, Cape Town, 28 March 2017.
Imraan Valodia, Cape Town, 17 January 2018.

4

The Measure of Mistrust

African Artisanal Gold Mining and the Geopolitics of the Barbarous Relic

Keith Breckenridge

In conversation and in print, Vishnu Padayachee was fond of elevating professional economists who had completed quantitatively demanding degrees and worked in the real economy (Padayachee and Sender 2018: 150) above the ranks of other academics and activists. Who can blame him? Yet this admiration for the professional quantitative expertise of the economists had few meaningful echoes in his own thinking. Vishnu's intellectual interests were intensely scholastic and historical, an aptitude most obvious in the obsessive reconstruction of the events and drivers of the African National Congress's (ANC) economic policy that produced *Shadow of Liberation* (Padayachee and Van Niekerk 2019). He was also a prodigious collector and reader of old books, with a specialist's familiarity with the intellectual history of South African economics. His life and his politics gave him a distinctive interest in a cluster of problems that have defined the economic history of this country: the mining corporations, central banking, the gold standard, Keynes's theories of monetary policy and their weak local appeal, and the global effects of Indian monetary history in shaping all of this. In a string of papers written with Bradley Bordiss, Keith Hart and Jannie Roussouw he produced a set of arguments that will shape the future understanding of South African capitalism (Bordiss and Padayachee 2011; Hart and Padayachee 2013; Padayachee and Bordiss 2013, 2015; Padayachee and Rossouw 2019). In each of these areas – the politics of gold mining, the obsessions of South African central bankers, the social and intellectual foundations of Afrikaner capitalism – I think there is plenty of opportunity for productive and ongoing debate.

In this chapter I want to examine the monetary history of gold, which lies at the heart of the critique of hard money, and in particular the optimistic belief in institutional trust that underpins the Keynesian argument for 'scientific monetary policy' (Keynes [1913] 2013b: 51). As Padayachee and Bordiss (2013: 825) observed of his attempts to dissuade Indian politicians from restoring monetary gold, it was Keynes who moved the explanation of British 'success away from the "barbarous relic" of mistrust represented by the gold standard and towards the trust, cooperation and shared resources that was the British banking system'. Yet, after half a century of dollar-supremacy, and a global system of quantitative finance dependent on it, geopolitical conflicts are renewing global demand for gold as money – especially in the countries that Keynes, Lehfeldt and Jevons described as sinks of precious metals (Jevons 1879; Keynes [1913] 2013b). This apparently insatiable 'barbarous' demand for gold as money is shredding the institutional and infrastructural foundations of African economies.

African gold mining
A global system of value, with African mines at its centre, has distinguished monetary gold for more than a millennium. This often-fabulous association between the continent and bullion has cloudy roots in the ancient mining of gold in the Nubian desert, but the stylised fact of the African origins of gold dates from the *hajj* of the Malian emperor, Mūsā, in the fourteenth century. His arrival in Cairo around 1324, with tens of thousands of slave retainers and tons of gold, was measured long afterwards in the metal's depressed price, and an enduring obsession with the geography of the gold mines of the Sahel possessed Arab and Christian geographers. By the fifteenth century gold provided a common regime of value, denominated in the Arab's 4.5-gram *mithqal* measure of gold dust, on both sides of the Sahara, and in much of the Mediterranean region. It was the rumours of the riches of the mines of Senegal and the Gold Coast, fostered by centuries of trade across the desert, that first attracted the Portuguese travelling around the bulge of West Africa in the fifteenth century, and the British and the French who followed them two centuries later (Curtin 1973; Garrard 1982; Gomez 2018; Lopez 1951; Thornton 1992).

In the twentieth century, the epicentre of the global system of value that was organised around gold shifted emphatically south. For almost the entirety of the twentieth century, the international market in gold was a monopoly of the South African deep-level mines, and of the richly capitalised, vertically integrated corporations that owned and managed them. One driver of this strange South African monopoly was the low, fixed price of gold, which remained, under the terms of the Bretton Woods agreement, at $35 per ounce from 1934 to 1971. The remorselessly declining real value of gold in these decades encouraged the South African mines to depress African wages; it also discouraged gold mining everywhere else. Over the course of the 1950s and 1960s the proportion of gold produced outside South Africa fell from 60 per cent to 25 per cent. This meant a continuous decline in mining in the major producing countries like Australia, Canada and the United States. Importantly, it also constrained gold mining on the rest of the African continent – including in the historically important regions of the Sahel, where small-scale mining remained basically unattractive throughout the Bretton Woods era (D'Avignon 2018; Hirsch 1968).

Over the last decade, and especially over the last five years as the price of gold has approached $2 000 an ounce, a new global pattern of gold exploitation has emerged. South Africans have watched with growing despair as thousands of desperate migrants have crept into old and abandoned mines, scavenging their architectures – and the towns, public infrastructures and economies around them – to feed an illegal gold market. The discontent stirred by the local power of these *zama zamas*, combined with the obvious complicity of the South African Police Service, triggered a national crisis in July 2022 after an alleged outbreak of gang rape in Krugersdorp. The national panic, and the grandstanding arrests of more than one hundred illegal miners, all faded away to nothing in yet another collapsed prosecution. Conspicuous official incompetence has only added to the sense of a uniquely South African post-extractive catastrophe (De Greef 2023). But this feeling of a very specific, gold-induced crisis on the Witwatersrand ignores the significance of what artisanal mining is doing elsewhere.

Across Africa, illegal and informal gold mining is reshaping national economies, political power and bureaucratic capacity. Aside from South Africa, illicit mining and the illegal export of gold are significant, and well documented, in twenty countries on the continent. Countries that do not mine much gold, like Burundi, Cameroon, Kenya, Rwanda, Togo and Uganda, are the sites of refineries that channel the metal to the opaque markets in Dubai. Meaningful statistics on the size of the total African workforce employed in illicit gold mining do not yet exist (Geenen, Stoop and Verpoorten 2021; Verbrugge and Geenen 2019), but the national estimates for individual countries are very large: more than half a million people work directly in unlicensed gold mines in each of the twenty countries referred to above. In Burkina Faso, the Democratic Republic of the Congo (DRC), Ethiopia, Ghana, Madagascar, Sudan and Tanzania carefully produced estimates suggest that more than one million people are directly employed in illicit gold mining. In Zimbabwe, serious researchers estimate that the artisanal mining workforce numbers more than one and a half million people. By contrast, the South African *zama zama* workforce is officially estimated at around twenty thousand people; our taxi industry, the most visible and ubiquitous employer in the country, employs about half a million people (International Crisis Group 2020).

One popular explanation for the power of illicit mining has been based on the idea of conflict resources, especially in the gold mining areas of eastern Congo and, more recently, in a huge field across the Sahel, from Darfur in Sudan to the area around the Tasiast open-cast mine in Mauritania (Chevrillon-Guibert, Gagnol and Magrin 2019; Tooze 2023). Financing from new mine resources created, in Paul Collier's influential phrase, a new 'opportunity for rebellion' (Collier and Hoeffler 2004), and the increased prices paid for many mined commodities after 2001 encouraged and resourced widespread violence and civil war (Berman et al. 2017; Collier and Hoeffler 2004). Public enthusiasm for this argument in the wealthy countries – carefully fostered by influential non-governmental organisations (NGOs), and surreptitiously endorsed by mining companies looking to exploit their customers' desire for clean hands – motivated the inclusion of Section 1502 in the Dodd–Frank Act of 2010, which prohibited US companies from sourcing minerals from conflict zones. These restrictions effectively hastened Congolese artisanal miners' move away from the '3Ts' (tin, tungsten and tantalum) to gold (Geenen 2014; Stoop, Verpoorten and Van der Windt 2018). Gold was formally included in the Dodd–Frank restrictions, but, as I will explain, it has financial and material qualities that frustrate the kinds of supply-chain due diligence that NGOs demand of the other metals.

There is, undeniably, something to the argument that artisanal gold mining sustains (and is sustained by) civil war. Well-documented examples of paramilitary control over gold stretch from the Rapid Support Forces' control of the Jabel Amer mines in Darfur (Bartlett 2016) to the Wagner Group's seizure of the Ndassima pit in the Central African Republic (The Africa Report 2023). There is more contested evidence of the Ugandan military's involvement in small-scale mining in the DRC in the 1990s, and, more recently, of Al Qaeda-affiliated militants in Burkina Faso occupying hundreds of mining sites in the north of the country (Autesserre 2012; Lewis and McNeill 2019; UN Security Council Panel of Experts 2001). Yet the scale of mining, with tens of thousands of sites spread across vast territories over long periods of time, makes the claim that conflict is the driver of artisanal mining implausible. Illicit gold mining has become a form of subsistence – and in many places (the DRC, Ghana, Sudan, Madagascar) the main form of non-farming employment. 'How many people in Burkina Faso can pay the school fees without artisanal mining?' the head of Burkina Faso's national union of gold miners asked Reuters' reporters in 2019. 'Our economy is gold mining. There is nothing else' (Lewis and McNeill 2019).

A related popular explanation of the dominance of illicit gold mining on the continent highlights the organising activities of flamboyant gangsters, who look to control production with more constrained enthusiasm for violence than the militias. Some of the journalists' fondness for the flamboyant gangsters is simply the techniques of compelling investigative journalism. As the *Al Jazeera* documentary 'Gold Mafia' (2023) so clearly shows, the shenanigans of figures like Kamlesh Pattni (who was a central actor in Kenya's Goldenberg scandal and remains active in Zimbabwe), Simon Rudland (the flamboyant owner of the Golden Leaf Tobacco Corporation [see amaBhungane 2022b]), and Uebert Mudzanire (an apostolic prophet and President Mnangagwa's envoy) make for compelling storytelling. Kimon de Greef's excellent *New Yorker* story on the *zama zamas* of Welkom is organised around the impressive (and terrifying) entrepreneurship of David 'One Eye' Ndlovu (aka Khombi /Kumbi) (De Greef 2023). Yet, again, there is a danger in overstating the activities of these gangsters to the point of confusion.

In every case, what distinguishes illicitly mined gold (much more than any of the many other illegally traded commodities) is that it is money, and, especially, that it has the secure cross-currency value that states, in particular, require. In Zimbabwe, the central bank conspires with gold smugglers (and money launderers from around the world) to ship the gold produced by thousands of informal miners to the opaque metal markets in Dubai. In Sudan, the control that Hemeidti's Rapid Support Forces exercised over the miners in Darfur from 2016 was endorsed by a prohibition on exports that required all sales of unrefined gold to be made to the central bank. Following the coup in 2019, gold merchants were allowed to sell directly to the markets in Dubai, but their foreign exchange earnings must be sold to the central bank in Khartoum at a 50 per cent discount on the black-market rate. Until it was sanctioned by the US government in 2021, Alain Goetz's refinery in Uganda, which mines no gold, was sustained by the removal of all taxes on gold exports in 2017; the country was exporting more than $2 billion worth of the metal, or roughly 40 per cent of total exports. In South Africa, the Rappa refinery associated with Rudland has been charged by the revenue collector, the South African Revenue Service (SARS), with a scheme to earn value-added tax (VAT) refunds by melting down Krugerrands and then exporting them as raw gold. Rappa has claimed R7 billion in VAT refunds for the export of more than eighty tons of gold (much of it purported to be sourced from artisanal miners in South Africa and elsewhere in the subcontinent). SARS claims that the gold was purchased from the Rand Refinery, as Krugerrand coins, and then illegally melted down into bars to qualify for the refund. The 14 per cent VAT exemption on Krugerrands is allowed because they are legal tender in South Africa, but it is also a crime to destroy or alter them (amaBhungane 2022a).

While scholars, NGOs and policy advisers in rich countries have called for the harmonisation of gold export taxes across the region to discourage smuggling, and for powerful donors to compel African states to formalise small miners' rights, artisanal gold has continued to grow as a powerful driver of institutional mistrust and state failure on the continent. Ghana provides a succinct model of how this works. Thousands of Chinese traders now work with hundreds of thousands of *galamsey* miners who have invaded the gold-bearing hillsides radiating out from Obuasi, the huge property abandoned by AngloGold Ashanti in 2014. Ghana now exports more gold than South Africa (a third of it directly from more than five hundred thousand *galamsey* miners). As is the case in South Africa, these undocumented and untaxed exports are an opaque and potent source of political mistrust. In 2017, after the environmental costs of the widely dispersed alluvial mines became increasingly obvious across the Ashanti region, Ghanaian media began to focus on the lost revenues from licensing and export taxes. Meanwhile, in Washington, AngloGold had filed a formal (and potentially very expensive) dispute against the Ghanaian government for failing to protect the Obuasi property from the *galamsey* miners. In August of that year the state duly began to take a much more aggressive, and paramilitary, approach to controlling the informal miners. But, like the South African drama, the results of the blowhard policing have only weakened public confidence in the state's commitment to legal regulation. This pervasive public misgiving was reflected in a series of video documentaries titled *Galamsey Economy* released between 2019 and the end of 2022, in which a Ghanaian investigative journalist recorded officials taking cash bribes to bypass the newly onerous licensing requirements for small-scale miners (see Arcton-Tettey 2022). This series culminated in November with a public showing of the third episode at the Accra International Conference Centre in which hundreds of viewers were treated to the sight of the deputy finance minister, Charles Adu Boahen (son of the famous historian), apparently accepting a $200 000 cash payment from a putative Gulf investor looking to secure a meeting with Vice President Bawumi (Mcternan and Smith 2017; Mensah 2022). Boahen was promptly sacked by President Akufo-Addo, but the sense that the institutions of democratic government are too weak to withstand the corrupting effects of rents from gold money remained.

Supply
The ubiquity of artisanal mining on the continent prompts careful consideration of the financial and institutional capacities of gold in our current moment. This also suggests that we should rethink the most influential accounts of gold's place in modern capitalism. Some of the most common elements are now blindingly obvious. At nearly $2 000 per ounce, the current international price is eight times what it was at the end of the 1990s, when it reached a low of $250 after two decades of slow and steady decline. The unregulated markets in raw gold in Dubai are drawing exports from across the continent that match new, well-resourced private demand from many countries in the Gulf and across Asia. Recently, Reuters has reported that the refineries in Dubai (which receive no shipments from the continent's formal mining companies) processed nearly four hundred and fifty tons of illicit, unrefined gold

during 2016, then valued at more than $15 billion, from African sources (Lewis, McNeill and Shabalala 2019; Lezhnev 2021; Marks and Alamin 2023). In the five years since that report was published, the gold price in dollars has nearly doubled – and many of the currencies of the supplying countries have collapsed.

On the supply side, hundreds of millions of potential workers on the continent have few compelling alternatives for employment. The wages earned by the manual labourers who do the actual mining – in Ghana, Sudan, eastern DRC, South Africa – are impressively constant at less than $5 per day. The $120 per month that millions of artisanal miners now earn across the continent in 2023 compares disconcertingly with the $220 per month (in 2023 dollars) that South African black miners earned (exclusive of their living costs) in 1969, *before* wages began rapidly to increase. Yet artisanal miners today are more likely to compare their work and wages with their kin working in agriculture, where earnings, often shared with a family, are generally closer to $1 per day. There is much, as I will show below, that distinguishes gold mining from the other forms of work available, but one element, in particular, is the seductive possibility of a bounty that will lift workers out of poverty. As the name *zama zama* (try, try) used in Southern Africa suggests, one of the real drivers of the mass engagement with artisanal mining is a lottery effect, what Sandra Calkins has described as the dream of the lucky strike: 'that God-willing they would find cars, stone houses, or new wives in the soil' (Calkins 2016; Chevrillon-Guibert, Gagnol and Magrin 2019: 12). What makes this windfall strategy feasible is that workers are generally paid from their own ore. The popular technique of mercury amalgamation (although wasting as much as 50 per cent of the captured gold, and poisoning people and water sources) allows individual workers to control the final stages in the production of dense, high-value ore, and to capture any windfalls, however unlikely they may be (Bansah 2022; Calkins 2016; Crowley 2014; Geenen, Stoop and Verpoorten 2021).

Informal mining is also supported by a uniform network of informal finance. Migrant workers, traders and suppliers lend funds to miners to purchase the devices, chemicals and food they need. In Ghana much of the working finance is now provided by Chinese traders, who collaborate with local miners and land-controlling aristocrats to fund licences, excavators and the trommels used to separate grains of sand; in the Sahel (where the gold can appear in nugget form) migrant workers from the Gulf purchase expensive metal detectors; in the DRC gold traders provide advances for the basic equipment and provisions required by teams of miners; and in South Africa workers also borrow money from traders and gangsters to sustain long periods of work underground (Calkins 2016; Crawford and Botchwey 2017; De Greef 2023; Geenen 2014). It is these informal debts – paired with the hope of the lottery payout – that bind workers to the job under often intolerable conditions, including violence and brutal policing. Unlike the controls over foreign exchange and gold-money, what distinguishes these systems of finance is the absence of formal banks and the state.

A host of official and semi-official rent-seekers thrive above and around the miners' production. Aristocrats, gangs and politicians commonly tax the miners, and – in the DRC and South Africa – they have sometimes forced them to work without pay. The police and the military, everywhere, extract transit payments either directly from the miners, or from the traders and financiers who earn the real money from mining. Intriguingly, the most successful of the apex entrepreneurs who control regional flows of gold draw on elaborate forms of apostolic celebrity to repurpose their wealth. After the public drama of the Goldenberg prosecutions, Kamlesh Pattni was reborn in the Redeemed Gospel Church as Brother Paul, and became a pastor in his own congregation; Uebert Mudzanire, the protagonist in *Al Jazeera*'s gold-washing documentary, is a self-described prophet and founder of the Spirit Embassy ministry in Manchester, UK; David One-Eye Kumbi, sentenced to life imprisonment for murder over a failed gold sale, is organising prayer sessions of his apostolic church in prison. Sara Geenen's informants describe an ex-miner in Kamitunga, eastern DRC, a 'very rich person and role model', who is the president of the miners' association and 'pastor in the "Ministère du combat spirituel"' (Geenen 2014: 186). Nor is the religious reworking of gold mining a pentacostal monopoly: Calkins's informants in Sudan describe 'a divine being, an Islamic God, who was held with planting the nuggets in the ground for certain ordained prospectors' (Calkins 2016). Followers of George Simmel might argue that these entertaining variations on the prosperity gospel work to domesticate and normalise the disturbingly abstract and alienated powers of money – in particular, of gold's ability to act across time and place, without regard to the circumstances of its creation. They will certainly point to the similarities between the universal obsession with money and modern religious revivalism. As Simmel observes, the 'wild scramble for money, the impulsiveness that money – in contrast with other central values, for example landed property – spreads over the economy and indeed over life in general ... approaches that of a religious mood' (Simmel 2004: 235). But it is also difficult to avoid the feeling that these religious entrepreneurs are simply scoundrels, scrambling for opportunities to leverage their success in raising rents from the gold trade.

The global supply of informally mined gold derives, principally, from a powerful match between the continent's geology and its distinctive demography. Gold is mined in tens of thousands of small sites, by relatively small numbers of workers, in each of these national regions. In eastern DRC, for example, there are more than two thousand seven hundred individual mines, each employing one hundred to two hundred workers. The same pattern of open, mobile, dispersed expansion and settlement is visible wherever gold is found in the ground. Katja Werthmann in Burkina Faso (2009, 2012), Boris Verbrugge and Sara Geenen in the DRC (2019), and Raphaëlle Chevrillon-Guibert, Laurent Gagnol, and Géraud Magrin in Sudan (2019) have separately described open mining frontiers developing beyond the administrative territory of already very weak states that overwhelm the property leases and titles of mining companies. These frontiers of work provide earnings to masses of unemployed and displaced people. Women, forced out of subsistence farming or formal work by conflict or poverty, participate actively on this frontier, with many researchers estimating that they make up a third of the total workforce. This is true in the Sahel, where women work in the mining camps and carry a specific reputational burden not shared with the male workers (Werthmann 2009). In each region an irrepressible human frontier exploits borderlands, surpassing shattered and dangerous transport infrastructures to move gold into well-established smuggling networks. While many states make a formal effort to register and regulate artisanal mines, none of these systems currently works in practice, and the miners (and officials) exploit their indifference to laws that derive from distant administrative centres.

Conflict over property rights arrangements – with contested claims of ownership between the state, aristocrats and local communities that share only their hostility to private, individualised and abstracted titles – creates the opportunity for these new subterranean claims. In occupying and working a claim, artisanal miners assert a strange, new, individualised right to the resources in the ground, but, in asserting this claim, they recognise a range of local institutions and tribunals – typically by paying fees and taxes. 'The gold miners, knowing they are technically "illegally" (according to the Mining Code) working in an industrial concession,' Geenen notes, 'therefore look for other sources of legitimacy' (Geenen 2014; 189; see also Klein 2022; Werthmann 2012). But there are also clear limits to the regulatory authority of these institutions. National and customary laws that have been designed to strengthen the claims of artisanal miners and local rights also contain clauses requiring the rehabilitation of agricultural land, which are observed only in the breach. The property claims of many large, industrial miners have been shredded by similar processes of mobile, distributed, individualised encroachment that dissolve boundaries and repurpose existing infrastructures. AngloGold Ashanti's decade-long unsuccessful struggle to control access to its large (and very expensive) Obuasi property in Ghana is probably the most visible of these processes of dispersed, and irresistible, encroachment. But similar unrelenting white-anting frontiers – where the informal miners and waves of violence have managed to turn employees and officials to their interests – have been documented in Burkina Faso, the DRC and South Africa (Faku 2023; Geenen 2014; Reuters 2022).

Demand
While the demographic and institutional features of African economies are important determinants of the main features of the gold frontier, the most potent drivers lie on the demand side of the global trade: in particular, in the sustained, elevated prices of the metal at source. It is gold's close monetary relationship with the dollar (half a century after the collapse of the fixed Bretton Woods dollar-gold exchange) that has created insatiable demand for the metal. Current demand, it is important to note, derives from countries that Jevons, Keynes and Lehfeldt described as the gold sinks of Asia: China, India, Turkey, Uzbekistan (Jevons 1879; Keynes [1913] 2013b).

The effects of this demand are felt on the gold frontier in an unusually double-sided manner. First, in the elevated, international prices for refined bullion in Dubai that attract miners, traders and smugglers to the gold frontier. And, second, in the local prices of unrefined gold at its source. For – quite unlike the global commodities like cocoa and coffee that African farmers produce, or the other metals that informal miners have generated – unrefined gold earns a price at source that is the same as, and *often higher* than, the metropolitan price (Calkins 2016; Crowley 2014; Geenen 2014; International Crisis Group 2019; Verbrugge and Geenen 2019). This price premium is a consequence of gold's many-sided uses as money – 'the choice it offers', as Simmel observes, 'increases its value' (2004: 212). The compact monetary form of gold in eastern DRC, Johannesburg, or western Sudan has specific additional uses for the illicit movement of private wealth, tax avoidance and, especially, money laundering: gold has an undiscounted capacity to wash the source of wealth, wherever it is generated.

The South African Chamber of Mines and the World Gold Council have long promised to provide a method for metallurgical fingerprinting of refined gold, without success. The most current forms of provenance endorsed by the London Bullion Market Association rely entirely on paperwork from the licensed refineries used by the large mines. These documentation systems have only been in existence since 2012, and cover only a small fraction of the total global supply. Gold passes continuously between jewellery, coins and bars, in private hands. That the Swiss and Emirati refineries, and private and central banks, all have a material interest in maintaining this anonymity makes it unlikely to change (Crowley 2014; Loeb 2018). As Khadija Sherife observed in her recent report, using the Panama Papers, on the transfer of wealth from the DRC, whereas 'currencies are attached to regulatory systems, reserve banks, and, ultimately, nationalities, gold is without identity, borderless and ever valuable' (Sharife 2016). Importantly and distinctively, these special features of gold are more valuable the greater the distance from the highly liquid, opaque, digitised and international financial markets in the metropolitan centres. That the local money supply – in countries like Zimbabwe and the DRC – has often been almost entirely dollarised by the collapse of central bank currencies only adds to the monetary functions and value of gold dust.

Half a century after divorce ended the unhappy marriage that (the reluctant) Maynard Keynes had negotiated with Harry Smith at Bretton Woods, the relationship between gold and the dollar remains geopolitically potent. Global dollar ascendancy, released from the constraints of the fixed price of gold, grew steadily – from the eurodollars of the 1960s and petrodollars of the 1970s to Japanese and Chinese purchases of exploding US government debts in the 1980s. The Federal Reserve Bank's use of dollar swap lines to manage regional liquidity crises after the 2008 crisis arguably created the global 'scientific standard' of central bank-managed money that Keynes had first proposed in 1923 (Keynes 2013a; Skidelsky 2005; Tooze 2018). Yet, this political arrangement, as Keynes well understood, depends on the delicate fabric of trust between banks, nationally and internationally. 'A preference for a tangible gold currency,' he argued in his defence of its prohibition in colonial India, was a 'relic of a time when governments were less trustworthy in these matters than they are now' (Keynes 2013b: 51; Skidelsky 2005: 196).

Yet, (as Keynes was reminded in the bitter negotiations with his American partners in the 1940s) institutional trust, especially across international boundaries, has long been wildly unevenly distributed in the global economy. In most developing countries, the private holders of financial assets have good historical reasons to mistrust the intentions and the capacity of their state-controlled monetary institutions. In many Islamic countries, doubts about the central banks' commitment to the 'scientific standard' are coupled with religious prohibition on interest-bearing assets. For the last twenty years, beginning long before the inflationary crisis in 2018, Turks imported more than one hundred and fifty tons of gold each year, including the largest global imports of gold coins. In much of Keynes's barbaric world, one of the key drivers of these enormous investments is a society-wide convention that sequesters gold wealth in the hands of women. Recently, these long-established conventions for private investments in gold have been bolstered by central bank purchases and by the falling values of dollar-denominated long-term debts (Dempsey 2022; Gülseven and Ekici 2016; Lex Populi 2023).

A more important measure of the enduring potency of geopolitical mistrust has been the return to gold of the central banks with the largest holdings of dollar-denominated assets in the months since the Russian invasion of Ukraine. Twenty-five years after Gordon Brown announced that nearly two-thirds of the gold reserves of the Bank of England would be converted into a 'profit maximizing portfolio of currencies' (The Times 1999), the dependence of the dollar-denominated financial order on the cooperation of states and central banks has suddenly become obvious again. The blocking of nearly $350 billion of Russian sovereign and corporate assets – and the prospect of additional global conflicts in the future – has triggered a historically unprecedented scramble to rebuild gold reserves. The central banks of Asia purchased nearly seven hundred tons in the course of 2023, and their large purchases continue. These sterile assets once again endanger the 'scientific management' of cross-border liquidity crises that obsessed Bagehot, Keynes and Tooze – as they did in the last years of Bretton Woods.

This sudden return to gold is particularly startling, because it comes in the wake of the success of a new monetary 'toolkit' that dominated emerging market economies in the aftermath of the Covid-19 crisis. Tooze has shown that central banks had mastered a common set of tools over the previous decade, which they used to manage the liquidity problems that were triggered by the pandemic and its aftermath: borrow in local currencies; allow foreign exchange markets to manage speculative investment (and firms to manage their risks with interest rate derivatives); accumulate massive foreign reserves to absorb shocks; work with regional trading partners to distribute liquidity problems and solutions; and, in the event of existential crisis, turn back to capital controls (Tooze 2021). Writers in the Bagehot tradition (including Tooze, Keynes and Vishnu Padayachee) will see this evidence that 'practice had moved ahead of theory' as evidence of the pragmatic drivers of modern, scientific monetary policy (Tooze 2021: 166). Yet, the sudden return to gold suggests the frailty of the fabric of institutional trust in the face of geopolitical conflicts. Keynesians will argue, of course, that the real driver of the resurgence of mistrust (and the restoration of the monetary value of gold) is the central bankers' austere interest rate regime that punishes the holders of long-dated dollar-denominated assets. Some of that is, no doubt, important, but it is difficult to imagine the Asian central banks rushing back to US government debt when interest rates begin to settle again. Most unexpectedly, the barbarous relic has re-established itself as one of the key instruments of value outside the metropolitan centres, and Africans, once again, are at the centre of this new financial order.

References

The Africa Report. 2023. 'CAR – Cameroon: An Investigation into the Wagner Group's African Financial Model'. *The Africa Report*, 18 January. https://www.theafricareport.com/275235/car-cameroon-an-investigation-into-the-wagner-groups-african-financial-model/.

Al Jazeera. 2023. 'Gold Mafia: Episode 1: The Laundry Service'. *Al Jazeera Investigations*. https://www.youtube.com/watch?v=evWEuVR1XIs.

amaBhungane. 2022a. 'Gold "Scam" Robs SA of Billions, Says SARS'. *amaBhungane*, 3 February. Blog post. https://amabhungane.org/stories/220203-gold-scam-robs-sa-of-billions-says-sars/.

———. 2022b. 'The Laundry: How Shape-Shifting "Money Launderers" Infiltrated SA Banks (Part One)'. *amaBhungane*, 25 October. Blog post. https://amabhungane.org/stories/the-laundry-how-shape-shifting-money-launderers-infiltrated-sa-banks-part-one/.

Arcton-Tettey, B. 2022. 'Ghana: Large Crowds Throng AICC to Watch "Galamsey Economy" by Anas'. *Ghanaian Times*, 16 November. https://allafrica.com/stories/202211160344.html.

Autesserre, S. 2012. 'Dangerous Tales: Dominant Narratives on the Congo and Their Unintended Consequences'. *African Affairs* 111 (443): 202–22. https://doi.org/10.1093/afraf/adr080.

Bansah, P.K. 2022. 'Ghana's Artisanal Miners Are a Law Unto Themselves – Involving Communities Can Help Fix the Problem'. *The Conversation Africa*, 14 October. https://allafrica.com/stories/202210140001.html.

Bartlett, A. 2016. 'Conflict Extractivism in Darfur's Gold Mines'. *Peace Review* 28 (1): 46–54. https://doi.org/10.1080/10402659.2016.1130378.

Berman, N., M. Couttenier, D. Rohner and M. Thoenig. 2017. 'This Mine Is Mine! How Minerals Fuel Conflicts in Africa'. *American Economic Review* 107 (6): 1564–610. https://doi.org/10.1257/aer.20150774.

Bordiss, B. and V. Padayachee. 2011. '"A Superior Practical Man": Sir Henry Strakosch, the Gold Standard and Monetary Policy Debates in South Africa, 1920–23'. *Economic History of Developing Regions* 26 (sup 1): S114–22. https://doi.org/10.1080/20780389.2011.586411.

Calkins, S. 2016. 'How "Clean Gold" Came to Matter: Metal Detectors, Infrastructure, and Valuation'. *HAU: Journal of Ethnographic Theory* 6 (2): 173–95. https://doi.org/10.14318/hau6.2.013.

Chevrillon-Guibert, R., L. Gagnol and G. Magrin. 2019. 'Les ruées vers l'or au Sahara et au nord du Sahel: Ferment de crise ou stabilisateur?' *Hérodote* 172 (1): 193–215. https://doi.org/10.3917/her.172.0193.

Collier, P. and A. Hoeffler. 2004. 'Greed and Grievance in Civil War'. *Oxford Economic Papers* 56 (4): 563–95. https://doi.org/10.1093/oep/gpf064.

Crawford, G. and G. Botchwey. 2017. 'Conflict, Collusion and Corruption in Small-scale Gold Mining: Chinese Miners and the State in Ghana'. *Commonwealth and Comparative Politics* 55 (4): 444–70. https://doi.org/10.1080/14662043.2017.1283479.

Crowley, K. 2014. 'Deadly Illegal Mining Booms below the City of Gold'. *Moneyweb*, 24 April. https://www.moneyweb.co.za/archive/deadly-illegal-mining-booms-below-the-city-of-gold/.

Curtin, P. D. 1973. 'The Lure of Bambuk Gold'. *Journal of African History* 14 (4): 623–31.

D'Avignon, R. 2018. 'Primitive Techniques: From "Customary" to "Artisanal" Mining in French West Africa'. *Journal of African History* 59 (2): 179–97. https://doi.org/10.1017/S0021853718000361.

De Greef, K. 2023. 'The Dystopian Underworld of South Africa's Illegal Gold Mines'. *The New Yorker*, 20 February. https://www.newyorker.com/magazine/2023/02/27/the-dystopian-underworld-of-south-africas-illegal-gold-mines.

Dempsey, H. 2022. 'Gold Buyers Binge on Biggest Volumes for 55 Years'. *Financial Times*, 29 December. https://www.ft.com/content/e0983ebb-bbe0-4d33-8517-e19fa06e1a77.

Faku, D. 2023. '"Criminal Justice System Failing Miners": Sibanye-Stillwater Says Illegal Mining by Zama Zamas Presents a Growing Material Risk to Its Operations'. *BusinessLIVE*, 30 April. https://www.businesslive.co.za/bt/business-and-economy/2023-04-30-criminal-justice-system-failing-miners/.

Garrard, T.F. 1982. 'Myth and Metrology: The Early Trans-Saharan Gold Trade'. *Journal of African History* 23 (4): 443–61. https://doi.org/10.1017/S0021853700021290.

Geenen, S. 2014. '"Qui Cherche, Trouve": The Political Economy of Access to Gold Mining and Trade in South Kivu, DRC'. PhD thesis, University of Antwerp.

Geenen, S., N. Stoop and M. Verpoorten. 2021. 'How Much Do Artisanal Miners Earn? An Inquiry among Congolese Gold Miners'. *Resources Policy* 70: 101893. https://doi.org/10.1016/j.resourpol.2020.101893.

Gomez, M. 2018. *African Dominion: A New History of Empire in Early and Medieval West Africa*. Princeton: Princeton University Press. https://doi.org/10.1515/9781400888160.

Gülseven, O. and Ö. Ekici. 2016. 'The Turkish Appetite for Gold: An Islamic Explanation'. *Resources Policy* 48 (June): 41–9. https://doi.org/10.1016/j.resourpol.2016.02.006.

Hart, K. and V. Padayachee. 2013. 'A History of South African Capitalism in National and Global Perspective'. *Transformation* 81 (1): 55–85. https://doi.org/10.1353/trn.2013.0004.

Hirsch, F. 1968. 'Influences on Gold Production (Les Influences s'exerçant sur la production de l'or) (Factores Que Influyen Sobre La Producción Del Oro)'. *Staff Papers (International Monetary Fund)* 15 (3): 405–90. https://doi.org/10.2307/3866297.

International Crisis Group. 2019. *Getting a Grip on Central Sahel's Gold Rush*. Africa Report 282. Brussels: International Crisis Group.

———. 2020. *All That Glitters Is Not Gold: Turmoil in Zimbabwe's Mining Sector*. Africa Report 294. Brussels: International Crisis Group. https://www.crisisgroup.org/africa/southern-africa/zimbabwe/294-all-glitters-not-gold-turmoil-zimbabwes-mining-sector.

Jevons, W.S. 1879. *Money and the Mechanism of Exchange*. New York: D. Appleton and Company.

Keynes, J.M. 2013a. *A Tract on Monetary Reform. The Collected Writings of John Maynard Keynes*, Vol. 4. Cambridge: Cambridge University Press.

———. [1913] 2013b. *Indian Currency and Finance*. Cambridge: Cambridge University Press.

Klein, B.I. 2022. 'Local Institutions and Artisanal Mining: Governance Forms in the Goldfields of Madagascar'. *Journal of Rural Studies* 92 (May): 269–83. https://doi.org/10.1016/j.jrurstud.2022.03.030.

Lewis, D. and R. McNeill. 2019. 'Special Report: How Jihadists Struck Gold in Africa's Sahel'. *Reuters*, 22 November. https://www.reuters.com/article/uk-gold-africa-islamists-specialreport-idUKKBN1XW11C.

Lewis, D., R. McNeill and Z. Shabalala. 2019. 'Gold Worth Billions Is Smuggled out of Africa – New Analysis'. *Reuters*, 24 April. https://www.reuters.com/investigates/special-report/gold-africa-smuggling/.

Lex Populi. 2023. 'Gold Shines as Rate Declines Come Closer'. *Financial Times*, 24 March. https://www.ft.com/content/7a4b7737-7ee8-430f-9268-d9681beee733.

Lezhnev, S. 2021. *Conflict Gold to Responsible Gold: A Roadmap for Companies and Governments*. Briefing. Washington DC: The Sentry. https://thesentry.org/reports/conflict-gold-to-responsible-gold/.

Loeb, J. 2018. 'Tracing the Story of "Tainted" Gold'. *Engineering and Technology* 13 (3): 20–5. https://doi.org/10.1049/et.2018.0300.

Lopez, R.S. 1951. 'The Dollar of the Middle Ages'. *Journal of Economic History* 11 (3): 209–34. https://doi.org/10.1017/S0022050700084746.

Marks, S. and M. Alamin. 2023. 'Post-Coup Plan Puts Spotlight on Sudan Army's Economic Empire'. *Bloomberg.Com*, 29 March. https://www.bloomberg.com/news/articles/2023-03-29/post-coup-plan-puts-spotlight-on-sudan-army-s-economic-empire.

McTernan, B.A. and P. Smith. 2017. 'Galamsey Gamble'. *The Africa Report*, 23 May. https://www.theafricareport.com/814/galamsey-gamble/.

Mensah, K. 2022. 'Ghana: Akufo-Addo Moves Decisively to Sack Ofori-Atta Deputy. Will It Be Enough?' *The Africa Report*, 15 November. https://www.theafricareport.com/260295/ghana-akufo-addo-moves-decisively-to-sack-ofori-atta-deputy-will-it-be-enough/.

Padayachee, V. and B. Bordiss. 2013. 'Barbaric Gold and Civilised Banking: Keynes's *Indian Currency and Finance*. A View from the South after 100 Years'. *International Review of Applied Economics* 27 (6): 822–33. https://doi.org/10.1080/02692171.2013.839501.

———. 2015. 'How Global Geo-Politics Shaped South Africa's Post-World War I Monetary Policy: The Case of Gerhard Vissering and Edwin Kemmerer in South Africa, 1924–25'. *Economic History of Developing Regions* 30 (2): 182–209. https://doi.org/10.1080/20780389.2015.1051027.

Padayachee, V. and J. Rossouw. 2019. '"Volkskapitalisme" in the Transition to Democracy and Beyond'. *International Review of Applied Economics* 33 (1): 150–62. https://doi.org/10.1080/02692171.2019.1524040.

Padayachee, V. and J. Sender. 2018. 'Vella Pillay: Revolutionary Activism and Economic Policy Analysis'. *Journal of Southern African Studies* 44 (1): 149–65. https://doi.org/10.1080/03057070.2018.1405644.

Padayachee, V. and R. van Niekerk. 2019. *Shadow of Liberation: Contestation and Compromise in the Economic and Social Policy of the African National Congress, 1943–1996.* Johannesburg: Wits University Press.

Reuters. 2022. 'Burkina Faso: Gold Boom Vanishes as Militants Advance and Russians Leave'. *The Africa Report*, 28 November. https://www.theafricareport.com/263843/burkina-faso-vanishing-gold-boom-puts-livelihoods-at-risk/.

Sharife, K. 2016. 'Panama Papers Reveal Dubious Behaviour by DRC's Gold Traders'. African Network for Centers of Investigative Reporting. https://panamapapers.investigativecenters.org/drc/.

Simmel, G. 2004. *The Philosophy of Money*, edited by D. Frisby. 3rd edition. London: Routledge.

Skidelsky, R. 2005. *John Maynard Keynes, 1883–1946: Economist, Philosopher, Statesman.* New York: Penguin.

Stoop, N., M. Verpoorten and P. van der Windt. 2018. 'More Legislation, More Violence? The Impact of Dodd-Frank in the DRC'. *PLOS ONE* 13 (8): e0201783. https://doi.org/10.1371/journal.pone.0201783.

Thornton, J. 1992. *Africa and Africans in the Making of the Atlantic World, 1400–1680.* Cambridge: Cambridge University Press.

The Times. 1999. 'All That Glisters Is Not Sense'. *The Times*, 7 July.

Tooze, A. 2018. *Crashed: How a Decade of Financial Crises Changed the World.* New York: Penguin.

———. 2021. *Shutdown: How the Coronavirus Made a Financial Revolution.* New York: Penguin.

———. 2023. 'Chartbook 209# The Sudan Crisis and the Sahel Gold Rush'. Substack newsletter. *Chartbook*, 18 April. Blog post. https://adamtooze.substack.com/p/chartbook-209-the-sudan-crisis-and.

UN Security Council Panel of Experts. 2001. 'Report on the Illegal Exploitation of Natural Resources and Other Forms of Wealth of DR Congo'. *Reliefweb*, 12 April. https://reliefweb.int/report/democratic-republic-congo/report-panel-experts-illegal-exploitation-natural-resources-and.

Verbrugge, B. and S. Geenen. 2019. 'The Gold Commodity Frontier: A Fresh Perspective on Change and Diversity in the Global Gold Mining Economy'. *The Extractive Industries and Society* 6 (2): 413–23. https://doi.org/10.1016/j.exis.2018.10.014.

Werthmann, K. 2009. 'Working in a Boom-Town: Female Perspectives on Gold-Mining in Burkina Faso'. *Resources Policy* 34 (1–2): 18–23. https://doi.org/10.1016/j.resourpol.2008.09.002.

———. 2012. 'Gold Mining in Burkina Faso since the 1980s'. In: *Mining Frontiers in Africa: Anthropological and Historical Perspectives*, edited by K. Werthmann and T. Grätz. Köln: Rüdiger Köppe Verlag.

5

National Development and the Enlightenment Gaze
A Joint Project with Vishnu Padayachee

Bradley Bordiss

Vishnu Padayachee was the greatest intellectual mentor that I have been blessed with in my life. The eight articles that we wrote together, and my master's and PhD theses, were motivated by one great common intellectual hero, one great common hatred, and one great love for a development tool. We both loved the work of John Maynard Keynes. We both despised imperialism, particularly that of internationally mobile capital. And we were both passionate about national institutions as the instruments of development. In describing his own activism, Vishnu talked to me about his rejection of ethnic mobilisation, and about his conscious decision in the apartheid era to work in the trade union movement rather than join the progressive forces via the Natal Indian Congress. Where we differed in our intellectual foundations was that Vishnu was thoroughly well read in and committed to Marxist intellectual thought, while my own reading of Karl Marx remains shamefully weak.

By contrast, I was impressed by much older lines of thought – first by those writers concerned with the ethics and morality of economic phenomena in ancient Greece, and later by the great writers of the medieval period, who took some of the ethical concerns of Plato, Aristotle and others and framed them in the context of the God-centric thinking of the eleventh to thirteenth centuries. I was also impressed by the focus in the work of the mercantilists and neomercantilists on developing and protecting national sovereignty. While, naturally, the flow of learning was from the wiser, internationally recognised professor to his amateur, part-time-academic student, I am proud of having introduced

Vishnu to certain wonderful mercantilist and progressive national economics works, including Antonio Serra's *A Short Treatise on the Wealth and Poverty of Nations* ([1613] 2011), Thomas Mun's *England's Treasure by means of Forraign Trade* ([1664] 2006) and William Mitchell and Thomas Fazi's *Reclaiming the State: A Progressive Vision of Sovereignty for a Post-Neoliberal World* (2017), all of which enjoyed positive treatment in Vishnu's article 'Can Progressive Macroeconomic Policy Address Growth and Employment while Reducing Inequality in South Africa?' (Padayachee 2019). Employing the ideas of mercantilists and their post-Keynesian intellectual heirs, Vishnu answered this question in the affirmative.

Doing archival research for my PhD with Vishnu, it soon became apparent that the monetary policy debate between the antagonists Andries Bruwer and Jack Holloway was an archetypal clash with great relevance for today.[1] Holloway was the defender of the cosmopolitan, liberal Enlightenment project in economic policy. His arguments were rational and based on a belief in the steady progress that modernist economic liberalism would bring universally (Bordiss 2021). He declined the state-sponsored credit facility available to the South African government at Bretton Woods, and instead visited the major international private finance houses in London and New York, negotiating what would become the 1950 loan in London. Bruwer was inspired by pre-Enlightenment thinkers and those of the economic counter-Enlightenment. He thought that different policies were appropriate to different geographies, and that rural culture and traditions were important. He shared Karl Polanyi's 'sacred hatred' of universal free markets intruding into areas where they had no business being.[2] He loathed private finance and campaigned to nationalise the South African Reserve Bank (SARB).

Given Holloway's commitment to the Enlightenment global laissez-faire project, it is not surprising that there is little evidence of any economic intellectual influences on him prior to David Hume's justification for the international laissez-faire gold standard in 'Of the Balance of Trade' (Hume [1752] 2006). He accepted the arguments for a rational, global, equilibrium-seeking free market economy, which through the trajectory of thought of Adam Smith (1776) and David Ricardo ([1817] 1911), was embodied in the interwar period in the work of Edwin Kemmerer (1934), the Princeton University economics professor, who was a one-man International Monetary Fund twenty-five years before that institution was created, 'the money doctor' of the 1910s and 1920s. Holloway was committed to a globally applicable model.

Bruwer was the opposite. He drew his intellectual influences from the anti-merchant and anti-finance writings of Plato and Aristotle, from the moral teachings of the scholastics of the medieval period, and then from the mercantilists and national economists. In his book *Kapitalisme, Partypolitiek en Armoede* (1934) Bruwer set out how, following Aristotle, the church held production by a homestead to be superior to the selfishness of making profit and accumulating great wealth. But 'whereas in Ancient Greece merchants were frowned upon, in South Africa there is a special fast train for them' (Bruwer 1934: 2–3).[3] The reason that 'people did not think much of merchants, [was] because merchants don't *produce* anything' (1934: 3, emphasis added). Bruwer thought that Plato was the 'moral high point' of statecraft (1934: 4) and claimed that Plato was against inequality and the making of loans: 'The State must be self-sustaining, and interest is banned in Plato's *Republic*' (1934: 5). Furthermore, 'the greatest good is the good of the State, money making is unnatural because it leads to decadence' (1934: 6). Bruwer claimed that 'Aquinas was in favour of gold accumulation by the State for the purpose of defence' (1934: 9), and then went on to recommend the reading of Thomas Mun's *England's Treasure by Forraign Trade* and the mercantilist works of Gustav von Schmoller, Hermann Ignaz Bidermann and Baron Edmund von Heyking (1934: 9), and to summarise the mercantilist arguments. He noted disapprovingly that 'around 1500 [CE] religious checks upon wealth were weakened and money making became more acceptable' (1934: 11). Smith was treated less harshly because 'Adam Smith's faith in laissez-faire is based on his faith in the basic goodness of people, the opposite of Hobbes' (1934: 13). But, like Keynes, Bruwer was unimpressed with Jeremy Bentham's utility calculation:

> Benthamite calculation leads to the sweeping aside of questions of morality in economics ... 'Don't dream' says Bentham in his *Deontology* 'that a person would move his pinkie finger to do something for you, unless it is clear to him that there is some personal advantage in it for him' (1934: 15).

Bruwer spoke disparagingly of David Ricardo, 'a Dutch Jew, who, like his father, made a fortune on the London Stock Exchange', and particularly of Ricardo's views on how wages were determined by demand and supply, and of his argument that the only way to maintain wages was by people having fewer children, limiting the supply of workers (1934: 15). Bruwer pointed out that

> '[the] belief in free markets was not absolute in the nineteenth century ... both [Friedrich] List and [Henry Charles] Carey fought it ... laissez-faire – the naïve belief in natural law working everything out based on individualism – relied on deduction ... [and] was beaten by a school of economics which relied on inductive actions, namely the historical school (1934: 17).[4]

The virtue of the historical school was its focus on the company, not the individual (1934). Paraphrasing Marx, Bruwer said that 'the economic determines the social, and the social determines the moral', and a 'different economic organisation may totally shift the moral views of humanity' (1934: 19). His argument followed the line of the Catholic distributionist writers Pope Leo XIII and G. K. Chesterton, and of certain anarchists, that a socialist company, which does not require individualism and selfishness, might encourage more sociable and moral personalities.

Bruwer ended his first chapter by lamenting that the 'Ricardian school of economics and human nature was so rooted in selfishness that there was no hope left over for the masses of the people' (1934: 24). He explained that he was focusing on the history of the capitalist era that produced this Ricardian school, and the utilitarianism and marginal analysis that were based on it, to show how South Africa had got itself into the mess of the 1930s.

What lessons can we learn from the debate between Holloway and Bruwer?

Why should the debates over economic policy between two Afrikaner economists in the 1920s and 1930s have relevance today? What lessons can we learn from the debate between a laissez-faire globalist and an economic nationalist in ruling Afrikaner circles, just under a century ago? In these questions are the motivation and purpose of this chapter. Are there lessons from the Afrikaner nationalist economic debates in this earlier period for an African nationalism today? In the debates that I have had over the last couple of years with friends who answer in the negative, I have found that the rejection of both economic nationalism and political nationalism in general (and African nationalism in particular) is invariably rooted in their failure to meet the criteria of the Enlightenment.

Both nationalisms fall foul of the charge that it is their pre- or counter-Enlightenment qualities that disqualify them as models for the current post-Enlightenment world. The charges against economic nationalism are, of course, different from those against African nationalism. But I wish to argue that the criticism of both economic and African nationalism as essentially pre- or counter-Enlightenment is largely correct, and to argue the merits of their respective *positive* counter-Enlightenment qualities. I then want to propose that economic nationalism should be part of a humane African nationalist project.

First, I will extract the key elements of economic nationalist thought from both the mercantilist writers and the post-Adam Smith neomercantilists, to produce those elements of policy that should be a part of a humane African nationalist agenda.

Next, I want to mount a counter-Enlightenment defence of African nationalism as a political project. As a white South African of a certain vintage, I will leave a deep dive into African nationalism to those better placed to critique it. Instead of an investigation of African nationalism, I want to consider works that suggest a counter-Enlightenment *support* for it as a force for good on this continent, by first considering the elements of the Enlightenment project that are antithetical to nationalism in general, and to African nationalism specifically. Broadly I want to consider two types of criticism of African nationalism – the liberal and the Marxist. I want to assess their antipathy as that of the two children of the Enlightenment that they are.

Finally, given that modern African nationalism was born of a struggle against imperialism and colonialism, I want to consider how we may deal with neo-imperialism using the tools discussed in this chapter.

Useful elements of economic nationalist thought for the African nationalist toolbox

In its early forms, economic nationalism developed in Europe, China and Japan. Its European body of thought became known as mercantilism. In China, although ideas which we can call mercantilist were only fully developed by 'Wei Yuan after the First Opium War of 1839–42' (Helleiner 2021: 232) and most substantially by Sun Yat-sen in the early twentieth century, many of the basic supporting ideas have a much longer pedigree. National profit, or the prosperity of the country, was a principle known as *kokueki*. *Kokueki* thinkers saw a strong connection between the cultivation of a domain's wealth and its power. The phrase 'rich state, strong army' first appeared in the period of Warring States in China (453–221 BCE) in *The Book of Lord Shang* by Shang Yang: 'He who rules the state well consolidates force to attain a rich state and a strong army' (2021: 204). In contrast to European mercantilism, the Chinese version promoted state-run institutions, rather than private ones (2021: 204). In this tradition, Okubo Toshimichi was the mercantilist of the Meiji government who had the most impact in Japan (2021).

In Europe, 'economics was primarily an Italian science until the last quarter of the eighteenth century. Spain, France, and England divide second honours' (Schumpeter 1954: 162). Joseph Schumpeter thought that the Italian mercantilist Antonio Serra was the 'first to compose a scientific treatise ... on Economic Principles' (1954: 195), and the first to develop the idea of an increasing return to scale that he attributed to manufacturing. Serra considered that there were some factors which generated wealth over which a country could not exercise control, such as geographical position and mineral endowment, and four factors over which a country could exercise some control, namely production in numerous sectors of manufacturing, an enterprising population, extensive trade and effective government (Serra [1613] 2011).

Although Daniel Gaido (2016) holds that the mercantilist period involved a shift away from the moral concerns of the scholastic thinkers of the medieval era (Christian, Muslim and Jewish) towards examining the causes of economic phenomena theoretically, there is some evidence that mercantilists were still mindful of moral principles. Jean Bodin (1530–96) was repulsed by a might-is-right philosophy and thought it an insult to God (Bodin [(1568) 1997] cited in Monroe 2006: 139). Mun (1571–1641) began his great work (published posthumously in 1664) by imploring his son to learn 'two things: The first is Piety, how to fear God aright, according to his Works and word: The second is policy, how to love and serve thy country' (Mun [1664] 2006: 1).

I would propose that the first great principle of mercantilist thought was that '*full employment* was the major mercantilist goal' (Allen 1987: 448, emphasis added). Although Serra ([1613] 2011) did not emphasise it, Mun noted the benefits of full employment if one buys local rather than foreign goods: 'If in our rayment we will be prodigal, yet let this be done with our own materials and manufacturers ... where the excess of the rich may be the employment of the poor' (Mun [1664] 2006: 12). This was the difference between the positive example of Mughal India and the negative one of the British Raj that Utsa Patnaik and Prabhat Patnaik describe (Patnaik and Patnaik 2021).

The second, related main principle of the mercantilists is to focus on production. The great historian of economic thought, Mark Blaug, quotes E.A.J. Johnson's statement that 'the ultimate concern of the mercantilists was the creation of effective factors of production. Not 10% of English mercantilist literature is devoted to the ill-fated doctrine of the balance of trade' (Blaug 1985: 12). This focus includes the appropriate industrial policy to enhance production. Adam Smith, in his attack on this mercantilist principle, shifts the focus of policy away from the welfare of the producers and their workers to that of consumers: 'Consumption is the sole end and purpose of all production; and the interest of the producer ought to be attended to, only so far as it may be necessary for promoting that of the consumer' (Smith 1776: V.viii, 376). Neomercantilists and national economists have considered this shift in focus from production to consumption to be a mistake.

With the aim of getting to full employment, a second principle of mercantilism is a *multisector economy*. Mun emphasised the importance of developing a manufacturing ('artificial') sector, in addition to whichever 'natural' sectors exist in a country, such as mines, agriculture and fishing (Mun [1664] 2006: 17, 72). It is a mercantilist and national economist's trait to consider separately how a particular phenomenon or policy affects *different sectors*, in short to think *sectorally*. Serra ([1613] 2011) noted that whether or not a particular policy affects a country depends on the nature of the economy in that country. Mun pointed out that a multisector economy makes it more difficult for a hostile foreign power to be effective against another country than it would be if this hostile power only had to target sanctions on a specific sector of an enemy nation. This is a lacuna in the thinking of economists trained in a laissez-faire paradigm: often the failure to treat the very different sectors of the economy separately is at the heart of the failure of their models. It was the central strength of Keynes's 'The Economic Consequences of Mr Churchill' ([1925] 1952) over the Treasury view; the central strength of James Galbraith's (2012) account of inequality compared to Thomas Piketty's (2014); and a central strength of Hamilton's *Report on Manufactures* ([1791] 2012) and the works of Henry Carey (1856) (Helleiner 2021; Schumpeter 1954) over Adam Smith's *An Inquiry into the Nature and Causes of the Wealth of Nations* (1776).

In particular, the *development of manufacturing* is something that is stressed by most mercantilist thinkers (Stark 1944). Bodin was an early proponent of this measure, encouraging the importing of the raw materials necessary for manufacturing, and of making sure that both these and domestically found raw materials were developed into finished goods (Bodin [(1576) 1967] cited in Stark 1944: 67). As both Schumpeter (1954) and Marx (Reinert 2011) acknowledged, Serra was a pioneer in understanding the increasing returns to scale enjoyed by manufacturing, and these increasing returns to scale were a fundamental reason for Serra's championing of manufacturing as a means of wealth creation (Serra [1613] 2011). This discovery was then used by both Marx and List in their models of the economy (Hunt 2011). Both Giovanni Botero and Serra were also advocates of *beneficiation* (Hunt 2011), as was Mun ([1664] 2006). This is another important mercantilist principle. Predating the structuralists and the dependency theories of Raúl Prebisch, Walter Rodney, Samir Amin and Utas and Prabhat Patnaik by more than three centuries, Mun was conscious of focusing on producing and exporting those goods with a low-price elasticity of demand and also of the possibility of driving competition from a market with trade-war prices, in order for a country to dominate and capture a foreign market.

In the era of *industrialisation* Carey favoured small-scale manufacturing and thought that, unlike production on a large scale, it would encourage social stability and cohesion (Helleiner 2021). The Ethiopian neomercantilist Gebrehiwot Baykedagn (1924, cited in Helleiner 2021: 190) developed this idea, suggesting that industrialisation, by increasing the number of industrial workers who had built a sense of community among themselves, would lessen the power of soldiers in Ethiopia, if the industrial workers were many and the soldiers relatively few: 'Since the cooperation between the people will enable them to defend themselves, the officers and the soldiers will become the servants of the people rather than their masters. Recognizing that they will not be attacked, the people will not aspire to become soldiers and officers of the people' (Baykedagn cited in Helleiner 2021: 192).

The importance of the *institutions of the state* is another key element of mercantilist concern. Serra ([1613] 2011) emphasised the importance of a strong and competent judiciary, to which are appointed highly qualified and experienced judges. Mun ([1664] 2006) discussed the importance of granaries, banks and a well-maintained army as the key institutions of a country. Regarding reserves, Mun said that 'those Princes which do not providently lay up Treasure, or do immediately consume the same when they have it, will sodainly [suddenly] come to want and misery; for there is nothing doth so soon decay as Excessive Bounty [patronage], in using whereof they want the means to use it' ([1664] 2006: 90). Squandering reserves not only robbed a country of its reserves but rotted its morals.

Finally, as both Marx and Keynes pointed out, mercantilist writers tended to focus on the practical applicability of their models, rather than on their theoretical elegance. Marx compared the practical mercantilists to the theoretically inclined Adam Smith and his followers by means of an analogy with the 'external religiosity' of the Catholics compared to 'making religiosity the inner substance of man' of Luther (Marx cited in Wiltgen 1989: 51). Keynes ended his chapter on the mercantilists in his *General Theory* by noting that they 'preferred to see the truth obscurely and imperfectly rather than to maintain error, reached indeed with clearness and consistency and by easy logic, but on hypotheses inappropriate to the facts' (Keynes 1936: 371). This preference for the pragmatic over the ideological is the subject of *Concrete Economics* (Cohen and De Long 2016) on the neomercantilism of Alexander Hamilton.

Imperialism and mercantilism

A common misconception about mercantilist thought is that it promotes imperialism and colonialism. An example of this misconception in the public imagination is the Wikipedia article on the subject.[5] I have not yet found the source of this misconception, but it is regrettably pervasive. It is undeniable that the European imperialist and colonialist project expanded substantially during the mercantilist era, from the second half of the sixteenth century until the middle of the eighteenth century, and even that many mercantilist writers benefited from it. William Petty acquired fifty thousand acres of Irish land after Oliver Cromwell's conquest of Ireland (Routh 1989). Thomas Mun was a director of the East India Company and defended its export of precious metals in a 1621 essay (Mun [1664] 2006). Jean-Baptiste Colbert (1619–83) set up a French East India Company and a French West India Company in the 1660s 'to improve and exploit French colonies' (Coleman 1987: 472). But this does not mean that encouraging imperialism was in any way central to their work. Many of the mercantilists, and most of the neomercantilists, were specifically *anti-imperialist* in their writings. Neither Marc'Antonio

De Santis nor Botero wrote in support of imperialism (Hunt 2011), and it is difficult to read Serra's work as anything other than an anti-imperialist tract. After all, it was written while Serra was in gaol, probably for participation in the 1599 revolt against Spanish colonial rule (Hunt 2011). Even Mun and Petty did not spend any significant time defending or promoting imperialism. I can only find a single sentence promoting it in Mun ([1664] 2006: 13–14), and this may be juxtaposed with his praise of the Dutch for having thrown off the yoke of Spanish imperialism, which was a necessary condition for their development ([1664] 2006: 101).

In *Imperialism: The Highest Stage of Capitalism* ([1917] 2010), Lenin located the worst period of imperialism and colonialism in the last quarter of the nineteenth and the first quarter of the twentieth centuries. In this period, he wrote, 'imperialism emerged as the development and direct continuation of the fundamental attributes of capitalism in general. But capitalism only became capitalist imperialism at a definite and very high stage of its development' ([1917] 2010: 109). The era of imperialism that Lenin describes is one that coincided with the adoption of laissez-faire policies by Britain as the dominant world power, and their subsequent spread through other parts of the world. In dealing with this era of British-inspired free trade, Ha-Joon Chang (2007) points out that most of this 'free trade' was imposed through the barrel of a gun by the laissez-faire-promoting British imperialists. John Mearsheimer's *The Great Delusion: Liberal Dreams and International Realities* (2018) shows how the impulse to interfere in other people's countries is foundational to the American liberal Enlightenment mode of thought.

Liberals often deny this claim and propose that capitalism thrives best in the non-coercive environment of a liberal democracy. Merle Lipton made this case in *Capitalism and Apartheid: South Africa, 1910–1984* (1985) and Steven Pinker's *Enlightenment Now* (2018) is a later restatement of it. Earlier versions of Pinker's thinking, which argued that economic liberalism brought an era of peace and an end to imperialism, were challenged by Edward Herman and David Peterson (2012). The form of imperialism that Lenin ([1917] 2010) describes materialised as the policy of the Republican Party of the United States in Latin America in the 1920s (Rosenberg 1999). This policy sometimes involved customs-receivership in these countries, and later an arbitration role for the Chief Justice of the US Supreme Court. It was consistent with the policy of the earlier Democrat administration of Woodrow Wilson, who insisted that private finance be at the centre of German reconstruction after World War I, an idea that contributed to the calamity that followed (McNeil 1986; see also Dayer 1976).

Most, but not all, neomercantilist thinkers were explicitly anti-imperialist. Eric Helleiner (2021) shows that although List ([1842] 2011) was better known and followed in the West, it was the anti-imperialism of Carey that endeared him to the neomercantilist thinkers of the Global South. Carey (1898–1959) thought that free trade eroded the social bonds of community by eroding the power of association. He thought that too many English thinkers were materialist utilitarians, focusing narrowly on material wealth and conceiving of humans as 'only an animal that will procreate, that must be fed, and that can be made to work – an instrument to be used by trade'. He prioritised the national community (Helleiner 2021), and thought that neomercantilism could be a tool for expelling imperialism:

> India will grow rich, and rapidly grow, when India shall become independent, and shall protect herself against the radical error of the English system [laissez-faire]; but until she shall do so: until she shall acquire power to place the consumer by the side of the producer: she must remain poor ... so long as she must remit twenty millions to pay interest, and raise so many other millions to pay armies and officers, while compelled to cultivate the poorest soils with the worst machinery, neither [population nor wealth] can increase (Carey cited in Helleiner 2021: 159).

This theme is picked up by Utsa and Prabhat Patnaik in their *Theory of Imperialism* (2017). It explains the impact of Carey on the Ethiopian Gebrehiwot Baykedagn (1886–1919) in his work promoting neomercantilist in that country.

The clash of Enlightenment and pre- and counter-Enlightenment ideas

Enlightenment thinking, which is so often offended by pre-Enlightenment mercantilism and by counter-Enlightenment nationalism, has been summarised recently by Pinker in his book *Enlightenment Now* (2018). Quoting Immanuel Kant, he defines the Enlightenment as 'humankind's emergence from its self-incurred immaturity, its lazy and cowardly submission to the dogmas and formulas of religious or political authority' (Kant [1784 (1991)] cited in Pinker 2018: 7). He points out that the convention is that the Enlightenment was born in the last two-thirds of the eighteenth century, and 'spilled into the heyday of classic liberalism in the first half of the 19th' (2018: 8). He identifies four themes of Enlightenment thinking: reason, science and humanism, based on the individual, and progress.

'The foremost is reason. Reason is non-negotiable,' he states (2018: 8). This is, of course, not to say that previous eras did not employ reason as central to their systems of thought. Thomas Aquinas, Al-Ghazali and Maimonides all valued reason; however, unlike the reason of the Enlightenment thinkers, who tended to be influenced by either materialist or Benthamite utility considerations, the medieval thinkers did not argue solely on materialist grounds, but considered the welfare of the soul within the context of a religious paradigm. This element was crucially missing from much Enlightenment rationality.

Defining his third element, humanism, Pinker notes that 'the thinkers of the age of reason and the Enlightenment saw an urgent need for a secular foundation for morality, because they were haunted by a historical memory of centuries of religious carnage' (2018: 10). He stresses that the foundation of what we call humanism privileges the individual over all groups: 'It is individuals, not groups, who are sentient – who feel pleasure and pain, fulfilment and anguish' (2018: 10). The natural consequence of Enlightenment humanism, according to Pinker, is that we are to abandon our tribe, our nation and other groups and 'are forced into cosmopolitanism: accepting our citizenship in the world' (2018: 11).

Pinker's fourth element of the Enlightenment is the belief in relentless progress. He attempts to disavow the dark side of this belief in rational, internationalist, relentless progress by disowning 'authoritarian high modernism' (2018: 12), but I would argue that this high modernism is an unavoidable ugly shadow of Enlightenment thinking. I will discuss this further below. Pinker's version of the Enlightenment is economic liberalism. Although he does not list it as one of the key elements of Enlightenment thinking, I would add a fifth element, namely a belief that this Enlightenment system of thought has a *universality* applicable throughout the world, regardless of social or geographic context. This universality was the basis of Hume's attack on the mercantilists' particular concern for national reserves in his essay *Of the Balance of Trade* ([1752] 2006), which constructed a model in which these reserves magically reached an international equilibrium. The universal model was considered superior to the national one.

Samir Amin (1931–2018) mounts a robust Marxist defence of Enlightenment modernity 'with its call to escape from supposed natural laws and to give full authority to the lawmaking citizen' (Amin 1998: 96–7).

> The modern era began with a philosophical break from that past (when people had 'divine commandments holding sway over them') ... Once political power was stripped of divine sanction, and the natural world was stripped of magical influences, the way to the free exercise of *human reason* was opened (1998: 95, emphasis added).

> The modern epoch is also the epoch of humanity's greatest achievements, accomplished at a pace immeasurably greater than that that marked premodern times. Modernity achieved enormous *progress* in material production and *scientific* knowledge ... the idea of *individuality* irreducible to membership in a familial or ethnic collectivity – these are all modern ideas (1998: 102, emphasis added).

> The Enlightenment established that the concepts of *reason* and emancipation are closely corresponding (1998: 103, emphasis added).

The challenge, of course, comes with crises that interrupt the Enlightenment obsession with progress. Then 'there is a great temptation to go back to a premodern stance ... [that] history takes place quite apart from their [human] activity' (1998: 99). In Chapter six of *Spectres of Capitalism*, Amin makes these Enlightenment arguments against a rising postmodernism, but they could equally be made against African nationalism, as Bill Freund does in *The Making of Contemporary Africa* (1998) and in his autobiography, *An Historian's Passage to Africa* (2021).

Amin set the Marxist Enlightenment view against both postmodernism and counter-Enlightenment elements. With the postmodern paradigm becoming dominant – a 'rising tide of vacuousness' – neoliberalism cohabits with a world of 'ethnic communalism, the spread of irrationality, religious cultism, the rising tide of violence, and all sorts of fanaticism' (1998: 102).

If Amin is one of the great Marxist thinkers of our time, Francis Fukuyama is one of its greatest liberals. His magnum opus *The End of History and the Last Man* (1992) is usually dismissed because of the liberal triumphalism that it sets out in the first fifty-one pages. If that was where the book ended, then this dismissal would be warranted, but the book contains three hundred and thirty-nine pages. Despite my happiness that liberalism was not the end of history, I defend Fukuyama because of his intellectual courage in raising the quest for *thymos* and the possibility that it may not be satisfied in our liberal Enlightenment world, and, I would add, not in a Marxist Enlightenment one either. Fukuyama explains that Socrates divided the soul into three parts: the passions, reason, and a third spiritual part which he called *thymos*. He is confident that passion and reason can find expression in a utility-obsessed liberal society. But what about *thymos*? How can this be satisfied in an Enlightenment-based society? Fukuyama has the honesty to admit that it might not be possible to do so. He goes through the various expressors of *thymos*: aristocrats and their wars of honour and dignity, great artists, captains of industry, sports stars, top politicians, and so on. Finally, in the penultimate chapter, he deals with community, and admits that liberal society is unable to generate the close-knit connection that religious communities were able to do.

This liberal (and Marxist) discomfort at not knowing what to do with a spiritual and communal yearning in an Enlightenment-driven world animates the work of another child of the Enlightenment, Elie Kedourie (1926–92). Informed by the dissolution of the Ottoman empire, and his family's experience of it, his book *Nationalism* (1960) chronicles the religious and ethnic fanaticism that sprang to life as nationalism filled the gap left by a crumbling empire. Kedourie argues that this empire was more tolerant of multi-ethnicity and a plurality of religions than the nation states that replaced it. In his lengthy foreword to *Nationalism in Asia and Africa* (1970), Kedourie applies these criticisms to the emerging national liberation efforts in Africa and Asia. He laments the shift in the definition of imperialism to the pejorative one described first by John Hobson ([1902] 2005) and later by Lenin ([1917] 2010). He disputes the motives that Hobson and Lenin ascribe to the imperialist powers: maintaining command over raw materials in the era of finance capitalled monopoly capitalism. Instead, he suggests that it was driven by the warrior aristocratic spirit within the imperialist countries. Kedourie fails to grasp that by preventing the development of industrial policy in the lands that they colonised, the imperialists were preventing development of those territories. He has almost nothing positive to say about the nationalism of the Global South. According to him, it was led by an indigenous elite educated in the West, and the very idea of nationalism was a Western import. In his view, the African nationalist Marcus Garvey was obsessed with race, and Gandhi's romantic view of Indian innocence and European corruption was delusional. He makes a point of quoting Gandhi selectively, so as to paint him as a religious fanatic (1970: 109).

Expanding on this theme of religious fanaticism accompanying nationalism, Kedourie draws a connection between the millennial religious fanatics and the fanatics described by the anarchist Michael Bakunin, and he shows how this dark power was often harnessed by the revolutionaries of national liberation movements. He discusses the Hitler-like evil inclinations of Mau Mau leader Dedan Kimathi, the religious fanaticism of Simon Kimbangu and the radical exclusionary religion of Simon-Pierre Mpadi in the Congo, the Jehovah's Witness John Chilembwe who led a rebellion in Malawi, and Frantz Fanon's celebration of revolutionary violence in Algeria, ending with the warning that the drug of national liberation 'may also excite its addicts to a frenzy of destruction' (1970: 147).

But is this the sum total of possibilities for counter-Enlightenment elements in an African nationalism? Banished, as Pinker, Amin, Kedourie and Freund might have it? Left dangling and unsatisfied, as Fukuyama would have it? Partha Chatterjee (1986) and Cornel West and Panashe Chigumadzi (2022) suggest not. On the inside cover of his book *Nationalist Thought and the Colonial World* (1986), Chatterjee is introduced thus:

> In this book a leading Indian political philosopher criticises Western theories of Third World nationalism – both liberal and Marxist. He demonstrates how Western theorists, with their emphasis on the power of reason, the primacy of the hard sciences and the dominance of the empirical method, have assumed

that their presuppositions are universally valid, and, through the impact of Western education, have imposed concepts of nationalism on non-Western peoples to the detriment, if not destruction, of their own world views. The author explores the central contradiction that nationalism in Africa and Asia has consequently experienced: setting out to assert its freedom from European domination, it yet remained a prisoner of European post-Enlightenment rationalist discourse (Chatterjee 1986: cover text).

In the book, Chatterjee uses Antonio Gramsci's concepts of passive revolution, war of position and war of movement to consider three great Indian thinkers who gave birth to Indian nationalism: Bankimchandra Chattopadhyay (1838–94), as the great figure of the Moment of Departure; Mahatma Gandhi (1869–1948), as the great figure of the Moment of Manoeuvre; and Jawaharlal Nehru (1889–1964), as the great figure of the Moment of Arrival.

Our interest in this chapter is in the counter-Enlightenment figure Gandhi, who, rooted in a religious state of being, was the spiritual force behind Indian national liberation. Likewise, West and Chigumadzi, in their article 'Black Spirit, Black Struggle' (2022), consider three African theologians – the African American James H. Cone, the Kenyan-born John Mbiti and the South African Desmond Tutu. Contrary to the horror stories of religious fanaticism that Kedourie (1970) associates with African nationalism, West and Chigumadzi tell the story of the clash between a centred, rooted and religious tradition and experience on the African continent proposed by Mbiti, and the radical, revolutionary liberation theology of Cone in the US. 'Where Conian Black theology's main concern was critique, Mbitian African theology's was cosmos,' they claim, stating further that 'Tutu reconciled Black critique with African cosmos, and his Black theological praxis embraced embodied utterance, not only on the pulpit but also on the burning streets of apartheid South Africa's townships' (West and Chigumadzi 2022: 35). At Steve Biko's funeral, at which Tutu officiated, Tutu said of Biko:

> God called him to be the founder father of the Black Consciousness movement, against which we have had tirades and fulminations. It is a movement by which God, through Steve,

sought to awaken in the Black person a sense of his intrinsic value and worth as a child of God, not needing to apologize for his existential condition as a Black person, calling on Blacks to glorify and praise God that he had created them Black (West and Chigumadzi 2022: 35).

The point, for our purposes, is this: why should we be cowed by our Enlightenment thinking into accepting every religious, cultural, or even ethnic expression in the Global South as something destructive and reactionary? Are the emancipatory examples of Gandhi's and Tutu's religious connection with their people not an inspiration for a humane counter-Enlightenment African nationalism? Do we have to shudder in the face of counter-Enlightenment elements in national liberation movements, and long for the days of empire, as Kedourie (1960) suggests? Can we not, as an alternative, consider the positive aspects of the counter-Enlightenment and their application to African nationalism today?

Yes, the shadow of the Nazi version of counter-Enlightenment nationalism hangs over all of us, as a warning of how badly it can go wrong. But as Keynes himself warned about Enlightenment and counter-Enlightenment forces, 'if either cast the other out, life is diminished in its force' (Keynes [1933] cited in Skidelsky 1992: 487). In *Conversations with Isaiah Berlin* (1992) by Ramin Jahanbegloo, Berlin takes a position in favour of pluralism similar to that of Keynes as cited in Skidelsky (1992: 487) – seeking to balance the Enlightenment and counter-Enlightenment ideas: the counter-Enlightenment's 'most important influence on European thought is the belief that science and reason do not have all the answers, that to some central questions of value – ethical, aesthetic, social, political – there can be more than one valid answer' (Jahanbegloo 1992: 68).

In *Three Critics of the Enlightenment* (2013), Berlin presents studies of Giambattista Vico, Johann Georg Hamann and Johann Gottfried Herder. Vico was repulsed by the overly rational and positivist approach of Descartes, whom he charged with not understanding that mathematics was arbitrary. By contrast, he loved history, and the metaphor for conveying what he called 'poetic logic' (Berlin 2013: 82). His view of religion, of submitting to God's plan and accepting divine providence, seems close to that of West and Chigumadzi's account of Mbiti (2022). Berlin was attracted to Hamann's rejection of the super-rational, internationally applicable model of the world. Hamann postulated that 'God is not a mathematician, God is an artist' (Jahanbegloo 1992: 69), an idea developed by Oscar Wilde in *De Profundis* (Wilde [1905] 1948). Hamann was 'both sensual and pious' (Berlin 2013: 409), and rejected utility maximisation, 'as gardens come before the cultivation of fields, painting before writing, singing before speech, metaphors before reasoning, barter before trade' (Hamann cited in Berlin 2013: 404). Herder believed that each culture had its own centre of gravity, rejecting the one-size-fits-all rationalism of some Enlightenment thinkers (Jahanbegloo 1992: 69). Berlin credited Herder as the 'first person to emphasize that the need to belong to a community is a basic human need, just as strong as that for eating, drinking, warmth, security' (1992: 89–90). Herder rejected conquest and the idea of the superiority of one nation over another, and so may constitute a resource for progressive African nationalists. Berlin described Herder as focusing on culture and a shared language but 'fundamentally against all racist ideas' (1992: 101). And it is worth noting that, as one of the fathers of German nationalism, he was a passionate opponent of racism, colonialism and imperialism (Noyes 2015). Herder asked: 'Can you name a land where Europeans have entered without defiling themselves for ever before defenceless, trusting mankind, by the unjust word, greed, deceit, crushing oppression, diseases, fatal gifts bought?' (Herder cited in Berlin 2013: 228). This is powerfully important, as it suggests that the ideas of Hamann and Herder do not inevitably lead through the God-defying and power-obsessed Friedrich Nietzsche and Johann Gottlieb Fichte to the Nazis. It is by no means inevitable that the Black Consciousness that Tutu defended earlier in his life (West and Chigumadzi 2022) leads to a dark and excluding African nationalism. The counter-Enlightenment thought that started with Hamann and Herder could just as easily have led to a humane German romanticism, had the disasters of World War I, the Treaty of Versailles, the austerity imposed by the agents of American reparations and the collapse of the German banking system from 1931 onwards not taken place. Yes, we must be wary of the potential of a counter-Enlightenment dark side; but an insistence that we never stray from rational universalism is taking Enlightenment thinking too far.

Keynes expressed his awareness that his Enlightenment thinking had led him away from truth in his lecture to his Cambridge friends in 1938 titled 'My Early Beliefs' (Keynes 1949). Moral questions were regarded as 'entirely rational and scientific in character' (1949: 86). Not in a materialist or Benthamite sense, but certainly within the parameters of Enlightenment thought, Keynes claims that he and his friends 'were among the last of the Utopians ... who believed in a continuing moral progress by virtue of which the human race already consists of reliable, rational, decent people, influenced by truth and objective standards' (1949: 98–9).

> In short, we repudiated all versions of the doctrine of original sin, of there being insane and irrational springs of wickedness in most men. We were not aware that civilisation was a thin and precarious crust erected by the personality and the will of a very few, and only maintained by rules and conventions skilfully put across and guilefully preserved. We had no respect for traditional wisdom or the restraints of custom. We lacked reverence, as [D.H.] Lawrence observed and as Ludwig [Wittgenstein] with justice also used to say – for everything and everyone. It did not occur to us to respect the extraordinary accomplishment of our predecessors in the ordering of life ... As cause and consequence of our general state of mind we completely misunderstood human nature, including our own. The rationality which we attributed to it led to a superficiality, not only of judgment, but also of feeling ... The attribution of rationality to human nature, instead of enriching it, now seems to me to have impoverished it (1949: 99–101).

There is a deliciously counter-Enlightenment feel to Keynes's essay 'Economic Possibilities for Our Grandchildren', written in 1930:

> When the accumulation of wealth is no longer of high social importance, there will be great changes in the code of morals. We shall be able to rid ourselves of many of the pseudo-moral principles which have hag-ridden us for two hundred years, by which we have exalted some of the most distasteful of human qualities into the position of the highest virtues. We shall be able to afford to dare to assess the money-motive at its true value. The love of money as a possession – as distinguished from the love of money as a means to the enjoyments and realities of life – will be recognised for what it is, a somewhat disgusting morbidity, one of

those semi-criminal, semi-pathological propensities which one hands over with a shudder to the specialists in mental disease ... I see us free, therefore, to return to some of the most sure and certain principles of religion and traditional virtue – that avarice is a vice, that the exaction of usury is a misdemeanour, and the love of money is detestable, that those walk most truly in the paths of virtue and sane wisdom who take least thought for the morrow. We shall once more value ends above means and prefer the good to the useful. We shall honour those who can teach us how to pluck the hour and the day virtuously and well, the delightful people who are capable of taking direct enjoyment in things, the lilies of the field who toil not, neither do they spin (Keynes [1930] 1952: 369–72).

Despite, and perhaps even because of, his foundations firmly within a Marxist, humanist, internationalist paradigm, Vishnu was particularly enamoured with this quote in the last six months of his life. As he found more time for self-reflection, and mindful of his love of leisurely lunches with friends, students and colleagues, Vishnu planned to write an article with me responding to both the above quotation from 'Economic Possibilities for Our Grandchildren' and the book by Robert Skidelsky and his son, Edward Skidelsky, *How Much is Enough? Money and the Good Life* (2012), in which we planned to wrestle with these pre-Enlightenment thoughts on religious virtue and, no doubt, through Vishnu's involvement, a post-Enlightenment humanism. Alas, this was not to be.

Notes

1. Andries Johannes Bruwer (1896–1983) was born on a farm in the Karoo, the eldest son of a wealthy farmer. He obtained a BA from Victoria College (later Stellenbosch University) in 1915, an MA from Harvard in 1920 (with a thesis on 'Currency, Banking and Exchange in South Africa'), and a PhD from the University of Pennsylvania in 1922 with the thesis 'Protectionism in South Africa'. He was chairman of the Board of Trade and Industry from 1924 to 1932, and of the Rand Water Board from 1955 to 1968.

    John Edward (Jack) Holloway (1890–1979) worked in a clothing shop in order to pay for his education at Victoria College. He received his PhD in economics from the London School of Economics in 1917. Holloway was the director of Census and Statistics (what is today Statistics South Africa) from 1925 to 1937,

secretary of finance of the Union of South Africa from 1937 to 1950, ambassador to Washington from 1954 to 1956 and high commissioner in London from 1956 to 1958.
2. 'Sacred hatred' was a term used by Polanyi's wife to describe her husband's motivation (described in Hejeebu and McCloskey 1999: 309).
3. All translations of the original Afrikaans quotes from Bruwer (1934) are by the author.
4. This is a reference to the work of Gustav von Schmoller, which Bruwer recommended reading; he was the leader of the 'young' German historical school and 'rejected both Marxism and Liberalism' (Screpanti and Zamagni, 2005: 190–1).
5. See https://en.wikipedia.org/wiki/Mercantilism.

References

Allen, W.R. 1987. 'Mercantilism'. In: *The New Palgrave Dictionary of Economics*. Vol. 3, edited by J. Eatwell, M. Milgate and P. Newman. London: Macmillan.

Amin, S. 1998. *Spectres of Capitalism: A Critique of Current Intellectual Fashions*. New York: Monthly Review Press.

Berlin, I. 2013. *Three Critics of the Enlightenment: Vico, Hamann, Herder*. London: Pimlico.

Blaug, M. 1985. *Economic Theory in Retrospect*. 4th edition. Cambridge: Cambridge University Press.

Bodin, J. [1568] 1997. *Response to the Paradoxes of Malestroit*, translated and edited by H. Tudor and R.W. Dyson. London: Bloomsbury.

———. [1576] 1967. *Six Books of the Commonwealth*. Oxford: Basil Blackwell.

Bordiss, B. 2021. 'Shaping Monetary Policy and Development in South Africa: The Role of Jack Holloway and Andries Bruwer, from 1914 to 1950'. PhD thesis, University of the Witwatersrand.

Bruwer, A.J. 1934. *Kapitalisme, Party-politiek en Armoede*. Bloemfontein: Nasionale Pers.

Carey, H.C. 1856. *The Harmony of Interests: Agricultural, Manufacturing and Commercial*. New York: Myron Finch.

Chang, H. 2007. *Bad Samaritans: The Guilty Secrets of Rich Nations and the Threat to Global Prosperity*. London: Random House.

Chatterjee, P. 1986. *Nationalist Thought and the Colonial World: A Derivative Discourse*. London: Zed Books.

Cohen, S.S. and J. B. de Long. 2016. *Concrete Economics: The Hamilton Approach to Economic Growth and Policy*. Boston: Harvard Business Review Press.

Coleman, D.C. 1987. 'Colbert, Jean Baptiste'. In: *The New Palgrave Dictionary of Economics*. Vol. 1, edited by J. Eatwell, M. Milgate and P. Newman. London: Macmillan.

Dayer, R.A. 1976. 'Strange Bedfellows: J. P. Morgan & Co., Whitehall and the Wilson Administration During World War I'. *Journal of Business History* 18 (2): 127–51.

Freund, B. 1998. *The Making of Contemporary Africa: The Development of African Society Since 1800*. London: Macmillan.
———. 2021. *An Historian's Passage to Africa: An Autobiography*. Johannesburg: Wits University Press.
Fukuyama, F. 1992. *The End of History and The Last Man*. New York: The Free Press.
Gaido, D. 2016. 'Rudolf Hilferding on English Mercantilism'. *History of Political Economy* 48 (3): 449–70.
Galbraith, J.K. 2012. *Inequality and Instability: A Study of the World Economy Just Before the Great Crisis*. New York: Oxford University Press.
Hamilton, A. [1791] 2012. *Report on the Subject of Manufactures*. Neuilly sur Seine: Ulan Press.
Hejeebu, S. and D. McCloskey. 1999. 'The Reproving of Karl Polanyi'. *Critical Review* 13 (3–4): 285–314.
Helleiner, E. 2021. *The Neomercantilists: A Global Intellectual History*. New York: Cornell University Press.
Herman, E.S. and D. Peterson. 2012. 'Steven Pinker on the Alleged Decline of Violence'. *International Socialist Review* 86. https://isreview.org/issue/86/steven-pinker-alleged-decline-violence/index.html.
Hobson, J.A. [1902] 2005. *Imperialism: A Study*. New York: Cosimo.
Hume, D. [1752] 2006. 'Political Discourses'. In: *Early Economic Thought: Selected Writings from Aristotle to Hume*, edited by A.E. Monroe. New York: Dover.
Hunt, J. 2011. 'Introduction'. In: *A Short Treatise on the Wealth and Poverty of Nations*, by A. Serra. London: Anthem Press.
Jahanbegloo, R. 1992. *Conversations with Isaiah Berlin*. London: Halban.
Kant, I. [1784] 1991. *An Answer to the Question: What is Enlightenment*. London: Penguin.
Kedourie, E. 1960. *Nationalism*. London: Hutchinson.
———. (ed.) 1970. *Nationalism in Asia and Africa*. New York: New American Library.
Kemmerer, E.W. 1934. *Kemmerer on Money*. London: George Routledge and Sons.
Keynes, J.M. [1925] 1952. 'The Economic Consequences of Mr Churchill'. In: *Essays in Persuasion*. London: Rupert Hart-Davis.
———. [1930] 1952. 'Economic Possibilities for our Grandchildren'. In: *Essays in Persuasion*. London: Rupert Hart-Davis.
———. 1933. 'National Self-Sufficiency'. *Studies: An Irish Quarterly Review*. 22 (86): 177–93.
———. 1936. *The General Theory of Employment, Interest, and Money*. New York: Harcourt, Brace and World.
———. 1949. 'My Early Beliefs'. In: *Two Memoirs*. London: Rupert Hart-Davis.
Lenin, V.I. [1917] 2010. *Imperialism: The Highest Stage of Capitalism*. London: Penguin.
Lipton, M. 1985. *Capitalism and Apartheid: South Africa, 1910–1984*. Aldershot: Wildwood House.

List, F. [1842] 2011. *National System of Political Economy: Three Volumes in One.* New York: Cosimo.

McNeil, W.C. 1986. *American Money and the Weimar Republic: Economics and Politics on the Eve of the Great Depression.* New York: Columbia University Press.

Mearsheimer, J. 2018. *The Great Delusion: Liberal Dreams and International Realities.* New Haven: Yale University Press.

Mitchell, W. and T. Fazi. 2017. *Reclaiming the State: A Progressive Vision of Sovereignty for a Post-Neoliberal World.* London: Pluto Press.

Monroe, A.E. (ed.). 2006. *Early Economic Thought: Selected Writings From Aristotle to Hume.* New York: Dover.

Mun, T. [1664] 2006. 'England's Treasure by Forraign Trade'. In: *Early Economic Thought: Selected Writings from Aristotle to Hume*, edited by A.E. Monroe. New York: Dover.

Noyes, J.K. 2015. *Herder: Aesthetics Against Imperialism.* Toronto: University of Toronto Press.

Padayachee, V. 2019. 'Can Progressive Macroeconomic Policy Address Growth and Employment while Reducing Inequality in South Africa?' *Economic and Labour Relations Review* 30 (1): 3–21.

Patnaik, U. and P. Patnaik. 2017. *A Theory of Imperialism.* New York: Columbia University Press.

———. 2021. *Capital and Imperialism: Theory, History, and the Present.* New York: Monthly Review Press.

Piketty, T. 2014. *Capital in the Twenty-First Century.* Cambridge, MA: The Belknap Press of Harvard University Press.

Pinker, S. 2018. *Enlightenment Now.* London: Allen Lane.

Reinert, S.A. 2011. 'Introduction'. In: *A Short Treatise on the Wealth and Poverty of Nations* by A. Serra. London: Anthem Press.

Ricardo, D. [1817] 1911. *The Principles of Political Economy and Taxation.* London: J.M. Dent and Sons.

Rosenberg, E.S. 1999. *Financial Missionaries to the World: The Politics and Culture of Dollar Diplomacy, 1900–1930.* Cambridge, MA: Harvard University Press.

Routh, G. 1989. *The Origin of Economic Ideas.* London: Macmillan.

Schumpeter, J.A. 1954. *History of Economic Analysis.* New York: Oxford University Press.

Screpanti, E. and S. Zamagni. 2005. *An Outline of the History of Economic Thought.* Oxford: Oxford University Press.

Serra, A. [1613] 2011. *A Short Treatise on the Wealth and Poverty of Nations.* London: Anthem Press.

Skidelsky, R. 1992. *John Maynard Keynes: The Economist as Saviour 1920–1937.* London: Macmillan.

Skidelsky, R. and E. Skidelsky. 2012. *How Much is Enough? Money and the Good Life.* London: Allen Lane.

Smith, A. 1776. *An Inquiry into the Nature and Causes of the Wealth of Nations.* Oxford: Oxford University Press.

Stark, W. 1944. *The History of Economics in its Relation to Social Development*. London: Kegan Paul, Trench, Trubner and Co.
West, C. and P. Chigumadzi. 2022. 'Black Spirit, Black Struggle'. *Boston Review*, 22 December. https://www.bostonreview.net/articles/black-spirit-black-struggle/.
Wilde, O. [1905] 1948. 'De Profundis'. In: *The Works of Oscar Wilde*, edited by G.F. Maine. London: Collins.
Wiltgen, R. 1989. 'The Evolution of Marx's Perspective of Mercantilism'. *International Journal of Social Economics* 16 (7): 48–56.

6

The Richness of Development Measures in Post-Apartheid South Africa?

Dorrit Posel

In the introduction to one of his edited books, *The Development Decade? Economic and Social Change in South Africa, 1994–2004*, Vishnu Padayachee warned that 'measurement, data and definitions should not be allowed to deflect the [development] discourse into narrow, technical, culs-de-sac' (Padayachee 2006: 4).[1] This short chapter reflects on some of the 'deflections' that gained traction after the end of apartheid; it considers why issues of 'measurement, data and definitions' can be important for informing the development discourse; and it describes how the range of development measures in South Africa has expanded over time.

Issues of definition and measurement in the development discourse

Issues of calibration have featured prominently in research and policy debates in South Africa, particularly during the earlier years of the democratic transition, frustrating political economists such as Padayachee, who worried that this dialogue obscured the many problems at hand. A 'preoccupation' with data, however, was not surprising, given the censored and inconsistent nature of data collected during the apartheid decades (Christopher 2011; Wilson and Horner 1996). This had instilled a deep mistrust of the credibility of quantitative data among many researchers and policy-makers (Posel 2017; Seekings 2001), increasing the responsibility placed on quantitative researchers to interrogate the reliability of data analysed. The first detailed household survey that was representative of all of South Africa (including the former 'bantustans' or 'homelands'), was conducted only in 1993. In the years that followed, surveyors and users of quantitative micro-data had to embark on a steep learning curve to probe, and where possible improve, the quality of data collected, as well as strengthen the ways in which these data were analysed (Posel 2017).

The data collected in the nationally representative household surveys are also the source of a range of 'official statistics', published by the national statistical agency (Statistics South Africa), including rates of unemployment, job creation, poverty and inequality. These statistics provide some of the key indicators used to measure the effectiveness of socio-economic policy, and thereby assess government performance. Given their significance, the veracity of the statistics – whether they show an improvement or a deterioration – is likely to be closely scrutinised in both the public and political arenas, and interventions in these debates require paying close attention to how the indicators are defined and generated, both at the cross-section and over time.

Debates over the measure of unemployment and employment
The ways in which issues of definition and measurement have deflected attention away from policy-intensive discussions are perhaps most clearly illustrated in the attention given to the unemployment and employment numbers in South Africa (for example, Alenda-Demoutiez and Mügge 2020; Casale, Muller and Posel 2004; Klasen and Woolard 1999; Nattrass 2000; Posel, Casale and Vermaak 2014; Standing, Sender and Weeks 1996).

Since 1998, Statistics South Africa has confined the official measure of unemployment to a 'strict' definition, which includes only those adults who have taken 'active steps to look for work or to start some form of self-employment' (Statistics South Africa 1998: 1). The grounds for excluding those who report wanting to work but not actively looking for work (or a 'broad' unemployment measure) are two-fold. First, this approach is consistent with that adopted in many (developed) countries. Second, by not actively searching for work, it is argued that individuals fail to signal that they actually want to work (and so are likely to misreport their true employment intentions) (Statistics South Africa 1998). However, in the context of very high rates of unemployment, an analysis of longitudinal national data shows that (a) the modal job-finding strategy in South Africa is through friends and relatives (which is not classified as active job search) (Posel, Casale and Vermaak 2014); (b) active searchers are no more likely to transition into employment than those who are not actively searching for work (Posel, Casale and Vermaak 2014); and (c) there is considerable churning between the two states of unemployment (Verick 2012).

The question of the appropriate definition of unemployment is not just a technical concern in South Africa. In many countries, the difference between the strict and the broad rates of unemployment is very small (Suryadarma, Suryahadi and Sumarto 2007). But in South Africa the gap between these two unemployment rates has often exceeded ten percentage points in the decades since the transition to democracy.

The debate about the 'true' size of unemployment has also included questions about the credibility of the unemployment numbers. During the 2000s, scepticism about the scale of unemployment was expressed by several important politicians. In 2005, for example, the then minister of finance, Trevor Manuel, commented that if the unemployment rate was really as high as it was measured to be using the broad definition, 'there'd be a revolution' (IOL 2005). Thabo Mbeki, the president at the time, was similarly distrustful, even of the number of people measured as 'strictly' unemployed, writing:

> In March 2004 there were at least 4 million South Africans walking about in our villages, our towns and cities 'actively looking for work'. This is such a large number of people that nobody could possibly have missed the millions that would be in the streets and village paths 'actively looking for work' in all likely places of employment. It, therefore, seems quite unlikely that the Stats SA figure is correct, if indeed it used the standard international ILO definition to determine the unemployment rate (Mbeki 2005).

The flipside of disbelief in the unemployment count was a debate over whether the employment numbers for South Africa were credible. The primary concern was that the national micro-data underestimated employment because respondents were reluctant to report on work if it was irregular, seasonal or informal (for example, Devey, Skinner and Valodia 2006). To reduce possible under-reporting, the questions used to collect employment activity were modified in 2000, with the changeover from the annual 'October Household Surveys' to the semi-annual 'Labour

Force Surveys', with far more prompts provided to respondents detailing types of work beyond regular wage or self-employment.[2] From October 1999 to September 2000, approximately one million more workers – and specifically domestic workers, the informal self-employed and subsistence farmers – were identified in the national micro-data, some of which probably reflects changes in how information on employment was captured (Casale, Muller and Posel 2004). Nonetheless, even by adopting a very broad definition of employment (people needed to have worked for only one hour in the previous week to be included among the employed), South Africa's official unemployment rate continued to increase, and the size of South Africa's informal sector remained puzzlingly small relative to the extent of unemployment in the country.

While some questioned whether employment in South Africa was being under-counted, others argued that official statistics overestimated the extent of job creation. In the run-up to the 2004 national election, for example, the government's claim that 'the economy created two million net new jobs since 1995' was met with disbelief by a wide range of commentators, who found it difficult to reconcile this claim with high and rising rates of unemployment and reports of large-scale retrenchments over the same period.[3] The resolution to this controversy required close analysis of the data sources that were used to derive official statistics on job creation. This revealed that while employment numbers had increased, the 'real' increase – net of changes in how employment was defined and captured – was closer to 1.4 million jobs from 1995 to 2003 (Casale, Muller and Posel 2004). Moreover, alongside this rise in employment, poverty among the employed had increased (Casale, Muller and Posel 2004), highlighting the type of work that had grown over the period.

Debates over measures of income and the rate of poverty
Technical debates about the measurement of income – and by implication, the rate of poverty – also featured prominently in the economic development discourse following the democratic transition. This perhaps is also not surprising, at least partly because reliable information on income is very difficult to collect.

The micro-data from the national household surveys are routinely used to generate official estimates of poverty in South Africa. This is because these surveys capture income from a wide range of employment types (including informal employment), and they also provide information on other sources of income received, including from social grants and remittances. However, survey respondents are often reluctant to divulge how much income they receive, and questions on income are plagued by high levels of non-response, particularly among people at the lower and upper tails of the income distribution (Posel and Casale 2006). To elicit more information, survey questions often prompt respondents to report their income in 'brackets' if they refuse to provide a 'point' estimate. But this then requires a method to reconcile two different kinds of income reports into a single measure, provoking considerable technical discussion and debate among researchers in South Africa (for example, Vermaak 2012; Von Fintel 2007).

Providing respondents with the opportunity to report income in categories reduces, but does not eliminate, the problem of non-response or the possibility that individuals under-report how much income they earn or receive. As with the unemployment numbers, the reliability of poverty rates estimated using the national micro-data has therefore been challenged. For example, it is generally accepted that poverty rates increased or remained constant up to 2000, and that they then declined with the expansion of the social grant programme in South Africa. However, the extent of the decline was rigorously debated by researchers, with data from an alternative source showing far lower poverty rates and a stronger decline over time (for example, Meth 2006; Van der Berg, Louw and Yu 2008).

The government's response also questioned the credibility of poverty statistics, but mostly because it was argued that money-metric measures ignored increased access to services (including water, sanitation, electricity, housing and health care), or the 'social wage'. In the early 2000s, the gross value of the social wage was estimated to be R72 billion per year, with about 55 per cent targeted at the poorest 40 per cent of households (Aliber and O'Donovan 2003). By disregarding the social wage, poverty estimates therefore underestimated the improvement in socio-economic well-being over the post-apartheid period.

Going beyond income: Complementary measures of development in post-apartheid South Africa

In addition to measurement issues, money-metric indicators of well-being typically do not capture the value of services or in-kind benefits received within the household, and the quality of life more generally. They also only provide estimates of average resource access in households, thereby concealing any inequalities within the household.

Alongside debates about how best to define and measure income and the rate of poverty, a range of studies in South Africa therefore started to explore alternative and complementary ways of describing economic status and well-being more broadly. Some of these analyses expanded money-metric indicators to include other dimensions of deprivation and poverty, using information collected in the national household surveys. 'Multidimensional' indicators provided a more holistic representation of 'human poverty' by encompassing not only income, but also access to basic services, nutrition and school enrolment within the household (for example, Klasen 2000; Rogan 2016). A growing body of literature also started to explore precarious livelihoods by focusing on questions of food security, hunger and under-nutrition (for example, Hendricks 2014; May and Timæus 2014).

Other studies examined subjective indicators of the quality of life, a development made possible by the inclusion of a range of subjective questions in several national household surveys (for example, Kollamparambil 2020; Møller 1998; Posel and Casale 2011; Posel and Rogan 2016). In contrast to their responses to questions about income earned or received, individuals are far more willing to provide information on how they assess their economic status or how satisfied they are with life. In addition, subjective indicators are individually ascribed, and they therefore overcome the limitations of money-metric indicators that can only provide measures of average resource access in the household (Posel 2021).

Conclusion
In contrast to the first post-apartheid decade, the credibility of socio-economic indicators has rarely been challenged in recent years. This could be the effect of both politicians and the public becoming inured to high rates of unemployment and poverty, or the result of progress made in improving, authenticating and enriching the quality of indicators derived from the national micro-data. While drawing attention away from substantive discussions on appropriate policy responses, this note suggests that the 'deflection' of the development discourse to questions of measurement and definition has not been without merit.

Notes

1. This is not to suggest that he was opposed to quantitative analysis. In his capacity as head of the School of Development Studies at the University of KwaZulu-Natal from 2009 to 2011, Vishnu Padayachee was very supportive of my building a new computer lab for the teaching of quantitative methods in the school – from finding the physical space for it and overseeing the appointment of a project manager, to procuring artwork to hang on its walls.
2. In asking about people's activities in the previous week, the new survey instrument included detailed categories of work (from running a business or working for wage, doing work as a 'domestic worker for a wage, salary or payment in kind' and working on their own plot of land, to even 'catch[ing] fish, prawns, shells, wild animals or other food for sale or family food', undertaking 'any construction or major repair work' on their or their family's home or business, and 'beg[ging] for money or food in public'.
3. The government's claims can be found in 'Employment II: The Myth of Jobless Growth' (ANC 2004); 'Doomsayers Take Liberties with Facts on Employment' (Erwin 2004); and criticism in 'Unions and Researchers Slam Government over Claims of Jobs Growth' (Bell 2004); 'Erwin Digs In His Heels on Job Increase Data' (Wray 2004); and 'DA Rubbishes ANC Jobs Claims' (Dawes 2004).

References

Alenda-Demoutiez, J. and D. Mügge. 2020. 'The Lure of Ill-fitting Unemployment Statistics: How South Africa's Discouraged Work Seekers Disappeared from the Unemployment Rate'. *New Political Economy* 25 (4): 590–606.

Aliber, M. and M. O'Donovan. 2003. *The Social Wage in South Africa: A Review on Behalf of the Social Cluster Task Teams on Free Basic Services and the Comprehensive Social Security Framework*. Pretoria: Human Sciences Research Council.

ANC (African National Congress). 2004. 'Employment II: The Myth of Jobless Growth'. *ANC Today* 4 (9): 5–11.

Bell, T. 2004. 'Unions and Researchers Slam Government over Claims of Jobs Growth'. *Business Report* 15 February.

Casale, D., C. Muller and D. Posel. 2004. '"Two Million Net New Jobs": A Reconsideration of the Rise in Employment in South Africa, 1995–2003'. *South African Journal of Economics* 72 (5): 978–1002.

Christopher, A.J. 2011. 'The Union of South Africa Censuses 1911–1960: An Incomplete Record'. *Historia* 56 (2): 1–18.

Dawes, N. 2004. 'DA Rubbishes ANC Jobs Claims'. *This Day*, 8 March.

Devey, R., C. Skinner and I. Valodia. 2006. 'Definitions, Data and the Informal Economy in South Africa: A Critical Analysis'. In: *The Development Decade? Economic and Social Change in South Africa, 1994–2004*, edited by V. Padayachee. Cape Town: HSRC Press.

Erwin, A. 2004. 'Doomsayers Take Liberties with Facts on Employment'. *Sunday Independent Business Report*, 15 February.

Hendricks, S. 2014. 'Food Security in South Africa: Status Quo and Policy Imperatives'. *Agrekon* 53 (2): 1–24.
IOL. 2005. 'Manuel Is Too Glib About Unemployment'. *IOL*, 28 February. https://www.iol.co.za/business-report/opinion/manuelis-too-glib-about-unemployment-749442.
Klasen, S. 2000. 'Measuring Poverty and Deprivation in South Africa'. *Review of Income and Wealth* 46 (1): 33–58.
Klasen, S. and I. Woolard. 1999. 'Levels, Trends and Consistency of Measured Employment and Unemployment in South Africa'. *Development Southern Africa* 16 (1): 3–35.
Kollamparambil, U. 2020. 'Happiness, Happiness Inequality and Income Dynamics in South Africa'. *Social Indicators Research* 21 (1): 201–22.
May, J. and I. Timæus. 2014. 'Inequities in Under-five Nutritional Status in South Africa: What Progress Has Been Made?' *Development Southern Africa* 31 (6): 761–74.
Mbeki, T. 2005. 'Letter from the President'. *ANC Today* 5 (20): 20–6.
Meth, C. 2006. *Income Poverty in 2004: A Second Engagement with the Van der Berg et al. Figures*. School of Development Studies Working Paper 47, School of Development Studies, University of KwaZulu-Natal.
Møller, V. 1998. 'Quality of Life in South Africa: Post-apartheid Trends'. *Social Indicators Research* 43 (1): 27–68.
Nattrass, N. 2000. 'The Debate about Unemployment in the 1990s'. *Studies in Economics and Econometrics* 24 (3): 73–89.
Padayachee, V. (ed.). 2006. *The Development Decade? Economic and Social Change in South Africa, 1994–2004*. Cape Town: HSRC Press.
Posel, D. 2017. 'Enriching Economics in South Africa: Interdisciplinary Collaboration and the Value of Quantitative-qualitative Exchanges'. *Journal of Economic Methodology* 24 (2): 119–33.
———. 2021. 'Intra-household and Inter-personal Comparisons of Subjective Well-being'. *Applied Research in Quality of Life* 16 (6): 2527–9.
Posel, D. and D. Casale. 2006. *Who Replies in Brackets and What Are the Implications? An Analysis of Earnings Data in South Africa*. Economic Research Southern Africa Working Paper 7, University of KwaZulu-Natal.
———. 2011. 'Relative Standing and Subjective Well-being in South Africa: The Role of Perceptions, Expectations and Income Mobility'. *Social Indicators Research* 104 (2): 195–223.
Posel, D., D. Casale and C. Vermaak. 2014. 'Job Search and the Measure of Unemployment'. *South African Journal of Economics* 82 (1): 66–80.
Posel, D. and M. Rogan. 2016. 'Measured as Poor versus Feeling Poor: Comparing Money-metric and Subjective Poverty Rates in South Africa'. *Journal of Human Development and Capabilities* 17 (1): 55–73.
Rogan, M. 2016. 'Gender and Multidimensional Poverty in South Africa: Applying the Global Multidimensional Poverty Index (MPI)'. *Social Indicators Research* 126 (3): 987–1006.

Seekings, J. 2001. 'The Uneven Development of Quantitative Social Science in South Africa'. *Social Dynamics* 27 (1): 1–36.

Standing, G., J. Sender and J. Weeks. 1996. *Restructuring the Labour Market: The South African Challenge. An ILO Country Review*. Geneva: International Labour Office.

Statistics South Africa. 1998. *Unemployment and Employment in South Africa*. Pretoria: Statistics South Africa.

Suryadarma, D., A. Suryahadi and S. Sumarto. 2007. 'Measuring Unemployment in Developing Countries: The Case of Indonesia'. *Labour* 21 (3): 541–62.

Van der Berg, S., M. Louw and D. Yu. 2008. 'Post-transition Poverty Trends Based on an Alternative Data Source'. *South African Journal of Economics* 76 (1): 59–76.

Verick, S. 2012. 'Giving Up Job Search During a Recession: The Impact of the Global Financial Crisis on the South African Labour Market'. *Journal of African Economies* 21 (3): 373–408.

Vermaak C. 2012. 'Tracking Poverty with Coarse Data: Evidence from South Africa'. *Journal of Economic Inequality* 10: 239–65.

Von Fintel, D. 2007. 'Dealing with Earnings Bracket Responses in Household Surveys: How Sharp Are Midpoint Imputations?' *South African Journal of Economics* 75 (2): 293–312.

Wilson, F. and D. Horner. 1996. *Lessons from the Project for Statistics on Living Standards and Development: The South African Story*. Living Standards Measurement Study Research Paper 5. Washington DC: World Bank.

Wray, Q. 2004. 'Erwin Digs In His Heels on Job Increase Data'. *Business Report*, 23 February.

7

The Political Economy of Nationalism and Populism
South Africa, India and the United States

Gillian Hart

One of Vishnu Padayachee's final publications was his powerful chapter in *Race, Class and the Post-Apartheid Democratic State* titled 'Harold Wolpe and the (Failed) Transformation of South African Capitalism' (Padayachee 2019). Drawing on and extending his earlier critical engagement with the Varieties of Capitalism (VoC) literature (Padayachee 2013a), he maintained that, although the VoC approach addresses broad systemic relations, especially in relation to influences upon the state and the market, its emphasis is on the varieties of institutions rather than the nature of capitalism itself. As he eloquently put it,

> from a Marxist perspective, there are notable absences in terms of deeper consideration of the class relations underpinning capitalism and the historically and socially different national and international forms that it adopts. This is not simply a matter of saying that the VoC approach is not Marxist but, rather, that it is relatively, if not absolutely, negligent of other approaches, especially from across other social sciences, that are both standard, richer and are more or less concerned with the same problems as the VoC approach (Padayachee 2019: 100).

He also challenged the VoC approach for its relative lack of attention to Asian, Eastern European, African and Latin American case studies. Pointing out that local and national histories always participate in the movement of world history, Vishnu went on to reject firmly any notion of South African exceptionalism. Rather, he argued, South Africa exemplifies – in an extreme form – 'some of the central tendencies of that long history, the features of which have included race, inequality and migration' (2019: 103).

Moving to an analysis of how South African capitalism has and has not changed in the post-apartheid era, Vishnu maintained that it has 'come to resemble more closely an Anglo American variant of capitalism, albeit with some older hybrid features in place' (2019: 114). He called attention as well to the forces driving nationalism and xenophobia:

> The ANC's actual strategy combined openness to neoliberal globalisation with policies that strengthened the opposition between the 'rainbow nation' and other Africans. South Africa's poor citizens, faced with the enrichment of a black elite and their own continuing economic exclusion, were asked to identify with apartheid's beneficiaries against their African neighbours, so contributing to the growing xenophobia evident in the post-apartheid era (2019: 115).

Along with close attention to the relations of class to race and nationalism, Vishnu also harked back to his earlier essay on corporate governance in South Africa to underscore the centrality of gender – more specifically what he called a cult of alpha-male leadership (Padayachee 2013b).

Rereading Vishnu's critique and reconstruction of the VoC literature has underscored for me a strong sense of affinity with his work, despite differences in our research projects. My current research focuses on the political economy of intensifying nationalisms and populist politics since the end of the Cold War in South Africa, India and the United States. The question to which it is addressed is why, instead of the widely presumed and celebrated global triumph of neoliberal capitalism combined with secular liberal democracy, we have witnessed not just resurgent nationalisms, virulent racisms and populist politics, but also ferocious battles between these forces and proponents of liberal democracy and secularism in these and other societies.

Drawing on and extending an argument in my book *Rethinking the South African Crisis* (2013), I point to the emergence of two distinct but related forms of neoliberal hegemony since the end of the Cold War: a liberal, technocratic form that seeks to *neutralise* the popular antagonisms often exacerbated by neoliberal capitalism (exemplified by Thabo Mbeki, Bill Clinton, Barack Obama and Cyril Ramaphosa), and a populist form that seeks to *mobilise* these antagonisms through articulations of nationalism with racial, religious, nativist, gendered and other forms of difference, while also keeping them under control (exemplified by Jacob Zuma, Narendra Modi and Donald Trump). What have been set in motion are warring tendencies between these mutually inflammatory forms of hegemony and the economic, political and social forces that constitute them. At the same time, these escalating battles have assumed distinctively different – but mutually illuminating – forms in different nation-states.

This approach calls into question a widely held view that the rise of the right signifies 'the protracted failure, both in design and delivery of third-way style of "progressive neoliberalism" on each side of the Atlantic' (Peck and Theodore 2019: 258), and related calls for left populism (for example, Mouffe 2018) or 'progressive populism' (Fraser 2019). In my view, these approaches vastly underestimate the analytical and political complexities and dangers of the present conjuncture (Hart 2019). They also overlook the slippages, openings and contradictions from which alternatives might emerge.

The political economy of nationalism and populism: A global conjunctural frame

To comprehend the dynamics of warring tendencies, I develop a critical comparative framework that is grounded in Antonio Gramsci's conjunctural analysis, while also stretching and reworking it in very different spatio-historical contexts from his own engagement with Italian fascism in the 1920s and 1930s. This frame (a) views South Africa, India and the US neither as pre-given national units nor as variations of a pre-existing broader process, but rather as historically specific yet interconnected sites in the production of worldwide processes; and (b) pays close attention to the relation of these national formations to the forms of imperialism in different spatio-historical conjunctures – with 'conjuncture' understood not just as a period or a 'slice of time', but as an accumulation of contradictions. The focus is on multiple, changing articulations of nationalism in relation to historically specific dynamics of capitalist accumulation, class differentiation and class struggle – and compels attention to articulations of race and racism, gender, sexuality, caste and religion as inseparably and actively constitutive of *both* class processes and nationalisms through the workings of bourgeois hegemony.

The frame is organised around a set of key *global conjunctural moments*, defined as major turning points when interconnected forces at multiple levels and spatial scales in different regions of the world – both structural and contingent – have come together to generate new conditions with worldwide implications and reverberations. One such moment was the end of the Cold War. To understand the generation of warring tendencies in many regions of the world, we have to go back to earlier global conjunctural moments – most immediately, the late 1940s and the late 1960s and early 1970s, but also the *longue durée* processes of racial capitalism, settler colonialism and imperialism through which South Africa, India and the US were formed as nation-states. In a forthcoming book provisionally titled *Warring Tendencies: Populist/Liberal Battles in a Global Frame*, I argue for the importance of understanding how racially inflected nationalisms and populist politics have taken shape in relation to changing forms of liberalism since the end of the Cold War, and I trace the deeper roots of these antagonistic tendencies.

The remainder of this chapter summarises two ways in which I have used this framework. Pointing to when and how populist movements in South Africa and India have taken control of state power since the end of the Cold War, I pose the question 'why did it take so long for a demagogic figure like Trump to ascend to power, given the long histories of racism and right-wing Christian nationalism in the United States; the ravages of neoliberal forms of capitalism; and the abandonment of the working class by the Democratic Party?' (Hart 2020: 239). And I suggest how situating current debates over Christian nationalism in the US in a global conjunctural frame can shed light on these debates, as well as on the political economy and cultural politics of anti-secular religious nationalisms in India and South Africa (Hart 2021).

Why did Trumpism take so long to emerge?
The question of why Trumpism took so long to emerge sprang initially from my efforts to understand widespread popular support for Zuma since the early 2000s (Hart 2013), which then led me to a rich and deeply informative Indian literature on the rise of Hindutva and the takeover of the state by Modi's Bharatiya Janata Party. What also came into view was the resurgence of right-wing nationalism and populist

politics in many other regions of the world, especially in the post-Cold War period. It was in relation to all of these that the electoral triumph of Trumpism in 2016 appeared as a belated victory in the US of forces that had been actively in play in different regions of the world for some time.

I was struck as well by Mike Davis's observation that 'with the help of Breitbart and the alt right, [Donald Trump] essentially ran in Patrick Buchanan's old shoes' (Davis 2017: 153). While I completely agree with Davis's observation, the question remains as to why it took so long for Buchanan's shoes to gain traction. Buchanan was a key figure on the Christian Right – a self-described paleo-conservative – who ran for the US presidency on a Christian nationalist platform in 1992, 1996 and 2000, deploying the 'America First' slogan made popular by fascist sympathisers in the 1930s. In the last of these elections, he ran against none other than Trump in the primaries. Trump dropped out of the race but pocketed the slogan for future use. The global conjunctural frame lets us see Trumpism neither as an aberration nor as the inevitable consequence of the failures of 'progressive neoliberalism', as some have argued, but as a live though latent possibility that required a particular configuration of forces – both structural and contingent – in order to burst forth.

Working back from the end of the Cold War, the frame focuses on (a) the conjuncture of the late 1940s and the emergence of Cold War-era projects of accumulation and hegemony – apartheid in South Africa; Nehru's project of development, secular democracy and non-alignment; and Fordism in the US; and (b) the multiple processes through which these projects imploded from the late 1960s onwards, giving way to the neoliberal counter-revolution – albeit in spatio-historically specific ways. The distinctive forms and timing of destructive forces unleashed in the post-Cold War era – including the rise of right-wing forms of nationalism and populist politics – are to be found in the wreckages of Cold War-era projects in South Africa, India and the US.

Also of great importance, I suggest, is that the early 1980s signalled the emergence of new forms of US imperialism marked by significant shifts in the interconnected financial and military relations of the US to different regions of the non-Western world. One can discern three very broad regional patterns of financial reconfiguration – closely linked to the neoliberal counter-revolution but not reducible to it – all of which generated massive capital inflows into the US from the 1980s that helped drive intensified militarism under Ronald Reagan: the rise of China as a major exporter of cheap consumer goods, and purchaser of US Treasury Bonds; the growing interconnections between petroleum and armament corporations following the OPEC oil price rise that fed into energy conflicts in the Middle East; and the debt crisis of the early 1980s in many Latin American and African countries that led to the imposition of stabilisation and structural adjustment policies, including the opening up of capital markets that propelled huge outflows of capital – much of which landed up on Wall Street. South Africa and India were not incorporated into any of these broad regional realignments with the US for reasons having to do with their very different relations to the Soviet Union. Non-alignment was a key element of the Nehruvian Consensus, although following India's defeat in the war with China in 1962 the Nehru regime moved into a closer relationship with the Soviet Union. For Euro-America, South Africa operated as a bulwark against communism in Africa – and was a major player in the proxy wars of the 1980s. Together, however, South Africa and India let us see Cold War-era projects of hegemony falling apart in slow motion in the course of the 1980s, setting in place the conditions for the 1990s and beyond, when neoliberal forms of capitalism and hegemony came into relation with intensified articulations of nationalism to generate populist politics – albeit in dramatically different ways – as well as the accession to state power of populist forces.

Drawing on the global conjunctural framework, I suggest that the answer to the question of why Trumpism took so long to emerge in relation to South Africa and India hinges crucially on these changing forms of US imperialism. Global interconnections in turn need to be understood in relation to forces operating in the realms of everyday life, through mediations of hegemonic processes that were thrown into chaos and crisis in the 1970s, and then transformed from the 1980s under Reagan. In summary, I propose the following key arguments:

(a) During the chaotic 1970s, Fordism fell apart more rapidly than either apartheid or the Nehruvian Consensus under the combined pressures of movements from the left and the right that gathered force during the 1960s; the capitalist crisis that intensified through the 1970s; and mounting political crises associated with the Vietnam War, followed by revolutions in Iran and Nicaragua, and the Soviet invasion of Afghanistan.

(b) Reagan's accession to power in 1981 represented the dismantling of Fordist hegemony, the consolidation of a project grounded in a new right-wing coalition, and the emergence of new forms of US imperialism driven both by global financial restructuring and the proxy wars outlined earlier, in which the fiercely anti-communist Christian Right that coalesced in the 1970s (but which goes back to the 1920s) played a central role.

(c) With the end of the Cold War, there was a sharp rupture in the right-wing coalition between the Christian Right and neo-conservatives that swept Reagan to power. Tensions within the Christian Right further undermined Patrick Buchanan's bid for state power on a populist platform.

(d) Another key part of the explanation of how resurgent right-wing populist movements were held in check is that, in the face of shrinking employment, stagnant incomes and escalating inequality, the mass of the US population was caught up in a frenzy of consumerism and spiralling debt – driven by financial deregulation under Reagan and Clinton, asset price inflation and massive foreign capital inflows that lowered the cost of debt, and enabled in crucially important ways by the tsunami of cheap consumer goods from China and Chinese purchasing of Treasury Bonds.

(e) The 9/11 attacks – part of the 'unfinished business' of the proxy wars of the 1980s (Mamdani 2004) – took the wind out of the sails of isolationist nationalist movements like Buchanan's by unleashing waves of militant patriotism combined with Islamophobia. During the Bush II administration the Christian Right became deeply embedded in the White House. In addition, the wars in Iraq and Afghanistan were accompanied by what Ellen Moore, in *Grateful Nation* (2017: 11) calls 'militarized common sense' through which military valorisation is infused into everyday civilian life.

(f) According to Dylan Riley, 'the crisis of the neo-liberal hegemonic formula can be dated precisely to October 3, 2008, when the $700 billion Troubled Assets Relief Program (TARP) [the huge bailout of the banks] revealed the hypocrisy of its free-market ideology' (Riley 2017: 25). Although multiple contingencies played into Trump's election, Riley maintains, it was these 'deeper shifts in the political economy of the country [that] made it possible for Trump to emerge in a context where the existing hegemonic project seemed exhausted' (2017: 30). Drawing on the global conjunctural framework, I suggest that the 2008 financial meltdown blew the lid off US neoliberal hegemony in ways that include – but extend well beyond – the hypocrisy of TARP. Most immediately, it also exposed the fragility of a consumer debt dynamic that is peculiar to the US because of its imperial position. In addition, this was the moment when Obama assumed power, unleashing powerful racist forces that found expression in the right-wing Tea Party uprising, and when the wars in Iraq and Afghanistan had been thoroughly discredited.

The confluence of these contradictions created a conjunctural moment in which Buchananesque articulations of racist nationalism and nativism could take root and metastasise during the Obama years – a process driven not just by Trump, but by the much wider global networks of right-wing white Christian nationalism in which Stephen Bannon remains situated. Bannon can be seen as the organic intellectual of Trumpist coalition, engaged not just in helping to constitute a cross-class, predominantly white movement out of the mounting popular antagonisms that brought Trump to power, but also deploying white Christian nationalist ideology to powerful effect in producing a conception of the world that resonates in certain respects with Hindutva. Yet the deep, profound contradictions within and through which Trumpism has been playing out in practice make it far more analogous to the tension-ridden forces at work in South Africa than to the relative coherence of the right in India, which I discuss more fully in my forthcoming book.

The violence that erupted following Trump's loss of the 2020 election exemplifies how populist strategies of mobilising popular antagonisms can and do spiral out of the control of the more 'moderate' elements of the social bloc – in this instance the Republican Party. In the conclusion to this chapter, I will return to reflect more broadly on the current conjuncture. Before doing so, we need to dig more deeply into the anti-secular religious nationalisms so powerfully on display in the US and India – and that also compel us to attend more closely to related processes in South Africa.

The political economy of anti-secular religious nationalisms

A useful starting point is an intense debate in the US over the religious character of support for Trumpism. Many take for granted that white evangelicals comprise the foundation of 'the base'. According to widely cited statistics, Trump won more than 80 per cent of the white evangelical vote in 2016; in 2020, exit polls indicated that 76 per cent of the 28 per cent of voters who identified as either white evangelical or white born-again Christian voted for Trump (Rubin 2020). A contrary view is that Trump's core support

> does not come from white evangelicals as such, but from an overlapping group of not necessarily evangelical, and not necessarily white, people who identify at least loosely with Christian nationalism: the idea that the United States is and ought to be a Christian nation governed under a reactionary understanding of Christian values (Stewart 2020).

The reference to 'not necessarily white' is significant, in the light of higher levels of Trump support by Latinx and black voters in 2020 than in 2016. Developed most forcibly by Katherine Stewart in her book *The Power Worshippers: Inside the Dangerous Rise of Religious Nationalism* (2019), this view is gaining growing support.

From a comparative perspective I have found the small but growing literature on Christian nationalism simultaneously compelling and in urgent need of further development. Most immediately, this work literally brought home to me that the US version draws on some of the same theological sources that informed white Christian nationalism in South Africa – most notably the influential ideas of the neo-Calvinist theologian and former Dutch prime minister Abraham Kuyper (1837–1920). Although helping to clarify why the Trump years have felt so eerily familiar to one born and raised in apartheid South Africa, recent work on Christian nationalism is very narrowly focused on the US – in effect reiterating American exceptionalism and abstracting from US imperialism. In addition, the liberal thrust of recent efforts to understand Trumpism in terms of Christian nationalism precludes comprehension of the articulations of race, religion and nationalism with capitalism and class – and hence the profound contradictions through which these interconnected forces play out in practice.

More generally, I suggest that we need a dialectical understanding of Christian nationalism as part of a hegemonic project, intimately linked with US imperialism and forms of racial capitalism – and that this also requires going beyond the US-centric focus of this literature. Drawing on the global conjunctural frame, I will now suggest in broad outline how religious nationalisms in South Africa and India can extend the work on US Christian nationalism and help to illuminate the escalating crisis in the US.

In part this requires returning to Gramsci, who charted by far the most useful way of relating politics and religion to class struggle My own efforts to move along this path are informed by Indian scholars of Hindutva discussed below, and by Fabio Frosini's brilliant reading of Gramsci on religion and politics:

> With the First World War and the Soviet Revolution a phase of 'frenetic' and 'totalitarian' integration of subaltern classes is opened, where 'liberal' modalities will be, in various degrees, abandoned or downsized, passing to the politics of permanent mobilization of the whole population...The bourgeoisie, reduced to the role of pure preservation...takes hold of the religious myths of subalterns and uses them as the engine of the passive inclusion of the masses into the state: the politics of total mobilization absorbs the vindication of the people's participation in power, the politics of colonial expansionism replies to the socialist egalitarian demand. Bourgeois universalism, devoid of any proper content, absorbs the common sense of subalterns and re-organizes its meaning. In this way bourgeois power incorporates the utopian energy of popular religious universalism, rendering it functional to its own expansion (Frosini 2013: 183).

Gramsci's focus, of course, was on the rise of fascism in Italy, which he located in a broader European context. Yet we need to recognise the end of World War I as a global conjunctural moment marked not only by the Bolshevik Revolution and indeed the Spanish flu pandemic, but also by popular uprisings all over the world – as well as by conservative forms of backlash and escalating nationalisms. It was within this context of the inter-war conjuncture that religious nationalisms in South Africa, India, the US and other regions of the world took hold – and are crucial to grasping key dimensions of the present conjuncture. Of necessity very briefly, let me turn now to outlining some key contours of these processes.

The resurgence of religious nationalisms in many regions of the world from the mid-1970s onwards discussed below – many of which continue to reverberate in the present – has its roots in the inter-war years. Formed in the mid-1920s, Hindutva took inspiration from Italian fascism and later Nazism. Combining blood-and-soil nationalism with mythologies of Muslim tyranny, it was driven by 'anxieties among large sections of the upper caste elites as they were pressed by the upsurge of lower castes from one side and the rise of a multi-religious, multi-caste nationalism that was becoming a veritable mass-movement with Gandhi's shepherding of the Congress, especially after 1919', as Aijaz Ahmad (2015: 182) makes clear. Drawing explicitly on Gramsci's conjunctural analysis, Ahmad underscores as well how 'if the October Revolution inspired the colonial peoples into a praxeological belief in mass uprisings against colonial state apparatuses, that same revolution instilled in the propertied classes of our countries the fear that the anti-colonial revolution may indeed proceed uninterruptedly to an anti-capitalist one' (Ahmad 2000: 165).

In South Africa, Dan O'Meara (1983) has shown how Kuyper's politico-theological claims of divinely ordained nations helped to drive the redefinition of white Afrikaner nationalism as Christian nationalism in the early 1930s. Spearheaded by the Broederbond, which described itself as 'born out of the deep conviction that the Afrikaner nation has been planted in this country by the Hand of God' (O'Meara 1983: 71), white Christian nationalism was closely linked with the project of *volkskapitalisme* (people's capitalism), and together they were explicitly aimed at containing class struggle. White Christian nationalism in turn formed the moral justification for the apartheid regime (1948–90) – while also providing a target of moral outrage for the anti-apartheid movement, an important component of which was framed in religious terms.

The rise of Hindutva in India and white Christian nationalism in South Africa bears directly on US debates over white evangelicalism versus Christian nationalism. By far the most influential view, exemplified by Frances FitzGerald's *The Evangelicals* (2017), holds that their anti-evolution campaign, culminating in profound humiliation in the 1925

Scopes 'monkey trial', drove conservative white evangelicals back into apolitical churches, and that they only emerged as a political army of cultural warriors in response to liberal Supreme Court rulings on school prayer, pornography and abortion in the 1960s and 1970s. A distinctively different interpretation by Alan Lichtman in *White Protestant Nation* (2008) maintains that modern conservatism, combining Christianity with private enterprise, took shape in the decade after World War I as a form of nationalism:

> At the core of right-wing politics in the 1920s and beyond was an anti-pluralistic ideal of America as a unified, white Protestant nation...Virtually every dispute over radicalism, loyalty, reproduction, race, immigration, sexuality, crime, permissiveness, creationism, and school prayer had its forerunner in the '20s. So too did forms of right-wing political mobilization...Since World War I, conservatives have been cultural, religious, and at times racial nationalists, dedicated to protecting America's superior civilization from racially or culturally inferior peoples, foreign ideologies, sexual deviance, ecumenical religion, or the encroachment of so-called one-world government (Lichtman 2008: 2–4).

These conservatives exempted capitalism from the charge of cultural corruption, thus opening 'a space within which big capital could unite politically with ordinary shopkeepers, farmers, and workers' (2008: 5). The predominantly white cross-class coalition of Trump support occupies precisely this space.

Turning now to the post-World War II conjuncture: with the exception of apartheid, Cold War-era projects were defined by liberal secularism and nominally inclusive nationalisms, the contradictions of which contributed to the implosion of these projects. As noted earlier, an important part of opposition to apartheid was cast in religious terms. More generally, 'Christianity has been a key component of South African nationalisms – both black and white' since the nineteenth century, Daniel Magaziner (2010: 11) reminds us; he also illuminates the process through which many were led to 'a total redefinition of the Christian faith in the South African context, from one complicit in colonization and dispossession to a message of assured liberation' (2010: 11).

These multiple rearticulations of Christianity as part of political struggles in South Africa highlight the importance of Nikhil Pal Singh's argument that liberal appropriation of Martin Luther King has rendered him 'part of a mythic nationalist discourse, even as it obscures his significantly more complex, worldly, and radical politics' (Singh 2004: 3). Singh goes on to note that King came to attack 'the presumptions of the "amazing universalism" of the American dream he had championed only a few years before' – coming to argue instead 'that the U.S. nation-state was neither a stable mediator of social antagonisms nor the ultimate horizon of black hopes for justice' (2004: 14). In the process King became more closely allied with other key figures in the black liberation struggle in the US who rejected liberal narratives of inclusive nationalism, turning instead to 'a combination of grassroots insurgency with global dreams' (2004: 219).

The resurgence of religious nationalisms needs to be situated explicitly in relation to the crisis of Cold War-era projects in the late 1960s and early 1970s, succinctly summarised by Leo Panitch as

> a time when increased inter-capitalist competition, rampant inflation, falling rates of profit and spreading speculation against the dollar were conjoined with a worldwide upsurge against American imperialism, while the core capitalist countries themselves were shaken not only by waves of industrial militancy, but by the eruption of youth and black protests in the streets, as the war in Indochina became a US disaster (Panitch 2000: 10).

Popular struggles were not, however, confined to core capitalist countries, and this was *also* a time of global resurgence of fundamentalist religious movements. Emerging in the mid-1970s in many regions of the world, these movements fiercely challenged secular liberalism and 'aimed at recovering a sacred foundation for the organization of society – by changing it if necessary', as Gilles Kepel (1994: 2) has pointed out. In addition to Evangelicals, these movements included Hindutva, political Islam, anti-secular Zionists and Catholic charismatics. They serve as a reminder that the growing political power of Christian nationalism in the US during the 1970s was part of worldwide processes and takes us back to a Gramscian understanding of class struggle in relation to the politics of religious nationalisms. What is distinctively peculiar about the

US is how, in the 1980s, the Christian Right was a driving force behind the emergence of new forms of US imperialism through its active engagement with proxy wars in different regions of the non-Western world – including Southern Africa (Hart 2020: 253–4). These imperialist reconfigurations are also deeply interconnected with dynamics of political-economic and spatial restructuring in the US since the 1980s, along with intensifying class, racial and spatial inequalities – and hence with the mounting antagonisms we are now witnessing between liberal and populist forms of neoliberal hegemony.

The Christian nationalist takeover of the Republican Party under Trump was fully on display during the invasion of the Capitol on 6 January 2021, as Sarah Posner (2021) makes clear in her chilling account of the Christian Right's invocation of the wrath of God and Jesus over the theft of the election from Trump and his people. Despite rifts within the Republican Party since Trump's departure to his kingdom by the sea in Florida, conflicts between populist and liberal forces in the US have, if anything, amplified in recent years, with Trump's rivals such as Ron DeSantis ramping up their ferocious attacks on liberal secularism and multiculturalism. In short, even if Trump were to disappear, the forces he helped to unleash remain alive and well – and it is to these forces rather than the figure of Trump himself that we need to attend. Much the same can be said of Zuma and Modi, as I will argue in my forthcoming book.

Concluding reflections

Returning to Vishnu's critique of the VoC literature and his firm rejection of any notion of South African exceptionalism, I would like to conclude by reflecting briefly on three ways in which the comparative conjunctural analysis outlined in this chapter resonates with his work.

First, this analysis lends unequivocal support to Vishnu's insistence that, far from being exceptional, South Africa participates in and contributes to interconnected economic, political and social processes under way in other regions of the world – albeit in an extreme and specific form. At the same time, situating South Africa in relation to the US underscores the 'exorbitant privilege' (Eichengreen 2011) that the dominance of the dollar continues to bestow on the US, despite the peril posed to American financial imperialism by the current refusal of Republicans in the House of Representatives to raise the debt ceiling – a topic on which Vishnu would undoubtedly have delivered some deliciously acerbic comments.

Second, the comparative conjunctural approach shares key elements with the critique and alternative to VoC that Vishnu pioneered – including the imperative to combine political economy with cultural politics and practices (or heterodox economics and the humanities), and a refusal of methodological nationalism.

A third, related affinity is 'the centrality of history and of the global dimension in any account of capitalist development', as Vishnu put it, but always in conjunction with close attention to local specificity and dynamics – in other words, 'accounts that are located in a deep understanding of how things have changed [in specific settings] . . . over time and in a rapidly changing global context' (Padayachee 2013a: 28).

References

Ahmad, A. 2000. *Lineages of the Present: Ideology and Politics in Contemporary South Asia*. London: Verso.

———. 2015. 'India: Liberal Democracy and the Far Right'. In: *The Politics of the Right: Socialist Register*, edited by L. Panitch and G. Albo. London: The Merlin Press.

Davis, M. 2017. 'The Great God Trump and the White Working Class'. *Catalyst* 1: 151–71.

Eichengreen, B. 2011. *Exorbitant Privilege: The Rise and Fall of the Dollar and the Future of the International Monetary System*. New York: Oxford University Press.

FitzGerald, F. 2017. *The Evangelicals: The Struggle to Shape America*. Toronto: Simon & Schuster.

Fraser, N. 2019. *The Old is Dying and the New Cannot Be Born: From Progressive Neoliberalism to Trump and Beyond*. London: Verso.

Frosini, F. 2013. 'Why Does Religion Matter to Politics? Truth and Ideology in a Gramscian Approach'. In: *The Political Philosophies of Antonio Gramsci and B.R. Ambedkar: Itineraries of Dalits and Subalterns*, edited by C. Zene. New York: Routledge.

Hart, G. 2013. *Rethinking the South African Crisis: Nationalism, Populism, Hegemony*. Pietermaritzburg: University of KwaZulu-Natal Press.

———. 2019. 'From Authoritarian to Left Populism? Reframing Debates'. *South Atlantic Quarterly* 118 (2): 307–23.

———. 2020. 'Why Did It Take So Long? Trump-Bannonism in a Global Conjunctural Frame'. *Geografiska Annaler: Series B, Human Geography* 102 (3): 239–66. https://doi.org/10.1080/04353684.2020.1780791.

———. 2021. 'Decoding "The Base": White Evangelicals or Christian Nationalists?' *Studies in Political Economy* 102 (1): 61–76.

Kepel, G. 1994. *The Revenge of God: The Resurgence of Islam, Christianity and Judaism in the Modern World*. University Park, PA: Pennsylvania State University Press.

Lichtman, A.J. 2008. *White Protestant Nation: The Rise of the American Conservative Movement*. New York: Atlantic Monthly Press.

Magaziner, D. 2010. *The Law and the Prophets: Black Consciousness in South Africa*. Athens, OH: Ohio University Press.

Mamdani, M. 2004. *Good Muslim, Bad Muslim: America, the Cold War, and the Roots of Terror*. New York: Pantheon.

Moore, E. 2017. *Grateful Nation: Student Veterans and the Rise of the Military Friendly Campus*. Durham, NC: Duke University Press.

Mouffe, C. 2018. *For a Left Populism*. London: Verso.

O'Meara, D. 1983. *Volkskapitalisme: Class, Capital, and Ideology in the Development of Afrikaner Nationalism, 1934–1948*. New York: Cambridge University Press.

Padayachee, V. 2013a. 'Introducing Varieties of Capitalism into the South African Debate'. *Transformation* 81–2: 259–90.

———. 2013b. 'Corporate Governance in South Africa: From "Old Boys Club" to "Ubuntu"'? *Transformation* 81–2: 5–32.

———. 2019. 'Harold Wolpe and the (Failed) Transformation of South African Capitalism'. In: *Race, Class and the Post-apartheid Democratic State*, edited by J. Reynolds, B. Fine and R. van Niekerk. Pietermaritzburg: University of KwaZulu-Natal Press.

Panitch, L. 2000. 'The New Imperial State'. *New Left Review* 2: 5–20.

Peck, J. and N. Theodore. 2019. 'Still Neoliberalism?' *South Atlantic Quarterly* 118 (2): 245–65.

Posner, S. 2021. 'How the Christian Right Helped Foment Insurrection'. *Reveal*, 30 January. https://revealnews.org/article/how-the-christian-right-helped-foment-insurrection/.

Riley, D. 2017. 'American Brumaire'. *New Left Review* 103: 21–32.

Rubin, J. 2020. 'What the Election Tells Us about Religion in America'. *The Washington Post*, 12 November. https://www.washingtonpost.com/opinions/2020/11/12/what-election-tells-us-about-religion-america/.

Singh, N.P. 2004. *Black Is a Country*. Cambridge, MA: Harvard University Press.

Stewart, K. 2019. *The Power Worshippers: Inside the Dangerous Rise of Religious Nationalism*. New York: Bloomsbury.

———. 2020. 'Trump or No Trump, Religious Authoritarianism Is Here to Stay'. *New York Times*, 16 November. https://www.nytimes.com/2020/11/16/opinion/trump-religion-authoritarianism.html?action=click&module=Opinion&pgtype=Homepage.

8

The Economics of the Feasible in a Democratic South Africa
Anglo American and Economic Policy

Gavin Keeton

Pre-1990: The last decade of apartheid

Anglo American can claim some credit for the role it played in preparing (mainly white) South Africans for the political changes unleashed by President F.W. de Klerk's February 1990 unbanning of the African National Congress (ANC) and the release of Nelson Mandela. This it did in two ways. The first was political, with its chairman, Gavin Relly, leading a group of (mainly Anglo-linked) business leaders to meet with the ANC in Zambia in September 1985. While President P.W. Botha reacted to the visit with fury, interaction between the ANC leadership in exile and the business leaders was warm. But Relly noted his concern afterwards that the ANC seemed to have no thoughts about the economic policies it would implement if in power, other than support for the Freedom Charter and, flowing from this, nationalisation of the 'commanding heights' of the economy.

The second role played by Anglo American, nominally economic but with important political implications, was the widespread dissemination of its scenario planning exercise titled *The World and South Africa in the 1990s* (Sunter 1987). The scenarios it presented correctly predicted the collapse of the Soviet Union and argued that South Africa must choose between two possible future scenarios. The first was the 'High Road' of sustained economic growth and increased prosperity, which, it was argued, required a market-oriented economy open to global competition. Importantly, it required, too, a fully inclusive democracy. The alternative 'Low Road' scenario of apartheid, sanctions and economic stagnation could lead only to declining living standards, increased unrest and eventual political change, but from a far weaker socio-economic position.

The scenarios were presented by Anglo executives Clem Sunter, Michael Spicer and Jim Buys to several hundred audiences in the second half of the 1980s. It is hard now to remember the hope this presentation ignited in white South Africans, numbed by the states of emergency declared by the government in the mid-1980s, by economic sanctions, and by a daily TV diet of reports of violent protests. Sunter presented the scenarios to Nelson Mandela in Pollsmoor Prison, and Spicer and Buys presented them to the ANC in Maputo. President de Klerk asked Sunter to present them to the Cabinet twice. Sunter later joked that he thought the right-wing members of the Cabinet must have thought they'd misunderstood the insistence on inclusive democracy as a critical ingredient for success!

Perhaps it was because of these early interactions, as much as Anglo's importance in the South African economy, that, after his release, among the first people Mandela met with was Relly. And fairly soon afterwards he established an informal series of dialogues with business leaders that met from time to time, at Mandela's request, at the Brenthurst home of Anglo's former chairman Harry Oppenheimer.

1990–94: The transition period
In the transition period from 1990 to the April 1994 elections, Anglo's economic thinking was set out each year in a *Chairman's Statement* (AAC 1990–95) that accompanied the corporation's annual report. The statement discussed key developments in its business interests, but significant chunks of the twelve-page (later sixteen-page) reports were devoted to thoughts about South Africa's political and economic future that one would not normally find being penned by business leaders. This willingness to publicly engage in controversial economic discourse reflected Anglo's size in the South African economy, but also a historical willingness to play a much larger societal role than just making profits. This role had been summed up by Anglo's founder, Sir Ernest Oppenheimer, in 1953 when – in reaction to shareholder concerns about Anglo helping to fund infrastructure development in Zambia – he stated: 'The aims of this Group have been – and they still remain – to earn profits, but to earn them in such a way as to make a real and permanent contribution to the well-being of the people and to the development of South Africa' (AAC 1993: i).

Unsurprisingly, the statements called for a market-oriented economy, focused on economic growth as the key requirement for sustainable poverty and unemployment reduction, and emphasised the importance of private sector investment in driving that growth and of deregulation, privatisation and lower corporate taxes in unleashing that investment. They warned of the risks to sustainable growth of large fiscal deficits, excessive bureaucracy and intrusive state intervention in business activity.

A common theme in each statement was the defence of Anglo's size and of the perceived dominance in South Africa of a relatively small number of conglomerates. The claim that Anglo controlled about half of the Johannesburg Stock Exchange was denied. The true number was calculated to be about 25 per cent, of which 20 per cent reflected companies Anglo had started from scratch or nurtured from humble beginnings. In steel and in pulp and paper Anglo had introduced competition against previous monopolies, and no Anglo companies other than 'the special case' of De Beers could be considered monopolies. Comparisons were made with other relatively small economies like Sweden, the Netherlands, Australia and (not a small economy) Germany, whose stock markets were also dominated by a small number of globally operating companies.

This theme also featured prominently in the endless round of seminars, conferences and breakfasts that dominated South African discourse during the transition period from 1990 to 1994. Inevitably Anglo's head of public affairs, Michael Spicer, was paired with the ANC's Tito Mboweni, and Mboweni would warn about the ANC's determination to 'dismember the conglomerates' that controlled the South African economy. Spicer would spiritedly defend Anglo's size and point to the large investments it was making as evidence of its confidence in the new South Africa. And the process would be repeated again and again.

At one of these conferences in Cape Town, Harvard University's Jeffrey Sachs (in possibly his only input into the South African policy discourse) listened to Mboweni and Spicer and concluded that competition policy was important. But scrap exchange controls, he told Mboweni, and corporate structures will change faster than you can imagine. How true this prediction proved to be, but not in the way Sachs imagined. The democratic South African government was unwilling to remove exchange controls, believing this would result in massive capital flight. Instead, it allowed first Billiton, then Anglo, and then SA Breweries, Old

Mutual and Dimension Data to move their primary stock market listings to London. A consequence of this move is that Anglo has today shed almost all its non-mining assets, and Old Mutual its non-financial assets. The other 'conglomerates' to which Mboweni referred back in 1990 were Sanlam, Liberty Life and Barlows, which have also substantially refocused their business interests. But while shareholders clearly benefited from the changed corporate structures, the impact on South African business dynamism was decidedly mixed. Certainly, the ability and willingness of South African business to engage in economic policy debate with the government was destroyed – a reality which Spicer (2016) laments in an article for the Helen Suzman Foundation.

The role of Anglo business executives, most especially Spicer, in engaging with the government on policy issues is set out in detail in Spicer (2016). Two other attempts deserve mention. The first, in 1992, was an Anglo document (summarised in AAC 1992) that discussed ways in which South Africa might have some quick successes in reducing poverty. The production of the document was coordinated by Mamphela Ramphele, an Anglo director, and was intended as a platform for dialogue with the ANC. The document argued that clean water and sanitation could be provided to twelve million rural South Africans, and that voluntary schemes of on-the-job training could be provided for youth, women and the unemployed at relatively low cost. It also covered the equalisation and improved delivery of pensions, health and nutrition, particularly school-feeding, education shelter, and rural development. It argued that some government budgets, such as education, would not need to be increased, 'because the scope for rectifying misallocation and waste is so great' (AAC 1992: 11). The 1992 *Chairman's Statement* concludes:

> Our studies suggest that a framework of this kind could bring tangible results within five or six years, at a cost roughly calculated at some R15 billion a year. That is clearly more than can be afforded at present. Additional spending on that scale would more than double the budget deficit and stultify growth ... But if we choose to follow macroeconomic policies that give balanced growth its head, the scope for addressing poverty is dramatically, and progressively, improved (AAC 1992: 11).

In the end, the document was presented to a delegation of ANC policy-makers led by Saki Macozoma as an intended tool for ongoing engagement. It was politely received, and a response and future meeting were promised, but nothing was ever heard from the ANC again.

Post-1994: Economic policy in the democratic era

The second, much more controversial, document, *Growth for All*, was published by the South Africa Foundation in February 1996. In meetings with President Mandela, business leaders had warned that they did not believe government policies would deliver the growth South Africa required to tackle poverty and unemployment, so Mandela invited them to set out what they believed needed to be done. *Growth for All* was the response. The economic sections were written by Old Mutual economists and the labour section by Anglo American. The document argued that a much faster reduction in the budget deficit was required to boost national savings and investment. Also, that a substantial further weakening of the rand exchange rate should be engineered (by lifting exchange controls and by Reserve Bank dollar purchases) to boost South Africa's global competitiveness and bring about the needed increase in domestic investment. Tighter fiscal policy and vigilant monetary policy would prevent the competitive benefits of the exchange rate weakening being eroded by higher inflation. Perhaps most controversially, the document called for a dual labour market, where existing labour regulations would apply only to existing businesses, but new businesses would operate under much more flexible hiring, firing and wage requirements.

The proposals were controversial even within the business sector. The bankers accused the mining sector (that is, Anglo American) of wanting to boost profits through the weaker exchange rate. In response, a 'windfall tax' on mining exports was included in the initial drafts of the document but was removed after vigorous opposition from Billiton's Brian Gilbertson. Anglo's industrial head, Leslie Boyd, asked incredulously whether the document was proposing that a business producing the same product as his own business should open next door operating under different conditions. 'Yes,' he was told, 'because it is in South Africa's interests to allow this.' He accepted the proposal.

The document was presented to President Mandela, who said it should be made public, and the immediate reaction within the ruling ANC-Congress of South African Trade Unions (COSATU)-South

African Communist Party alliance was outrage. COSATU responded with its own document (COSATU, NACTU and FEDSAL 1996) demanding the exact opposite of everything *Growth for All* had proposed. Labour Minister Mboweni slammed the call for a dual labour market. Alan Hirsch observes:

> Had the two documents [by the South Africa Foundation and COSATU] been the basis for an academic debate rather than a struggle for influence, it would not have been too hard to find common ground. But, following the publication of *Growth for All*, the tone of the debate was too strident, as if some participants saw it as a struggle for the soul of the ANC (Hirsch 2005: 96).

Importantly, Old Mutual, having previously accused Anglo of trying to claim credit for its work, headed for the hills, and with it went much of corporate South Africa's willingness to stick their heads over the parapet on matters of economic policy. The final nail in that coffin was President Thabo Mbeki's later bitter criticism of Anglo CEO Tony Trahar for what Trahar had intended to be constructive and positive comments about the improving investment climate in South Africa. The fact that Trahar had said 'political risk' in South Africa had diminished was said by Mbeki to be racist-speak for black government's not being able to govern properly (Bruce 2017; Terreblanche 2004). Spicer told Trahar that the incident was 'a boil that needed lancing'. 'Maybe,' the tough-as-nails Trahar responded, 'but I promise you it's not fun being the boil.'[1]

Accelerated by the London listings, a new generation of unengaged business leadership, and fragmented and weakly led organised business structures (see Spicer 2016), the era of business engagement in policy formulation in South Africa came to an end.

So why did ANC economic policy change course – or did it?
The reasons why the ANC seemingly abandoned its historically redistributive economic stance in favour of a more market-friendly, pro-growth macroeconomic approach have been extensively discussed by, among others, Vishnu Padayachee and Robert van Niekerk (for example, in Padayachee and Van Niekerk 2019). In more populist political debates on economic policy and 'radical economic transformation', Mandela and Finance Minister Trevor Manuel have often been accused of having 'sold

out' to white capitalism. There is an underlying suggestion that they were 'bought off' by big business. Where else did the Growth, Employment, and Redistribution (GEAR) policy (National Treasury 1996) come from?

The first reaction to this claim is a reminder that reducing the budget deficit and restoring macroeconomic balances was a constant theme in all ANC policy documents after 1990 (see Hirsch 2005). GEAR simply accelerated the process. The explanation for the fiscal conservatism that underlay GEAR and previous ANC policy documents lies not at all in a 'market-friendly approach', but rather in the ANC's huge fear that if things went wrong economically, South Africa would have to turn to the International Monetary Fund and the World Bank for bailouts, and economic sovereignty would be lost (see Green [2008: 369–70] for an eloquent and detailed discussion of these fears). Manuel and Mbeki were determined to avoid such an outcome where, Manuel told Pippa Green (2008: 370), 'you end up in the pouches of these people'.

The underlying message of such claims is the belief that what was implemented after 1994 was in fact business-friendly economic policy. But while business was happy with the reduction in fiscal deficits, the post-1994 labour, industrial, procurement and empowerment policies, as well as the gradual collapse of the state-owned enterprises providing critical infrastructure for business operations and exports, were far from 'business-friendly' developments. Indeed Spicer (2016) laments business's unwillingness to stand up to the government in the face of the gradual erosion of its competitiveness, preferring to find ways in which individual businesses could adapt, without regard for the implications for the overall business environment and ultimately for economic growth. Today's economic stagnation is the consequence.

Conclusion

That a business such as Anglo American engaged so actively in economic policy discourse during and after apartheid in the manner described in this chapter is unusual. This willingness declined after the London listing in 1999 and its resultant dramatic restructuring, which substantially reduced the importance of South Africa to its global operations. New leadership replaced those executives who had played such a public role in the tumultuous last decade of apartheid and the transition to democracy, and with them the willingness to criticise government policy or offer alternative visions for economic success disappeared. This was echoed throughout big business in South Africa.

It can be argued that this is how democracies are meant to run, and unelected business leaders have no right to attempt to use their economic might to influence political decisions. It can also be asked, however, whether South Africa today does not sorely miss those powerful voices who can challenge the government and offer alternatives, at a time when its economy stagnates, and critical institutions like Eskom crumble.

Note

1. Personal communication between Trahar and the author.

References

AAC (Anglo American Corporation of South Africa Ltd). 1990. *Chairman's Statement*. Johannesburg: Anglo American Corporation.
———. 1991. *Chairman's Statement*. Johannesburg: Anglo American Corporation.
———. 1992. *Chairman's Statement*. Johannesburg: Anglo American Corporation.
———. 1993. *Chairman's Statement*. Johannesburg: Anglo American Corporation.
———. 1994. *Chairman's Statement*. Johannesburg: Anglo American Corporation.
———. 1995. *Chairman's Statement*. Johannesburg: Anglo American Corporation.
Bruce, P. 2017. 'Why Thabo Mbeki Was Wrong and Tony Trahar Was Right Back in 2004'. *Rand Daily Mail BL Premium*, 25 October. https://www.businesslive.co.za/rdm/politics/2017-10-25-peter-bruce-why-thabo-mbeki-was-wrong-and-tony-trahar-was-right-back-in-2004/.
COSATU (Congress of South African Trade Unions), NACTU (National Council of Trade Unions) and FEDSAL (Federation of South African Labour Unions). 1996. 'Social Equity and Job Creation: The Key to a Stable Future'. *Africa Focus*. http://www.africafocus.org/docs96/saf9605.ec1.php.
Green, P. 2008. *Choice Not Fate: The Life and Times of Trevor Manuel*. Cape Town: Penguin.
Hirsch, A. 2005. *Season of Hope: Economic Reform under Mandela and Mbeki*. Pietermaritzburg: University of KwaZulu-Natal Press.
National Treasury, 1996. *Growth, Employment and Redistribution: A Macroeconomic Strategy*. https://www.treasury.gov.za/publications/other/gear/chapters.Pdf.
Padayachee, V. and R. van Niekerk. 2019. *Shadow of Liberation: Contestation and Compromise in the Economic and Social Policy of the African National Congress, 1943–1996*. Johannesburg: Wits University Press.
South Africa Foundation. 1996. *Growth for All: An Economic Strategy for South Africa*. Johannesburg: South Africa Foundation.

Spicer, M. 2016. 'The Business Government Relationship: What has Gone Wrong?' *Focus: The Journal of the Helen Suzman Foundation* 78: 3–19.
Sunter, C. 1987. *The World and South Africa in the 1990s*. Cape Town: Human & Rousseau.
Terreblanche, C. 2004. 'Mixed Reaction to Mbeki's Broadside on Anglo'. *IOL*, 12 September. https://www.iol.co.za/news/politics/mixed-reaction-to-mbekis-broadside-on-anglo-221697.

9

An Unfinished Research Agenda on the South African Reserve Bank
Linking Academic Scholarship and Monetary Policy

Jannie Rossouw

The South African Reserve Bank (SARB) is the oldest central bank in Africa, established in terms of the Currency and Banking Act (No. 31 of 1920). It opened its doors for business on 30 June 1921 in Pretoria (SARB 1971) and celebrated its centenary in 2021. The SARB therefore looks back on a long and illustrious history.

The historical development of the SARB and its approach to policy implementation are interests that Vishnu Padayachee and I shared. Vishnu and I met in 1996, when he was appointed to the board of the SARB as a non-executive director. I served as secretary of the SARB at that time. As the most junior non-executive director, Vishnu's board seat was at the bottom of the board table, next to mine. In the years of his service as a non-executive director, he progressed in seniority and moved towards the top of the table. When he stepped down from the board, he was the most senior non-executive director and had a board table seat next to the deputy governors.

Despite his many other interests, Vishnu also developed an interest in the history of monetary policy and the institutional history of the SARB during his years of service on the board. As he and I shared these interests, a fruitful friendship developed. Often, I called him around 6.15 a.m. for an early-morning discussion, with Vishnu answering the telephone with a 'Hallo, what's up?'

Our first major project was my PhD (Rossouw 2008) on matters pertaining to inflation rate accuracy and credibility, and the SARB's successes or otherwise in containing inflation, completed under Vishnu's supervision. Subsequently, we published several research papers together on a variety of matters, mostly in the sphere of monetary policy and central banking. Inevitably, we had to consider the 1980s; a period when the autonomy and independence of the SARB were under serious pressure (see, for example, Rossouw and Padayachee 2011). This was also the decade in which South Africa suffered its highest annual rate of inflation. Clearly, political interference in monetary policy and low inflation cannot be reconciled.

Recently I assessed our joint research output in accredited journals, some of which we also co-authored with other colleagues, academics and students. Vishnu and I were very productive, as I counted more than fifteen such outputs on which our names appear jointly, with or without other researchers (see, for example, Bordiss, Padayachee and Rossouw 2021; Bosch, Rossouw and Padayachee 2015, 2017; Padayachee and Rossouw 2007, 2019, 2021; Rossouw and Padayachee 2008, 2009, 2011, 2021; Rossouw, Padayachee and Bordiss 2015; Rossouw, Padayachee and Bosch 2009, 2011; Rossouw, Padayachee and Mondi 2019).

One of these research papers was in Afrikaans, my mother tongue (Padayachee and Rossouw 2010). Vishnu was particularly proud of this paper, as he had previously published in French and Czech, in addition to his vast research output in English.

I have also written about Vishnu, for instance an obituary with Bradley Bordiss published in a special edition of the journal *Economic History of Developing Regions* (Bordiss and Rossouw 2021). And I completed the manuscript that Vishnu and I were working on at the time of his death (Rossouw and Padayachee 2022). I wish to thank Jeremy Grest, the editor of *Transformation*, for his assistance in getting this manuscript through the review process and accepted for publication. This was probably one of the last papers to be published under Vishnu's name.

Vishnu and I considered various questions pertaining to central banking and monetary policy that receive scant attention in academic scholarship. These questions include the link between monetary policy and aspects such as institutional structures and internal decision-making processes of central banks; the Common Monetary Area (CMA); and seigniorage emanating from currency in circulation.

Seigniorage relates to the income accruing to central banks owing to their currency liability to the public. However, when Vishnu and I discussed research in this area of central banking and monetary policy, it soon transpired that the first two challenges to agree on were the definition of seigniorage, and the basis for its calculation, as is explained later in this chapter. Initially we focused on the fact that the impact of monetary policy decisions receives wide coverage in the literature, while the processes and systems of monetary policy decision-making receive scant attention. It soon became clear to us that this void in the literature runs much deeper and wider; hence the aspects we identified as potential research projects. We agreed that these aspects of central banking would be the basis of fruitful future research as a series of papers or a book.

Evolution of decision-making structures in the SARB
The Currency and Banking Act that established the SARB in 1920 designated the board of directors as the formal decision-making structure of the central bank. This decision-making structure was retained in the South African Reserve Bank Acts (No. 29 of 1944 and No. 90 of 1989). The legislation, and regulations framed in terms of the legislation, also provided for ordinary general meetings of stockholders/shareholders.[1] The Currency and Banking Act made reference to stockholders of the SARB, rather than shareholders. The term 'stockholders' was replaced by the term 'shareholders' of the SARB in the South African Reserve Bank Amendment Act (No. 49 of 1989). The shareholders have very limited decision-making powers in regard to the activities of the SARB.

In 1956 the South African Reserve Bank Act (No. 29 of 1944) was amended with the insertion of a new Section 6 *bis* (South African Reserve Bank Amendment Act [No. 45 of 1956]), which provided for the delegation of powers by the board of the SARB to the governor, the deputy governor, or any officer of the SARB. Vishnu and I considered undertaking research on the question of the discharge of day-to-day management responsibilities by the executive and staff of the SARB and its board prior to the provision for such delegation, but no academic or other literature exists on this subject. Such research is therefore impossible.

The delegation of powers by the board of directors never identified the governor of the SARB as its CEO. This interpretation is confirmed by the writings of E.H.D. Arndt, the deputy governor of the SARB from 1951 to 1961. Arndt stated of the governor of that time (M.H. de Kock): 'I have known Mike de Kock intimately since 1922 ... he looked upon himself merely as *primus inter pares* – the first among equals' (cited by Botha 2022: 34).

In 2010, the South African Reserve Bank Amendment Act (No. 4 of 2010) demarcated the oversight functions of the board of the SARB, with the remainder of the management functions entrusted to the management of the central bank in terms of the legislation. This superseded the previous delegation of powers by the board.

The Currency and Banking Act of 1920 and the subsequent enabling legislation, the South African Reserve Bank Act of 1944 which replaced the legislation of 1920, provided only for the appointment of a governor and a deputy governor at the SARB. The number of deputy governorships was subsequently increased to three, resulting in a culture of committee decision-making replacing individual responsibility for decisions.

The Governors' Executive Committee is the most senior internal executive committee of the SARB. It commenced as an informal meeting of the governor and deputy governors after the appointment of G.P.C. de Kock as governor and was necessitated by the increase in the number of deputy governors. Before the existence of this committee, the governor and deputy governors took individual responsibility for decisions in their respective areas of oversight.

Given the extensive body of academic literature on individual responsibility vis-à-vis in-committee decision-making, Vishnu and I planned to research the question of whether the use of committees improved the quality of decision-making in the SARB. After all, matters should only be referred to committees for consideration in those instances where deliberation results in better decisions than when taken by individuals. Nevertheless, Vishnu and I were in complete agreement that one area of in-committee decision-making adopted by the SARB was an improvement on the previous system used. This related to the Monetary Policy Committee (MPC), which enhanced the public understanding of questions such as where monetary policy decisions are taken; by whom these decisions are taken; when such decisions are taken; and why such decisions are taken.

Despite the improvements ushered in by the MPC and its deliberations, Vishnu and I held the view that general public agreement will never be reached on the appropriate monetary policy stance in South Africa, or for that matter in any other monetary jurisdiction. Even he and I sometimes disagreed on the monetary policy stance of the SARB. Without putting words in his mouth, I can say that I am an inflation hawk. My view can be summarised as *inflation is ungood*™.

Other decision-making structures of central banks, and the lack of academic benchmarking of such structures, intrigued Vishnu and me. It is unclear why these issues receive scant attention, as central banks must surely be able to draw on each other's best practice. Given this void in the academic literature, our first objective was to assess whether the structure of the SARB is aligned with decision-making structures in other central banks; whether it enhances the quality of decision-making vis-à-vis individual decision-making responsibility; and whether it possibly impedes agility, thus prolonging decision-making processes. Analysis and comparison of the institutional frameworks for decision-making at central banks will be a fertile field for future research, which I wish I could tackle in conjunction with Vishnu, given our shared interest in these matters.

The Common Monetary Area and monetary policy
The CMA agreement between South Africa, Eswatini, Lesotho and Namibia receives scant attention in academic research, despite its importance in the context of the monetary policy decisions of the SARB.

In terms of the CMA agreement, all four member countries have their own central banks with the power to set monetary policy and issue their own currency, but the currencies of Eswatini, Lesotho and Namibia are pegged at one-to-one exchange rates with the South African rand, and therefore also to one another. The practical implication is that the SARB formulates monetary policy for the CMA countries (see, for example, Maziva 2016).

The CMA countries also use the South African national payment and settlement system for the settlement of interbank transactions and claims. The precondition is that the exchange rate peg should be retained, as the payment system does not provide for exchange rate differences. If any CMA country wishes to relinquish the currency peg, a precondition will be the prior development of its own payment and settlement systems.

A further characteristic of the CMA agreement is that the South African rand circulates freely as legal tender in Eswatini, Lesotho and Namibia. South Africa compensates those countries in terms of a seigniorage sharing agreement for such circulation within their respective borders. Seigniorage sharing by South Africa is limited to the CMA partner countries, thus excluding other countries such as Zimbabwe where the rand circulates (albeit without any formal agreement).

Vishnu and I viewed the CMA agreement as a fertile topic for future research, with a focus on two areas in particular. The first is the seigniorage sharing agreement, which is discussed in more detail in the next section.

The second area is much more contentious, dealing with the fact that the SARB is the *de facto* (albeit not the *de jure*) central bank for all CMA countries. As the MPC of the SARB sets monetary policy for all four countries, Vishnu and I considered the contentious possibility of the CMA countries being granted the opportunity to appoint a representative as a member of the MPC. To this end, we considered the benefits and disadvantages of the identification of one of the governors of the three central banks of the CMA countries to such a position, perhaps on the basis of rotation or length of service as governor of one of the three central banks. This would be a major change from the current approach, in which an MPC comprises only SARB officials. Vishnu and I reached no final view or conclusion from our discussions, but such an appointment might have a fortuitous unforeseen consequence: a CMA appointee to the MPC might help to protect the SARB against political interference from the South African government, as happened in the 1980s (see, for example, Rossouw and Padayachee 2021; Rossouw, Padayachee and Mondi 2019). The SARB might need the support of the CMA in the protection of its autonomy and independence against its own government's whims, as was the painful reality in the 1980s.

Seigniorage

Monetary policy decisions of central banks receive extensive attention in the academic literature, while their other 'visible' responsibility, namely the issuance of currency, receives very little coverage. Vishnu and I agreed that we should focus on filling this void in developing our understanding of seigniorage emanating from currency in circulation in the broader context of monetary policy. I took a first step, albeit without Vishnu, on this journey, when I recently published in Afrikaans a paper on banknotes and seigniorage (Rossouw 2022). However, much more has to be done to develop a body of academic literature on this topic.

The first research challenge is agreement on the definition of seigniorage, while the second challenge is agreement on the basis for its calculation. Definitions of seigniorage obtained from various discussions and from the literature differ considerably, from a broad to a narrow definition. Broader definitions imply larger amounts earmarked as seigniorage, while narrower definitions imply the collection of smaller amounts in the form of seigniorage. A broad definition of seigniorage is 'the excess of the face value ... [of currency] ... over the cost of production of currency' (Van der Merwe et al. 2014: 21; see also Bain and Howells 2003: 22; De Beer and Shikwane 2021: 113), which recalls the historic definition used by Wim Vanthoor (1997) in respect of coin. Vanthoor shows that the origins of seigniorage are to be found in the difference between the cost of production and the issuance value of coin, but that it subsequently also encompassed banknotes. The implication is that seigniorage is to be calculated on currency in circulation, that is, banknotes and coin. However, the question is how to do the calculation.

An alternative definition for seigniorage focuses on high-powered money, rather than just the currency component. If the 'sovereign' has the sole right to issue currency and receives economic value from that right, should such a right not also apply equally to the sole right to supply electronic money used for settlement? Bank reserves held at the central bank give the central bank the capacity to hold more interest-bearing assets, and so acquire economic value, just as currency notes on issue do.

Vishnu and I never finalised our views on the preferred calculation of seigniorage, but we discussed a preference for a definition of seigniorage based on the rate of return on the currency in circulation, rather than a definition based on changes in the stock of currency in circulation (see, for example, European Central Bank 2017). We planned to assess the linkages between seigniorage and monetary policy once we agreed on the definition and the basis for its calculation. The different definitions mentioned in the literature confirm the fact that little research has been done on any possible linkage to monetary policy.

The next challenge is to clarify the CMA seigniorage sharing agreement. This agreement compensates the CMA partner countries for their lost seigniorage on South African rands circulating within their borders. The compensation payable by South Africa to its partner countries is based on an *estimate* of the value of rands in circulation in each of Eswatini, Lesotho and Namibia (as no data are available on the actual quantity of rands circulating in each of those countries), multiplied by two-thirds of the annual yield on a portfolio of South African government bonds. To the extent that the rands in circulation in Eswatini, Namibia and Lesotho are overestimated, the seigniorage sharing agreement includes an element of development aid.

Seigniorage sharing is reported annually in the *Estimates of National Expenditure* as an expenditure item of the South African National Treasury (National Treasury 2021). The SARB does not publish any calculation or estimate of seigniorage emanating from currency in circulation. My estimate for seigniorage is calculated on the basis of interest earned on currency in circulation, after adjustment for cost of production and circulation. On this basis seigniorage amounts to R1 193 million for the SARB for its 2019/20 financial year (Rossouw 2022).

The South African government shares in two ways in the profits of the SARB, which include the income from seigniorage. First, the SARB pays income tax on any profit. Second, any profit earned by the SARB after taxes, dividends and reserve allocation have been deducted is paid to the South African government by means of a surplus distribution to the National Revenue Fund.

Seigniorage is earned by the SARB in respect of South African currency circulating in Eswatini, Lesotho and Namibia, but the payments to those countries are made by the South African government. It can therefore be argued that the payment of seigniorage to Eswatini, Lesotho and Namibia should be a commitment of the SARB, rather than the South African government, to ensure a better reflection of seigniorage earned and the commitment paid from it, although the actual amounts paid will not change.

The payment for 'Common Monetary Area compensation' (seigniorage) for the 2019/20 fiscal year amounted to some R787 million (National Treasury 2021: 108). This is equal to nearly two-thirds of the estimated seigniorage of the SARB. The seigniorage sharing agreement therefore clearly includes a large amount of development aid in favour of South Africa's CMA partners.

The preliminary conclusion is that South Africa is too generous in its compensation of CMA countries. Such generosity should rather be identified as development aid and should not be hidden as seigniorage sharing. At least South Africa would then get the necessary recognition as one of the most generous donor countries in the world, particularly when this aid is seen in conjunction with the development aid hidden in the revenue sharing agreement of the Southern African Customs Union.

Conclusion

This chapter shows that the institutional structures of central banks and the decision-making structure of the SARB in support of monetary policy decisions are fertile areas for future research. Likewise, much more research is required before any final conclusions can be drawn about the advantages and disadvantages of the appointment of a member of the MPC from the CMA countries. However, it is obvious that any pressure on the SARB to be subservient to a political agenda, as was the case in the 1980s, will heighten the attractiveness of such an appointment.

The CMA seigniorage sharing agreement is also fertile ground for further research. No academic literature exists on this matter. The initial focus of such research will be to enhance the general understanding of the agreement, followed by an analysis of the development aid component of the agreement. A likely conclusion, however, seems to be that South Africa should identify development aid and pay it directly, rather than disguising it as seigniorage sharing.

This chapter also argues that seigniorage should be researched in more detail. Despite its importance in the revenue streams of central banks, there is no consensus on the basis for its calculation. One way to reach agreement on international best practice for the calculation of seigniorage is for central banks to report such income as a separate line item.

Vishnu and I set out a research agenda for ourselves and showed some progress, evidenced by our recent papers in the sphere of central banking. Now Vishnu has left us, and this research agenda can be summarised as 'unfinished business'. In pursuing this research agenda, I shall miss 'Hallo, what's up?' around 6.15 in the morning.[2]

Notes

1. An Extraordinary (Special) General Meeting was called once (in 2002) to consider the delisting of SARB shares from the Johannesburg Stock Exchange.
2. The views expressed in this chapter do not reflect the position of the University of the Witwatersrand, either now or in the past.

References

Bain, K. and P. Howells. 2003. *Monetary Economics: Policy and Its Theoretical Basis*. New York: Palgrave Macmillan.

Bordiss, B., V. Padayachee and J. Rossouw. 2021. 'Two of the Most Eventful Years in the History of the South African Reserve Bank: William Henry Clegg and Johannes Postmus and the 1931–1932 Crisis'. *Economic History of Developing Regions* 36 (2): 1–19.

Bordiss, B. and J. Rossouw. 2021. 'Professor Vishnu Padayachee, 1952–2021'. *Economic History of Developing Regions* 36 (2): 122–3.

Bosch, A., J. Rossouw and V. Padayachee. 2015. 'Inflation Perceptions and Inflation Expectation in South Africa: Trends, Determinants and Comparisons (2006–2010)'. *Southern African Business Review* 19 (1): 1–21.

———. 2017. 'Towards a Formal Link between Inflation Perceptions and Inflation Expectations'. *South Africa Review of Economics and Finance* 9 (2): 167–200.

Botha, J. 2022. 'Down Memory Lane: Past Presidents, 1925–1963'. *Economic Society of South Africa*. https://www.essa.org.za/about/past-presidents/.

De Beer, L. and J. Shikwane. 2021. 'Note on Banknotes and Coin in South Africa'. *Quarterly Bulletin* 301 (September). Pretoria: South African Reserve Bank.

European Central Bank. 2017. *What is Seigniorage?* https://www.ecb.europa.eu/ecb/educational/explainers/tell-me/html/seigniorage.en.html.

Maziva, R. 2016. 'The Rand Currency Monetary Area: An Option for De-dollarisation in Zimbabwe'. MBA research project, University of Pretoria. https://repository.up.ac.za/bitstream/handle/2263/59870/Maziva_Rand_2017.pdf?sequence=1&isAllowed=y.

National Treasury. 2021. *Budget 2021: Estimates of National Expenditure*. Pretoria: National Treasury.

Padayachee, V. and J. Rossouw. 2007. 'A Study on Inflation Credibility among Students at the University of Pretoria'. *South African Journal of Economic and Management Sciences* 10 (2): 145–54.

———. 2010. 'Vergoedingsneigings in die Openbare Sektor te midde van Volgehoue Inflasie – 'n Ekonomiese Perspektief' (translated as 'Remuneration Trends in the Public Sector during Sustained Inflation – an Economic Perspective'). *Tydskrif vir Geesteswetenskappe* 50 (2): 169–86.

———. 2019. '"Volkskapitalisme" in the Transition to Democracy and Beyond. *International Review of Applied Economics* 33 (1): 150–62.

———. 2021. 'The Political Economy of South Africa's Constitutional Road to Central Bank Independence (1993–1996)'. *Transformation* 105: 74–97.

Rossouw, J. 2008. 'Inflation in South Africa: 1921 to 2006: History, Measurement and Credibility'. PhD thesis, University of KwaZulu-Natal.

———. 2022. ''n Eeu van Sentrale Banknote in Suid-Afrika: Ekonomie, Koste en Voordele. (translated title: 'A Century of Central Bank Notes in South Africa: Economy, Cost and Benefits'). *SA Tydskrif vir Natuurwetenskap en Tegnologie* 41 (1): 2–11.

Rossouw, J. and V. Padayachee. 2008. 'South African Price Changes and Inflation since 1974: A Note on the Testing of Inflation Accuracy'. *South African Journal of Economic and Management Sciences* 11 (2): 229–46.

———. 2009. 'Measuring Inflation Credibility: Results of a First Representative South African Sample'. *South African Journal of Economics* 77 (2): 314–31.

———. 2011. 'Reflecting on Ninety Years of Intermittent Success: The Experience of the South African Reserve Bank with Inflation since 1921'. *Economic History of Developing Regions* 26 (Suppl. 1): 53–72.

———. 2021. 'The Independence of the South African Reserve Bank: Coming Full Circle in 25 Years?' In: *The Political Economy of Central Banking in Emerging Economies*, edited by M. Yağcı. London: Routledge.

———. 2022. 'Transition in Decision-making in the South African Reserve Bank: An Area of Interest to Vishnu Padayachee (1952–2021)'. *Transformation* 108 (1): 59–79.

Rossouw, J., V. Padayachee and B. Bordiss. 2015. 'Central Banks and Fractional Reserve Banking: Money Creation out of Nothing?' *African Review of Economics and Finance* 7 (2): 105–31.

Rossouw, J., V. Padayachee and A. Bosch. 2009. 'Links or Disconnect: A First Consideration of Inflation Expectations and Inflation Credibility, with Specific Reference to South Africa: Analysis of Survey Data'. *South African Journal of Economic and Management Sciences* 12 (4): 475–92.

———. 2011. 'A Comparison of Inflation Expectations and Inflation Credibility in South Africa: Results from Survey Data'. *South African Journal of Economic and Management Sciences* 14 (3): 263–81.

Rossouw, J., V. Padayachee and L. Mondi. 2019. 'Inflation Targeting in Context of "Nationalisation" Debate'. *New Agenda* 72: 19–23.

SARB (South African Reserve Bank). 1971. *A Short Historical Review*. Pretoria: South African Reserve Bank.

Van der Merwe, E.J., S. Mollentze, T.L.A. Leshoro, J. Rossouw and C. Vermeulen. 2014. *Monetary Economics*. 2nd edition. Cape Town: Oxford University Press.

Vanthoor, W.F.V. 1997. *European Monetary Union since 1848: A Political and Historical Analysis*. Brookfield: Edward Elgar.

Vishnu with his parents, Umkomaas, c.1962.

Vishnu at his birthday party, 1965.

Naidoo Memorial High School prefects, 1969. Vishnu top right.

Vishnu's childhood home in Umkomaas, photo 2021.

The *mado*, Vishnu's den as a teenager, photo 2021.

Vishnu with his daughter, Sonali, and his wife, Nishi, 2019.

Umkomaas, showing the town, SAICCOR factory, and Roseneath area, c.2000.

Staff at the Institute for Social and Economic Research at the University of Durban-Westville, 1987.
Back row: Mark Byerley, Stephen Gelb, Karen Kohler, Jenny Smit, Bharati Parekh, Anne Vaughan, Winona Venter, Tim Quinlan, Selvie Moodley, Surie Seeramaloo, Kogi Naidoo, Vishnu.
Front row: Maurice Makhatini, Priya Banwari, John Butler-Adam, Doug Hindson.

The Combined Staff Association (COMSA), University of Durban-Westville, 1987. Back row: Alan Brimer, Vishnu Padayachee, Prem Singh, Kastur Bhana, Surendra Bhana, Trish Gibbon, Jairam Reddy, Dasrath Chetty. Front row: Robert Morrell, John Butler-Adam, Mala Singh.

Jairam Reddy, Mala Singh, Vella Pillay and Vishnu, Durban, c.1995.

The wall at Ike's Books, Greyville, Durban, 2002.

Imraan Valodia and Vishnu at the World Social Forum, Mumbai, 2004.

Ike Mayet at his bookshop, Chapel Street, Overport, Durban, 1989.

Vishnu sorting books on the floor at Ike's Books, c.2004.

African Guernica by Dumile Feni, 1967.

Rajend Mesthrie and Vishnu at the Franschhoek Literary Festival, 2011.

Raj Patel, Sharad Chari, Vishnu, Imraan Valodia and Mark Hunter at a Cuban art evening at Ike's Books, 2004.

Author Peter Alegi, with Henry 'Black Cat' Cele, Glenn Cowley and Vishnu at the launch of *Laduma* at Ike's Books, 2004.

Julian May, Jo Rushby and Vishnu at Christmas lunch at Ike's Books, c.2005.

Author Lewis Nkosi and Vishnu at the launch of *Mandela's Ego* at Ike's Books, c.2007.

Vishnu with Madhubani painter Chano Devi in Bihar, India, 2004.

Showers Mawowa and Vishnu at a School of Development Studies event, UKZN, c.2009.

Bill Freund and Francie Lund, School of Development Studies, UKZN, c.2004.

Nompumelelo Nzimande, Vishnu and Linda van Staden, UKZN graduation, c.2009.

Vishnu at Wits University, c.2016.

Bradley Bordiss, Vishnu, Basil Moore and Sibs Moore at Wits University, c.2018.

Maynard Govender at the launch of *Shadow of Liberation*, Westville, Durban, 2019.

Vishnu, Patsy Pillay and Robbie van Niekerk, London, 2019.

Jannie Rossouw and Vishnu at a research interview with F.W. de Klerk, at the FW de Klerk Foundation, Plattekloof, 2019.

Rajend Mesthrie and Vishnu at the *Scenes from the South* exhibition (in honour of J.M. Coetzee), Amazwi Museum, Makhanda, 2020.

Attendees at the symposium in honour of Vishnu at Wits University, 2022. Back row: Eddie Webster, Keith Breckenridge, Seeraj Mohamed, Janet Cherry, Alec Erwin, Robbie van Niekerk, Bradley Bordiss, Rajend Mesthrie, Goolam Aboobaker, Adam Aboobaker, Omar Badsha, Gavin Keeton, Jannie Rossouw, Pundy Pillay. Front row: Ruth Castel-Branco, Rob Morrell, Imraan Valodia.

10

Heterodox Economics and Macroeconomic Policy-making
A Critical Review of Vishnu Padayachee's Contribution to Fiscal Policy

Seeraj Mohamed

I will start this discussion of Vishnu Padayachee's contribution to economic thinking about fiscal policy in South Africa with the rejection of the Macroeconomic Research Group (MERG) report (MERG 1993) by the economic leadership of the African National Congress (ANC) and its Department of Economic Planning (DEP). I start with MERG because accounts of the viciousness of the rejection of it by the ANC economic leadership, with the support of Nelson Mandela and Thabo Mbeki, have been repeated so often that it has become, among progressive economists in South Africa, historically iconic (akin to the assassination of Julius Caesar). The economic elites of the ANC's DEP each had a chance with their daggers. Dear Vishnu, who had played a key role in MERG along with the other drafters of its report, were subjected to this pre-scripted humiliation. Ben Fine (cited in Padayachee and Van Niekerk 2019: 99) describes the events as involving 'a long sequence of witnesses for the prosecution (i.e., department heads) [who] uniformly marched into the discussion of the document and routinely and ridiculously rubbished it in what could only be described as a badge of loyalty'.

Padayachee and Robert van Niekerk (2019: 101) describe what Vishnu and his MERG comrades felt:

> The shock at the rejection of the MERG economic policy recommendation and the manner of it was acutely felt by the drafters of the MERG report, especially as they had all at various

times since the 1980s (in some cases earlier) been so warmly held within the embrace of the senior ANC leadership.

The depth of their pain may have been intensified by the knowledge that Trevor Manuel and his poorly trained, unprepared and overstretched ANC economics team would have been behind the rejection of MERG (Freund 2021; Van Amerigen 1995). Padayachee and John Sender report that Vella Pillay, the head of the MERG project, had been 'abrasive' with the ANC economics leadership and members of this DEP team. They argue that Pillay's abrasiveness was justified, explaining that he was a 'well trained professional economist ... who was forced to discuss economic policy with people who have no understanding of the determinants of investment and employment in capitalist economies but have eagerly swallowed a few weeks of training provided to the African National Congress's ... Department of Economic Policy by J.P. Morgan and other corporate ideologues'. They say that 'Vella had no hesitation in vigorously questioning the competence and integrity of many members of the ANC's Department of Economic Policy (DEP), including some who went on to become ministers or senior civil servants in the post-apartheid government' (Padayachee and Sender 2017: 17). Three decades later, in their well-researched book *Shadow of Liberation*, Padayachee and Van Niekerk confirm Pillay's view of the ANC economics leadership and the DEP: 'Our findings reveal that the ANC economic team too eagerly imbibed a few weeks of crash-course training in economics provided to them by the World Bank, JP Morgan and other corporate ideologues' (Padayachee and Van Niekerk 2019: 229).

Padayachee and Van Niekerk's view of this team is not only disparaging but also claims that they flouted the ANC's 'social democratic and redistributive tradition' and the standards of democracy and accountability of the South African democratic movement (2019: 230–1). They describe the attitude of the ANC's DEP as follows: 'A culture lacking in democracy and accountability but high on ego and arrogance were key features of the DEP's approach in the transition years' (2019: 116, nn. 230–1). They report that this culture carried over into the new government. The secret formulation of the Growth, Employment and Redistribution (GEAR) macroeconomic strategy document (RSA 1996) and the announcement that it was 'non-negotiable' (Michie and Padayachee 1998: 626) provide further evidence of this arrogant culture. However, they reject conspiracy theories such as those claimed by economists such as Patrick Bond and Sampie Terreblanche (2019: 232). Instead, they point to support for neoliberal policies coming from Western governments, the International Monetary Fund (IMF) and the World Bank, and most importantly from South African big business and the mainstream media houses.

These unfortunate historical developments are key to understanding the approach to fiscal policy adopted by the South African government and the role of the National Treasury as custodian of the government's budget. The ANC's underprepared economic leadership and members of the DEP team would enter into the post-apartheid government with a determination to continue following the market-oriented approach to economic policy initiated by the apartheid government during the 1980s. They further entrenched neoliberal economic ideology with the adoption of GEAR as the government's economic policy approach. Under the leadership of Trevor Manuel as finance minister, the National Treasury asserted its dominance as the 'alpha' government department, which was able to intimidate and silence other government departments into compliance. Manuel and his DEP colleagues were able to use the ANC's approach of 'cadre deployment' to ensure that the Department of Finance (later the National Treasury) and the South African Reserve Bank (SARB) would be staffed with hand-chosen, like-minded people, including former mass democratic movement activists, who would relentlessly drive a neoliberal approach to macroeconomic policy. This group went on to employ economists trained in mainstream, neoclassical economics to provide technical analyses to lend support to this conservative approach. They also often imbibed through them an arrogant culture based on the view that the National Treasury was the only well-run and capacitated government department, which had a duty to shepherd and cajole the other departments into line.

Vishnu witnessed the consolidation of neoliberal macroeconomic thinking within the National Treasury and its approach to macroeconomics, including fiscal policy. He criticised and challenged this approach to macroeconomics and these policies throughout his remaining years. His article with Jonathan Michie, 'Three Years after Apartheid: Growth, Employment and Redistribution?' in the *Cambridge Journal of Economics* (Michie and Padayachee 1998) reports on the poor performance of the GEAR strategy in generating growth and domestic and foreign investment. He and Michie highlight the fact that GEAR's greatest weakness was its inability to create new jobs. With reference to the impact of the austere approach to fiscal policy in GEAR, they say that 'while GEAR succeeded in meeting its stringent fiscal targets (a budget deficit of 4% of GDP in 1996), the gap between promise and delivery in terms of social and infrastructural services widened' (1998: 632). This article concludes with the statement that 'it is becoming apparent that a programme truly to reconstruct and develop the South African economy and society will require something very different from the sort of economic orthodoxy represented by the "Growth, Employment and Redistribution" (GEAR) document' (1998: 634).

Padayachee and Van Niekerk (2019: 104) describe MERG as an economic policy framework that follows a 'broadly Cambridge or Post-Keynesian approach in the tradition of Keynes, Robinson, Kaldor, and Kalecki – where effective demand failures and the possibility of under-full-employment equilibrium are recognised as key problems'. It may seem unnecessary (but I will do so anyway) to point out that Vishnu advocated for this heterodox economics approach and the macroeconomic policies and programmes, such as MERG, associated with it. And, as the affirmative answer to the question in his 2019 journal article 'Can Progressive Macroeconomic Policies Address Growth and Employment while Reducing Inequality in South Africa?' indicates, he continued to support this 'progressive' macroeconomic policy approach in general and believed it was essential for South Africa. This article also indicates that he continued to support, and regularly pointed to, the approach and solutions of the programme outlined in the MERG document as the correct macroeconomic policies for South Africa.

According to Padayachee and Van Niekerk (2019), the MERG programme envisaged a first phase where relatively large state expenditure on social and physical infrastructure investment (in housing, health, education and physical infrastructure) would increase economic growth, which would crowd in and catalyse a second phase of more intense private sector investment. The MERG report covered supply-side issues such as health, education, housing, labour market policy, industrialisation and trade, among others. The economic impact was modelled and, according to Padayachee and Van Niekerk (2019: 105), 'the approach was fully consistent with the required macroeconomic balances'. They pointed out that MERG stresses the importance of 'prudent and risk averse fiscal, monetary and balance of payments management' (MERG [1993] cited in Padayachee and Van Niekerk [2019: 105]).

When taking into account the concern with macroeconomic balances and with prudent and risk-averse fiscal, monetary and balance of payment management in the MERG report, it is important to realise the large differences between neoliberal and heterodox macroeconomic approaches. The monetarist revolution that displaced Keynesian approaches to macroeconomic policy included the important shift from full employment as the major goal of macroeconomic policy to concerns with keeping inflation low and ensuring price stability. The neoliberal macroeconomic approach dismissed fiscal policy as ineffective, and monetary policy became the dominant tool of macroeconomic policy. It favoured independent central banks as the custodians of monetary policy. In effect, the adherence to neoliberal macroeconomic policy meant that theoretically, governments' hands were tied when there were economic downturns that led to decreases in demand, increasing unemployment and declines in investment. It would be the task of the central bank to ensure price stability. Of course, in practice many governments embarked on the use of fiscal policy, such as increased expenditure and tax cuts, to stimulate the economy during downturns. Neoliberal policies led to deregulation of finance that allowed private sector debt to increase, and at the same time government debt rose rapidly because their neoliberal policies caused governments to shift from taxing corporations and the rich to borrowing from them. The central bankers, who are supposed to be less affected than governments by political pressure, have been forced to become increasingly discretionary due to the increasing financial fragility resulting from financial liberalisation since the late 1970s (Mastromatteo and Esposito 2015).

On the other hand, heterodox macroeconomists continue to support fiscal policy playing the dominant role and full employment as the main goal of macroeconomic policy. The concern with macroeconomic balances and prudent fiscal management in MERG fits within a heterodox perspective very different to the neoliberal view that sees increased government expenditure as inflationary and fiscal policy as ineffective. The mainstream view also expresses concern about growing government expenditure requiring higher levels of debt that would crowd out private borrowers and cause lower levels of private investment. MERG's approach was based on an understanding of the South African economy, and it developed a programme wherein government expenditure on infrastructure and improved basic services would be both redistributive and a stimulator of economic growth.

The macroeconomic approach of MERG economists was that government investment could crowd in private investment and stimulate increased economic activity within society. Padayachee and Harry Zarenda (1996: 186) mention that 'the crowding in of private investment has even been accepted by the World Bank'. Padayachee (1997: 33) criticises the World Bank's acceptance of the potential for 'crowding in' of public expenditure on infrastructure while continuing to advocate fiscal austerity. He argues: 'However, the Bank's warning that such investment should not put budgetary targets at risk by raising recurrent government expenditure seemed to ignore inevitable interactions between capital and current expenditure, especially in education, health and related types of social spending.'

The overall effectiveness of macroeconomic policy would be in relation to supply-side interventions in health, education, industrialisation, and so on. The MERG report envisaged that the macroeconomic balances would occur within a dynamic, growing environment where initially government consumption and investment spending would support increased economic activity, reduced unemployment, health- and education-induced growth in productivity of workers, and government support to both widen and deepen industry. Padayachee (2019: 10) explains the relation between monetary and fiscal policy and supply-side factors and macroeconomic interventions as follows: 'Post-Keynesians also pay attention to the matter of the proper coordination and timing of the different strands of macroeconomic policy as well as coordination within each – especially fiscal policy coordination – to bring about more effective policy impacts on demand and distribution.'

Ultimately, MERG was a vision of how to address the legacy of unemployment, poverty and inequality of colonialism and apartheid, and bring about transformation of the South African economy. The targets of economic policy, including macroeconomic policy, would be progressive redistribution and increasing employment in a growing economy. The target of the neoliberal macroeconomic policy that had become increasingly influential within the ANC's DEP and elements of its leadership was the size of the government's budget deficit and debt. Neoliberal economists favoured a reduction in the size and influence of the state. Their basic neoclassical theory and models do not include the state. For example, the equilibrium of prices and demand that is at the centre of neoclassical theory and is geometrically represented by simplistic supply and demand curves that require multiple unrealistic and very far-fetched assumptions, has no state – just private buyers and sellers.[1] State actions that may influence equilibrium and prices are generally described as distortionary. In the real world (and it may help at this point to think of the South African economy at the time when the MERG project was under way), terms such as 'free market' and 'market-friendly' are generally untrue ideological rhetoric. These ideologically loaded terms do not take into account many extremely obvious characteristics of society and the economy, such as the domination of markets by very few large corporations, the high levels of unemployment and inequality, and the role of racism, misogyny, class and other biases in shaping economic outcomes.

The heterodox approach recognises the impact of the past on the present and the effect of path dependence in shaping future outcomes. This notion of path dependence is implicitly present in the theory and macroeconomic models of heterodox economics. On the other hand, neoclassical economic theory and models usually abstract from time. The approach to transforming the South African economy within MERG and in Vishnu's writings recognises the interaction between unemployment, poverty and inequality, and the need to change the structure of the economy to support a progressive economic growth path. Within their common heterodox economic perspective is the recognition that not only the structure of the economy, but also the health, education, living conditions and opportunities of individuals have an impact on the outcomes and can constrain the future economic growth path. Therefore, there is a massive difference between neoliberal economic views and heterodox economic views on fiscal policy with regard to the importance and affordability of expanding expenditure in order to improve the living conditions and economic opportunities of the poorest households. Neoliberal economists generally treat such actions narrowly as government expenditure and focus almost entirely on the size of the budget deficit and government debt when arguing to constrain or reduce such expenditure. Heterodox economists view these actions to alleviate suffering and increase economic opportunities as essential not only for economic justice but also for shifting the economy onto an improved growth path, where more people are involved in economic activity and capable of increased productivity, aggregate demand expands, and the size of the economy grows.

Heterodox economists support an active role for the state, not only to narrowly rectify market imperfections but because they recognise the inherent instability of capitalist economies and financial markets. The depth of the schism between heterodox and neoliberal economic perspectives is further understood when one considers their different views on the stability of capitalist economies and how they define the role of the state. Padayachee (2019: 9) explains that 'in contrast to Marxist and post-Keynesian economists, the vast majority of mainstream economists believe that the capitalist system is endogenously stable and that crises arise from exogenous shocks'. This point takes one back to Padayachee and Sender's (2017) explanation of the 'abrasiveness' of the head of the MERG project towards the likes of Manuel and the DEP. One imagines Vella Pillay's frustration, not only as a highly experienced professional economist but also as a heterodox economist who was forced to converse with neoliberal economics converts who, despite their experience as activists in South Africa, were compelled to talk a new language of economics constrained by a laissez-faire world view. Their new world view would have them think unrealistically about the role of the state. They would have had to convince themselves that if the state stepped back from the economy, then the market would (somehow, perhaps magically) solve South Africa's horrendous unemployment and inequality problems.

Padayachee (2019) points out that before the global financial crisis of 2008, neoliberal economists and their mainstream economic theories and models did not view inequality as a destabilising factor. The unfortunate outcome of the approach of the neoliberals in the DEP (which remains the view of the National Treasury today) towards fiscal policy is that redistributive policies and the provision of services and grants to the poor are just a government expense that should be curtailed and considered from the perspective of affordability. However, addressing South Africa's high levels of unemployment and inequality was central to the views of liberation movements in their struggle against apartheid. For the economists who drafted the MERG report, including Padayachee, addressing unemployment and inequality would be vital for macroeconomic stability and economic development in South Africa.

The ANC economics leadership and DEP, with the help of the apartheid government and big business, the World Bank, the IMF and Western governments, accepted neoliberal economic views relatively soon after the unbanning of the ANC. The economic views on fiscal policy expressed in public by Mandela and the leaders of the DEP, Manuel and Tito Mboweni, became more focused on narrow concerns of affordability and the size of the government's budget deficit, rather than adopting the more dynamic approach to fiscal balances that would be implicit in a heterodox approach such as that of MERG. It is important to recognise that as these ANC leaders shifted towards common ground with the leaders of the apartheid government, big business and the financial sector in their support for neoliberal economics, their economic perspectives became increasingly constrained. The behaviour of big business and finance, which dominate most markets of the South African economy and had been so close to the apartheid government that they joined its state security structures in the 1980s, was no longer an important concern in their economic thinking and planning, particularly with regard to macroeconomics and fiscal policy. Their approach was reduced to thinking about the government's budget and the levels of government debt and deficit as factors that would affect business confidence. The National Treasury today still talks about government debt crowding out private borrowers.

As a result of this neoliberal turn within the ANC economics leadership in the early 1990s, documents such as the ANC's 'Ready to Govern' (ANC 1992) and even the Reconstruction and Development Programme (RDP) (ANC 1994) that discuss the importance of redistributive programmes to address basic needs and increase economic opportunities also propose a neoliberal approach to macroeconomic balance and price stability. Padayachee and Van Niekerk (2019: 115) show that 'by the time the final version of the RDP was accepted, it was not a radical document'. They say that trade and macroeconomic policies, including the independence of the Reserve Bank, 'closely tracked Washington Consensus thinking' (2019: 115). Notwithstanding this insertion of neoliberal economic thinking on trade and macroeconomics into the ANC's RDP base document (ANC 1994), the government's RDP *White Paper on the Reconstruction and Development Programme* (RSA 1994) shifted the economic policy discourse even further towards neoliberal conservatism and austerity.

In their analysis and critique of the RDP *White Paper*, Padayachee and Zarenda (1996: 192) argue that

> in general, the new government appears to have prioritised fiscal and monetary discipline as key elements in (what might best be described as) a programme of economic stabilisation. In our view this has severely constrained the realisation of the broader social and developmental objectives of the RDP.

This critique of the RDP *White Paper* builds on the alternative approach to fiscal policy outlined in the MERG report. Asghar Adelzadeh and Padayachee (1994: 4) discuss the approach to fiscal policy in the MERG report as follows:

> The maintenance of a sound fiscal balance (as the MERG Report 1993: 47 points out) should not be constraining, but enabling and facilitating. The real question is how that balance is managed. A co-ordinated economic programme can effectively utilise both the revenue and expenditure aspects of fiscal policy to achieve some of its main objectives, namely to create employment, develop the infrastructure, provide basic needs, reduce the concentration of wealth and improve income distribution, and finally help achieve sustainable economic growth.

Adelzadeh and Padayachee (1994: 4–5) explain that the major focus in the RDP *White Paper* is on fiscal discipline, which translates into an approach they describe as 'narrow fiscal conservatism'. The RDP *White Paper* requires all levels of government to reduce expenditure. They warn that the implication of this 'narrow fiscal conservatism' is that the large social expenditure required to fund the RDP would have to be financed through reallocation of government expenditure within the constraints of the government's existing budgets. This government expenditure would be further constrained because the RDP *White Paper* commits the government to maintaining or even reducing direct taxes. The unfortunate neoliberal shift meant that rather than viewing redistributive welfare policies within a dynamic heterodox framework, the focus of fiscal policy took on the neoliberal goals of liberalising the economy and improving business confidence.

Conclusion

The fiscal conservatism and narrow neoliberal perspective that were inserted into the RDP *White Paper* and were a core aspect of the GEAR strategy remain very much part of the approach that underpins the government's fiscal policy. The government continues to view fiscal policy through a narrow neoliberal lens, which means abandoning a developmental and interventionist role for the state to shift the economy onto a sustainable and more just economic growth path. The approach of the National Treasury and the government is to maintain austerity, not increase taxes, and shift the focus away from the serious limitations of its fiscal policy by promoting structural reforms aimed at promoting increased liberalisation and business confidence.

Even during the economic crisis caused by the Covid-19 lockdowns, the government maintained its fiscal consolidation approach to fiscal policy and pointed to structural reforms as the answer to South Africa's economic problems. Vishnu was the second signatory of an open letter signed by more than two hundred economists asking President Cyril Ramaphosa and his Cabinet to do more to alleviate suffering related to Covid-19 lockdowns.[2] The reason his name was at the top of the list of signatories was because the drafters of the letter knew that when other economists of all stripes saw that he had already signed it they would be more likely to add their signatures.

While the government reported that it would provide a R500 billion rescue package in response to the Covid-19 pandemic, it remained concerned to limit expenditure and the budget deficit. R200 billion of the R500 billion was in the form of an unsuccessful government loan guarantee scheme. The actual use of the budget to stimulate the economy was relatively small. Vishnu once again was the first signatory on a letter signed by more than one hundred economists, submitted to the Standing Committee on Finance (SCOF). The letter asks the SCOF to reject the 2020 Supplementary Budget and warns the SCOF that 'it would be a dereliction of duty for Committee Members to vote in favour of a budget that reduces government expenditure by R230 billion over two years when the country needs a targeted injection of resources to mitigate the damage caused to households, workers and businesses by the COVID-19 crisis'.

With regard to the R500 billion rescue package, the letter points out that 'instead of R500 billion, the Budget presents a net increase to non-interest spending in the current year of just R36 billion. This is because, of the R145 billion targeted at COVID-19-related expenditure, R109 billion is funded through the suspension of baseline allocations and reprioritisations'.

The neoliberal approach to fiscal policy embedded in the GEAR strategy has fostered an austerity mindset within the government. This mindset has been so influential that it has constrained the government's funding of policies and programmes to alleviate the suffering of the majority of South African households, even during the Covid-19 pandemic. Over the past two-and-a-half decades, this austerity mindset has compelled the government to under-resource industrial and agricultural sector development, including land restitution, as well as maintenance and investment in infrastructure.

As mentioned above, a key strategy of MERG's proposal was an initial phase of intense social and physical infrastructure investment. The strategy posited large-scale government investment in the provision of housing, basic services, health and education. The members of MERG expected these investments to begin to address the deep legacy of poverty and deprivation across South Africa. They also believed that these investments by the government would provide an injection of financing into the economy that could stimulate aggregate demand from households and stimulate investment by private sector businesses. MERG saw the potential growth in aggregate demand as having the ability to catalyse a new type of growth among a much larger number of people and over a wider geographical spread in South Africa. The increased demand for bricks, cement, steel, glass and other inputs for infrastructure, plus increased demand for furniture, fittings and appliances, could spur mass investment and economies of scale in production of higher value-added manufactured goods within the country. MERG's vision was to change the South African economic growth path from extraction and export of primary commodities and slightly beneficiated mineral products to providing for the needs of the entire population in a way that would increase employment and aggregate demand.

The approach to economic growth in the neoliberal GEAR programme was very different. With regard to macroeconomic policy, the approach adopted in GEAR continues to be the government's approach two-and-a-half decades later. The major concern of the government was to signal the credibility of its macroeconomic policies to the rentiers who operated in global financial markets. The level of investment in social and physical infrastructure would be constrained by the government's focus on keeping the budget deficit, government debt and inflation low. In line with monetarist and neoclassical macroeconomic theory, the government believed that fiscal policy was not effective in increasing economic growth and combating unemployment. It also believed that increased public sector borrowing would crowd out private borrowers from credit markets, which would lead to lower levels of private investment. The rhetoric around the ineffectiveness of the government, poor capacity in local governments and the inefficiencies inherent in state-owned enterprises became rooted in public discourse very early in the democratic era.

The ANC's economic leadership that so forcefully rejected the MERG report may have done so because it feared that if the government had adopted it, the programme it proposed could be a massive failure. The neoliberal macroeconomic framework that informed government policies would have reinforced these fears. The government seemed to have fallen for the self-fulfilling prophecies of public sector inefficiency and corruption. It probably imagined that there would be huge government wastage, causing inadequate investment in infrastructure development, bankrupt and poorly performing state-owned corporations, and higher levels of government deficits and debt. The GEAR strategy lamented the 3 per cent growth levels at the time it was published and predicted that the government's implementation of GEAR would achieve 6 per cent economic growth and the creation of 400 000 jobs per annum. Notwithstanding the fact that the economy has not performed even close to the levels predicted by GEAR, there has been consistent application of this unfortunate neoliberal approach to macroeconomic policy throughout the period since 1996. However, the outcome today looks very much like the fears of failure that probably led to the rejection of the MERG programme.

Looking back at macroeconomic policy in South Africa, Padayachee (2019: 3) asserts that

> the neo-liberal economic policies that the African National Congress-led government surprisingly adopted in 1996 in order to assuage global markets sceptical of its historical support for dirigiste economic policy, have simply not worked. Appropriate

progressive macroeconomic interventions are urgently needed to head off the looming prospect of a failed state in the country which Nelson Mandela led to democracy after his release from prison in February 1990.

Corruption, state capture and poor management in the public sector may be important explanations for the poor state of the South African economy. However, the massive role of neoliberal ideology in the poor economic outcomes experienced in South Africa has to be acknowledged. At a macroeconomic level, the belief that private investment would grow if the government kept out of the way of the private sector and kept its deficits low was obviously incorrect. Instead, it is an important macroeconomic reason for the poor economic growth and employment performance of the South African economy.

After the global financial crisis of 2008, mainstream macroeconomists began to coalesce around a new view of fiscal policy that was closer to heterodox economic views on fiscal policy. Jason Furman (2016), who was the chair of President Barack Obama's Council of Economic Advisers at the time, says that unlike the old mainstream views on fiscal policy, the new view does not treat fiscal policy as ineffective. He says research and evidence support the new mainstream economics view that discretionary fiscal stimulus can be 'very effective', because rather than crowd out private investment it will crowd in private investment. He says the new view of fiscal policy also appreciates that 'fiscal space is larger than generally appreciated because stimulus may pay for itself'. The South African government has remained steadfastly committed to the older view of fiscal policy embedded in GEAR.

In its dogged pursuit of a primary fiscal surplus, the government has not given the economy time to recover after the Covid-19 pandemic. It justifies its austerity approach by using the term 'fiscal consolidation'. Fiscal consolidation in South Africa means real reductions in government expenditure, which translates into outcomes such as real reductions in social spending, higher learner-to-teacher ratios and fewer nurses and doctors per patient. This austerity mindset dominates government fiscal policy even after the devastation of the pandemic.

The government introduced a social relief of distress grant of R350 during 2020 because of the increased suffering caused by Covid-19, saying this was a temporary grant. However, it was forced to reintroduce the grant after the violent social unrest in July 2021 that caused billions of rands in damage overnight. Unfortunately, the austerity mindset within the government remains so strong that it has worked to reduce the number of beneficiaries of the grant by making the process of qualifying for the grant more difficult, and it has not adjusted the grant for inflation after it was extended through to March 2024. The possibility of more violent protests in the future, and the large cost to the economy and fiscus of these protests, is very likely to materialise because of extraordinarily high levels of poverty and inequality in South Africa. The government's rush to achieve a primary fiscal balance could very well end up once more costing society and the economy the kinds of pain and damage associated with the July 2021 social unrest.

The government fails to realise that its fiscal consolidation fiscal policy, rather than creating conditions for growth and investment, hurts growth, discourages investment and increases unemployment. This is a view that heterodox economists have expressed in frustration for decades, and for which some influential mainstream macroeconomists have recently begun to present evidence. An IMF working paper by Yan Carrière-Swallow, Antonio David and Daniel Leigh (2018: 23) reports that

> the effects of fiscal consolidation on economic activity in advanced and emerging market economies may thus be more similar than typically assumed ... Fiscal consolidations undertaken in periods of economic booms and slumps do not have significantly different estimated effects on economic activity in LAC [Latin American and Caribbean] economies. Their effects are contractionary in both cases.

Antonio Fatás and Lawrence Summers (2018) show that fiscal consolidation has a significant impact on economic growth and is very likely to have caused higher debt to GDP levels. They report that

> the large size of the effects points in the direction of self-defeating fiscal consolidations ... Attempts to reduce debt via fiscal consolidations have very likely resulted in a higher debt to GDP ratio through their long-term negative impact on output ... If the negative effects of fiscal consolidation are long lasting,

countries can enter a negative loop where attempts to reduce government debt are not effective because of the reductions in GDP. As GDP falls permanently, attempts to reduce debt via reductions in spending or increases in taxes lead to a higher debt to GDP ratio (Fatás and Summers 2018: 238).

Neoliberal macroeconomic ideology has forced a short-term perspective on the government's planning and budgeting. The myopic concern with maintaining low deficits and debt levels has consistently hobbled the ability to implement programmes informed by longer-term visions for the economy, because neoliberal austerity fiscal policies had been inserted into programmes such as the RDP and the National Development Plan (SA GCIS 2012). Vishnu's work warned policy-makers of this error-ridden path and offered heterodox macroeconomic policy as a viable alternative.

Even though Vishnu did not publish much specifically on fiscal policy and did not enter into the intensified fiscal policy debates within post-Keynesian macroeconomics taking place since the global financial crisis, he contributed much to keeping the heterodox approach adopted by MERG on macroeconomic policy present in economics discourse, debates and academia in South Africa, and in his numerous publications in international journals. His contribution is really important, because there are so few heterodox economists within South Africa and most economics courses taught at South African universities are mainstream. And, as Padayachee (2019: 4) points out 'those supportive of alternative heterodox policy ideas are often and quickly labelled macroeconomic populists or madmen (not least in contemporary South Africa)'. His stature and his contributions to economics in South Africa remain such that they allow the relatively few heterodox economists (those who have more insight into 'the determinants of investment and employment in capitalist economies' [Padayachee and Sender 2017: 17]) more space to challenge the narrow and simplistic neoliberal macroeconomic views on fiscal policy.

Notes

1. And the 'invisible hand' or fictitious 'Walrasian auctioneer' who magically and instantaneously matches all buyers and sellers to ensure supply and demand equilibrium.
2. The letter is available at https://drive.google.com/file/d/1d8Qmd8oQ_Bb69 MP1SSlmGIB95n9sG9w6/view.

References

Adelzadeh, A. and V. Padayachee. 1994. 'The RDP White Paper: Reconstruction of a Development Vision?' *Transformation* 25: 1–18.

ANC (African National Congress). 1992. *Ready to Govern: ANC Policy Guidelines for a Democratic South Africa*. Johannesburg: African National Congress.

———. 1994. *Reconstruction and Development Programme Base Document*. Johannesburg: Umanyano Publications.

Carrière-Swallow, Y., A.C. David and D. Leigh. 2018. *The Macroeconomic Effects of Fiscal Consolidation in Emerging Economies: Evidence from Latin America*. International Monetary Fund Working Paper WP/18/142. Washington DC: International Monetary Fund.

Fatás, A. and L.H. Summers. 2018. 'The Permanent Effects of Fiscal Consolidations'. *Journal of International Economics* 112: 238–50.

Freund, B. 2021. *An Historian's Passage to Africa: An Autobiography*. Johannesburg: Wits University Press.

Furman, J. 2016. 'The New View of Fiscal Policy and Its Application'. Paper presented at the Conference on Global Implications of Europe's Redesign, New York, 5 October.

Mastromatteo, G. and L. Esposito. 2015. *The Two Approaches to Money: Debt, Central Banks, and Functional Finance*. Levy Economics Institute Working Paper 855. Annandale-on-Hudson, NY: Bard College.

MERG (Macroeconomic Research Group). 1993. *Making Democracy Work: A Framework for Macroeconomic Policy in South Africa*. Cape Town: Centre for Development Studies, University of the Western Cape.

Michie, J. and V. Padayachee. 1998. 'Three Years after Apartheid: Growth, Employment and Redistribution?' *Cambridge Journal of Economics* 22 (5): 623–35.

Padayachee, V. 1997. 'The Evolution of South Africa's International Financial Relations and Policy: 1985–95'. In: *The Political Economy of South Africa's Transition: Policy Perspectives in the Late 1990s*, edited by J. Michie and V. Padayachee. London: The Dryden Press.

———. 2019. 'Can Progressive Macroeconomic Policies Address Growth and Employment while Reducing Inequality in South Africa?' *Economic and Labour Relations Review* 30 (1): 3–21.

Padayachee, V. and J. Sender. 2017. 'Vella Pillay: Revolutionary Activism and Economic Policy Analysis'. *Social Scientist* 45 (3–4): 17–40.

Padayachee, V. and R. van Niekerk. 2019. *Shadow of Liberation: Contestation and Compromise in the Economic and Social Policy of the African National Congress, 1943–1996.* Johannesburg: Wits University Press.

Padayachee, V. and H. Zarenda. 1996. 'Macroeconomic and Labour Market Policies for Employment Generation in South Africa'. *Metroeconomica: International Review of Economics* 47 (2): 172–96.

RSA (Republic of South Africa). 1994. *White Paper on the Reconstruction and Development Programme.* Pretoria: Republic of South Africa.

———. 1996. *Growth, Employment and Redistribution: A Macroeconomic Strategy.* Pretoria: Republic of South Africa.

SA GCIS (South African Government Communication and Information Services). 2012. *Our Future – Make It Work: National Development Plan 2030.* https://www.gov.za/sites/default/files/gcis_document/201409/ndp-2030-our-future-make-it-workr.pdf.

Van Ameringen, M. 1995. *Building a New South Africa. Volume 1: Economic Policy.* Ottawa: International Development Resource Centre.

11

South African Capitalism
Conversations with Vishnu Padayachee

John Keith Hart

Vishnu Padayachee and I met in Cambridge in 1995. He invited me to Durban two years later. We became friends and intermittent writing partners for twenty-five years. In *Self in the World: Connecting Life's Extremes* (Hart 2022), I highlight the need to connect pairs that often seem to be opposed and unreachable, one from the other – individual and society, local and global, personal and impersonal, informal and formal, life and ideas, real and virtual – more effectively than the last century's institutions conventionally allowed. Accordingly, I begin with some observations concerning our personal relationship and place Vishnu as a man in his city, before turning to our professional activities. Some key joint publications are then summarised. These had a common theme – the need to place South Africa's development in African and world economic history through the concept of 'national capitalism'.

In the essay's third section, I update the full cycle of national capitalism's rise and fall at the global level in the light of its collapse now in the early 2020s. I believe that we are entering a period comparable to what Winston Churchill (1948) called 'the second thirty years war' (1914–45), when four decades of financial imperialism driven by unfettered global capital flows ran up against its inevitable contradictions. I conclude with some remarks about South Africa's current crisis and Vishnu's example as a beacon in the engulfing darkness.

We must extend our political perspective beyond national boundaries to participate in global solutions more appropriate to humanity's predicament now. This was always the point of my conversations and writings with Vishnu.

Partners in Durban

We met at Cambridge University's African Studies Centre, where I was the director, and hit it off immediately, spending the evening exploring our common interests in cricket, C.L.R. James, M.K. Gandhi and the Indian Ocean world. Soon afterwards, Vishnu invited me to Durban, the largest Indian city abroad. I have been fascinated by India since I was a teenager and made two unsuccessful attempts to carry out research there. My focus has been on the North Atlantic quadrilateral formed by the slave trade, colonial empire and unequal development – Europe, West Africa, the Caribbean and the United States. Vishnu now offered an opportunity to combine Africa and India in one place.

I spent a month in Durban and Cape Town, checking out African Studies programmes there. Durban instantly enchanted me with its mixed white, brown and black population. The Indian Ocean, port and beach had a special appeal. The atmosphere in Vishnu's School of Development Studies (SDS) at the University of KwaZulu-Natal (UKZN) was relaxed and amiable; it was a socially engaged place in a world dominated by finance. UKZN had a beautiful campus on a hill overlooking the city. I came back often. I have worked at the interface between anthropology and development in twenty-four countries and published a book on the political economy of West African agriculture (Hart 1982). Vishnu was a development economist and historian of South Africa with an internationalist perspective. We shared a lot more besides.

We began writing together with a paper on South Africa's Indian businessmen after apartheid (Hart and Padayachee 2000). Vishnu obviously knew a lot more about this than I did, but I did most of the final writing. We later cooperated on a collection edited by Vishnu, *The Political Economy of Africa* (Padayachee 2010), and embarked on a history of South African capitalism seen in national and global perspective (Hart and Padayachee 2013). We talked, pooled our reading and enjoyed the good life – taking breakfast in a colonial hotel or sipping sauvignon blanc on the veranda of Ike's Bookshop while exploring similarities and differences in our journeys through life. Despite (or because of?) being apart more often than together, we sustained the most creative and lasting intellectual partnership I have ever had.

The conclusions of our article on South African capitalism (Hart and Padayachee 2013) were too mild then and are out of touch now. We wrote it before Jacob Zuma's corruption of the country was as obvious as it is now. We highlighted three features of the post-apartheid era: the shift from the minerals–energy complex to services, with consequences for the forms of capitalism; African National Congress (ANC) government policy, especially on black economic empowerment and African immigration; and white capital flight as the main threat to South Africa's political economy.

Vishnu's family roots in Umkomaas were hard to miss, although I have no direct knowledge of them.[1] My focus here is on Durban; but I am aware of how those local roots shored up the diversity of his commitments at home and abroad. Manchester played a similar role in my world travels (Hart 2003).[2] Durban has become pivotal to how I live in the world and Vishnu was my guide and mentor there. I emphasise how Vishnu, as one of its most prominent citizens, created new institutions, networks and collaborations in the city that were an extension of his unique social personality.

In 2008, Vishnu told me he had seen a 'fantastic' apartment on South Beach while purchasing books from its departing owner. I bought it. My Paris family has spent vacations there, and sometimes longer stays, ever since; and my wife Sophie has become an ethnographer and historian of Durban in her own right (Chevalier 2015, 2019). The building was 1930s art deco, with panoramic views.

There are not many Vishnus around who can generate progressive, cooperative and interactive social relations with many people and places. He was a citizen of the world, but with durable anchorage close to home. The Killie Campbell Museum and Library is in a colonial mansion on a hill with monkeys swinging between trees in its extensive gardens – a beautiful place where one evening a book launch was hosted. The University of KwaZulu-Natal Press had just published a book on a Muslim Indian reading group in Durban during the 1950s. The Pakistan ambassador gave a speech to a well-dressed crowd of Indians, whites and fewer blacks, a multiracial gathering of Durban's elite. Vishnu was in his element as a university professor, bookshop owner, Africana collector and clearly an integrated member of the Durban community. Soon after, I heard a rumour that the Durban city council wanted to acquire the place as the mayor's residence. I raised it with Vishnu, who dismissed the idea with a shrug, saying, 'the university has an unbreakable contract; in any case, we would never let it happen'. I was left to wonder who 'we' were.

In time, I was impressed by the Durban bourgeoisie to which he belonged, a sort of medieval class that ran and cared for its city. For example, Vishnu led the development of a local museum dedicated to the history of labour struggles there. But the local ANC politicians had other ideas, and we eventually saw the writing on the wall. Vishnu responded to his class's defeat by diversifying his engagements and interests. What he built in Durban proved to be more fragile than had once seemed likely. He was proud of Gandhi's impact on his city and country, but did not study him, focusing rather on the history of Indian migration and labour in Natal (Padayachee and Morrell 1991) with obvious links to my own work in West Africa (Hart 1973). He also studied the history of South African non-white associations, especially in cricket (Desai et al. 2002), while I explored the networking opportunities provided by the digital revolution (Hart 2022).

Two crowning achievements stand out from Vishnu's mature local career – the formation of the SDS and Ike's Books and Collectables, where he first worked with bookbinder Ike Mayet, its founder, and then relaunched the store in 2000 with Julian May. Both institutions were very good at doing what they were supposed to. The SDS was an internationally renowned centre in its field, and Ike's is a local award-winning treasure. It looks and feels like a museum, but an extraordinarily user-friendly one, lacking any pressure to buy, converse or participate in events. Its book launches are convivial and political. What made each special was its intimate social atmosphere; he would have demurred, but both places took their character from Vishnu.

Vishnu organised his life at its Durban peak in a daily sequence. He got up at 4 a.m. for email, reading and administration, then took his daughter to school and turned up at UKZN around 8 a.m. The morning was for department meetings, some lectures and informal chat. Everyone gathered in a dedicated room for coffee around 10 a.m. Companions for lunch and a regular public seminar at 12 p.m. were readily available. Vishnu put in two to three hours each afternoon for one-on-one discussions and official meetings. He then drove to Ike's bookshop and chilled out in its congenial surroundings, ordering first editions and socialising with customers. He returned home around 6 p.m. for an evening meal with his family, went to bed early and set the alarm clock for 4 a.m. Organising his life in a regular sequence of compartments was essential. I fitted into its cracks, outside holidays.

Vishnu combined this routine with being a director of the South African Reserve Bank, taking care of individual students and colleagues, prolific reading, research and publishing (as a single author, collaborator and editor); and he hosted conferences and seminars and travelled widely to them. On my first visit, he introduced me to his 'two young stars', Ashwin Desai and Adam Habib. He later transferred his share of the joint ownership of the bookshop with Julian to his British assistant, Jo Rushby. The SDS was much reduced by a vice chancellor who envisaged UKZN as the leading black African university, and its best-known members left for the University of the Witwatersrand, including Vishnu. Ike's is flourishing under new management.

Vishnu's last personal venture, the Validation Clearance Bureau – with a South African-born Lebanese entrepreneur, Neville Kerdachi – pioneered a banking system aimed mainly though not exclusively at black small and medium enterprises, to speed up slow invoice payments to the self-employed; there are some 250 000 black small and medium enterprises in South Africa. The system can be set up anywhere and has won approval from the Bank of International Settlements and the World Bank. Since 2000, my own research has been increasingly on issues relating to money (Hart 2000, 2022). We were never short of things to discuss.

Main publications and themes
Vishnu and I soon established a periodisation from the 1860s for placing South African capitalism in world history, featuring national capitalism's global rise and fall:

1770s–1850s	Bourgeois and industrial revolutions
1860s–early 1870s	Origins of national capitalism
1880s–1914	First age of financial imperialism (globalisation 1.0)
1914–45	First age of revolutions, war and economic collapse[3]
1945–70s	Golden age of national capitalism under state management
1980–2020	Second age of financial imperialism (globalisation 2.0)
2021–?	Second age of revolutions, war and economic collapse

From its foundation in 1910, South Africa aspired to build a national economy based on a relationship between the state, industry and finance. Its racial premises have now been officially abandoned, along with the ANC's Cold War communism (exchanged for neoliberalism until now). It faces an escalating world crisis as a malfunctioning, corrupt and racially divided society.

The World Economic Forum ranked 141 countries in *The Global Competitiveness Report* in 2013 (Schwab 2013). South Africa was number 50 overall. In regard to specific rankings, the country was, on the one hand, ranked at 2 for the efficacy of corporate boards, 4 for financial market development, 13 for management schools and 17 for air transport infrastructure; on the other hand, it was ranked at 97 for electricity supply, 130 for pay and productivity, 130 for life expectancy and 133 for education system. A world-class business environment was surrounded by among the lowest human development conditions. Inequality in South Africa has increased since the ANC came to power.[4] South Africa's three per cent average annual growth rate then was under half that of the seven African countries in the world's top ten fastest-growing economies. Any economy has its specific history and institutions; but South Africa's trajectory has usually been examined *sui generis*, whereas it has long been an integral part of global development.

'National capitalism' is the synthesis of the nation-state and industrial capitalism, an attempt to manage money, markets and accumulation through central bureaucracy for a community of citizens. It fostered the rise of large business corporations, and its main symbol has been a monopoly currency. This system became general after World War I, when states turned inwards to manage their economies. Its apogee was social democracy after 1945. National capitalism has been in decline since the 1970s. Today's global crisis consists of the terminal disjuncture between national capitalism and neoliberal globalisation. World society is growing closer together and more unequal at once. South Africa is such a world in microcosm.

Indian business in South Africa after apartheid
More than a century ago, Indian indentured labourers came to South Africa to work in Natal's sugar industry. After their contracts expired, they moved into small trade, fishing, manufactures and the like. In the interwar period, South Africa's biggest Indian-owned firm, the Moosas'

firm, entered shipping and the import-export trade, even establishing one of the earliest national cinema chains. After 1945, South Africa turned inward, imposing high tariff barriers and allowing some Indians to manufacture clothing and manufactures for the home market on an expanded scale.

When official apartheid ended, Indian businesses moved into hotels, metal products and the transport industry. Some drew on South Africa's financial sophistication and cheap labour with extraordinary success, forming alliances with old white money, black political power, foreign Asian capital and global diasporas to dominate some sectors at home and move aggressively abroad. I summarise here two examples.

Rajen Pillay was the managing director of Coastal Group, a fashion fabric manufacturer registered in Mauritius. In 1992 he set up the Afro-Asian Trading Company to strengthen links with Asia, especially Indonesia. Coastal was mainly owned by an Indonesian multinational run by an old friend of his father, a pioneering manufacturer of processed foods and a world traveller. The company built large garment factories in KwaZulu-Natal and one in Botswana, and grew cotton in what is now Limpopo Province, importing polyester yarn from Indonesia. Gigantic runs of cloth were sold mainly in Europe and America. The firm's slogan was 'Globally Oriented–Locally Dominant' (GOLD). Share capital worth $70 million was raised through South African loans. Then Southeast Asia's 1998 financial crisis wiped out most of the parent company's assets and Coastal failed.

Harish Mehta's grandfather was employed by Gandhi as a printer. Universal Printing was established in 1924; his father headed the firm and included his sons in the business. Harish joined it in 1978 when it employed twenty-two people. He acquired a printing diploma in London, went to college in the US, became a citizen there and worked for the NCR corporation. On returning home, against his father's wishes, he hired an American consultant to make Universal a modern corporation. It needed R300 million (then $50 million) for new equipment. Harish coopted First National Bank with 25 per cent of shares in the company, and two black empowerment companies also with 25 per cent. One partner brought banking know-how, the other lucrative government contracts. The family kept control with 50 per cent plus one more share.

Universal acquired contracts for printing the Rugby World Cup programme, the government's mid-term report and the national telephone directory. It bought a huge web offset press and then an even larger one. Harish Mehta joined First Asian Investment Corporation as founding chairman and bought The Lion Match Company from South African Breweries. The matches are made in Durban and shipped throughout the southern hemisphere.

Both men had fathers who owned substantial family businesses and went abroad for training and experience. Both had global ambitions and maintained strong roots in KwaZulu-Natal. Rajen Pillay relied heavily on international partners, while Harish Mehta looked within South Africa for them. The Indian diaspora is a highly dynamic force in world society today. South Africa's Indians were active in the world during the apartheid era, developing a rich cosmopolitan history of their own.

The Political Economy of Africa
Vishnu and I worked together closely (with some others) on this volume (Padayachee 2010), addressing the real possibilities for African development after its poor performance in the previous half-century. Western economic models often ignore Africa's diversity when peddling economic nostrums of dubious merit. We looked forward to the time when Africa's economies would be grounded in local conditions. The current shift in power from the West to Asia and a more plural world economy favour such a project. We jointly wrote the introduction and a chapter placing South African national capitalism within regional development and in Africa more generally (Hart and Padayachee 2010; Padayachee and Hart 2010).

Our introduction (Padayachee and Hart 2010) sought to overcome three obstacles to effective thinking about Africa's development. The first is a tendency to lump its regions together in a vague abstraction, 'Africa', which becomes the object of general theories that swing between polarised extremes. African union still has a long way to go; we should rather engage with its diversity now. The second obstacle is 'development', truly a leap from one idea to its negation – colonialism to independence or capitalism to socialism? History's big breaks are always moderated by a gradual shift between plural institutions found across time and space. Our third concern was with political agency. African politicians and pundits often talk of development as a free choice from a smorgasbord – to follow the American, Russian, Korean or Chinese route, regardless of local and global conditions. The problem is to keep more than a single idea in one's head at once, to think dialectically about contrasting pairs – national/global, state/market, here and now as part of other times and places. 'Africa' is a territory for Africans, Arabs, Asians and Europeans alike, not just the home of a race, possibly marching towards economic and political union. Dreams of African emancipation have global, not only regional or racial, implications. Orthodox economics can never embrace such concrete notions of Africa.

Moeletsi Mbeki (2009) asked why Africans remain so much poorer than the rest of the world. He blames African political elites who, from the slave trade onwards, have enriched themselves at their own people's expense by serving foreign powers interested only in exploiting local people and resources. This accumulation without development depends on home-based politicians. Enrichment of a few Africans with political connections is a pay-off by white corporations for not nationalising their assets. Mbeki reminds us that the ANC was always marginal to the anti-apartheid struggle, and now relies on powerful paymasters to rule. It clings to power without any economic programme for advancing the poor mass of South Africa's citizens.

The limits of 'national capitalism', and especially the reduced significance of its place in a region and continent, are the focus of our joint chapter (Hart and Padayachee 2010). Mbeki's development model is consolidation of the home market for industry;[5] he links this to investment in its citizens' education and skills and insists that bureaucracies must be genuinely committed to all citizens, an idea pioneered by Hegel in *The Philosophy of Right* ([1821] 1967). 'National capitalism' was the dominant social form of the last century; look where it got the world. We accept Mbeki's critique but reject his strategy, since it could not capitalise on South Africa's advantages. We prefer to look to large regional trading blocs protecting nation-states from 'the markets', while freeing up their internal commerce.

South Africans notably, but people everywhere, have generated a plethora of social movements – civil society for short – capable of by-passing corrupt bureaucracies while reaching out to the world. These are political, commercial, technological, religious, artistic and intellectual movements, while national politicians today ignore what ordinary people already do for themselves. Both civil society and politicians lack an overarching vision comparable to what made Pan-Africanism the world's most inclusive political movement from 1900 to the 1950s.

The ANC's actual strategy combines neoliberal globalisation with opposing its 'rainbow nation' to other Africans, conceived of as local competition. South Africa's poor citizens are invited to identify with the beneficiaries of apartheid against their African neighbours who supported them in the struggle to abolish it. Thabo Mbeki's bid for African leadership courted the political class that has failed Africa since independence. His vision excluded the popular forces of civil society. African peoples have moved long distances without borders for centuries and still do, despite their rulers' attempts to force them into national cages. Most African economies are now held to be 'informal' as a result. State regulations are routinely ignored, half the population and most economic activities are labelled 'criminal', and government efforts are wasted on trying to apply unenforceable rules.

The proven historical answer to this chaos is classical liberalism, the drive to establish the widest area of free trade and movement in a regional federation with minimal regulation by the authorities. Neoliberal globalisation insists on discrediting this recipe for combining free trade with protection. For Southern Africa, both its large and small members, the boundaries of commerce and public intervention should be pushed beyond national limits. John Maynard Keynes showed how international liberalism and social democracy at home are not contradictory.

Economic democracy needs a more proactive strategy, starting with sorting out the confusion of internal barriers to trade in the Southern African Development Community (SADC). Instead of a mid-century model of industrial development, we would base South Africa's (and Africa's) economic future on rapid global growth in digitised cultural services such as entertainment, education, media, software and information, conducted through financial, communications and transport infrastructures and the physical means available – construction, energy and minerals. As Daniel Bell (1991: 225) once observed, 'the national state has become too small for the big problems in life and too big for the small problems'. One solution is subsidiarity, a feature of federalism, devolving power to the lowest effective authority. South Africa should revive its own federal past while reaching out to its smaller neighbours.

A continental single currency and central bank are wildly inappropriate now. Existing regional associations must simplify administration and eliminate conflict between rules at different levels. The African Union and its economic arm, the New Partnership for Africa's Development

(NEPAD) could try to persuade international bodies that Africa's poverty is a drag on the global economy. For infant industries to develop, Africa needs special protection for a time. Arguments like these will not be persuasive coming from fifty-five nation-states, mismanaged as they are now. Africa's educated classes could try moving beyond blaming colonialism for Africa's current ills and inspect domestic politics today more critically.

National capitalism versus neoliberal globalisation
It took us a decade of research and conversation to write the article 'A History of South African Capitalism in National and Global Perspective' as an antidote to what we took to be the insularity of South Africans' discourse on their own country (Hart and Padayachee 2013). Traditional South African capitalism was a stunted, colonial form that left the economy hopelessly unbalanced and unable to generate growth of output and employment (Feinstein 2005). The minerals–energy complex and later attempts to develop manufacturing are rapidly being replaced by the services sector. 'Big men' no longer dominate boardrooms; but the group-holding, pyramid structure and extensive crossholding directorships persist. Criticism of black economic empowerment has been severe: its beneficiaries become wealthy through boardroom deals, and none of them has started a large new business. The South African Communist Party, a partner of the ANC in government, concurs, stating: '[This] comprador class ... does not create jobs; it relies on special share deals, affirmative action quotas, fronting, privatization and trading on its access to state power' (SACP 2006: 32).

In contrast to massive net inflows of foreign capital during globalisation 1.0, the third feature of South African capitalism today is white capital flight. Twenty per cent of GDP has left the country since 1994, legally and illegally. South African firms' failure to invest at home means that corporate savings are at their highest level. They either send their money abroad or sit on the cash. Either way, little capital finds its way into domestic investment and employment creation.

The post-war decades of social democracy and socialism held that moral and material progress go together; the state delivers to all its citizens and economic growth results. The neoliberal counter-revolution was its antithesis, reverting to a pre-industrial system of favouring rents and distribution over production. The social contract was replaced by an ethos of 'take what you can and run'. Despite this, China, India, Brazil and, in its own way, even South Africa struggle to develop welfare states to moderate the risks to new workers moving to the cities.

How does the ANC's South Africa compare with its predecessor? South African capitalism traditionally had a markedly 'neo-feudal' character, marked by a cult of alpha-male leadership, cronyism between firms, banks and government, a relative absence of competition, weak democracy in the workplace, and no culture of small and medium enterprises. Its roots lay in British colonialism, rural Afrikanerdom and white racial oppression. That the ANC has nothing to say about this is a national tragedy. Any proposal for how to resolve the problem must engage with both its external and internal dimensions.

We believe that a sustainable future for Africa, or at least its southern region, must be central to South Africa's search for a successful economy, and vice versa. Other African countries may disagree however, given the ANC's history of rejecting them. Its embrace of nationalism and neoliberal globalisation together, to the detriment of both, has done lasting damage to regional integration. The chance for South Africans to play a leading role in a new Pan-Africanism may have already passed.

My subsequent reflections on national capitalism
The current break in world history goes far deeper than the postwar replacement of social democracy and socialism by neoliberalism. A world-historical process that began in the 1860s is ending now. In between, there have been two phases of financial imperialism each lasting four decades. The first ended in World War I and its grisly aftermath. Governments soon provided new legal conditions for the operations of large business corporations. A bureaucratic revolution ushered in mass production and consumption. Today's financial crisis is about more than just credit boom and bust.

I sketch here national capitalism's origins, growth and decline, adding that a global approach should inform any solutions to South Africa's current crisis. Its icon was a national monopoly currency in a fragmented world with many of them. The social organisation of money that we lived by in the last century is fast unravelling now. Business corporations were at first allied with national governments, but they have superseded them. Private property has shifted from persons to huge abstractions (states and corporations) and from things to ideas (intellectual property).

Xenophobic dictators, national governments, regional trade federations and transnational corporations are locked in a struggle for world domination. As a result, market fundamentalism has split into two main forms – for and against joining the world (Hart 2018). The historical compromise between big money and political power that constituted national capitalism has been resolved by their unification, with capitalists or politicians variously in charge.

The 1860s and early 1870s saw a transport and communications revolution (steamships, continental railways and the telegraph) that decisively opened up the world economy. Political revolutions gave the leading powers – Britain, France, Germany, Austria, Russia, the US and Japan – institutional means of organising industrial capitalism. Karl Marx ([1867] 1970) published *Capital* and the first workers' international was formed. This suggests that world society was already integrated, but international trade then accounted for under one per cent of GNP in most countries; the division of the world into high- and low-wage economies defined by race occurred later, around 1900 (Lewis 1978).

Modern capitalism has always rested on an unequal contract between owners of money and those who make and buy their products. This requires effective punishment of workers who withhold their labour or buyers who fail to pay. The owners need governments, laws, prisons, police, even armies for this. The machine revolution was pulling unprecedented numbers of workers into the cities, where criminal gangs controlled large areas, adding a new dimension to crowd control. The period's political revolutions were founded on an alliance between capitalists and the traditional enforcers to form governments capable of managing all this.

The 1970s were a watershed. Almost all money exchanged internationally until then was for goods and services purchased abroad. 'Stagflation' encouraged neoliberal conservatives to revive 'the market', not 'the state', as the agent of economic strategy. The vast bulk of international exchange today is of money for money in different forms. Foreign exchange alone has a daily turnover of $6 trillion. Production and sale of commodities and political management of currencies and trade have given way to an autonomous global circuit of capital. Ronald Reagan and Margaret Thatcher's counter-revolution against post-war egalitarianism restored financial imperialism. Society conceived of as decentralised networks (federations) contradicts the political recipe of a closed hierarchical entity (the nation-state).

Where are the levers of democratic power now that national economic management has failed? In both globalisation 1.0 and 2.0, market forces were unleashed inside national societies, leading to unrestrained accumulation and inequality. Finance capital internationalised economic relations and people moved everywhere. The first era organised production in a bureaucratic revolution; national bureaucracies are now dismantled by neoliberal globalisation and the digital revolution. In both phases autocracy increased. The West won the Cold War and lost the world. Keynes's monetary legacy should now be revived under very different historical circumstances (Hart 2009).

Thomas Jefferson saw three main threats to democracy: governing elites, organised religion and commercial monopolies (Hardt 2007). He called the last 'pseudo-aristocrats' and 'monarchists', since their project for world domination had no room for democracy. He failed to get freedom from monopoly into the Bill of Rights. Corporations sought the constitutional rights of individual citizens but were denied them. Later the railroads tried once more and this time they succeeded (Hartmann 2009).

The race is on to save the human commons, culture and ecology from corporate private property, not just by conserving the earth's natural resources or saving public services from privatised agencies. Behind closed doors – real power never seeks publicity – transnational corporations claim that national capitalism is decadent and must be replaced. Nation-states are corrupt and ineffective; national laws are irrelevant and unenforceable; and national citizens are lazy and disaffected. The digital revolution has promoted information services at distance whose transmission is almost costless. The US, born in resistance to corporate monopoly, now uses coercive methods to 'persuade' small countries in international bodies to support a trade-related intellectual property treaty shoring up corporate profits.

World society now resembles the Old Regime that the bourgeois revolution was supposed to have disposed of (Hart 2002). Monopoly rent extraction has replaced production of commodities for profit in capital accumulation. Liberal democracy has become its antithesis, autocracy. An impersonal public sphere is indispensable to living in society. But individuality and moral purpose have vanished from politics in the leading countries (Hart 2005). Free global capital flows have subordinated politics to markets for decades.

National capitalism failed because complacent voters handed over government to the rich and money escaped the controls imposed after 1945. The causes are many: neoliberalism and its lawless global money circuit; the reduced powers and legitimacy of nation-states; the breakdown of the post-war international order; free money for rich insiders versus stagnant wages, debt and austerity for the rest; the rise of the corporations; the digital revolution, globalisation and fintech; growing autocracy and xenophobic nationalism. Dissenters must decide what the sides are and do their best for democracy. Humanity is sleepwalking into a disaster.

There is a history of the relationship between money and power. Despite a barrage of propaganda claiming that we now live in an age of science and democracy, our dominant institutions are still those of agrarian civilisation. These are territorial states, embattled cities, landed property, warfare, racism, bureaucracy, limited literacy, impersonal money, long-distance trade, work as a public value, world religion and the nuclear family. Industrial capitalism's flawed potential to increase the opportunity for humanity's emancipation from unequal society was temporary. The idea of a *nation* represents a desire to escape from modern history.

The new plutocrats are no longer interested in wealth for conspicuous consumption (Veblen [1899] 2021), but only for achieving political power. They would stamp out democracy while hiding behind its classical slogans. For dictators and the self-made mega-rich alike it's about brute power – making humanity bow down before oppressors who, if necessary, will take off into space or hide in underground bunkers.

Big-time accumulation of capital now relies on extracting rents (transfers sanctioned by political power they have bought). The Wall Street bank Goldman Sachs retrieved from the US Treasury at full face value the $90 billion lost by insurance giant AIG in the 2008 crash. Elon Musk, the richest man in the world, built up his companies with government loans and now campaigns against taxation. These rent-seekers are not punished for stealing from the public. They are bailed out by our taxes and held up as shining examples of super-rich consumption to a public that has exchanged equal citizenship for identity politics and reality TV.

The chief problem for these dictators, corporate CEOs and billionaires is not how to make money but how to figure out what will stop the guards killing their employers when the balloon goes up.[6] The main chance for us is to mobilise global networks to develop a democratic world society, learning from networked 'alter-globalisation' movements

(Pleyers 2010) inspired by the 2001 World Social Forum in Porto Alegre, and relying on being more humane and faster than them.

The modern world has seen three huge waves of population growth – in Europe (1830–1930), Asia (1945–2000) and Africa, whose share of the world population's −7.5 per cent in 1900 (half its share of the world's inhabitable land) – is projected to reach 40 per cent in 2100. Asia's share, now 60 per cent compared to Africa's 15 per cent, will be similar to Africa's. The rest will be under 20 per cent. This will be the greatest demographic transition ever and just maybe the end of a racist world order.

What are all those young urban Africans going to do when they grow up, assuming that sheer numbers can beat the corrupt old men who rule them? The winners in any previous world have the most to lose in the next one, and the previous losers will gain the most. The Asian manufacturing exporters already know that Africa's demographic explosion will sustain the world economy. Westerners are stuck in the world they made in the nineteenth century; they are growing older and resent the younger non-whites whose taxes pay for their pensions.

South Africa aped its racist twin in celebrating itself as exceptional without any of the US's historical justification based on its global influence. For a few years, South African civil society won global support when fighting racism for democracy's sake. Nelson Mandela was the world's most admired politician; but the idea of a 'rainbow nation' was yoked to national capitalism in its death throes. His country's estrangement from the rest of Africa only amplifies its domestic ruin. To save its own skin, the ANC wants to drag South Africans onto the next world war's losing side. But South Africa shares something else with the US, the likely winner of that war – geographical isolation between two oceans where continents start and end.

Many of us old academics believed in our youth that the West was decadent and found hope in the struggle of the postcolonial insurgents. South Africa came late to that struggle with considerable advantages; it is now a basket case. Vishnu Padayachee was not mainly a good economist. He believed in civil society, not political parties; was an internationalist historian; and built alternative social and economic institutions all his adult life. He taught Durban workers economics in night classes. The ANC, then in exile, had him marked down as a potential troublemaker. At a conference in York he was collared by a well-known Stalinist thug, later a minister in Mandela's government (one of six Indians), who demanded: 'Are you a Trot[skyite] or something? What are you teaching economics to the workers for? The Party know what's best for them!' Vishnu made a quick exit.[7]

Without our long conversation, I would never have found my mature intellectual politics or renewed the hope I once cherished for Africa's future. Older South Africans should take courage from their active part in displacing apartheid in the 1980s and share their experience with the African kids who, like Generation Z everywhere, know they have been dealt a terrible hand. They might save the world, but they can't do it alone.

Notes

1. See Chapter 2 in this volume by Rajend Mesthrie for a description of Vishnu's life in Umkomaas.
2. I supported United, and Vishnu Spurs.
3. It was the second age after 1776–1815, which coincided instead with an economic boom.
4. The World Economic Forum now boosts government and corporate greenwashing, not global inequality.
5. A position first articulated by Lenin (1899).
6. The late Roman emperors were familiar with this problem.
7. Vishnu Padayachee, personal communication with the author.

References

Bell, D. 1991. *The Winding Passage: Sociological Essays and Journeys*. New Brunswick: Transaction Books.
Chevalier, S. 2015. 'Food, Malls and the Politics of Consumption: South Africa's New Middle Class'. *Development Southern Africa* 32 (1): 118–29.
———. 2019. 'The Politics and Moral Economy of Middle-class Consumption in South Africa'. In: *Conspicuous Consumption in Africa*, edited by D. Posel and I. van Wyk. Johannesburg: Wits University Press.
Churchill, W. 1948. *The Second World War: Volume 1*. London: Houghton Mifflin.
Desai, A., V. Padayachee, K. Reddy and G. Vahed. 2002. *Blacks in Whites: A Century of Cricket Struggles in KwaZulu-Natal*. Pietermaritzburg: University of Natal Press.
Feinstein, C. 2005. *An Economic History of South Africa: Conquest, Discrimination and Development*. Cambridge: Cambridge University Press.
Hardt, M. 2007. 'Jefferson and Democracy'. *American Quarterly* 59 (1): 41–78.
Hart, K. 1973. 'Informal Income Opportunities and Urban Employment in Ghana'. *Journal of Modern African Studies* 11 (3): 61–89.

———. 1982. *The Political Economy of West African Agriculture*. Cambridge: Cambridge University Press.

———. 2000. *The Memory Bank: Money in an Unequal World*. London: Profile Books.

———. 2002. 'World Society as an Old Regime'. In: *Elite Cultures: Anthropological Perspectives*, edited by C. Shore and S. Nugent. London: Routledge.

———. 2003. 'Manchester on My Mind: A Memoir'. *Global Networks* 3 (3): 417–36.

———. 2005. *The Hit Man's Dilemma: On Business Personal and Impersonal*. Chicago: Prickly Paradigm Press.

———. 2009. 'The Great Revolutions are Monetary in Nature: Mauss, Polanyi and the Breakdown of the Neoliberal World Economy'. *Storicamente* 5. https://storicamente.org/hart.

———. 2018. 'After 2008: Market Fundamentalism at the Crossroads'. *Cultural Anthropology* 33 (4). https://journal.culanth.org/index.php/ca/article/view/ca33.4.03.

———. 2022. *Self in the World: Connecting Life's Extremes*. Oxford: Berghahn Books.

Hart, K. and V. Padayachee. 2000. 'Indian Business in South Africa after Apartheid: New and Old Trajectories'. *Comparative Studies in Society and History* 42 (4): 683–712.

———. 2010. 'South Africa in Africa: From National Capitalism to Regional Integration'. In: *The Political Economy of Africa*, edited by V. Padayachee. London: Routledge.

———. 2013. 'A History of South African Capitalism in National and Global Perspective'. *Transformation* 81–2: 55–85.

Hartmann, T. 2009. *Unequal Protection: How Corporations Became 'People' – and How You Can Fight Back*. Oakland: Berrett-Koehler.

Hegel, G.W.F. [1821] 1967. *The Philosophy of Right*. Oxford: Oxford University Press.

Lenin, V.I. 1899. *The Development of Capitalism in Russia: The Formation of a Home Market for Large-scale Industry*. https://www.marxists.org/archive/lenin/works/1899/devel/.

Lewis, W.A. 1978. *The Evolution of the International Economic Order*. Princeton: Princeton University Press.

Marx, K. [1867] 1970. *Capital: The Critique of Political Economy: Volume 1*. London: Lawrence and Wishart.

Mbeki, M. 2009. *Architects of Poverty: African Capitalism Needs Changing*. Johannesburg: Pan Macmillan Africa.

Padayachee, V. (ed.). 2010. *The Political Economy of Africa*. London: Routledge.

Padayachee, V. and K. Hart. 2010. 'Introducing the African Economy'. In: *The Political Economy of Africa*, edited by V. Padayachee. London: Routledge.

Padayachee, V. and R. Morrell. 1991. 'Indian Merchants and Dukawallahs in the Natal Economy, *c.*1875–1914'. *Journal of Southern African Studies* 17 (1): 71–102.

Pleyers, G. 2010. *Alter-Globalization: Becoming Actors in a Global Age*. Cambridge: Polity.

SACP (South African Communist Party). 2006. *Bua Komanisi* 5 (1), Special edition on State Power.

Schwab, K. (ed.) 2013. *The Global Competitiveness Report, 2012–13: Full Data Edition.* Geneva: World Economic Forum.

Veblen, T. [1899] 2021. *The Theory of the Leisure Class.* Independently published.

12

Reflecting on Ideas, History and Institutions in South African Social Policy through the Prism of Vishnu Padayachee's Method

Robert van Niekerk

'Of Clement Attlee... I was an admirer. He was a serious man and a patriot. Quite contrary to the general tendency of politicians in the 1990s, he was all substance and no show. His was a genuinely radical and reforming government.' With his folded arms in his formal blue jacket and with that studiously inquiring gaze, Vishnu marvelled with me at these observations on the UK post-war prime minister Clement Attlee. The profound irony and incongruity of these words coming from Margaret Thatcher (1995: 69), of all people, who systematically dismantled Attlee's landmark welfare state post-war legacy, was (of course) not lost on Vishnu. There was very little that Vishnu shared with Attlee. The latter was a quietly tenacious and determined post-war Labour Party leader and unlikeliest of revolutionaries. Famously taciturn, Attlee was once disparagingly referred to by Churchill, to whom he lost the 1945 election by a landslide, as 'a modest man with much to be modest about' (Churchill 1954). By contrast, Vishnu was a romantic by comportment, with a debonair flair. This he reconciled, with some aplomb, with being a studiously toiling intellectual of major progressive purpose, influence and consequence.

What Attlee and Padayachee did share, in their starkly different ways, was an unswerving personal and political integrity. A commitment to understanding and implementing 'big ideas' of economic and societal transformation. Including ideas such as the function and purpose of the redistributive welfare state, perhaps among the most maligned concepts in the South African policy lexicon. Our discussion on the significance of the welfare state's primary lesson centred on the challenge of institutionalising redistributive public goods that were shared by all social classes – such as the National Health Service ushered in by Attlee's government – and the importance of universalisation as a mechanism to achieve it. A key problem of South African social policy was a failure to financially desegregate our public goods, leading to extreme inequality in provision of health and education. Simply put, this was because the majority of severely impoverished citizens could not afford private health care or 'Model C' (let alone private) education. There was thus a need to remove cost barriers through the application of the principle of universalism in access to shared public goods, such as proposed through the system of National Health Insurance (NHI). The question was, did we possess the ethical political leadership that could sustain such an institution, given our societal trust deficit since the Zuma years?

What Vishnu and Attlee shared was a passionate belief in the humane transformation of the lives of the most economically and socially subjugated, made possible through the redistributive policy interventions of a democratic state and which was the measure above all else of the good society – whether dressed in the preferably dashing red of democratic socialism (Vishnu) or the modest crimson of post-war social democracy (Attlee).

In the many years of our friendship and intellectual collaboration, an enduring topic that surfaced was how South Africa's dividend of constitutional democracy following the destruction of apartheid, with the shared intentions (we thought) of implementing the social democratic Freedom Charter, could have been so squandered by the time of the disastrous Zuma years of the 2010s.

Our book *Shadow of Liberation* (Padayachee and Van Niekerk 2019), developed over several years, attempted a historicised explanation that could contribute to the emergence of new ideas which could help to re-foster progressive policy frameworks aimed at more fundamental social change, rooted in a democratic, ethical, political ethos. It brought together Vishnu's interest in economic policy with my interest in social policy and excavated a longer history of imaginative policy ideas in South Africa on the construction of an egalitarian good society, stretching back to the anti-fascist 'wars years' of the 1940s.

In this chapter I set out and engage with some of the historical and institutional lessons of the eras of the 1940s and the 1990s, two landmark periods for understanding social change in modern South Africa, as a means of indicating the method and spirit of open, historicised inquiry that animated Vishnu's progressive scholarship.

What went wrong and how could the lessons learnt be translated into new ideas?

To reclaim the – or perhaps *a* – humane, social democratic vision of the good society, understood here as the universal provision of public goods such as education, health and welfare by a democratic state which constitutionally protects political, civil and social rights through calibrated economic policy interventions in the market, we need to understand how that original vision and the 'big policy ideas' it represented did not come to fruition: why those ideas failed and how. One method of doing this is to relate those 'big ideas' to past historical attempts at implementing progressive policies within specific historical and institutional contexts, racialised and then deracialised in the South African case.

In a paper on the historical antecedents of heterodox economic thinking, Vishnu argued that

> [it] surely wouldn't be a wasted effort for the Left to dedicate some energy to working through radical social democracy and complementary heterodox macroeconomic models, including post-Keynesianism – whether we see these approaches as just interim measures on the path to socialism or as the ultimate state and form of the good society (Padayachee 2019: 18).

I offer my own response to this important injunction, by reflecting on redistributive social policy, specifically government policies on health, welfare and education aimed at universally meeting the social needs of citizens and thereby establishing an egalitarian 'good society'. I examine the eras of the 1940s and the 1990s and attempts to implement such government social policies in the context of institutions of governance that mediated and then subverted progressive policy intentions, leading to policy failure (when related to the intended policy objectives).

A review of literature in the post-1994 democratic era on the development of inclusive social policies reveals that commentators on the Left attribute the failure of egalitarian social policies to have their intended outcomes to the fiscal conservatism of the new democratic government led by the African National Congress (ANC). This fiscal conservatism was argued to be at variance with macroeconomic and social policy proposals developed by the ANC in the pre-democratic era that, by contrast, were radical and redistributive (see, for example, Adelzadeh 1996; Alexander 2002; Bond 1996, 2000; Bond, Pillay and Sanders 1997; Fine 2019; Marais 1997, 2001; McKinley 1997; Saul 2005). The literature tends to treat social policy-making in the period of the democratic era as a *tabula rasa*, however, largely failing to connect it with previous historical attempts at inclusive social policy-making and to draw comparisons with these previous attempts, such as the period of liberal social reforms of the 1940s.

Such critiques also fail to take into account the significant impact of the proposed reforms to governance and fiscal institutions, which were being negotiated between the leaders of the ANC and the National Party (NP) in the Convention for a Democratic South Africa (CODESA) in the immediate pre-democracy period between 1991 and 1993. These multiparty political negotiations over new governance and fiscal institutions occurred in parallel with the development of progressive, redistributive economic and social policies by civil society groups and activists in the unbanned liberation movements broadly.

It is arguably here as well that the problem can be found of effecting fundamental social change by implementing egalitarian social policy ideas through governance institutions originally established for *not* effecting such social change.

The expansion of the four provinces and the Bantustans of the apartheid era into nine new provinces, as a new institution of governance in the democratic era, is of particular significance. The creation of these nine provinces, established as the key implementing agency of national government economic and social policy based on the principle of fiscal decentralisation, was an expedient concession by the ANC in the CODESA negotiations in 1993 to the late apartheid-era NP government. According to the late F.W. de Klerk, the then leader of the NP, the NP was committed to dismembering the central wielding of state power by a new democratic government, through the 'establishment of strong and entrenched regional governments with adequate budgets' and 'vested with wide and meaningful powers and functions' (Calgary Herald 1992). The ANC had initially resisted the further fragmentation of the state implied by the proposals of the NP, counter-proposing the maintenance of the existing four provinces – the Transvaal, Orange Free State, Cape and Natal. The ANC view was that regional government should be decided by a constitution-making body following the 1994 elections (ANC 1993).

The ANC eventually agreed with the NP to leave the determination of the function and structures of the provinces to a Commission on the Demarcation of States/Provinces and Regions. Severely constrained by time due to the impending 1994 elections, this commission used nine economic development regions proposed by the late apartheid-era Development Bank of South Africa (DBSA) as the basis for determining the nine new provincial boundaries. The DBSA model was based on late apartheid-era ethnicised spatial planning aimed at modernising the Bantustan system. The final agreement in 1993 between the ANC and the NP was a tiered model of 'cooperative governance' between national government, provincial government and local government (Spitz and Chaskalson 2000).

A path-dependency was established consequent on the policy decisions negotiated over governance and fiscal institutions at CODESA. These decisions, which institutionally refragmented the post-apartheid polity from four into nine provinces based on late apartheid-era development planning, arguably moved even further away from the idea of a post-apartheid 'unitary' and also 'non-racial' state contained in the ANC's 'Constitutional Principles for a Democratic South Africa' policy framework (ANC 1991). Ironically the latter had been the bedrock of the ANC's strategy in the liberation struggle era, in opposition to the ethnicised, racially fragmentary and black labour-subordinating intentions of the Bantustan system established under Grand Apartheid through the Promotion of Bantu Self-Government Act (No. 46 of 1959). The fiscal arrangements originally negotiated at the CODESA negotiations in the 1990s resulted in a hybrid system of fiscal federalism in the democratic era that gave the nine new provincial governments control of social spending without ring-fencing spending on health or welfare, while policy development and coordination was reserved for the national government. The nine provinces were, in effect, allocated a cumulative block grant, including for social spending, which was determined using a formula aimed at achieving interprovincial equity. Once they 'received' this grant from the national government, provinces were entitled to allocate the funds according to their own provincially determined priorities, alongside the nationally agreed upon norms and standards. The new post-election ANC government simultaneously adopted a market-privileging economic development strategy and emphasised fiscal containment in its policy pronouncements. This, in significant part, was intended to extract it from the problem of 'unfunded mandates' that particularly impacted upon under-resourced and under-capacitated provinces such as the Eastern Cape, which had inherited the Transkei and Ciskei legacies of underdevelopment.

Here, arguably, are the institutional roots of what now can increasingly be characterised as provincial political fiefdoms, with social spending on provincial health, education and welfare subjected to the vagaries of the political elites constituting the provincial cabinets appointed by and accountable to their political party, not to the provincial electorates they are elected to serve. The creation of nine new provinces which incorporated the pre-existing Bantustans and their fragmented, racialised civil services as integral units accounted not only for the weak institutional capacity of some provinces, but for the 'crowding out' of social expenditure in favour of expenditure on a civil service and a political bureaucracy to sustain each province as a functioning entity. The trend is evident from the period since the advent of democracy, with a rise of cumulative expenditure on provincial civil servants from 52 per cent in 1996/97 to 55 per cent in 1997/98 to 60 per cent in 2021/2022 (Wehner 2000: 54–55; see also Parliamentary Budget Office 2022). By 2015 the government was spending 38 per cent of its budget on the public sector wage bill, amounting to R450 billion annually. This is in comparison to under 25 per cent spent on the wage bill in the other BRICS countries (Brazil, Russia, India and China) (Fin24 2015). Primary individual beneficiaries of state spending in the social sectors increasingly are a new class of politicians and high-income-earning civil servants linked to the state apparatus.

These policy developments represented, furthermore, an abandonment of the redistributive and fiscally expansive economic and social policies focused on building developmental infrastructure, as advocated by the Macroeconomic Research Group (MERG) appointed by the ANC in 1993. MERG (1993: 48) argued for a 'slim but strong state' with the 'need for a substantial increase in government spending on human development, social infrastructure, and the expansion of productive economic capacity. Such an increase is a prerequisite for the achievement of high economic growth rates'. Vishnu Padayachee described the overall MERG strategy as follows:

MERG envisioned a two-phase, 'crowding-in' approach to South Africa's development. The latter was built around a powerful state-led social and physical infrastructure investment programme focusing on housing, education, health and physical infrastructure investment as the growth drivers in the first phase, followed by a more sustainable growth phase which would see private-sector investment kick in more forcefully as growth picked up (Padayachee 2019: 8).

The MERG approach was also coterminous with the broadly social democratic Reconstruction and Development Programme (RDP) 'base document' proposals for a state-led development programme of the ANC and its alliance partners, also released in 1993 (ANC 1993, 1994b). As described in detail in *Shadow of Liberation* (Padayachee and Van Niekerk 2019), the new, fiscally austere economic policy framework called GEAR (Growth, Employment and Redistribution) displaced the broadly social democratic development strategy of MERG and the RDP, privileging economic stability and growth through the market as a precondition for social development in the post-apartheid era. The embrace of neoliberal orthodoxy represented a departure also from the principles enunciated in the ANC's own 1992 pre-election manifesto, 'Ready to Govern' (ANC 1992). The policies set out in this manifesto explicitly pledged equitable redistribution through social policies that were seen not only as forms of consumption but as a means of social investment, and which emphasised social rights to health, welfare and education. However, the pattern of government spending in the post-apartheid era saw spending increasingly directed towards civil servants with a reduction of capital spending, which decreased by as much as eight per cent between 2017 and 2018 (Statistics South Africa 2019).

History matters: Why social policies in the democratic era did not have egalitarian outcomes

The question that emerges, then, is why the social policies of the democratic era did not have their intended egalitarian outcomes once political rights had been achieved and a democratic state established. We would need to consider what were the other impediments to them achieving their intended outcomes, in addition to the rapid policy shift from a broadly social democratic-oriented to a neoliberal policy framework of development. A key factor concerns the continuities and discontinuities in the history of radical social policy reform and its possibilities. These occurred in at least two significant moments for social policy reform in South Africa: the 'war years' of the 1940s; and the period of transition from statutory apartheid to establishment of democracy, between 1990 with the unbanning of the ANC and 1999, the end of the first democratic administration under Mandela. In both these periods, a combination of external global political factors and internal receptivity by the minority white governing political party and liberation movements to inclusive, constitutional methods of political reform led to a convergence of thinking on the need for systematic dialogue about social policies that could shape a new post-segregation and then post-apartheid society. In the period of the war years of the 1940s, some common ground existed between the ANC, led by its radically reformist secretary-general Alfred Bitini Xuma, and the United Party, led by the liberal reformist Jan Smuts. Conditions induced by the global war against fascism led to joint support for the objectives of the anti-fascist Atlantic Charter of 1941. The Charter articulated the ideas of the Allied forces on a new post-fascist world order aimed at the global extension of democracy, welfare and labour rights. In the 1990s, by contrast, it was the global impact of the collapse of the Soviet Union in 1989 and the political stalemate reached between the ANC and the NP over control of state power that impelled the search for a negotiated political solution to the South African conflict (Van Niekerk 2013, 2017).

The significant dissimilarity between the two eras was that in the 1940s the denial of political rights to blacks meant that the extension of social rights to health, education and welfare was vulnerable to the political vagaries of the divided white minority electorate of the period. This electorate in the war years with exclusive access to political rights used its repressive monopoly of such rights to block attempts at more comprehensive social reforms that would benefit urban blacks (who took up labour positions made vacant by white men who had enlisted in the anti-fascist war effort in the 1940s) (Van Niekerk 2013).

In comparison, in the 1990s the precondition for acceptance of political negotiations as the strategy for creating a new political dispensation was the prior acceptance by the ANC and the NP, the key protagonists, of the undifferentiated extension of political rights to all citizens of South Africa. This meant that, unlike the situation in the 1940s, from 1994 onwards disenfranchised blacks could defend the social rights to education and health they had achieved through negotiations for a new political dispensation, by exercising their newly achieved universal political right to vote into power political parties that would advocate and implement social policies beneficial to their interests.

Continuities and discontinuities: The lessons of the 1940s applied to the 1990s

The values and principles that informed approaches to social policy, meanwhile, were revealed as a significant, if not decisive, influence on the development of inclusive social policies in both the 1940s and the 1990s. For example, in the early to mid-1940s the liberalisation of social policy in education was evident in the successful attempt by liberal reformer Jan Hofmeyr, then the minister of finance and education in the United Party government, to place African education under the general revenue account of the central government in 1945. Despite the continued inequity of racial differentiation in quality of schooling, the radical departure from previous practice of this policy initiative by Hofmeyr was that it established the principle of government responsibility for the education of *all* children of school-going age from a single tax base, regardless of race (MacQuarrie 1956).

In the apartheid era of the 1950s, the NP reversed this principle of state responsibility for education of all inhabitants of the country from a single tax base and reinstated the inequitable pre-war principle of funding for African education being determined by African tax-paying capability, through a separate racialised account. Combined with the introduction of the Bantu Education system in 1953 with the passing of the Bantu Education Act (No. 47 of 1953), aimed at the educational subservience of blacks, the application of this inequitable fiscal principle re-racialised the basis on which the system of education was provided.

In the early 1990s, the NP attempted to implement reforms to shore up its legitimacy in the black community, following protracted anti-apartheid mass mobilisation in favour of democratic rule based on a universal franchise. In the health care sector, the party implemented health policies that would devolve basic public health care provision to local government level, on the basis that communities would be able to access health care provision more effectively at this level. The principle of residualism informed the NP health policy reforms, with individuals expected to make provision for their health care needs through the market, and the state viewed as a last recourse for health care provision. The NP policy proposals specifically called, for example, on the need for 'individual responsibility for meeting health care needs' and 'cost-recovery through means testing' and 'encouragement of private sector provision', as stated in the National Policy for Health Act (No. 116 of 1990).

Consequently, the health policy reform attempts of the NP in the final period of apartheid rule were piecemeal. They failed to address the systemic problems of the health system related to skewed patterns of health funding between public and private provision, and the dominance of fiscal resource-draining tertiary-level health care provision. In contrast, the principle that informed the health care policies of the ANC and the broader opposition movement was state responsibility for provision of public health care as a constitutionally guaranteed social right of citizenship. The policy framework of the ANC advocated that 'every person has the right to achieve optimal health' and that a 'single governmental structure would co-ordinate all aspects of both public and private health care delivery', which would be 'accountable to the people through democratic structures' (ANC 1994a: 2).

When the ANC assumed government office in 1994, these redistributive policy intentions were significantly subordinated to the new fiscal federalist system of budgeting. The principle of health care to be provided universally as a social right, which traced itself to the social democratic-oriented African Claims policy statement of 1943 of the ANC led by Dr A.B. Xuma (ANC 1943), was thus not able to be implemented uniformly in the first post-apartheid government. This was in part due to the tenacity of the Bantustan legacy of underdevelopment, the weak administrative capacity for management of fiscal resources for health care in provinces with Bantustan legacies such as the Eastern Cape, and the scale of the fiscal resources required. The institutions of fiscal governance (established in the immediate post-apartheid period) combined with the refragmenting of the polity (through establishment of nine provincial administrations each controlled by a political elite ['cabinet'] appointed through the party apparatus) have conditioned the implementation of social policies in health, education and welfare, to parlous effect.

A comparison of the development of social policies in the eras of the 1940s and 1990s thus reveals the significant role played by constitutionally protected governance and fiscal institutions in mediating the implementation of inclusive social policies and the exercise of social rights, despite the universal extension of political rights of citizenship in the democratic era.

The fiscal and governance institutions established in the early 1990s transition period and the democratic era from 1994 onwards continue to mediate attempts at establishing inclusive outcomes in social policy. For example, the attempt to universalise health care through the current NHI Act (No. 20 of 2023), despite public distrust of state-owned enterprises, is unlikely to achieve its intended goals, if this fundamental problem of governance is not addressed.

This continuity in the historical problem – of institutions that were established for maintaining racial exclusion in the segregation and apartheid era being *ineffectively* repurposed for serving more inclusive, egalitarian purposes in the democratic era – is also illustrated in the provincial Western Cape Ministry of Health's concern expressed formally in 2019 in response to the draft NHI Bill (Western Cape Government Ministry of Health 2019). The Bill (which would become law in 2023) aimed to universalise the system of South African health care partly through nationally coordinating health care provision, through the National Department of Health. The consequence, in the view of the Western Cape Ministry of Health, would be the undermining of provincial departments' responsibility for controlling the funds provided through the nationally determined equitable share for providing health care in the province. Albeit under very different political conditions, these were precisely the same concerns about institutional control of provincial health care that eventually scuppered the plans of the landmark Gluckman Commission on a National Health Service in 1944 from coming to fruition. In the 1940s, the proposal of the Gluckman Commission for establishment of a universal health service by taking powers over fiscally draining general hospital services away from the four provincial administrations of the segregation era was rejected by Smuts, the prime minister and leader of the United Party at the time. The intention of the Gluckman proposal was to enforce a rationalised system of health care organisation throughout the three different levels of service delivery (national, provincial and local) and ensure the ending of provincial control over government health budgets, which were the bulk of public sector health care funding, and which provinces were empowered to use for purposes other than health (National Health Services Commission 1944; Van Niekerk 2016).

The implementation of the Gluckman proposal would have meant significant loss of provincial revenue and required a change to the constitution that had established the Union of South Africa in 1910. Smuts feared this would upset the narrow balance of power between English- and Afrikaans-speaking voters in the white electorate. Similarly, attempts by the last apartheid-era health administration, led by Rina Venter in the early 1990s, to devolve public health expenditure to local government levels by taking control and funding of tertiary hospitals away from provincial government failed, as it undermined the powers and control of the four provincial administrations over general hospitals, a significant source of their provincial revenue. To be effective, the plan driven by Venter would have needed to undermine the still existing apartheid constitution (albeit now deprived of any political legitimacy), which entrenched the fragmented delivery of health care across a number of authorities. This proved to be an Achilles heel, which the four provincial health administrations seized upon. As anticipated, strong provincial administrative resistance ensued against the attempt to undermine or dilute provincial powers over control of the health budget.

This was explained, somewhat melodramatically, by Venter, for the case of KwaZulu-Natal:

> In Natal there was a Peter Miller who was MEC [Member of the Executive Council] for Health – he fought me tooth and nail and then he used the KwaZulu-Natal/Buthelezi team – he did not want central government interference in any way – he went to Buthulezi *en hy het hom opgestiek* [he instigated him] – he told him 'this minister is going to go for an ANC policy' – they are going to destroy KwaZulu-Natal. So he [Buthulezi] ran to F.W. de Klerk – 'Do you know what your minister [of health] is doing? She's introducing ANC policies' – which was nonsense. The ANC at that stage had a centralised approach to health care – I was centralising and devolving at the same time – I had to centralise to get control and then devolve towards local government (Venter interview 1998).

The four provincial administrations in the late apartheid era used the same 1910 constitution first used to stymie the Gluckman universal health care reform proposal of 1944 to block the limited health policy reform attempts of Venter in the 1990s.

Déjá vu: Institutions and South African social policy reforms

History continues to repeat itself in South African social policy-making. When the ANC assumed government office in 1994 the fiscal and governance mechanisms negotiated at CODESA for a new political dispensation and enshrined in the new democratic constitution of 1996 undermined its ability to implement its social policies as intended.

Reflecting on these two historical periods of the 1940s 'war years' and the first post-apartheid government of the 1990s demonstrates furthermore that although political rights – the universal extension of the franchise – are a necessary condition for social rights to health, education and welfare, they are not a guarantor of such social rights. Poorly conceived fiscal and governance institutions can fundamentally undermine the intentions of social policy, even despite constitutionally guaranteed political and social rights. There is, however, also a subjective dimension without which even appropriate fiscal and governance institutions combined with political, civil and social rights would arguably render 'big ideas' such as implementing a redistributive, social democratic reform programme a failure. This is the dimension of consistent, ethical political leadership.

The ruinous Zuma years and the rapid evisceration of a social democratic-oriented possibility under the current ANC government – the complete abandonment in practice of the broad social democratic ideals of the Freedom Charter – suggest that new forms of ethical political leadership need to be nurtured and allowed to develop if the core goals of a genuinely non-racial, non-sexist, democratic and unitary South Africa are to be realised. Without such political leadership, all progressive policy intentions will flounder on the corrupting rocks of patronage, commodified self-gain and expediency, as is being currently demonstrated.

Whatever the past, my own musing on the future is that maintaining the current trajectory unchecked will probably eventually lead to severe conflict in South Africa, for which all the ingredients of comprehensively failed government institutions, increasingly violent political factionalism in the ruling party and its spin-offs relating to the patronage networks to access limited public resources, economic immiseration of the masses of people, and deep social polarisation will serve as the likely backdrop. Understanding how we got to this abysmal moment still matters and may help us to avert such a catastrophe.

Current political trends suggest the importance of coalition government as the primary institution of future democratic governance. Opportunities for a national policy dialogue on the kind of progressive, good society we aspire to will thus re-emerge. The ideas and ethical scholarly, political and personal practices and methods of Vishnu Padayachee demonstrate how this endeavour can be pursued. Embracing the progressive eclecticism and open scholarly inquiry aimed at achieving humane societal outcomes that characterised Vishnu's contributions offers us a point of departure. More specifically, as Vishnu himself argued in a final unpublished piece before his tragically untimely death:

> South Africa's transition to democracy and development is far from complete. That is one reason why I would maintain that the task of progressive economists, political economists and social scientists is to seek actively to re-build relationships with modernizing social movements in civil society, while at the same time, wherever possible, to exploit and expand the new spaces opened up at the level of the state by the triumph over apartheid oppression. In case this still sounds too vague, let me advance one possible, more specific task which could be taken on in this context. That would be to develop, debate and contest the theoretical frameworks, policy instruments, and organizational forms needed to give effect to an approach to South Africa's reconstruction and development (Padayachee 2021).

This task is now of inestimable value for the future and should animate all of us who seek to realise the promise of our constitutional democracy and the triumph over apartheid, which Vishnu dedicated his life to in his inimitable way. A mensch and dear friend and comrade, he continues to be much missed.

References

Adelzadeh, A. 1996. 'From the RDP to GEAR: The Gradual Embracing of Neo-liberalism in Economic and Social Policy'. *Transformation* 31: 66–95.

Alexander, N. 2002. *An Ordinary Country*. Pietermaritzburg: University of Natal Press.

ANC (African National Congress). 1943. 'African Claims in South Africa, including the "Atlantic Charter from the Standpoint of Africans within the Union of South Africa" and "Bill of Rights". Adopted by ANC Annual Conference

1943'. Document 29b. In: *From Protest to Challenge: A Documentary History of African Politics in South Africa 1882–1964: Volume 2: Hope and Challenge 1935–1952*, edited by G.M. Carter and T. Karis, 1987. Stanford: Hoover Institution Press.

———. 1991. *Constitutional Principles for a Democratic South Africa*. https://www.anc1912.org.za/policy-documents-1991-constitutional-principles-for-a-democratic-south-africa.

———. 1992. *Ready to Govern: ANC Policy Guidelines for a Democratic South Africa adopted at the National Conference*. https://www.anc1912.org.za/policy-documents-1992-ready-to-govern-anc-policy-guidelines-for-a-democratic-south-africa/.

———. 1993. *ANC Regional Policy*. Cape Town: Centre for Development Studies, University of Western Cape.

———.1994a. 'A National Health Plan for South Africa'. Prepared by the ANC Health Department with the support and technical assistance of the WHO and UNICEF. https://www.anc1912.org.za/policy-documents-1994-a-national-health-plan-for-south-africa/.

———. 1994b. *The Reconstruction and Development Programme*. Johannesburg: Umanyano Publications.

Bond, P. 1996. 'The Making of South Africa's Macro-economic Compromise'. In: *Development Strategies in Southern Africa*, edited by E. Maganya. Johannesburg: Institute for African Alternatives.

———. 2000. *Elite Transition: From Apartheid to Neoliberalism in South Africa*. Pietermaritzburg: University of Natal Press.

Bond, P., Y.G. Pillay and D. Sanders. 1997. 'The State of Neo-liberalism in South Africa: Economic, Social and Health Transformation in Question'. *International Journal of Health Services* 27 (1): 25–40.

Calgary Herald. 1992. 'De Klerk Lays Out Bottom-line Stand'. *Calgary Herald*, 13 October.

Churchill, W. 1954. 'Review: The So Austere, So Safe Clement Attlee by William Henry Chamberlin'. *Chicago Sunday Tribune Magazine of Books*, 27 June.

Fin24. 2015. 'Will Nene Crack the Whip on the Govt Wage Bill?' *Fin24*, 24 February. https://www.news24.com/fin24/budget/will-nene-crack-the-whip-on-the-govt-wage-bill-20150224.

Fine, B. 2019. 'Post-Apartheid South Africa: It's Neo-Liberalism Stupid!' In: *Race, Class and the Post-Apartheid Democratic State*, edited by J. Reynolds, B. Fine and R. van Niekerk. Pietermaritzburg: University of KwaZulu-Natal Press.

MacQuarrie, J.W. 1956. 'The New Order in Bantu Education'. *Africa South* 1 (1): 32–42.

Marais, H. 1997. 'The RDP: Is There Life after GEAR?' *Development Update* 1 (1): 1–19.

———. 2001. *South Africa: Limits to Change: The Political Economy of Transformation*. 2nd edition. London: Zed Books.

McKinley, D. 1997. *The ANC and the Liberation Struggle*. London: Pluto Press.

MERG (Macroeconomic Research Group). 1993. *Making Democracy Work: A Framework for Macroeconomic Policy in South Africa*. Cape Town: Centre for Development Studies, University of the Western Cape.

National Health Services Commission (Union of South Africa). 1944. *Report on the Provision of an Organised National Health Service for all Sections of the Union of South Africa (U.G.30)*. Pretoria: Union of South Africa.

Padayachee, V. 2019. 'Can Progressive Macroeconomic Policy Address Growth and Employment while Reducing Inequality in South Africa?' *Economic and Labour Relations Review* 30 (1): 3–21.

———. 2021. 'Intellectuals in South Africa: Initial Thoughts Drawing on My Experience'. 16 May, rough draft ideas, records of Robert van Niekerk.

Padayachee, V. and R. van Niekerk. 2019. *Shadow of Liberation: Contestation and Compromise in the Economic and Social Policy of the African National Congress, 1943–1996*. Johannesburg: Wits University Press.

Parliamentary Budget Office. 2022. *Fiscal Brief – October 2022: Financial Year Analysis (April–August 2022)*. https://www.parliament.gov.za/storage/app/media/PBO/Analysis_and_Reports/2022/5-october/28-10-2022/Fiscal_Brief.pdf.

Saul, J.S. 2005. *The Next Liberation Struggle: Capitalism, Socialism and Democracy in Southern Africa*. New York: Monthly Review Press.

Spitz, R. and M. Chaskalson. 2000. *The Politics of Transition: A Hidden History of South Africa's Negotiated Settlement*. Johannesburg: Wits University Press.

Statistics South Africa. 2019. 'Public-sector Capital Expenditure Continues to Fall'. *StatsSA*, 31 October. https://www.statssa.gov.za/?p=12705.

Thatcher, M. 1995. *The Path to Power*. London: Harper Collins.

Van Niekerk, R. 2013. 'Social Policy, Social Citizenship and the Historical Idea of a Social Democratic Welfare State in South Africa'. *Transformation* 81: 112–39.

———. 2016. 'The Politics of Universalising Health Care in South Africa: History, Policy, and Institutions'. *Transformation* 91, Special Issue: Democratic South Africa and the Politics of New Social Policies: 40–62.

———. 2017. 'A Hidden History of Social Democratic Thinking in the ANC, 1940–1962'. In: *The National Question in South Africa: A Hidden History*, edited by E. Webster. Johannesburg: Wits University Press.

Wehner, J. 2000. 'Fiscal Federalism in South Africa'. *Publius: The Journal of Federalism* 30 (3): 47–72.

Western Cape Government Ministry of Health. 2019. *Western Cape Comments on the NHI Bill*. https://www.westerncape.gov.za/assets/departments/health/PPHF/general_comments_on_nhi_bill_-_28_nov_2019.pdf.

Interview
Rina Venter, Pretoria, June 1998.

13

Locating Vishnu as Engaged Political Economist

A Personal Journey

Ben Fine

The original version of this essay (Fine 2022) began by specifying contemporary capitalism as globalised, financialised neoliberalism, having gone through three (logical, not necessarily sequential and separate) phases (shock therapy, third wayism and continuing interventionism by the state to promote financialised accumulation).[1] It then traced the trajectory of mainstream (development) economics from the marginalist revolution, highlighting the core presence of its technical apparatus (production and utility functions) and technical architecture (preoccupation with individual optimisation, efficiency and equilibrium). Such massive unrealistic reductionism was seen to have inspired a wealth of diverse heterodox alternatives that have been heavily and increasingly marginalised by the mainstream. The mainstream has, nonetheless, engaged in three phases of economics imperialism (colonisation of subject matter of other social sciences), with the latest incoherently combining its sacrosanct technical apparatus/architecture with whatever other variables it fancies, and careful theory increasingly displaced by increasingly sophisticated statistical methods loosely formulated in relation to theory.

Against this, now excluded, breakneck journey through the nature of contemporary capitalism and the history of economic thought, I pick up in the next section of this essay with an overview of the post-apartheid economy, seeing it as conforming to neoliberalisation, with its own characteristics involving the globalisation and financialisation of the core minerals-energy complex, and with an associated incorporation of a new black elite.[2] What is striking about the post-apartheid neoliberal transition is its speed, its extent and its lack of opposition. This is explained by a combination of loyalty to, and trust in, a tight leadership as it took a neoliberal turn; its command over the Tripartite Alliance (the African National Congress [ANC], the South African Communist Party [SACP] and the Congress of South African Trade Unions [COSATU]) but distrust in its supposed 'populism'; faith in, and commitment to, creation of a black bourgeoisie; and deference to leadership as the condition for self-advancement in whatever economic, political or personal arena. Centralised authoritarianism of the Nelson Mandela and Thabo Mbeki governments, together with their failure to deliver substantively for the majority, paved the way for neoliberalised politics par excellence in the form of Jacob Zuma and what has inappropriately been termed state capture (already captured but turned to more deeply entrenched corrupt practices). The loyalty to and trust in the ANC on the part of the people has been eroded through its abuse, with the result that the political credit with which to neoliberalise has been spent and the Tripartite Alliance has correspondingly unravelled within and across its three components. However, nothing has yet emerged to offer alternatives other than more of the same with a new face in charge, Cyril Ramaphosa, though one hardly free of personal wealth and compromise.

Essentially, then, progressive forces have been disempowered in the post-apartheid period, with corresponding systemic processes of disengagement of the potential for engaged and interdisciplinary scholarship or scholars. This overview frames the subsequent account in the chapter of post-apartheid economics and the role of Vishnu Padayachee within it.

The post-apartheid context

Get too close to your object of study and you cannot see the wood for the trees. Get too far away and, as a scholar, you are liable to impose inappropriate preconceptions. In my own work on South Africa, I benefited considerably from an initial distance from, if not ignorance of, as well as abhorrence for the apartheid system. I was also lucky in my first two readings, one by Duncan Innes on Anglo American (Innes 1983) and the other a government report on Eskom (RSA 1985). Although antagonistic to the notion of the US as being driven by a military-industrial complex, these readings did inspire me to characterise South Africa as a minerals-energy complex in light of the close and coordinated relations between South African mining capital and its associated conglomerates and the state and state enterprises (Fine and Rustomjee 1996).

In some respects, this specification is more easily recognised by setting aside the role of apartheid. For, jumping to the present, there is some virtue in understanding the neoliberalisation of South Africa without designating it primarily as 'post-apartheid', and so burdened by considerations of how apartheid is a lingering, even leading, burdensome determinant as opposed to a conditioning factor. Where the apartheid/post-apartheid division is particularly germane, however, is in the extent to which the apartheid economy, despite its global connections as a major mineral producer and exporter, was initially insulated from the early phases of neoliberalism. As a result, the post-apartheid economy is readily seen as complex in both having combined, or overlain, the different phases of neoliberalism and having done so, or having caught up with elsewhere, particularly – even astonishingly – rapidly.[3]

How it did so, and what it did, are heavily marked by the heritage of the apartheid economy, and the central role of the minerals-energy complex within it. As apartheid entered its transitional phase to formal democracy, the minerals-energy complex was already marked by a number of key features. The first of these, as already remarked, was a close, integral relationship between a small number of conglomerate mining houses and the state and its nationalised industries, constituting the core of the minerals-energy complex. Privately owned coal mines produced fuel for state-owned power stations at guaranteed profits, with the electricity used to extract and process ore for privately run gold mines. And a similar relationship existed in regard to coal exports, with quotas allocated by the state, transported by state-owned rail to state-owned ports for sale at premium prices. Comparable observations can be made for steel, and for South Africa's (unique, sanction-avoiding) coal-to-oil facility, SASOL, itself the basis for petrochemicals, and so on. In addition, though, especially in light of restrictions on the export of capital and informal or formal sanctions impeding inward investment, but more longstanding, was the extensive spread of conglomerate ownership across sectors not necessarily attached or linked to the minerals-energy complex core.

The second key feature historically, most sharply revealed by the formal adoption of apartheid in the post-war period by the National Party government, was the disjuncture between the economic power held within the minerals-energy complex, variously caricatured as English or foreign, and the political power that lay with Afrikanerdom. Uneasy compromises over the economy were reached, particularly through the growth of nationalised industries that served the minerals-energy complex and beyond. However, long before the apartheid period drew to a close, two major political developments were realised: while competitive conflicts still remained, large-scale conglomerate capital had been closely integrated, across the minerals-energy complex core; and, simultaneously, the representation of small-scale Afrikaner capital had been subordinated to large-scale capital. Consequently, for example, the 1970s witnessed a major expansion of the minerals-energy complex core, strongly coordinated by the state, in response both to the oil crisis and to the unprecedented increase in the price of gold following the breakdown of Bretton Woods.

The third feature, a major mechanism underpinning these economic and political developments, was the use of finance to promote Afrikaner capital, with English capital having long been integrated into (global) financial markets to meet the funding needs of large-scale mining operations. Consequently, the South African economy was marked by a particularly well-developed (internationalised) financial sector as apartheid ended.

Fourth, an enduring feature of the South African economy, with a few exceptions, has been the failure to have diversified out of the core strengths of the minerals-energy complex along value chains involving capital, intermediate and consumption goods. Initially, this was due to the disjuncture between economic and political power and the tentative, if growing, collaboration across political divides, as the economic power of large-scale Afrikaner capital, its integration with English capital, and its dominance over small-scale capital strengthened. By the time the strategy became politically feasible in the 1970s, the opportunity was taken to further consolidate the minerals-energy complex core in light of oil and gold price increases.

Traditionally, but totally wrongly, the failure to progress in consumption goods has been seen as a failure of import-substituting industrialisation (ISI), as if South Africa's industrialisation depended upon its consumer goods as opposed to its mineral-related sectors. But, in practice, ISI was never attempted in South Africa. Instead, if mistaken for ISI in retrospect, tariff protection to consumer industries was offered more or less on demand as a concession to small-scale (Afrikaner) industry (and agriculture) – as opposed to ISI proper, in which policy targets are intended to coordinate and integrate expansion of consumption goods, not just market relief. Significantly, as the apartheid period was winding down, government reports were clearly aware that continuing with tariff protection was counterproductive, and the only appropriate choices were to abandon it altogether or to supplement it with more extensive measures, a decision essentially postponed under the crisis conditions of the apartheid economy in the 1980s.

Such were the conditions, alongside gross social and economic inequalities, with which South Africa entered the post-apartheid period, or should we say its period of catch-up neoliberalisation as is readily seen in retrospect, leading to the crunching together of neoliberalism's three phases. First and foremost, particularly on the basis of its well-developed financial markets, the South African economy entered an intensive and extensive period of financialisation or, more exactly, economic and social restructuring heavily compromised by financialisation. It might even be considered a classic case, albeit with its own peculiar features.

In brief, financialisation involves the securitisation of streams of revenue that are then subject to speculative financial trading to make profits without producing, which can only be at the expense of the rest of the economy. South Africa's growth of financial assets over the post-apartheid period has, much like the global average, exceeded that of its national income by roughly three times, indicating a heavy role of finance in appropriating from, as opposed to underpinning, growth. Correspondingly, in South Africa during the post-apartheid period, the fastest growing sector has been finance, now putatively contributing 20 per cent to GDP as well as relatively few jobs and more inequality. Essentially this means, as finance itself produces nothing, that finance has stolen 25 per cent of real GDP, claiming it has contributed this to GDP (as 20 per cent is 25 out of 125), while in fact only leaving 80 per cent of actual GDP for other purposes.

As South African financialisation has gathered pace, the majority of its citizens have seen it drawn into their everyday lives through increasing, often stressed, indebtedness (whereas, previously, 40 per cent or so were denied any financial services at all – the most indebted and the most advantaged by financialisation are always the wealthiest). But the abiding impact has been the total deficiency of the financial sector in what mainstream economics designates as its major function, to mobilise and allocate investment (as opposed to speculation). During the post-apartheid period, despite its burgeoning financial sector, the overall level of real investment in the economy has rarely exceeded 20 per cent of GDP, something in the region of 10 per cent too little to meet the needs for economic and social development.

Consequently, the South African economy is best characterised by the five lows. It suffers from low investment, low productivity, low employment, low wages and low social provision. These lows can only be managed, not addressed nor even substantially ameliorated, until low levels of financialised investment are remedied. In the post-apartheid period, however, the financialised, neoliberalised globalisation of the economy has been geared towards the unbundling of conglomerates and their integration, especially the minerals-energy complex core, into multinational corporation activity (not least with offshoring), the outflow of capital (much of it illegally through transfer pricing on minerals, and, on occasion, even exceeding the domestic investment deficiency), and the holding of financial reserves for potential speculative purposes. In addition, the various machinations around black economic empowerment have primarily created a new black elite with (the connections for) the purpose of facilitating these developments through political influence or power, with corresponding parasitic rewards for integration into such restructuring.

In general, the neoliberalisation of the South African economy has been most prominently signalled by what is perceived to be austere macroeconomic policy, alongside trade liberalisation and other similar market-friendly policies. The description of such policies as neoliberal is appropriate, but they are as much the consequence as the cause of South Africa's neoliberalism. Most obviously, if you ignore or are complicit with capital flight, then it makes sense to raise interest rates and constrain government expenditure so that (potentially volatile) short-term inflows of capital can be used to balance long-term outflows. Turning a blind eye to the realities of economic restructuring inevitably leads to a logic of compensating for their effects by whatever means necessary.

However, the leap into neoliberalism also has to be managed politically and ideologically. Understandably, much attention has focused on the 'Faustian Pact' and the discrete steps involving the abandonment of the Macroeconomic Research Group (MERG) programme and the Reconstruction and Development Programme (RDP) after its rapid marginalisation once the ANC was in power, and the adoption of the non-negotiable Growth, Employment and Redistribution (GEAR).[4] MERG had been commissioned to formulate progressive economic policies, through a longstanding and senior ANC activist, Vella Pillay, who was requested by Mandela to lead the project of providing a progressive economic programme. The RDP was the ANC's declared programme. The effective abandonment of both MERG and the RDP was accompanied by correspondingly typical neoliberal political developments around centralised authority: power to decide and coordinate were rapidly devolved to the Ministry of Finance (and, subsequently, also to the Presidency) and, initially, paved the way for what was to follow, key ministries (finance and minerals and energy) and the South African Reserve Bank remaining with the National Party under the terms of the Government of National Unity. The mass democratic movement was effectively demobilised, and the SACP and COSATU were effectively incorporated as more or less willing partners in crime.

All of this is well known, and the various explanatory factors involved, from international conspiracy and coercion through to lack of professional economists and knowledge of economics by the leadership, have been well rehearsed so that emphasising one or another of them has some but limited merit; in general, these factors reinforced one another and ran together. Instead, what stands out, and yet is more readily missed, is just how rapidly and fully earlier aspirations evaporated alongside resistance to defend, let alone promote, them.

Here the material culture of South African politics comes to the fore. Entering the post-apartheid period, political cultures and organisations ranged across the entire spectrum, not only from left to right, but also from those of the Keynesian period (including both social democracy and Soviet communism, albeit increasingly in disrepute) to those across the three phases of neoliberalism. Initially, with the ANC in the lead and without denying the presence of some internal oppositions and conflicts, the Tripartite Alliance easily held these cultures together, drawing upon a single purpose, liberation and the prospective undoing of the inequities of apartheid, and an unprecedented degree of trust and loyalty – to the goals, to the organisations and to the leadership.

In this light, a determined faction within the leadership, presumed to be led by Mbeki, successfully adopted a neoliberal strategy in all but name. By bringing Mandela on board, a further aspect of material culture came into play, revolving around the processes of (individual) positioning in prospective outcomes. These processes went far beyond the (if heavily present) self-enrichment and climbing of this or that greasy pole. For access to position, power, wealth and/or influence depended upon unquestioned acceptance of trust and loyalty to the neoliberal turn and its leadership. Fail to support and you were out, bringing root and branch leadership momentum behind the shift and, further, requiring contempt, stigma and marginalisation for those who failed to fall in line.

Just imagine for a moment that alternative world in which the MERG proposals (MERG 1993) had been adopted and aggressively pursued by the leadership. Is there any doubt that those who turned against it on the leadership's instruction would have been fully supportive if the leadership had stuck with its initial intentions when commissioning MERG? And even spirited opposition from the ANC's opponents (the white and international establishment) in that alternative world could well have been more muted than was experienced from the ANC itself in reality, given MERG's own emphasis upon state intervention to promote private through public investment, as opposed to redistribution of, and assault upon, private ownership as such. Wherever they might have led, the MERG proposals were at most radical social democratic, and entirely compatible, if with some detail and rationale attached, with the ANC intentions that had prevailed previously. The shift in posture during negotiations may have reflected a fear that they could fail at the expense of formal democratisation and liberation, but it also seemed to reflect a preemptive strike on who was going to hold political (and economic) power, and how.

Deference to leadership, and the reasons and motives for it, explain how the neoliberal turn should be so rapid and full, with limited contestation.[5] No more than symbolically, it speaks to my own experience of meteoric rise and fall. From nowhere, I was elevated to a position of engaging with, and drafting policy documents for, the ANC. This, no doubt, arose out of my trusted connections, direct or indirect, with the Communist Party of Great Britain, Joe Slovo, and the British National

Union of Mineworkers and, subsequently, with MERG. Yet, as indicated, within a year or so of the latter being commissioned, Mandela was being instructed to disown the programme it proposed. At its presentation to the ANC, as a show of solidarity, one after another of the ministers or directors-general in waiting showed themselves to be heavily opposed to its policies, often with ignorance of their content in equal measure, even though MERG had genuinely been constructed to meet the ANC's perceived aspirations and commissioned as such.[6]

Following the presentation of the MERG proposals, then, the ANC's response was not just the rejection of a set of policy proposals but also of those who were associated with them. My own relations with the ANC and with the SACP came to a more or less abrupt halt. Immediately afterwards, there remained at most lingering calls for my support from the trade union movement and an (unexplained and anomalous) invitation to me to join the Presidential Labour Market Commission as one of four international expert advisers.

I was sufficiently naïve not to question why this had happened until long after the event. Understandably, I had not been happy with the direction taken by policy-making, and the rejection of MERG, in particular the way it was done. But, until I was prompted much later to rethink these developments, and more deeply, I saw this as the movement's choice and of no wider significance. It was only when MERG, and its role in the transition, became an object of merely historical interest that I was forced to think about the process involved and its role in what unfolded more generally. In short, left-wing economists, especially those associated with MERG and the like, were designated as *personae non grata*, treated contemptuously as unrealistic and buried in the past (of communism or even social democracy), and dismissed without serious consideration or debate. I felt this particularly in regard to Vella Pillay who, apart from leading the MERG project, had an outstanding record as both activist and practising economist, and who reasonably became both bewildered and embittered by the way he was treated by his erstwhile comrades.[7] And ultimately, or long before that, even those committed to progressive change from within government found themselves thwarted by the structures and dynamics involved, voluntarily or forcibly leaving for the private sector to pursue their ambitions alongside those who had done so for less altruistic reasons.

Such vignettes, writ large, tell us much about the evolution of neoliberalised South Africa. It is arguable that the direction taken by policy for the post-apartheid economy reflected a deep leadership distrust of the working class and its and other progressive organisations, in terms of being incapable of being fiscally or otherwise responsible (as opposed, laughably in retrospect, to a prospective black capitalist class). In addition, such postures may have given rise to antipathy to forms of provisioning that had the potential to create progressive organisations and demands – whether around economic or social provision. In short, the imperative was to command both policy and the policy-making process, the very antithesis of democracy and liberation. Such post-apartheid developments have heavily conditioned post-apartheid economics.

Post-apartheid economics: From unravelling to disempowered
Under apartheid, with a few significant exceptions, academic economics and its offshoots can best be described as mainstream, weak, outdated and liable to be complicit with apartheid imperatives. As no doubt in many other fields, those who managed to rise above these confinements would be inclined to seek training and careers for themselves abroad. Such loss of talent was inevitably reinforced by choice or necessity, in light of any compunctions about remaining and so being intellectually compromised by the ideologies and practices of apartheid. Even to the degree that there was some latitude in terms of academic freedom, heterodox economics would have been hard pressed to leverage a strong and stable position, with influence beyond academia, given the institutionalised pincer dominance of both apartheid and intradisciplinary orthodoxy.

Unsurprisingly, then, home-grown heterodox economics was extremely limited within South Africa (other than a small, acceptable current of neo-Austrianism), although the mainstream could and did certainly display its antipathy in principle to apartheid as obstructing the free and efficient operation of markets as a starting point for efficiency. Instead, then, heterodox political economy (and progressive social science more generally) drew upon a rich and eclectic combination of alternative overlapping influences, sources and themes. The first and foremost influence stemmed from the need to understand the nature and persistence of apartheid itself, and how it might best be contested. Second was the contributions of those individuals who had benefited from overseas education. Third was the role of progressive movements around the anti-apartheid movement and trade unions, and the protection offered to some degree by academic freedom, with a mix of institutions and specific individuals tending to be to the fore.

As a result, as the apartheid period was drawing to a close, political economy was often left to economic historians but drew heavily upon interdisciplinary contributions, with the most significant and high-quality of these contributions deriving from the outward reach of disciplines other than economics. The debate over the functionality of apartheid to capitalism between liberals and Marxists is a leading example, as is Wolpe's cheap labour power hypothesis (inspired by French anthropologists' discussions of articulation of modes of production). Also significant are the understanding of apartheid as being structured upon the tensions between foreign/English economic and national/Afrikaner political power (drawing upon Poulantzas), and the notion of apartheid as racial Fordism (imposing regulation theory on South Africa). There were also very important studies in economic history, especially relating to mining, agriculture, industrial and labour relations and migration.

In the transition from apartheid, the situation changed dramatically and quickly in terms of the balance of approaches, sources and subject matter. Foremost was the switch from understanding the relationship between capitalism and apartheid to formulating policy proposals for post-apartheid South Africa, with a general presumption, often implicit but occasionally explicit, that the basis of the post-apartheid economy would be some form of non-racial capitalism seeking to redress the inherited inequities of apartheid to a greater or lesser extent at a greater or lesser speed. Second, there was a deluge of mainstream contributions, dovetailing with those deriving from (corporate) think tanks, with sanctions and the stigma of apartheid no longer a barrier to the contribution of foreign participants, and the World Bank and the International Monetary Fund to the fore, heavily in liaison with the old regime (and its personnel) in the first instance, and with the new government, especially once GEAR was adopted. Third, if more as a minority sport of temporary symbolic value, was an at most temporary flourishing of heterodox economics, not least in relation to the preparation of the RDP, the role of MERG (in training black economists as its initial and prime task), and, particularly prominently, the Industrial Strategy Project (ISP).

The fate of the ISP offers some insight into the trajectory of post-apartheid heterodox economics. It was extraordinarily well resourced in terms of funds and personnel, and attracted some formal political support, not least through connections with Alec Erwin. Its intellectual inspiration was provided by one of its four co-directors, Raphie Kaplinsky, who hailed from the Institute of Development Studies at the University of Sussex, where Mbeki had formed ideas about dependency theory and economics that later had a considerable influence on his policies. Paradoxically, the ISP was to some degree the descendant of the Economic Trends Group (ET), led by Stephen Gelb, which had dissolved with his disgruntled departure from it. But what the ET and ISP had in common was a predilection for forcing the ill-fitting French regulation approach onto South Africa – racial Fordism for Gelb but, even more bizarrely (see below), post-Fordism, the *filière* approach and flexible specialisation (flec-spec) for the ISP. Kaplinsky had presumably picked up flec-spec from his Sussex colleague Robin Murray, who was its leading exponent in the UK.

The ISP's application of the flec-spec approach to South Africa was totally inappropriate as the core of a strategy for the post-apartheid economy in general and for industry in particular. It simply failed to acknowledge the overwhelming roles of the mineral-energy complex and finance, not least because they did not even begin to fit readily into the flec-spec framing. As a result, there was little, or false, diagnosis of the nature of the South African economy and, in particular, of the need to remedy the continuing historical failure to diversify out of the mineral-energy complex core as a strategy for industrial development. Training, support to niche sectors to upgrade, and the virtues of increased competitiveness were unduly exaggerated at the expense of dealing with levels of investment and economies of scale and scope across the major sectors of the economy.

Whatever its merits, the ISP disappeared more or less without influential trace. The point of recalling it is to highlight how the ISP engaged with much of what heterodox resources and influences there were in the immediate post-apartheid period, arguably at some expense to other approaches and influences, and with little or no impact upon building a broader constituency of heterodoxy in substance and personnel. However, the ISP did have considerable purchase over policy formulation (if not policy-making) at the Department of Trade and Industry (DTI), especially in promoting a sectoral approach and in misplaced over-emphasis on increasing trade with other African countries. Whatever the

DTI's success in the first, and easier, step of formulating a scatter-gun of policies, the second step of seeing these policies implemented has been hamstrung by lack of resources and political clout to implement its programmes other than piecemeal and ineffectively, and by the overwhelming deadweight of being hemmed in by the absence of any strategy to exert power over South Africa's major mineral-energy complex sectors and industries.

Consequently, the ISP is one early exception that proves the rule that heterodox economics in toto, let alone its interdisciplinarity, was entirely disempowered in the post-apartheid period. The fate of MERG is indicative, recalling that it was set up to train black economists. Not just MERG's proposals but its personnel and ethos had to be disempowered or disengaged. Continuing training and research projects, originating in SOAS (which had already trained many black economists through its separate distance learning programmes), with committed funding, failed to materialise simply because they would not receive a stamp of approval from the ANC leadership. This sheds some light on the idea that the adoption of neoliberalism more or less as soon as the ANC got into government is to be explained by its having no alternatives or alternative economists of its own. If so, the natural reaction would have been to seek to make up the shortfall, not to stand in the way of doing so (subject to the path-dependent rationale that, once neoliberalism was adopted, antipathy to heterodoxy inevitably became set in stone).

Sadly, post-apartheid economic policy has not only been abysmal but has also shifted from one casually informed framing to another, from GEAR at the outset to the National Development Plan and beyond currently. Heterodoxy has only managed to survive at the margins, thanks to the dedication of (at most small groups of) individuals in fragmented locations. With African economics, and training, dominated by the World Bank and its Oxford offshoot (the Centre for the Study of African Economies), the Economic Society of South Africa remains mainstream, and the discipline has been more or less untouched despite (a) the main source of the mainstream within academia, and beyond in media, think tanks and the like, deriving from apartheid origins; (b) the explosion of the demand for pluralism worldwide, especially after the global financial crisis, and its institutionalisation in many heterodox movements and organisations; (c) the increasing demand for decolonisation of academia; (d) the variety of demands deriving from

South African student movements; and (e) the unavoidable failings of the South African economy and polity.

However, more promising, as a late exception that also proves the rule about disempowered heterodoxy in the post-apartheid period, has been the successful campaign for a national minimum wage. It was sustained by a combination of outstanding academic research, communication, networking and campaigning, drawing strong if not uniform support from trade unions and political organisations, striking popular consciousness in times of low wages and high poverty and unemployment, and having the benefit of high-level intervention from government (Ramaphosa himself being brought on board).

Significantly, this rare, even unique, example of success has been closely associated with the late but welcome institutional breathing of life into heterodox economics in a South African context. Much of this has been spearheaded by the newly formed Institute for Economic Justice (IEJ), founded by the leading personnel in the academic campaign for the national minimum wage. The IEJ has a wide programme of academic research informing an equally wide-ranging set of policy issues. It has also been instrumental in promoting Rethinking Economics for Africa, an organisation of students at the University of the Witwatersrand (Wits) and a latecomer counterpart to the African Programme on Rethinking Development Economics, which for more than a decade attempted to fan the few sparks of heterodox economics into life in (South) Africa and beyond, campaigning for pluralism and alternatives in (the teaching of) economics.

Locating Vishnu

As much as these new initiatives are most welcome and important, and, hopefully, the shape of things to come, what still stands out in the South African context is just how much there has been a syndrome of 'so little, so late', a moniker that applies equally to economic and social development in the post-apartheid period. To some degree, all that has gone before points to the connections between these dual deficits. This applies in the context not only of South Africa (and its minerals-energy complex corporate restructuring, with incorporation of black economic empowerment more generally) but also of globalised, neoliberalised, financialised contemporary capitalism. This, after all, was the world into which the formally democratically liberated society was both released and, for the main part, captured through more or less willing surrender. To put it bluntly, compared to the successful initiative on minimum wages, and the current endeavours of the IEJ and of others that have gone before, where are those for health, education, agriculture, housing, and so on? This is not to say that nothing has occurred across these and other sectors coming from engaged, committed and conscientious scholars, but that the results in terms of impact have been weak, ineffectual and marked by a lack of strong, organised presence around home-grown (or any other) heterodox economics.

This is despite the concerted efforts of a few isolated institutional bases and a few dedicated scholars of ability, integrity and conscientiousness in research and teaching, of whom Vishnu is a leading example. It is surely telling that someone with his stature and experience should have been more or less forced out of his longstanding academic base in Durban and ended up at Wits, where heterodoxy has only just begun to find a degree of security, again thanks to those who kept it alive in the past against mainstream hostility, and those who have promoted it in the present (as was Vishnu's own mission upon arriving there, until his tragic, early death).

While, as a heterodox economist, it would be easy to label Vishnu as a post-Keynesian, this is slightly misleading. First, within that school, it is important to see his approach as more informal and discursive than attached to formal model-building and statistical methods (although empirical as well as other primary and secondary historical material was vital to his research). But, second, post-Keynesianism does not cover his much broader approach and contributions, which straddle and fall under the umbrella rubric of applied fields – historically, institutionally and empirically informed, extending far beyond the methods and scope of (post-Keynesian) economics and political economy.

So, no question, Vishnu ticks all the boxes of the scholarly part of the engaged (interdisciplinary) scholar. But the engaged part is more problematic, raising, in the first instance, the question of what it is to be an engaged scholar, potentially ranging in conceptualisation from some sort of organic intellectual through intellectual agitator-activist to policy adviser. Certainly, Vishnu was engaged, not least in having served on the board of the Reserve Bank. But why was it that he was not even more engaged, especially given his much broader range of talents than those of a scholar, incorporating management, administrative, practical and personal skills?

Some might seek an answer in Vishnu's own personality and character – his dedication to scholarship and his broader interests and activities that were so dear to him and made his lifestyle what it was. I consider this to be a case of blaming the victim. Vishnu's 'leisure' activities and leisurely manner to a large extent concealed an extraordinarily high level of hard, effective, dedicated work. More fundamentally, the thrust of what I have argued previously is that heterodox economists in post-apartheid South Africa were deeply structurally disengaged by much more general processes of disempowerment that rendered them neither wanted nor able to prosper. To paraphrase Karl Marx, the engaged scholar can only be made in circumstances that are not self-chosen.

Paradoxically, then, Vishnu's own personality (try never to let disappointment get in the way of enjoyment, for yourself or others), his capacities for collaboration and cooperation, and the breadth and depth of his contributions can give the impression of satisfaction rather than frustration with the levels and directions of his engagements as a scholar and otherwise. His experience and bitter disappointment, deriving initially from being an editor for MERG, gave him a head start in active antipathy to ANC economic policy-making (from a post-Keynesian perspective of inequality and inadequate effective demand and beyond). This placed him from the outset, anomalous appointment to the Reserve Bank apart, on the margins of policy-making engagement, but he remained dedicated to engagement where he could be both useful and retain his integrity. From this, so many of us benefited in joint work or simply amiable, informative discussions in light of a calm, determined persona, openness to the views and contributions of others, and apparent lack of bitterness.

Others, at all levels, have responded to the context of (scholarly) disengagement and disempowerment in a variety of ways, displaying one or more responses in mixed combinations, open to shifting over time. The options are and have been of being (over-)active, inactive, resentful, frustrated, envious or, to the extent of being in a position to do so, pursuing self-interest by becoming incorporated into the mainstream and establishment through combinations of political position, government or public sector appointment, or private sector pursuit of enrichment and/or – possibly more worthy – doing stuff, with various degrees of dishonesty and/or rationalisation/self-justification through appeal to pragmatism and realism.

In short, Vishnu's position derived not simply from his talents, integrity, conscientiousness, collegiality and hard work. He also finessed, with considerable aplomb, the personal, practical and intellectual tensions of being an engaged scholar in an age of scholarly disengagement. He was fully engaged, but not so much that he fell victim to the greasy pole or slippery slope. Hopefully, what he has left us in our memories and in his body of work will inspire more of the same, and contribute to renewal of an age of scholarly engagement which can prosper for the benefit of one and all.

Notes
1. Thanks especially to John Sender for his comments on the essay.
2. This section of the chapter is a drastic summary of half a lifetime's work, drawing in part on select references listed, if not necessarily cited (Ashman and Fine 2013; Ashman, Fine and Karwowski 2021; Ashman, Fine and Newman 2011; Fine 1994, 1995, 2009a, 2009b, 2012a, 2012b, 2016, 2022, 2023; Padayachee and Fine 2019), with occasional co-authorship with Vishnu, his frequent support and collaboration, and much discussion.
3. Recall that Harold Wolpe (1995) intervened in the post-apartheid debate to question whether the appeal of social democratic policy-making was blinding the mass democratic movement to the pitfalls of failing to challenge capitalist state power. Yet, social democracy was soon wiped from the policy agenda (Reynolds, Fine and Van Niekerk 2019). In passing, note that Wolpe is an early and leading example of a (dis)engaged scholar, as discussed in the final section of this chapter, in the field of education and its policy-making.
4. For the best account of this, see Padayachee and Van Niekerk (2019). See also the collection edited by Pons-Vignon and Segatti (2013).
5. Once again, my own experience is that there was a golden moment for self-advancement during the period of transition, with erstwhile students experiencing meteoric rises in positions of power, influence and wealth across public and private sectors – the low-hanging fruit for the qualified and the connected were bountiful.
6. Having drafted sections of the MERG report (MERG 1993) on education, health, housing and electrification, I was particularly at the rough end of harsh criticism. See Fine (2023) in response to Desai (forthcoming).
7. See Padayachee and Sender (2018). Thus, Pillay also falls into the category of (dis)engaged scholar discussed below, with a relatively rare movement (and balance of weight) from 'engaged' to 'scholar', rather than in the more common opposite direction.

References

Ashman, S. and B. Fine. 2013. 'The Meaning of Marikana'. *New Agenda* 51: 27–30.
Ashman, S., B. Fine and E. Karwowski. 2021. 'The Relevance of Financialization for African Economies: Lessons from South Africa'. SOAS Department of Economics Working Paper 245. https://www.soas.ac.uk/economics/research/workingpapers/file156232.pdf.
Ashman, S., B. Fine and S. Newman. 2011. 'Amnesty International? The Nature, Scale and Impact of Capital Flight from South Africa'. *Journal of Southern African Studies* 37 (1): 7–25.
Desai, A. forthcoming. 'The Politics of Economics in South Africa, 1990–94: The Case of the Macroeconomic Research Group'. *Journal of Contemporary African Studies*.
Fine, B. 1994. '"Politics and Economics in ANC Economic Policy": An Alternative Assessment'. *Transformation* 25: 19–33.
———. 1995. 'Flexible Production and Flexible Theory: The Case of South Africa'. *Geoforum* 26 (2): 107–19.
———. 2009a. 'Submission to the COSATU Panel of Economists on "The Final Recommendations of the International Panel on Growth" (The Harvard Panel)'. *Transformation* 69: 5–30.
———. 2009b. 'A Rejoinder to "A Response to Fine's 'Harvard Group Shores up Shoddy Governance'"'. *Transformation* 69: 66–79.
———. 2012a. 'Assessing South Africa's New Growth Path: Framework for Change?' *Review of African Political Economy* 39 (134): 551–68. Revised from B. Fine. 2011. 'New Growth Path – Elephant in the Room'. *The Shopsteward* 20 (4): 16–25.
———. 2012b. 'Chronicle of a Developmental Transformation Foretold: South Africa's National Development Plan in Hindsight'. *Transformation* 78: 115–32.
———. 2016. 'Across Developmental State and Social Compacting: The Peculiar Case of South Africa'. ISER Working Paper 2016/1. Grahamstown: Institute of Social and Economic Research, Rhodes University. https://eprints.soas.ac.uk/34148/1/iserwp.pdf.
———. 2022. 'Locating Vishnu as Political Economist, a Personal Account: The Director's Cut'. Unpublished essay, available from the author.
———. 2023. 'The Enigma of the Post-apartheid Economic Transition: Insights from the Fate of MERG and a Personal Journey'. Response to A. Desai. forthcoming. 'The Politics of Economics in South Africa, 1990–94: The Case of the Macroeconomic Research Group'. *Journal of Contemporary African Studies*.
Fine, B. and Z. Rustomjee. 1996. *The Political Economy of South Africa: From Minerals-Energy Complex to Industrialisation*. London and Johannesburg: Hurst and Wits University Press.
Innes, D. (1983) *Anglo American and the Rise of Modern South Africa*. London: Heinemann Educational.
MERG (Macroeconomic Research Group). 1993. *Making Democracy Work: A Framework for Macroeconomic Policy in South Africa*. Cape Town: Centre for Development Studies, University of the Western Cape.

Padayachee, V. and B. Fine. 2019. 'The Role and Influence of the IMF on Economic Policy in South Africa's Transition to Democracy: The 1993 CCFF Revisited'. *Review of African Political Economy* 46 (159): 157–67.

Padayachee, V. and J. Sender. 2018. 'Vella Pillay: Revolutionary Activism and Economic Policy Analysis'. *Journal of Southern African Studies* 44 (1): 149–65. https://doi.org/10.1080/03057070.2018.1405644.

Padayachee, V. and R. van Niekerk. 2019. *Shadow of Liberation: Contestation and Compromise in the Economic and Social Policy of the African National Congress, 1943–1996*. Johannesburg: Wits University Press.

Pons-Vignon, N. and A. Segatti. 2013. '"The Art of Neoliberalism": Accumulation, Institutional Change and Social Order since the End of Apartheid'. *Review of African Political Economy* 40 (138): 537–55.

Reynolds, J., B. Fine and R. van Niekerk (eds). 2019. *Race, Class and the Post-Apartheid Democratic State*. Pietermaritzburg: University of KwaZulu-Natal Press.

RSA (Republic of South Africa). 1985. *Report of the Commission of Inquiry into the Supply of Electricity in the Republic of South Africa*. Pretoria: Republic of South Africa.

Wolpe, H. 1995. 'The Uneven Transition from Apartheid in South Africa'. *Transformation* 27: 88–101.

14

Accounting for Some Recent Deaths in South Africa
Zombie Economics Blues

John Sender

I've lost a friend
And I'm under pressure
Can't stop singing this song
Cause I'm under pressure
— Oliver Mtukudzi, 'Under Pressure'

Too many people are dying in South Africa, especially in rural South Africa. At the same time, too, many brain-dead economic ideas are roaming the nation; they stalk *lekgotlas* and webinars in South Africa, their hackneyed melodies loudly trumpeting their claims that a 'new improved' snake oil will achieve 'inclusive growth' (and accelerate power generation) while soft-pedalling their responsibility for the mediocre performance of private sector investment and for the dismal recent trend in mortality rates. Aiming to silence these raucous claims would be over-ambitious; and it is even unrealistic to hope they might be persuaded to engage in serious debate over conflicting economic and political ideas, let alone contribute to a harmonious resolution of what the key issues are, and how to approach and resolve them.

This chapter has a more modest objective; I hope to reduce the noise, to pull the plug on a few performers who are dominating economic policy debates, because they hurt my ears with their over-amplified and flat renditions of the old conventional policy songs that Vishnu Padayachee helped me to criticise in 1993. Nearly three decades ago we both worked on the steering committee of the Macroeconomic Research Group (MERG) and, towards the end of 1993, the steering committee asked us to edit and finalise a draft of the MERG report (MERG 1993). It is sad that, after all these years, so many South African policy-makers (and economists and policy entrepreneurs) can continue to downplay, if not ignore, key economic arguments published by MERG.

Years of collaborative work have taught me that Vishnu was a remarkably tolerant and affable person. He was loyal to old comrades and was able to relish courteous interchanges with economists who had diverse backgrounds, training and experience. When later we worked together again to put the record straight about the influence of Vella Pillay on economic policy (Padayachee and Sender 2018), Vishnu was especially firm (and fair to a fault); he redacted any attempt to tarnish the halo worn by economists very close to the African National Congress (ANC) leadership, although he knew that they had not hesitated to join the board of the largest private health care group, to accept the blandishments of Goldman Sachs, JP Morgan, ABSA, AngloGold Ashanti, Old Mutual, Rothschild and so on, or to jump at the chance of working for well-funded institutions that rarely support progressive economists, such as Brookings, the Harvard Kennedy and Business Schools and the World Trade Institute in Switzerland.

I miss Vishnu's calm efforts to reign in my polemical propensities and will commemorate him here by highlighting a few recent policy interventions, rather than attributing South Africa's abysmal performance to the personal defects of individual politicians and intellectuals. It was certainly not Vishnu's style, for example, to dismiss individuals such as Trevor Manuel and Alec Erwin, by calling them 'confirmed neoliberals' (Bond 2021), or to ridicule Alan Hirsch because of his 'weak and one-sided' attempts to legitimise the ANC (Fryer 2006: 605). Vishnu's approach, which I struggle to follow in this chapter, was much closer to the nuanced practice of those historians and moral philosophers who, even when writing about the worst fascist horrors of the 1940s, refuse to think in Manichean terms or to adopt the shorthand solution of demonising easily identified perpetrators (Zbinden and Todorov 2004).

I begin with a mournful overture to set the scene. Readers are reminded about the appalling scale of death from HIV/AIDS. I also insist that in the period since 1990, discussed below under the heading 'Pandemic I', the number of *preventable* deaths in South Africa has been horrifically high, in both absolute and relative terms. More recently, as discussed under the heading 'Pandemic II', South Africans, especially those living in poorer rural communities, have suffered from relatively high Covid-19 mortality rates and there has been an accelerating failure, especially in some of the poorer provinces, to reduce mortality thanks to the failure to vaccinate the poorest rural children against the common diseases continuing to kill them.

The monopolisation of the supply of Covid-19 vaccines by rich countries is said, especially in nationalistic speeches delivered to other African leaders, to have made a major contribution to this suffering and to the inadequate rate of vaccination in South Africa. This claim will briefly be discussed (and compared to earlier conspiratorial claims about the evil intentions of foreign pharmaceutical corporations exporting harmful antiretroviral potions). More generally, I argue that the inadequate policy responses to Pandemic I and Pandemic II appear to have some similarities. These may partly be explained by, and are certainly consistent if not complicit with, the malign influence of mainstream economists on South African thinking about state intervention in the health and other sectors.

I end the chapter – with what has now become the refrain of an old classic tune – by emphasising differences between the MERG report's approach to policy issues and the arguments that many economists currently make when discussing public expenditure on health (and other forms of state intervention). The final words are a strained search for a silver lining, for reasons to be less pessimistic about possibilities for positive economic outcomes.

How the living die: Pandemic I
The number of deaths from HIV/AIDS per 100 000 people in South Africa peaked in 2006 at 663, before falling to 251 in 2019. In other African countries, the average mortality rate from HIV/AIDS has been very much *lower* – about one-third of the mortality rate from HIV/AIDS in South Africa; and the comparable rate for all upper-middle-income countries is lower still – below 9 per 100 000 in 2019.[1] It can readily be seen that South African government policy has had a direct and dramatic effect on these trends in AIDS-related deaths.

While deaths from HIV/AIDS increased at a terrifying speed between 1997 and 2006, after 2006 there was a remarkable decline in HIV/AIDS and tuberculosis mortality.[2] This decline can be directly attributed to *new policies* adopted by the South African authorities (as well as to the support of some international donors). The government reluctantly agreed – after five years of bullying, prevarication and litigation – to begin to distribute antiretrovirals (ARVs) (Johnson et al. 2022). As late as 2004, fewer than 50 000 South Africans were receiving ARVs and, although 4.6 million people did manage to gain access to ARVs by 2018 (equivalent to about 60 per cent of the population living with HIV), the inordinate delay in improving free access to ARVs caused the death of many hundreds of thousands of black African adults (and thousands of children), especially those living in the rural areas of the poorer provinces (Achoki et al. 2022; Burger, Burger and Van Doorslaer 2022; Kabudula et al. 2021).

These dismal facts are well known, as are the names of the most prominent national and provincial ANC leaders who, by stubbornly denying the efficacy of ARVs while slandering activist critics of denialism, may be considered responsible for so many deaths. But what was the broader ideological context encouraging widespread fear of ARVs and welcoming the advice of economists claiming that pharmaceutical treatment was unaffordable? Hein Marais provides an answer to some of the contextual questions; he notes that denialist claims were not only warmly applauded by almost *all* ANC parliamentarians,[3] but 'scarcely any ANC figure of note publicly broke ranks, including stalwarts revered for their independence of thought and the courage of their convictions' (Marais 2012). When the ANC's National Executive Committee (NEC) met in March 2002 to discuss AIDS policy, there was a general rush to rebuke and rebuff Nelson Mandela because he had made statements critical of Thabo Mbeki's (and Peter Mokaba's) position on ARVs. At the end of the meeting the NEC issued a statement asserting that these drugs 'could not be provided in the public health system because of prohibitive costs' (Heywood 2005: 15–16; Jobson 2013).

Trade union leaders such as Cyril Ramaphosa, as well as key employers including the Chamber of Mines, sympathised with Mbeki's rejection of the results of rigorous academic medical research – on the spurious grounds that such research fuelled racist sexual stereotypes and the stigmatisation of miners (Webster 2022). Many of Mbeki's feelings and prejudices were even more widely shared; in 2006 (according to reliable Afrobarometer results), about two-thirds of South Africans who were ANC supporters approved of the government's handling of AIDS

– Mbeki's national job approval rating was even higher, at 77 per cent (Lodge 2015). Probably a large majority of young people had become convinced that the internationally accepted scientific research on HIV/ AIDs 'reflected deeply entrenched white racist beliefs and concepts about Africans and black people' (Lawson 2008: 263).

Popular support for lethal policies intensified when intellectuals (as well as opportunist political leaders at national and provincial levels) began to fan scattered but glowing embers of nationalist sentiment. The malevolent foreign forces many intellectuals identified as threatening the nation were not just the usual suspects (the CIA and the pharmaceutical multinational corporations), but also the World Health Organization – accused of 'pushing' ARVs in South Africa – while ignoring their dangerous side effects.

It is not difficult to point to other epidemics in Africa (such as Ebola in Liberia) where much of the population, equally or more traumatised by a long history of violence, displacement and corruption, could readily be persuaded (by radio reports, for example) that corrupt domestic and foreign elites – supported by UN agencies and the CIA – were recruiting nurses to inject poisons (Epstein 2014). In rural South Africa, historians and anthropologists regard the range and complexity of popular beliefs and prejudices about AIDS as bewildering, with too little understood about the origins and impact of these beliefs (Delius and Glaser 2005).

There is, however, clear evidence that a high proportion of those currently living with HIV/AIDS have continued to make use of traditional healers, even when they are receiving ARVs; moreover, because they relied on treatment from traditional health practitioners *before* seeking help from conventional medical practitioners, a very large number of South Africans prolong the period when they risk infecting others (Mothibe and Sibanda 2019). Official policies and institutions are funding and encouraging traditional healers while promoting African spirituality, thereby increasing the morbidity and mortality risks associated with delayed treatment; the South African government's stated objective in 2022 was to remove South Africans' historical bias – their long-standing preference for high-cost Western health care over older (and cheaper) care traditions.[4]

In addition to the Directorate of Traditional Medicine established within the National Department of Health, generously funded South African think tanks serve as platforms for prominent intellectuals to lament all forms of 'imposed alien modernity' and to promote an African Renaissance (Netshitenzhe 2015). Wishful thinking about solidarity with other African countries, and assertions about the benefits of south-south and especially regional cooperation, are highlighted in these think tanks' discussions about reducing the costs of epidemics, for example in the policy conclusions published by the Mapungubwe Institute for Strategic Reflection (Mazibuko 2019). The Human Sciences Research Council supports the work of researchers on the Covid-19 epidemic who advocate a switch to 'people's science', while criticising the role of 'Western' theories and 'Western medical experts' (Bank and Sharpley 2020: 7, 19). Steven Friedman is one of South Africa's most respected public intellectuals. During the Covid-19 epidemic, he also found fault with 'curative medicine valued by the west' and now advocates an alternative approach based on learning from African countries, contextually appropriate forms of 'peoples science', communal ties and traditional African healers (Friedman 2021: 114–17).[5]

It should come as no surprise that both the MERG report (which included the proposal for a National Health Service focusing on primary and preventative provision), as well as later NGO proposals made in the 1990s for the immediate distribution of ARVs, were denounced because they were 'Western'. For example, economists at Stellenbosch University who remained well connected to key state institutions responsible for economic policy in the 1990s (as well as earlier and later) resorted to xenophobic arguments to reject the MERG proposals – on the grounds that they were mainly produced by foreigners (Kentridge 1993).

Proposals for new forms of state intervention were also rejected on other grounds, especially by deploying the tired old arguments of reactionary rhetoric (Sender 1994). For example, those economists dogmatically committed to reducing public expenditure and to fiscal conservatism latched onto the useful assumption that the cost per life-year gained if ARVs were to be distributed to adults would always remain too high (much higher than the cost per life-year gained by promoting abstinence, for example). Yet, they simply failed to take account of the massive reductions in the fiscal burden of HIV treatment that would follow from a scale-up in the distribution of low-cost ARVs (Forsythe et al. 2019). Their argument was that treating adults with ARVs was not cost-effective; in the financially constrained South African public health system this high-cost policy should be rejected as too risky, as unaffordable and impossible (Creese et al. 2002; Marseille, Hofmann and Kahn 2002; Regondi and Whiteside 2012). Others opposed general distribution of ARVs using cruder xenophobic arguments, based on the prejudiced assumption that making these drugs available to immigrant workers was both undesirable and unaffordable (De Gruchy and Vearey 2020).

Many well-known economists subscribed to these impossibility theses, probably because they were unable to imagine that standard ARV treatment costs could possibly fall from about R3 420 per month in 1998 to less than R120 per month in 2009; this imaginative failure was consistent with many other pessimistic (and self-fulfilling) prophecies made by influential advisers to the ANC. These advisers firmly believed that, for the foreseeable future, the South African state would lack the capacity and experience to intervene to promote a domestic supply of low-cost generics, far less to protect and support a nationalised national champion to produce generics – such as the Brazilian national pharmaceutical manufacturer, Farmanguinhos, that partnered so successfully with the public procurement agency CEME (Urias 2019).[6]

Other advisers preferred playing the third-worldist victim card, refusing opportunities to take advantage of readily available supplies from suspect multinational corporations – even when these were offered at lower costs than imported generics (Geffen and Cameron 2009; Lawson 2008). Nationalistic opposition to multinationals involved posturing and not much else. It was not complemented by any practical initiatives to secure South Africa's access to low-cost essential medicines; the policy agenda *excluded* imposing tariffs, using compulsory licences (as in Brazil and Thailand), or providing support to the exercise of Trade-Related Aspects of Intellectual Property Rights (TRIPS) Agreement transition periods (Wilson 2009). Instead, the Pharmaceutical Manufacturers Association in South Africa, the US government and lobbyists for multinational pharmaceutical corporations were at the same time both demonised and appeased; policy-makers bent over backwards to follow the hoary old advice that their overriding priority should be to avoid any restrictions on corporations or commitments to public expenditure that might have a negative effect on '*private sector confidence*' – a mysterious imaginary creature, part Santa Claus and part Tooth Fairy – that would continue to have a remarkably strong influence on the prospects for growth in South Africa (Krugman 2012).

The development of successful import-substituting industries, whether they were to manufacture pharmaceuticals or any other technologically complex goods, would have required massive public investment in tertiary education and in research and development, as attempted in both India and Brazil. Investment on the required scale has never been seriously considered or attempted in South Africa; and, indicatively, the relatively tiny number of doctoral researchers and PhD graduates produced in the country is one clear measure of *inadequate* state intervention in research capacity-building. By 2017, South Africa had only produced about 1 300 doctoral graduates in science and engineering (compared to about 10 500 in Brazil and 24 500 in India); the number of full-time researchers per million people in South Africa is half that in Brazil and only one-fifth the number in Malaysia, while South Africa is ranked 64th in the world in terms of the number of doctorates produced per million people (Government of India 2020; Wolhuter et al. 2020). The research base to maintain or increase agricultural output and employment in South Africa has been severely eroded, even though most of the poorest people live in rural areas. Massive reductions in state support – for example to the Agricultural Research Council – have diminished excellent prospects for a less narrowly conceived and more viable industrialisation strategy (Cramer, Di John and Sender 2022; Sender 2016).

How the living die: Pandemic II
The AIDs pandemic prefigured the distribution of mortality and morbidity recorded during the next (Covid-19) pandemic, as well as some of the dubious policy responses, nationalistic posturing and xenophobic outbursts that appeared in 2020. The well-known problem of finding reliable estimates of the resulting number of deaths has not been solved. The Medical Research Council and University of Cape Town professionals conclude that 'there is an urgent need to re-engineer the civil registration and vital statistics system ... [because] there is considerable uncertainty around what proportion of the excess deaths was due to COVID-19 (directly or indirectly)' (Bradshaw et al. 2022: 6). This urgent need has still not been addressed (Maqungo et al. 2022).

Statistics South Africa, like the official statistical agencies in other African countries, has only been able to publish data on deaths of those that are more than three years old – its most recent publication on cause-of-death refers to 2018 data (Statistics South Africa 2021), probably because it lacks the resources to recruit enough staff to process the forms (Dorrington et al. 2021). Not only has there been an inordinate delay in the publication of cause-of-death statistics, but their usefulness to policymakers has also been reduced because the gap between the reports of officially tabulated Covid-19 deaths and the true number of these deaths appears to be widening over time, with especially severe underestimates in poor provinces such as Limpopo and Mpumalanga (Bradshaw et al. 2022: 5). Under-investment in the vital registration system means that the total number of deaths recorded on the National Population Register (NPR) is also unreliable; it is widely acknowledged that not all deaths are registered on the NPR, especially in rural areas and especially if deaths take place outside hospitals, if the deceased is under the age of five, or if he or she lacks a South African birth certificate or identity document (Price et al. 2019; Whittaker et al. 2021).

What evidence there is does suggest that South Africa, despite implementing a severe lockdown on its relatively young population, has had *higher excess death rates* per 100 000 than most other countries in the world, including a comparable upper middle-income country such as Brazil. The excess death rate per 100 000 population has tracked the death rate from Covid-19 closely and has, unsurprisingly, been very much lower in South Africa's richer provinces (such as the Western Cape) than in poorer provinces (such as the Eastern Cape) (Bradshaw et al. 2022). Even within the Western Cape, the risk of dying from Covid-19 has been much higher in the poorest districts (Hussey et al. 2021). People living in the lowest-income rural households appear to be much more vulnerable to Covid-19 than other South Africans (Yu 2023).

By 2021, Covid-19 had probably overtaken HIV as the leading cause of death in South Africa and, by May 2022, it is likely that Covid-19 had caused the death of about 260 000 people (Geffen and Low 2022). But the full impact of the pandemic on excess mortality, particularly for the poorest South Africans in the poorest areas, will only become evident in the future; 'collateral deaths (in terms of missed diagnoses or treatment, for example) arising from lockdowns and the overburdening of the health system during the various waves remain unknown' (Bradshaw et al. 2022: 5). But there is already evidence that between 2019 and 2020 the state was unable to protect access to primary-level care, including immunisation, contraception and testing for tuberculosis and HIV.[7] These reductions in access to key services will inevitably result in increasing morbidity and mortality for the poor. Problems were certainly more severe in the poorer provinces. Mpumalanga and the Eastern Cape, for instance, experienced especially large falls in contraception prescriptions and in the percentage of children fully immunised at one year of age (Barron et al. 2022; Bradshaw et al. 2022; Pillay et al. 2021). This reduced access to care will have a cumulative and long-term negative impact on health that will 'dwarf the damage done by COVID-19' (Burger and Ngwenya 2021: 862).

The mechanisms propelling unvaccinated children towards both a short-run deterioration in cognitive development and lower standards of living in the medium term have been well documented in India (Summan, Nandi and Bloom 2022). In South Africa, lockdowns exacerbated a longstanding problem; immunisation coverage had been stagnant since 2014 (with more than 40 per cent of South African children incompletely vaccinated in 2016). Reasons for the new, Covid-related decline in the immunisation rate – a fall of as much as 50 per cent in some rural areas – include not only the poverty of some children's households, but also vaccine stock-outs (Iwu-Jaja et al. 2022; Ndwandwe et al. 2021).[8] Poor people may be unwilling to bear the expense of travelling to attend clinics where they do not receive treatment because there is 'poor stock management', and it is not surprising that poorer people are much less likely to immunise their children than richer households. The *Financial Times* reported at the end of May 2022 that 'vaccination sites remain poorly advertised, are hard to get to, and close too early for workers and those in poor areas to reach them' (Cotterill, Barnes and Burns-Murdoch 2022). Immigrants not only suffer from inconvenient access and stock-outs but also from 'denial of treatment, and in some instances name-calling and outright discrimination by frontline health workers' (White and Rispel 2021: 1293). As already noted, the intelligentsia have not always resisted the temptation to respond to popular fear by deploying nationalist, xenophobic and anti-immigrant arguments in response to pandemics; these responses, in South Africa and elsewhere, appear to have grown as Covid-19 spread (Steenberg et al. 2023). Some of the rural intelligentsia, who continue to affirm that traditional healers, or eucalyptus-infused steam (IOL 2021), can provide an adequate response to Covid-19, may also have provoked vaccine hesitancy among the poor (Mphekgwana, Makgahlela and Mothiba 2021).

Stuck in the orthodox groove playing old policy refrains

By the end of January 2023, only about one-third of South Africa's population was fully vaccinated. The number of administered Covid-19 vaccine doses per one hundred people was very low relative to many other African countries – including Rwanda, Morocco, Cape Verde, Botswana, Tunisia, Egypt, Mozambique, Mauritania, Côte d'Ivoire, Liberia, Zimbabwe, Sierra Leone and Angola.[9] Recent failures to vaccinate vulnerable people and children against Covid-19 have triggered old, familiar and unconvincing policy proposals. It is not clear, for example, that the nationalistic proposals to increase South Africa's capacity to produce vaccines domestically rather than continue to rely on imports, or that posturing demands to reduce the rents secured by intellectual property rights, will solve the failure to vaccinate many poor rural people. Vietnam has been just as reliant on imported vaccines as South Africa but managed to vaccinate virtually its entire population.[10] Even after Covid-19 vaccine supplies and domestic vaccine production had been ramped up, these supplies certainly did *not* reach all of the unvaccinated – and over-supply soon became a problem. By the end of 2021 the government was compelled to request Johnson & Johnson and Pfizer to delay delivery of Covid-19 vaccines, because it had *too much* stock (Gonzalez 2022; Khan 2023; Mukherjee 2021). By mid-2022, the Gqeberha plant in the Eastern Cape established to produce Aspenovax was forced to consider closure, because it had no orders from South Africa's Department of Health (or anyone else). At the end of 2022, the installed Aspenovax production lines were still idle, and the company had received no orders for its own brand of Covid-19 vaccinations (Becker 2022).

If we are not convinced that getting rid of the malign influence of foreign patent owners will improve Covid-19 vaccination rates in South Africa, another school of policy advisers is at hand to offer us an (old) solution that remains surprisingly popular in debates about public health (and electricity) provision.[11] For example, the usual suspects in Washington (the International Finance Corporation) and a large JSE-listed logistics corporation (Imperial) have offered a time-honoured solution to the Covid-19 pandemic. Their remedy involves bypassing the 3 500 state-funded and 'financially unsustainable' primary health care clinics and substituting a new private sector health provider. The International Finance Corporation will give a sweetener to Imperial to encourage new markets for the private sector – to provide more efficient testing, vaccination and 'quality' treatment of Covid-19 in specially manufactured primary health care units or modules. The aim is to install these modules in densely populated urban areas – not, of course, in those rural areas less attractive to private investors where access to services is far more limited (Arnoldi 2020). 'Nurse entrepreneurs' are subsidised to run these urban showcases for philanthrocapitalism, but uptake has been slow; only about one hundred clinics had been established by mid-2022. The national outcomes and the cost-effectiveness of these new units has not been established, but the Lancet Global Health Commission's exhaustive review of the evidence reached the conclusion that the interventions usually delivered by state-funded primary health clinics *are* cost-effective (Hanson et al. 2022).

Readily available evidence of the high costs and inefficiencies of the most important private sector health providers in South Africa is often brushed under the carpet. The South African state continues to subsidise the non-competitive corporations dominating the health sector. Nowhere else in the world is such a high percentage of total current expenditure on health accounted for by private insurance; but less than 17 per cent of the population benefit from the burgeoning facilities and resources that now absorb about half of health expenditure and 70 per cent of all health workers (Barber et al. 2018; Pauw 2022). The MERG report highlighted subsidies received by the private sector and predicted that private provision would, in a context of extreme income inequality, inevitably tend to the over-treatment of the wealthy and, by the criteria of social efficiency and equity, the inefficient crowding-out of the treatment of the impoverished. Our argument was that

> the private sector is never self-sufficient, but often benefits from direct subsidies, and is totally dependent upon medical personnel whose training has been publicly funded. Nor does the dependence upon private practice necessarily release funds for the use of the public sector; apart from the economic and political pressures that the private sector will place upon the public sector, it itself suffers from the diseases of modern commercial medicine – over-treatment, over-charging and over-administration, not to mention . . . over-litigation (MERG 1993: 106).

Some rather similar conclusions about over-treatment were reached (decades later, after an absurdly lengthy and high-cost investigation) by the Competition Commission's 'Health Market Inquiry Report', published in 2019, which stated that 'the combination of healthcare practitioners acting as agents for ill-informed individuals requiring healthcare and the perverse incentives associated with the largely fee-for-service remuneration environment facilitated supplier-induced demand; this was the key driver for increases in healthcare utilisation and costs' (Solanki, Cornell, Besada et al. 2020: 89).

The social costs of private provision and over-treatment are particularly evident in the South African data on maternity services. In the private sector the caesarean section (CS) rate is one of the highest in the world at 73 per cent – the public sector CS rate (24.7 per cent) is closer to the global norm. There are *no* obstetric indications for the extremely high CS rate in the private sector, suggesting that sections are often performed to suit the convenience or pockets of providers (Solanki, Cornell, Daviaud and Fawcus 2020). About 60 per cent of all pregnant women relying on the public sector must give birth in community health centres or district hospitals, but many of these institutions (especially in remote rural areas) are unable to respond to a life-threatening need for a CS because the required theatre facilities and staff are not available (Pattinson et al. 2015). The solution proposed is that the private sector should be offered contracts to provide CS services under the new National Health Insurance scheme, but it is not at all clear how such proposals will overcome perverse incentives to over-treat or solve the current inability of an under-staffed and under-resourced public sector to monitor contracts with private providers.

The most widely discussed, piloted and accepted policy proposals to achieve universal health care involve contracting private sector providers to 'strengthen' primary health care facilities (Pauw 2022). Senior policy analysts at one of South Africa's most influential think tanks continue fiercely to defend the relative 'excellence' of private health care on the familiar grounds that it is impossible for the state to manage anything, especially health services. But they do (inconsistently) suggest an important new role for the state; low-cost medical schemes and insurance policies should be introduced and should receive additional subsidies so that the poor can become members, too – using their share of 'tax-funded health vouchers' (Roodt and Fleming 2018: 1; Settas 2020).

These recommendations to 'include' the poor, alongside the fashionable promotion of new mobile and telemedicine technologies, have effectively increased ideological pressure for patients 'to take greater responsibility for their own health' and, especially, to cover the costs of health provision by paying their health insurance premiums digitally. The MERG report anticipated some of these pressures and reactions:

> Privatisation ... creates or reinforces those interest groups (whether in the service of, or served by the system), who also have the economic and political power and voice to undermine and shift government intent. The medical profession has proved itself to be powerful, as have the insurance companies that organise the finance for private schemes. In addition, there will always be economic and political pressures from those who receive or benefit from private medicine to be the beneficiaries of direct or indirect subsidies equivalent, or even preferential to, those allocated to the public sector, and for the latter to be a target for reduced expenditure and further privatisation (MERG 1993: 109).

What the authors of the MERG report obviously failed to anticipate was the feebleness of 'government intent', the ANC's unwillingness to discipline, or even negotiate fiercely with, the handful of large corporations dominating health expenditure and the market for new forms of debt or insurance. Some MERG economists also *overestimated* the ANC's capacity to commission and make effective policy use of alternatives to mainstream economic arguments. In the early 1990s it was hard to imagine how very rapidly all alternative negotiating positions and policies would be ditched, or that the old orthodox arguments would so rarely be questioned in Cabinet and NEC discussions.

If this chapter has had any success in isolating and exposing the crackle produced by worn-out economic ideas, then it may be possible to hear a far more hopeful tune, there all along but buried under the clashing cymbals of post-apartheid policy advice. More hopeful and upbeat tunes are being sung in South Africa – by the chorus of voices that together represent the rise and the impact of such critical and independent organisations as the National Minimum Wage Research Initiative, the Treatment Action Campaign, Section 27 and Collective

Voices Against Health Xenophobia, and publications such as *Groundup* Opinion Pieces and *Spotlight*.[12] The contributions of this chorus were also not anticipated or given sufficient emphasis by the MERG report. South African civil society still continues to produce activist authors and progressive academics who, like Vishnu, are capable of arguing very effectively against economic illiteracy and orthodoxy.

Notes

1. See https://ourworldindata.org/hiv-aids#death-rates-are-high-across-sub-saharan-africa.
2. Statistics South Africa has never been able to publish reliable and up-to-date national cause-of-death statistics, but there is little doubt that in the period after 1997 millions of adults and children died as a result of HIV/AIDS, and that HIV/AIDS mortality trends did decline – after 2006 (Pillay-Van Wyk et al. 2016).
3. Pregs Govender and Barbara Hogan were isolated and honourable exceptions.
4. See https://www.gov.za/AfricanTraditionalMedicineDay2022.
5. Jay Naidoo, an even more celebrated public intellectual, advocates learning from Uttar Pradesh – and pushes a cocktail of ivermectin and vitamins (Hogg 2023).
6. Development economists espousing impossibilist and pessimistic assumptions are discussed at length in Cramer, Sender and Oqubay (2020).
7. Falls in the supply of condoms available in primary health centres pre-date the onset of Covid-19, but the decline in distribution accelerated between 2021 and 2023 (Tomlinson 2024). Subsidies to new 'empowered' private sector condom providers such as the 'Black Industrialist' Gemilatex (DTIC n.d.) have failed to reverse drastic reductions in public sector provision.
8. See also Baleta (2020); SA Corona Virus Online Portal (2022).
9. See https://www.statista.com/statistics/1221298/covid-19-vaccination-rate-in-african-countries/.
10. South Africa's COVID vaccination rollout began a little earlier than in Vietnam, but widely distributed imports soon allowed the latter to catch up and rapidly overtake the sluggish record of the former.
11. Proposals for increased investment in South Africa's power generation – in the context of a 'weakened state apparatus and its vulnerability to corruption' – usually conclude by repeating the old suggestion that 'a more market-orientated policy approach will be necessary' (Crompton and Matsika 2021: 301). Some criticisms of popular proposals for unbundling Eskom to pursue the utopian future of *private* clean energy are discussed in Baigrie (2022). The risks and consequences for the rural poor of allowing free access to the solar off-grid market, including 'new private-sector monopolies, mostly foreign owned and/or backed by sources of international finance and investment', are

discussed in Baker (2023: 218). Evidence of inefficiencies and high social costs caused by privatising water supply in England have been discussed by Buse and Bayliss (2022).
12. See https://groundup.org.za/category/opinion_and_analysis/; https://www.spotlightnsp.co.za/.

References

Achoki, T., B. Sartorius, D. Watkins, S.D. Glenn, A.P. Kengne, T. Oni, C.S. Wiysonge, A. Walker et al. 2022. 'Health Trends, Inequalities and Opportunities in South Africa's Provinces, 1990–2019: Findings from the Global Burden of Disease 2019 Study'. *Journal of Epidemiology and Community Health* 76(5): 471–81.

Arnoldi, M. 2020. 'IFC Backs Imperial Rollout of Modular Covid-19 Screening, Treatment Units'. *Engineering News*, 23 September. https://www.engineeringnews.co.za/article/ifc-backs-imperial-rollout-of-modular-covid-19-screening-treatment-units-2020-09-23/.

Baigrie, B. 2022. 'Eskom, Unbundling, and Decarbonization'. *Phenomenal World*, 14 February. https://www.phenomenalworld.org/analysis/eskom-unbundling-and-decarbonization/.

Baker, L. 2023. 'New Frontiers of Electricity Capital: Energy Access in Sub-Saharan Africa'. *New Political Economy* 28 (2): 206–22.

Baleta, A. 2020. 'Dramatic Drop in SA's Immunisation Rates'. *Spotlight*, 24 June. https://www.spotlightnsp.co.za/2020/06/24/dramatic-drop-in-sas-immunisation-rates/.

Bank, L. and V.N. Sharpley. 2020. 'The State and the People in Rural South Africa in the Time of COVID'. *Africa Insight* 50 (2): 4–22.

Barber, S.L., A Kumar, T. Roubal, F. Colombo and L. Lorenzoni. 2018. 'Harnessing the Private Health Sector by Using Prices as a Policy Instrument: Lessons Learned from South Africa'. *Health Policy* 122 (5): 558–64.

Barron, P., H. Subedar, M. Letsoko, M. Makua and Y. Pillay. 2022. 'Teenage Births and Pregnancies in South Africa, 2017–2021 – a Reflection of a Troubled Country: Analysis of Public Sector Data'. *South African Medical Journal* 112 (4): 252–58.

Becker, Z. 2022. 'As Orders Slow to a Halt, J&J Partner Aspen May Have to Redirect Manufacturing Efforts: Report'. *FiercePharma*, 11 August. https://www.fiercepharma.com/manufacturing/jj-covid-19-partner-aspen-pharmacare-faces-empty-production-lines-orders-slow-halt.

Bond, P. 2021. 'Can South Africa Urgently Evolve, from Victim-globalisation to Passive-deglobalisation to Active-localisation?' *CADTM*, 29 November. https://www.cadtm.org/Can-South-Africa-urgently-evolve-from-victim-globalisation-to-passive.

Bradshaw, D., R. Dorrington, R. Laubscher, P. Groenewald and T. Moultrie. 2022. 'COVID-19 and All-cause Mortality in South Africa – the Hidden Deaths in the First Four Waves'. *South African Journal of Science* 118 (5–6). https://doi.org/10.17159/sajs.2022/13300 .

Burger, C., R. Burger and E. van Doorslaer. 2022. 'The Health Impact of Free Access to Antiretroviral Therapy in South Africa'. *Social Science and Medicine* 299: 114832.

Burger, R. and M. Ngwenya. 2021. 'The Economics of Health in South Africa'. In: *The Oxford Handbook of the South African Economy*, edited by A. Oqubay, F. Tregenna and I. Valodia. Oxford: Oxford University Press.

Buse, K. and K. Bayliss. 2022. 'England's Privatised Water: Profits over People and Planet'. *BMJ*. 378: o2076. https://doi.org/10.1136/bmj.o2076.

Cotterill, J., O. Barnes and J. Burn-Murdoch. 2022. 'Why Africa's First Covid Vaccine Factory Struggles to Find Customers'. *Financial Times*, 30 May.

Cramer, C., J. Di John and J. Sender. 2022. 'Classification and Roundabout Production in High-value Agriculture: A Fresh Approach to Industrialization'. *Development and Change* 53 (3): 495–524.

Cramer, C., J. Sender and A. Oqubay. 2020. *African Economic Development: Evidence, Theory, Policy*. New York: Oxford University Press.

Creese, A., K. Floyd, A. Alban and L. Guinness. 2002. 'Cost-effectiveness of HIV/AIDS Interventions in Africa: A Systematic Review of the Evidence'. *The Lancet* 359 (9318): 1635–43.

Crompton, R. and R. Matsika. 2021. 'Energy in South Africa'. In: *The Oxford Handbook of the South African Economy*, edited by A. Oqubay, F. Tregenna and I. Valodia. Oxford: Oxford University Press.

De Gruchy, T. and J. Vearey. 2020. '"Left Behind": Why Implementing Migration-aware Responses to HIV for Migrant Farm Workers is a Priority for South Africa'. *African Journal of AIDS Research* 19 (1): 57–68.

Delius, P. and C. Glaser. 2005. 'Sex, Disease and Stigma in South Africa: Historical Perspectives'. *African Journal of AIDS Research* 4 (1): 29–36.

Dorrington, R.E., D. Bradshaw, R. Laubscher and N. Nannan. 2021. *Rapid Mortality Surveillance Report 2019 & 2020*. Cape Town: South African Medical Research Council.

DTIC (Department of Trade, Industry and Competition). n.d. *Black Industrialist and Exporter Profiles Directory*. http://www.investsa.gov.za/wp-content/uploads/2022/08/BIE-PROFILES-DIRECTORY-2022.pdf.

Epstein, H. 2014. 'Ebola in Liberia: An Epidemic of Rumors'. *New York Review of Books*, 18 December.

Forsythe, S.S., W. McGreevey, A. Whiteside, M. Shah, J. Cohen, R. Hecht, L.A. Bollinger, and A. Kinghorn. 2019. 'Twenty Years of Antiretroviral Therapy for People Living with HIV: Global Costs, Health Achievements, Economic Benefits'. *Health Affairs* 38 (7): 1163–72.

Friedman, S. 2021. *One Virus, Two Countries: What COVID-19 Tells Us About South Africa*. Johannesburg: Wits University Press.

Fryer, D. 2006. 'Review: *Season of Hope: Economic Reform under Mandela and Mbeki* by Alan Hirsch'. *International Affairs* 82 (3): 604–605.

Geffen, N. and E. Cameron. 2009. *The Deadly Hand of Denial: Governance and Politically-instigated AIDS Denialism in South Africa*. Working Paper, Centre for Social Science Research, University of Cape Town.

Geffen, N. and M. Low. 2022. 'Two Years into the Covid Disaster, Where Do We Stand?' *Groundup*, 12 May. https://www.groundup.org.za/article/two-years-into-covid-disaster-where-do-we-stand/.

Gonzalez, L.L. 2022. 'J&J Delays Could Leave South Africa Paying for COVID-19 Vaccine Doses'. *devex*, 10 October. https://www.devex.com/news/j-j-delays-could-leave-south-africa-paying-for-covid-19-vaccine-doses-104154.

Government of India. 2020. *Research and Development Statistics, 2019–20*. New Delhi: Ministry of Science and Technology. https://dst.gov.in/sites/default/files/Research%20and%20Deveopment%20Statistics%202019-20_0.pdf.

Hanson, K., N. Brikci, D. Erlangga, A. Alebachew, M. De Allegri, D. Balabanova, M. Blecher, C. Cashin et al. 2022. 'The Lancet Global Health Commission on Financing Primary Health Care: Putting People at the Centre'. *The Lancet Global Health* 10 (5): e715–72.

Heywood, M. 2005. 'The Price of Denial'. *Development Update* 3 (5): 1–27. https://markheywood.com/the-price-of-denial/.

Hogg, A. 2023. 'Jay Naidoo: What Happens to the Covid Vaccine-injured? Why SA Needs Another TRC'. *BizNews*, 12 March. https://www.biznews.com/undictated/2023/03/12/jay-naidoo-covid-vaccine-sa-needs-another-trc.

Hussey, H, N. Zinyakatira, E. Morden, M. Ismail, M. Paleker, J-L. Bam, L. London, A. Boulle et al. 2021. 'Higher COVID-19 Mortality in Low-income Communities in the City of Cape Town: A Descriptive Ecological Study'. *Gates Open Research* 5: 90. https://doi.org /10.12688/gatesopenres.13288.1.

IOL. 2021. 'Conspiracy Theories on Covid-19 Vaccine Can Be as Deadly as Virus Itself'. *IOL*, 29 January. https://www.iol.co.za/news/opinion/conspiracy-theories-on-covid-19-vaccine-can-be-as-deadly-as-virus-itself-8adf871e-2d9e-4d6a-8e43-ae188308ac52.

Iwu-Jaja, C.J., P. Jordan, N. Ngcobo, A. Jaca, C.D. Iwu, M. Mulenga and C. Wiysonge. 2022. 'Improving the Availability of Vaccines in Primary Healthcare Facilities in South Africa: Is the Time Right for a System Redesign Process?' *Human Vaccines & Immunotherapeutics* 18 (1): 1926184.

Jobson, R. 2013. 'When the ANC Jeered Mandela'. *Groundup*, 12 December. https://www.groundup.org.za/article/when-anc-jeered-madiba/.

Johnson, L.F., G. Meyer-Rath, R.E. Dorrington, A. Puren, T. Seathlodi, K. Zuma and A. Feizzadeh. 2022. 'The Effect of HIV Programmes in South Africa on National HIV Incidence Trends, 2000–2019'. *Journal of Acquired Immune Deficiency Syndromes*. https://doi.org /10.1097/QAI.0000000000002927.

Kabudula, C.W., B. Houle, D. Ohene-Kwofie, D. Mahlangu, N. Ng, H. Van Minh, F.X. Gómez-Olivé, S. Tollman et al. 2021. 'Mortality Transition over a Quarter Century in Rural South Africa: Findings from Population Surveillance in Agincourt 1993–2018'. *Global Health Action* 14 (sup 1): 1990507. https://doi.org/10.1080/16549716.2021.1990507.

Kentridge, M. 1993. *Turning the Tanker: The Economic Debate in South Africa*. Johannesburg: Centre for Policy Studies.

Khan, T. 2023. 'Government Has a Massive Surplus of Vaccine Doses: Round of Covid-19 Booster Shots Available as Demand Dwindles'. *Sowetan*, 26 January. https://www.sowetanlive.co.za/news/south-africa/2023-01-26-round-of-covid-19-booster-shots-available-as-demand-dwindles/.

Krugman, P. 2012. 'Death of a Fairy Tale'. *New York Times*, 26 April. https://www.nytimes.com/2012/04/27/opinion/krugman-death-of-a-fairy-tale.html.

Lawson, L. 2008. *Side Effects: The Story of AIDS in South Africa*. Cape Town: Double Storey.

Lodge, T. 2015. 'The Politics of HIV/AIDS in South Africa: Government Action and Public Response'. *Third World Quarterly* 36 (8): 1570–91.

Maqungo, M., N. Nannan, B. Nojilana, E. Nichols, D. Morof, M. Cheyip, C. Rao, C. Lombard et al. 2022. *Can Verbal Autopsies Be Used on a National Scale? Key Findings and Lessons from the South Africa National Cause-of-Death Validation Study*. https://doi.org/10.21203/rs.3.rs-2349584/v1.

Marais, H. 2012. 'Making Sense of the Indefensible'. *Mail & Guardian*, 5–12 April. http://mg.co.za/article/2012-04-05-making-sense-of-the -indefensible.

Marseille, E., P.B. Hofmann and J.G Kahn. 2002. 'HIV Prevention before HAART in Sub-Saharan Africa'. *The Lancet* 359 (9320): 1851–6.

Mazibuko, Z. (ed.). 2019. *Epidemics and the Health of African Nations*. Johannesburg: Mapungubwe Institute for Strategic Reflection.

MERG (Macroeconomic Research Group). 1993. *Making Democracy Work: A Framework for Macroeconomic Policy in South Africa*. Cape Town: Centre for Development Studies, University of the Western Cape.

Mothibe, M.E. and M. Sibanda. 2019. 'African Traditional Medicine: South African Perspective'. In: *Traditional and Complementary Medicine*, edited by C. Mordeniz. London: IntechOpen.

Mphekgwana, P.M., M. Makgahlela and T.M. Mothiba. 2021. 'Use of Traditional Medicines to Fight COVID-19 during the South African Nationwide Lockdown: A Prevalence Study among University Students and Academic Staff'. *The Open Public Health Journal* 14 (1): 441–5. https://doi.org/10.2174/1 874944502114010441.

Mtukudzi, O. 1990. 'Under Pressure'. Album track on *Chikonzi (Messenger!)* by Oliver Mtukudzi and The Black Spirits. Johannesburg: Sheer Sound.

Mukherjee, P. 2021. 'Slow Covid-19 Vaccine Uptake Means SA Has To Halt Orders'. *BusinessDay*, 24 November. https://www.businesslive.co.za/bd/national/health/2021-11-24-slow-covid-19-vaccine-uptake-means-sa-has-to-halt-orders/.

Ndwandwe, D., C.A.Nnaji, T. Mashunye, O.A. Uthman and C.S. Wiysonge. 2021. 'Incomplete Vaccination and Associated Factors among Children Aged 12–23 Months in South Africa: An Analysis of the South African Demographic and Health Survey 2016'. *Human Vaccines & Immunotherapeutics* 17 (1): 247–54.

Netshitenzhe, J. 2015. 'Theorising the South African Renaissance Ideal'. In: *Roundtable on the Role of Intellectuals in the State-Society Nexus*. Johannesburg: Mapungubwe Institute for Strategic Reflection. https://mistra.org.za/mistra-media/rountable-on-the-role-of-intellectuals-in-the-state-society-nexus/.

Padayachee, V. and J. Sender. 2018. 'Vella Pillay: Revolutionary Activism and Economic Policy Analysis'. *Journal of Southern African Studies* 44 (1): 149–65. https://doi.org/10.1080/03057070.2018.1405644.

Pattinson, R.C., J.D. Makin, Y. Pillay, N. van den Broek and J. Moodley. 2015. 'Basic and Comprehensive Emergency Obstetric and Neonatal Care in 12 South African Health Districts'. *South African Medical Journal* 105 (4): 256–60.

Pauw, T.L. 2022. 'Catching Up with the Constitution: An Analysis of National Health Insurance in South Africa Post-apartheid'. *Development Southern Africa* 39 (6): 921–34.

Pillay, Y, S. Pienaar, P. Barron and T. Zondi. 2021. 'Impact of COVID-19 on Routine Primary Healthcare Services in South Africa'. *South African Medical Journal* 111 (8): 714–19.

Pillay-Van Wyk, V., W. Msemburi, R. Laubscher, R.E. Dorrington, P. Groenewald, T. Glass, B. Nojilana, J.D. Joubert et al. 2016. 'Mortality Trends and Differentials in South Africa from 1997 to 2012: Second National Burden of Disease Study'. *The Lancet Global Health* 4 (9): e642–53.

Price, J., M. Willcox, C.W. Kabudula, K. Herbst, K. Kahn and A. Harnden. 2019. 'Home Deaths of Children Under 5 Years in Rural South Africa: A Population-based Longitudinal Study'. *Tropical Medicine & International Health* 24 (7): 862–78. https://doi.org/10.1111/tmi.13239.

Regondi, I. and A. Whiteside. 2012. 'Fiscal Space for Health: Assessing Policy Options in South Africa'. *Journal of Contemporary Management* 1 (1): 14–26.

Roodt, M. and M. Fleming. 2018. *South Africa's National Health Insurance Scheme*. Johannesburg: South African Institute of Race Relations.

SA Corona Virus Online Portal. 2022. *South Africa COVID-19 and Vaccine Social Listening Report*, 21 March 2022. Report 41. https://sacoronavirus.co.za/2022/03/23/south-africa-covid-19-and-vaccine-social-listening-report-21-march-2022-report-41/.

Sender, J. 1994. 'Economic Restructuring in South Africa: Reactionary Rhetoric Prevails'. *Journal of Southern African Studies* 20 (4): 539–43.

———. 2016. 'Backward Capitalism in Rural South Africa: Prospects for Accelerating Accumulation in the Eastern Cape'. *Journal of Agrarian Change* 16 (1): 3–31.

Settas, M. 2020. 'Covid-19 and the Case against a State-run National Health Insurance'. *Daily Maverick*, 13 September. https://www.dailymaverick.co.za/opinionista/2020-09-13-covid-19-and-the-case-against-a-state-run-national-health-insurance/.

Solanki, G.C., J.E. Cornell, D. Besada, R.L. Morar and T. Wilkinson. 2020. 'The Competition Commission Health Market Inquiry Report: An Overview and Key Imperatives'. *South African Medical Journal* 110 (2): 88–91.

Solanki, G.C., J.E. Cornell, E. Daviaud and S. Fawcus 2020. 'Caesarean Section Rates in South Africa: A Case Study of the Health Systems Challenges for the Proposed National Health Insurance'. *South African Medical Journal* 110 (8): 747–50.

Statistics South Africa. 2021. *Mortality and Causes of Death in South Africa: Findings from Death Notification 2018*. Pretoria: Statistics South Africa.

Steenberg, B., A. Sokani, N. Myburgh, P. Mutevedzi and S.A. Madhi. 2023. 'COVID-19 Vaccination Rollout: Aspects of Hesitancy in South Africa'. *Vaccines* 11 (2): 407. https://doi.org/10.3390/vaccines11020407.

Summan, A., A. Nandi and D. Bloom. 2022. *A Shot at Economic Prosperity: Long-term Effects of India's Childhood Immunization Program on Earnings and Consumption Expenditure*. Discussion Paper DP17386. London: Centre for Economic Policy Research.

Tomlinson, C. 2024. 'Dramatic Decline in Condom Distribution in SA, New Figures Show'. *Spotlight*, 2 April. https://www.spotlightnsp.co.za/2024/04/02/condom-distribution-in-south-africa-has-dropped-dramatically-over-the-last-five-years/.

Urias, E. 2019. 'The Potential Synergies between Industrial and Health Policies for Access to Medicines: Insights from the Brazilian Policy of Universal Access to HIV/AIDS Treatment'. *Innovation and Development* 9 (2): 245–60.

Webster, E. 2022. 'Choosing Sides: The Promise and Pitfalls of a Critically Engaged Sociology in Apartheid South Africa'. In: *Critical Engagement with Public Sociology*, edited by A. Bezuidenhout, S. Mnwana and K. von Holdt. Bristol: Bristol University Press.

White, J.A. and L.C. Rispel. 2021. 'Policy Exclusion or Confusion? Perspectives on Universal Health Coverage for Migrants and Refugees in South Africa'. *Health Policy and Planning* 36 (8): 1292–306.

Whittaker, C., P.G.T. Walker, M. Alhaffar, A. Hamlet, B.A. Djaafara, A. Ghani, N. Ferguson, M. Dahab et al. 2021. 'Under-reporting of Deaths Limits Our Understanding of True Burden of Covid-19'. *BMJ* 375: n2239. https://doi.org/10.1136/bmj.n2239.

Wilson, K.R. 2009. 'A Manufactured Solution? The Transfer of Technology to Developing Countries for the Local Production of Affordable Antiretrovirals: Case Studies from Tanzania and South Africa'. PhD thesis, University of Toronto.

Wolhuter, C., Z.L. de Beer, E. Niemczyk, J. Botha, O. Gore, A. Marimo, M. Neethling, V. Santhakumar, J. Seleti, H.J. Steyn, B. Taylor and D. Vos. 2020. *Critical Issues in South African Education: Illumination from International Comparative Perspectives from the BRICS Countries*. https://directory.doabooks.org/handle/20.500.12854/70683.

Yu, D. 2023. 'Revisiting the COVID-19 Vulnerability Index in South Africa'. *Development Southern Africa* 40 (1): 91–108.

Zbinden, K. and T. Todorov. 2004. 'In Praise of Nuance: An Interview with Tzvetan Todorov'. *Salmagundi* 141–2: 3–26.

15

Regional Integration as an Instrument of Industrialisation
Perspectives from South Africa

Nicolette Cattaneo

Since the 1980s, regional integration policy in Southern Africa has been impeded by problems associated with overlapping membership of regional organisations, unequal distribution of the costs and benefits of integration, polarised industrial development and implementation issues related to regional and national political economy factors. These have been exacerbated by tensions between agreements negotiated among African countries themselves and those negotiated with external countries or regional blocs, particularly the Economic Partnership Agreements (EPAs) with the European Union (EU). The relationship of integration arrangements on the continent to the multilateral trade architecture under the World Trade Organization adds another layer of complexity to the regional policy mix.

While debate on an appropriate framework for regional integration has evolved through various phases, a development integration narrative has been adopted by some regional configurations on the continent, notably the Tripartite Free Trade Area (TFTA).[1] In this view, economic integration is regarded as an instrument of industrialisation, with elements such as a regional industrial policy, cooperation in infrastructure development and, more recently, the promotion of regional value chains (RVCs) (Davies 2019; Ismail 2018). However, the most prominent integration initiative at present, the African Continental Free Trade Area (AfCFTA), has not made explicit reference to such an approach. Indeed, the status quo with respect to economic integration policy appears to be characterised by what Davies (2019: 8) has referred to as 'paradigmatic incoherence', a state of affairs that could result in regional integration failing to fulfil its potential as a developmental tool.

Recent contributions on African economic integration have criticised the evident adherence to a linear model of market integration, proceeding from a free trade area (FTA) to a customs union, common market and finally economic union.[2] In particular, concern has been raised over the weak provisions for a comprehensive industrialisation strategy in the policy mix (Davies 2019). Other commentators have pointed to a reluctance to assess appropriate mechanisms to facilitate an equitable distribution of the costs and benefits of integration in the context of the prevailing balance of power and interests, both within and between states.[3]

The Agreement to Establish the AfCFTA was launched in Kigali in March 2018 and entered into force in May 2019. Implementation was set for January 2020 but was delayed due to outstanding negotiating issues in Phase I (covering goods and services) and the onset of the Covid-19 pandemic.[4] The adoption of the AfCFTA Agreement while negotiations are still in progress provides an opportunity to revisit a number of key questions related to the architecture of economic integration in Africa and to explore its future trajectory.

What have been the origins, influences and evolving approaches to regional integration in Southern Africa and the rest of the continent? What has South Africa's impact on the regional integration landscape been during the same period? What are the prospects of a 'development integration' approach ultimately informing the evolution of the remaining AfCFTA negotiating processes?

A re-examination of the trade policy and regional integration agenda during and after the democratic transition in South Africa in a chapter dedicated to the scholarship of Vishnu Padayachee brings to mind three volumes of Vishnu's work, apart from the report of the Macroeconomic Research Group (MERG 1993), in which he was deeply involved. These are *The Political Economy of South Africa's Transition*, edited with Jonathan Michie (Michie and Padayachee 1997), *The Development Decade?* (Padayachee 2006) and *The Political Economy of Africa* (Padayachee 2010). Michie and Padayachee (1997) is of particular relevance for the present study, with its notable chapters by Trevor Bell on trade policy, which grapples with the reasons behind South Africa's trade liberalisation trajectory in the 1990s, Ben Fine on industrial and energy policy, and, importantly, Harry Zarenda on regional integration. At the time of the democratic transition, there were some marked shifts in the debate on regional integration.[5] The present chapter tries to situate these shifts against the background of evolving perspectives and influences on African economic integration more broadly.

In his paper 'The Spread of Economic Doctrines and Policymaking in Postcolonial Africa' (2014), Thandika Mkandawire, the former director of the Council for the Development of Social Science Research in Africa (CODESRIA) and an inspiration to more than a generation of African scholars, examines the relationship between economic ideas and policy-making on the continent in the past five decades. Mkandawire (2014: 171–3) identifies the shift from what he calls the 'structuralist-developmentalist and neo-Marxist perspectives of the 1960s and 1970s' during the phase of development planning, through the neoliberal period of the 1980s and 1990s (the structural adjustment phase), to a 'more eclectic combination of neo-institutionalism [and] growth orientation', in combination with a focus on poverty alleviation issues. Although the latter is termed the post-Washington Consensus (PWC) era, he emphasises that it is still situated within an essentially neoclassical framing of ideas. While gently chastising economists on the continent for a lack of self-reflection on the state of their discipline, Mkandawire also explores how domestic competencies were harnessed or oriented to carry out policy in each of the phases mentioned above.

It is evident that the evolution of approaches to regional integration on the continent is connected to the linkages between ideas and policies that have evolved more broadly. Mkandawire's analysis therefore provides a useful lens through which to look at regional integration policies and approaches on the continent during the three phases. At the same time, Vishnu Padayachee's work in this area, and particularly his 2016 paper, 'Ideas and Power: Academic Economists and the Making of Policy', provides an instructive complementary lens through which to consider South African perspectives on regional integration policy both during and after the democratic transition.[6]

The rest of this chapter is organised as follows. The next section considers the approaches to economic integration that have informed regional cooperation initiatives on the continent in relation to Mkandawire's (2014) analysis. The following section examines policy and perspectives on economic integration before and during the democratic transition in South Africa, as well as in the immediate post-apartheid period. The final section concludes the chapter with reference to the lessons that can be drawn from historical experience on the continent and elsewhere.

Regional integration in Africa: Origins, influences and evolving approaches

Kwame Nkrumah provided an early vision of Africa's integration at the Fifth Pan-African Congress held in Manchester in 1945 (Adedeji 2002; Adi and Sherwood 2003). In the immediate post-independence period, Nkrumah hosted the 1958 All Africa Peoples' Conference in Accra (Mazrui 2005) and was instrumental in the establishment of the United Nations Economic Commission for Africa (UNECA) that year, which championed African integration. The rationale for economic integration rested on the need to overcome the legacy of small fragmented markets on the continent. The emphasis was on development through industrialisation, with integration as a means of lowering the cost of protecting individual domestic markets (Adedeji 1970). Development through industrialisation was seen as best achieved through continent-wide economic planning (Green and Seidman 1968; Mkandawire 2014).

Nkrumah's vision for Africa's integration viewed the development of continental institutional structures as a priority. He was evidently critical of a vision of Pan-Africanism that rested on the emergence of regional organisations, a position that reportedly brought him into conflict with Julius Nyerere's approach to the federation of East Africa, among others (Kamata 2019; Mkandawire 1985). Following the failure to get the East African Federation off the ground, Nyerere energetically promoted regional economic integration in East Africa and later played a key role in the emergence of the Southern African Development Coordination Conference (SADCC), the precursor of the Southern African Development Community (SADC) (Mazrui 2005).

Apart from Pan-Africanist leaders such as Nkrumah and Nyerere, other early influences on African integration included Raúl Prebisch, the Argentinian structuralist economist, and early Latin American integration projects such as the Latin American Free Trade Association and the Central American Common Market (CACM), both created in 1960 (Adebajo 2014; Adedeji 2002; Davies 1992). In an early study of the CACM, Miguel Wionczek (1968) emphasised that from the outset the rationale for Latin American integration was not regional trade liberalisation and external tariff harmonisation per se, nor was economic integration seen as an end in itself. Rather, it was envisaged as a means to ensure 'accelerated diversification and industrialisation of the region's economy' and 'politically balanced regional economic development' (Wionczek 1968: 238).[7]

On the African continent, while the Organization of African Unity (OAU) was established in 1963 with Nkrumah and Nyerere among its key founders, the impetus for more concrete regional integration plans arguably came from UNECA, in part through its regional offices set up in the early 1960s (Adedeji 2002; Mazrui 2005). However, despite a proliferation of cooperation arrangements in the decade that followed, there was limited progress in the pursuit of a continental agenda for economic integration. Mkandawire (1985) notes that, by 1974, most post-independence regional cooperation initiatives had collapsed. The early East African Community, founded in 1967, was in a state of crisis and dissolved in 1977, in a further blow to Nyerere's ambitions for East African integration.

Integration schemes among developing countries elsewhere also fared poorly in this period, with the failure of projects in Latin America, Asia and the Caribbean (Vaitsos 1978). This was a result, inter alia, of inadequate attention to industrial planning and investment coordination, polarisation and the resulting uneven distributional effects of integration. In the early 1970s, these factors were compounded by political problems (such as conflict with the regime of Idi Amin in East Africa, tension between leaders in West Africa, and regional instability), together with emerging global economic crises (Adedeji 2002; Mazrui 2005). Hence scepticism intensified (from both mainstream and more heterodox perspectives) about the prospects for regional integration schemes on the continent.

Mkandawire (1985) and Constantine Vaitsos (1978) note the limited political economy analysis of the interest groups and actors involved in or benefiting from the process of economic integration. Vaitsos (1978) points to the resulting lack of attention paid to suitable mechanisms to address the distributional effects of integration and, like Adedeji (1970), highlights tensions between nationalist development projects and regional integration imperatives. The early architects of Latin American and African integration schemes were acutely aware of these issues, but despite some innovative mechanisms to promote industrial development (Wionczek 1968; Adedeji 1970), the political economy context impacted on their success.[8]

Nevertheless, calls for 'collective self-reliance' and economic cooperation among developing countries found renewed expression in debates in the 1970s on reconfiguring the global economic architecture and transformation of the UN system. These discussions culminated in the adoption of the *Declaration on the Establishment of a New International Economic Order* by the UN General Assembly in 1974 (Mkandawire 2005). In 1975, after a decade of dialogue initiated under the auspices of UNECA, the Economic Community of West African States (ECOWAS) was formed. This was followed by two further regional initiatives supported by UNECA, in collaboration with the OAU and the African Development Bank (ADB). The treaty establishing the preferential trade area (PTA) for Eastern and Southern Africa was signed in 1981, while the Economic Community for Central African States was created in 1983 (Adedeji 2002). Underpinning these developments, arguably the most ambitious statement of intent regarding economic development on the continent, the Lagos Plan of Action (LPA), was launched by African heads of state in April 1980 under the auspices of the OAU.

According to Adebayo Adedeji, the executive secretary of UNECA from 1975 to 1991 and the key architect of the LPA, the plan's immediate precursor was UNECA's *Revised Framework of Principles for the Implementation of the New International Economic Order in Africa* (Adedeji 1983). This provided the detailed intellectual and theoretical basis for the 1979 Monrovia Strategy and the LPA the following year. The importance attached to regional industrialisation is explicit in the LPA, with industrial financing and promotion of trade in manufactures as key elements. Transport and communications infrastructure is accorded special prominence, while the plan calls for 'preferential trade areas or institutions' to be established, with the formation of an African Common Market as the end goal (OAU 1980: 65).

Despite a compelling developmental approach to regional integration, with detailed strategies and target dates in key areas, the LPA was criticised for its lack of a comprehensive monitoring and implementation programme (Ismail 2018). Two decades after its launch, Adedeji (2002: 3) remarked that the LPA was 'observed more in the breach than in observance by African governments and openly vilified by ... the donor community and the IFIs [international financial institutions]'.[9] Within a short space of time, the context in which the LPA emerged had altered markedly as the neoliberal era took hold. This significantly affected the trajectory of regional integration policy in the 1980s and 1990s. The 1981 World Bank study *Accelerated Development in Sub-Saharan Africa: An Agenda for Action* (known as the Berg report) became, as Mkandawire (1985: 3) puts it, 'the main text of [the neoliberal] doctrine as repackaged for the African context'.

While advocating the standard International Monetary Fund policy prescriptions such as cuts in government expenditure, liberalisation and privatisation, the Berg report purported to 'accept the long-term objectives of African development as expressed ... in the Lagos Plan of Action' (World Bank 1981: v). The central message of the report was a focus on 'getting the prices right' to effect macroeconomic stabilisation and send the 'correct' signals to facilitate private sector investment (Mkandawire 2014). This would, in the Bank's view, obviate the need for national development planning and, indeed, even project planning, thereby slashing state intervention on the continent. Samir Amin (1982: 28) highlights the Berg report's assertion that the continent placed 'too much' emphasis on industrial development, to the detriment of agriculture.[10]

As the structural adjustment phase unfolded, regional cooperation plans were only encouraged by the IFIs if they were designed as stepping stones towards the eventual removal of all barriers to free trade and hence, ultimately, the effective elimination of intraregional trade preferences (Mkandawire 1985). Such an approach saw little need for regional industrial policy as part of an economic integration strategy. Indeed, in the neoliberal era, industrial policy became something that was practised but not preached by developed economies. The liberalisation approach contrasted starkly with the developmental integration character of the LPA and with early integration approaches in Latin America and Africa during the development planning period.

Meanwhile, the need for a focused implementation strategy for the LPA found expression only a decade later in the 1991 Abuja Treaty Establishing the African Economic Community (AEC). The first objective of the AEC emphasises 'the integration of African economies in order to increase economic self-reliance and promote an endogenous and self-sustained development' (OAU 1991: 8). Regional economic blocs would be created where none existed and these would merge with existing blocs into a continental economic community. Each region was to begin with the creation of an FTA, followed by a customs union, then a common market and a monetary union. This shift to a more explicit linear model of integration characterised by progressive regional trade liberalisation is exemplified by the trajectories of two regional groupings with contrasting initial approaches but significant overlapping membership that emerged in the early 1980s: SADCC and the PTA.

SADCC was officially formed by the Frontline States of Southern Africa in April 1980, the same month that the LPA was launched.[11] Among SADCC's original aims were the reduction of economic dependence particularly, but not only, on South Africa, together with balanced regional development (SADCC 1980). While SADCC's origins date back to the mid-1970s, its formation was given further impetus by South Africa's counterplan for a 'Constellation of Southern African States' (CONSAS) later that decade (Mkandawire 1985), and the intensification of the apartheid regime's policy of regional destabilisation (Kibble and Bush 1986). The limited success of formal integration schemes in the 1970s, particularly the collapse of the early East African Community, influenced the founders of SADCC. The organisation was thus initiated as a loose association to promote cooperation and coordination rather than formal economic integration. More specifically, it followed a functional integration approach, facilitating sectoral and project cooperation in fields such as transport, agriculture and food security, mining, energy and tourism. The main priority was the transport and communications sector, since dependence on South Africa was particularly acute in this area. Greater emphasis on intraregional trade and industrialisation only emerged later.

Unlike the PTA, SADCC was not initially one of the building blocs of a continental integration arrangement under the auspices of the OAU. Indeed, SADCC's early origins as 'donor-driven' were critiqued, although it eventually became recognised as a building bloc of the AEC. In 1992, SADCC transformed itself into the Southern African Development Community (SADC) and moved towards trade integration. The SADC Trade Protocol was signed in 1996, with the phased-in implementation of an FTA to be completed by 2008. The first fifteen-year Regional Indicative Strategic Development Plan (RISDP) emphasised the goal of deeper integration, prioritising the formation of a customs union and further movements up the ladder of integration (SADC 2003). There has since been considerable debate about whether SADC's future trajectory should involve deepening integration via a move to a customs union and beyond.

The PTA, by contrast, moved more quickly up the ladder of integration and was replaced by the Common Market for Eastern and Southern Africa (COMESA) in 1994, with the formation of an FTA in 2000, followed by the launch of a customs union in 2009. From the late 1980s, therefore, there was greater adherence to a model of market integration with a focus on regional trade liberalisation. While integration schemes clearly involved a broader agenda than just trade integration, a lack of attention to regional industrial policy persisted. For example, in SADC's first RISDP, industrialisation did not appear as a 'priority intervention area' in its own right. Although SADC's 1992 theme document, 'SADC: Towards Economic Integration' (see Davies 1992), put forward 'development integration' as the organisation's underlying approach, the neoliberal integration trajectory evident in the first RISDP is worth quoting in full:

> The RISDP focuses on promoting trade, economic liberalisation and development as a means of facilitating trade and financial liberalization, competitive and diversified industrial development and increased investment through the establishment of a SADC Common Market. In order to attain this goal, SADC will need to accelerate and complete the formation of a free trade area; begin negotiations for the establishment of a customs union, which will be followed by a common market; enhance competitiveness through industrial development and increased productivity in all sectors; harmonize policies, legal and regulatory frameworks for the free movement of factors of production; and implement policies to attain macroeconomic stability and build policy credibility (SADC 2003: Executive summary).[12]

By the early 2000s, eight regional groupings had emerged that were recognised by the African Union (AU) as building blocs of a continental economic community (Ismail 2018).[13] However, problems of overlapping membership, together with the disruption caused by the EPA negotiations with the EU, lent impetus first to the TFTA and then more broadly the AfCFTA negotiations.

South Africa and the region: From destabilisation to 'development integration'

In the 1980s, economic cooperation arrangements in Southern Africa reflected the divide between apartheid South Africa and its majority-ruled neighbours. Two groupings in the region dated back to the colonial period and always included South Africa. These were the Southern African Customs Union (SACU) and Common Monetary Area (CMA). The other two, the PTA and SADCC, which emerged in the early 1980s, excluded South Africa, with SADCC specifically intended to counter the apartheid regime's regional dominance and destabilisation.

South Africa in SACU: The pre-transition period

The 1910 Customs Union Agreement between South Africa and Botswana, Lesotho and eSwatini (BLS) allowed for the free movement of goods and a common external tariff, adherence by BLS to South Africa's tariff laws and a revenue-sharing arrangement under which the smaller partners were paid a fixed share of the common customs and excise revenue pool, based on estimates of their revenue for 1906–1908 (McCarthy 1994). From the mid-1920s, South Africa used the tariff to pursue its own industrial development objectives. As such, the SACU agreement remained a revenue-sharing instrument from the BLS perspective, while South Africa benefited from access to the captive market of its neighbours as it sought to industrialise.

The achievement of independence of BLS in the second half of the 1960s led to the renegotiation of the Customs Union Agreement. Their main concerns were the revenue-sharing formula (still based on their average imports in 1906–1908), polarised industrial development, and the impact of South African-determined tariffs on consumer prices without counterbalancing employment creation and industrial activity emerging (Cattaneo 1998). The 1969 SACU agreement called for an accord 'designed to ensure the continued economic development of the customs union area as a whole ... [with] arrangements [that] encourage the development of the less advanced members of the customs union and the diversification of their economies' (Department of Commerce 1969: Preamble).

It provided for revised revenue-sharing arrangements, a Customs Union Commission to facilitate consultation, and clauses that ostensibly allowed BLS to protect the development of infant industries and 'industries of major importance' (Articles 6 and 7 respectively). The revised revenue-sharing formula contained a multiplier of 0.42 and accounted for duties that would have been earned on BLS imports from South Africa. Both aspects were evidently designed as 'compensation' for the price-raising effects of the common tariff that was set by South Africa (Walters 1989). These revenue-sharing arrangements were of significant benefit to the smaller countries.

However, from an industrialisation perspective, the development pretensions of the 1969 SACU agreement were somewhat murkier. In particular, the ability of the smaller partners to invoke Articles 6 and 7, providing for the protection of key industries, was hindered by a 'Secret Memorandum' to the 1969 agreement attaching conditions to these clauses. For example, in the case of Article 7, the Memorandum reads:

> In regard to paragraph (2) ... [regarding] any proposals for an increase in customs duty ... it is specifically to be understood that industries should be able to supply the qualitative requirements of the common customs area and that they should be in a position to supply *at least about sixty per cent of the quantitative requirements of the area* before tariff protection in terms of this section would be considered ... (Secret Memorandum n.d.: 13, emphasis added).

As Rob Davies (1994) remarks, in addition to the unworkable conditions above, other strategies were used to block industrial projects in BLS and Namibia that sought to supply the South African market, unless they filled some minor gap in the country's industrial sector. These included regulatory hurdles, retaliation by South African producers and pressure on retailers.

By the late 1970s, the regional environment in which SACU operated had evolved considerably. In November 1979, then Prime Minister P.W. Botha made his call for a 'Constellation of Southern African States' (CONSAS) at a conference of government officials, politicians and business leaders in Johannesburg. The South African government hoped that CONSAS would further its economic, political and security goals in the region by providing a buffer of compliant neighbouring states as part of its 'total strategy' of survival. Since BLS were tied to South Africa in the Customs Union, it was envisaged that they would join CONSAS. However, Pretoria's initiative failed, as its neighbours eschewed a grouping that sought to include the 'homelands' (Transkei, Bophuthatswana, Venda and Ciskei, collectively known as TBVC) as 'independent' entities. While SADCC was launched by the Frontline States in April 1980, CONSAS was formed later that year with only South Africa and TBVC as members (Cattaneo 1990).

The other arm of the apartheid regime's regional strategy, military and economic destabilisation, intensified in the early 1980s in the form of covert operations in support of the Resistencia Nacional Moçambicana (RENAMO) in Mozambique and União Nacional pela Independência Total de Angola (UNITA) in Angola, overt military raids and economic blockades. The human and economic cost to Angola, Mozambique and BLS in particular was severe, as was the broader impact on the region's infrastructure and industrial development prospects (Cattaneo 1990; Kibble and Bush 1986).[14]

South Africa's share of the SACU customs pool declined from 96.1 per cent in 1969/70 to 54.8 per cent in 1990/91. This was largely due to significant transfers to Namibia and TBVC in the 1980s, Botswana's increased imports at the start of the 1990s, and the formalisation of Namibia's membership of SACU on independence (Maasdorp and Whiteside 1993; McCarthy 1994). From the perspective of the smaller SACU countries, concerns about revenue-sharing, industrial development and loss of fiscal discretion remained. As the democratic transition unfolded it was evident that a complete renegotiation of the SACU agreement was necessary.

Regional integration debates during the democratic transition
The debate on a post-apartheid regional economic architecture during the transition period is systematically addressed in the MERG background paper on regional cooperation and integration (Davies et al. 1993). This seems a fitting point of departure, given Vishnu's involvement in the MERG project and the apparent connection between the fate of MERG and the evolution of ideas and policy-making more broadly during and immediately after the transition.[15]

According to Davies et al. (1993), there appeared to be broad agreement at the start of the 1990s that a democratic South Africa's participation in a formal Southern African regional arrangement was desirable. South African government officials and business sector constituencies, together with existing regional organisations, as well as the OAU, UNECA and the World Bank, expressed support for formal integration that went beyond sectoral or functional economic cooperation. For example, the chairman of Standard Bank, Henri de Villiers, called for the formation of a 'Southern African Economic Community', reportedly stating that 'natural polarisation' could improve efficiency, and that mechanisms to ensure an equitable distribution of the benefits could easily be incorporated into such an arrangement (Joffe 1990).

Statements from the mass democratic movement also indicated support for a programme of economic integration in a post-apartheid setting. At a SADCC event in August 1990, ANC secretary-general Alfred Nzo called for 'self-reliant regional economic associations ... to promote greater interaction ... and give us greater bargaining power in our relations with the outside world'; Nzo emphasised the need 'to take into account both ... existing inequalities and the legacy of destabilisation' and 'develop productive activities' in less developed regions and countries (cited in Davies 1991: 2–3). An ANC discussion document for the July 1992 policy conference stated that 'the ANC is strongly in favour of promoting both cooperation and regional economic integration after apartheid' (cited in Davies 1992: 20). However, there was a tendency in the discourse of this period to refer to cooperation and integration interchangeably, and the terms 'common market' and 'economic union' loosely, without reference to their precise economic meanings.[16] It is thus not clear what, if any, rationale lay behind the apparent consensus.

As Davies et al. (1993) note, more divergent views soon began to emerge on the economic desirability of a Southern African regional union. The views of business and South African officials became more tempered, while regional organisations such as SADC began their move towards deeper integration with the expectation that a democratic South Africa would join the fold. In South Africa, Reserve Bank Governor Chris Stals counselled against 'vast new common markets' on account of 'too great a divergence between the stages of development of the various countries, making it impossible to integrate the economies and placing a huge burden on the more advanced nations' (Davies et al. 1993: 33; Financial Times 1992). A discussion document prepared for the South African Chamber of Business the same year suggested that 'ability to compete on overseas markets' rather than 'penetration of African markets' was the greater policy imperative, and that functional cooperation should be favoured over formal integration (Leistner 1992: 1).

However, it was still not clear how many of these diverse views and conclusions were derived, which theoretical paradigm or practical experiences they drew on and whether they had been adequately deliberated. As a result, the MERG background paper identified two key questions for the democratic movement in South Africa to address: should a programme of economic cooperation or formal integration be supported and, if integration was chosen, then which framework should inform this, given the various underlying approaches that were evident, but had not been systematically analysed (Davies et al. 1993).

Davies (1992) suggests that three broad frameworks or paradigms have been associated with the transition debate on Southern African regional integration: the neoclassical (market or trade integration) paradigm, functional integration and development integration. The functional and development integration approaches evolved as the most prominent perspectives among developing countries in the context of the 1960s (during Mkandawire's 'development planning phase'), while a neoliberal-flavoured market integration approach became a feature of the structural adjustment period. The latter has since evolved into confusion about what African regional integration seeks to be in the PWC phase: a tool for industrialisation and development, a counter to the entrenchment of hegemonic trading blocs elsewhere, or a stepping stone to free trade in a liberalised multilateral trading system.

In the market integration model, regional integration is typically viewed as a way to foster broader and deeper liberalisation by developing countries. This is the thrust of a World Bank (1991) study during the transition period that appears to support trade integration in Southern Africa to the extent that it would facilitate the multilateral trade liberalisation of member states, rather than because of any particular benefits of regional integration per se. By contrast, a substantive 1993 study by the ADB envisages a regional integration approach comprising both trade integration and sectoral cooperation, cautioning that market integration should proceed more slowly, as the benefits of regional trade liberalisation would be unevenly distributed. In particular, 'without in-built design of compensatory mechanisms to distribute regional gains (i.e., a regional investment and development policy) the pattern of their accrual, left to market forces alone, would mainly benefit South Africa ... in the short and medium term' (ADB 1993: 319). However, 'a strong interventionist thrust towards planning resource allocation and investment on a regional basis ... would seem to be impracticable, inconsistent with SAPs, and untimely ... Of course, significant public intervention will be necessary in southern Africa. But ... its role must be to create the regional policy environment that will enable market-based integration to work' (ADB 1993: 303–4).

Thus, while the ADB study acknowledges a role for intervention in what is fundamentally a market-driven approach to integration, this role is seen as limited. This view is in line with the PWC approach of limited intervention by a 'facilitating state'. The PWC is associated with the market imperfections school of neoclassical economics, whose policy prescriptions are still free trade despite the analysis itself pointing to the case for a strategic trade policy (Deraniyagala and Fine 2006). There is little reference to regional integration as an instrument of industrialisation. Indeed, policies advocated for growth and poverty reduction more broadly in the PWC period became characterised by what Mkandawire (2014: 187) terms 'a state of disarray' and Rodrik (2006: 973) titled 'Washington confusion'.

Strategic approaches to integration among developing countries require mechanisms to address industrialisation imperatives and distributional impacts. Alternatives include functional integration, involving cooperation on joint projects to address underdeveloped production structures and infrastructure constraints. As Davies (1992) explains, such cooperation is a prerequisite for regional trade liberalisation, to avoid polarisation as well as the de-industrialisation of less developed partner countries. Cooperation on sectoral projects in areas such as transport, energy and infrastructure characterised SADCC's early approach. However, functional integration has been criticised for lacking a systematic focus on regional trade and industrial development.

Towards development integration
At the time of the transition, the MERG background paper on South Africa and the region (Davies et al. 1993) favoured a development integration framework in which regional integration is viewed as a vehicle for industrialisation. This approach goes beyond market integration to incorporate comprehensive regional industrial policy, together with infrastructure development and measures to promote a balanced distribution of benefits (Davies 1996, 2019).[17] Another important element is the prospect for the developing country bloc to present stronger joint positions in international forums.

Unlike the view that emphasised access to African markets as a lesser policy imperative, the MERG paper recognised the continent's and especially Southern Africa's importance for South Africa's manufactured exports. At the same time, it underscored the need to take account of the impact of the apartheid regime's destabilisation policies in the design of a regional integration strategy for the post-apartheid era. Similarly, in a 1993 article in *Foreign Affairs* on the ANC's proposed foreign policy goals, Nelson Mandela highlighted the need to address the inequitable relations that had emerged historically in Southern Africa:

> The regional economy that emerged under colonialism entrenched the domination of one country (South Africa) and incorporated other countries in subsidiary and dependent roles as labor reserves, markets for South African commodities,

suppliers of certain services (such as transport) or providers of cheap and convenient resources (like water, electricity and some raw materials). South Africa's visible exports to the region exceed imports by more than five to one ... While South Africans experienced discrimination and repression at home, southern Africa fell victim to apartheid's destabilization strategy, which left two million dead and inflicted an estimated $62.45 billion of damage on the economies of our neighbors (Mandela 1993: 90).

While Mandela reiterated the importance of the region for South Africa's manufactured exports, he argued that more balanced trade was essential. Additionally, despite the need for project cooperation in power and natural resource development, it was imperative to go further to emphasise industrialisation: 'Any program ... must be sensitive to the acute imbalances in existing regional economic relations. Any move towards a common market or economic community must ensure that industrial development in the entire region is not prejudiced' (Mandela 1993: 91–2). With respect to SACU in particular, revision of the 1969 Customs Union Agreement would be undertaken in a manner 'guided by broader considerations than the implications for the South African treasury', and in particular with a view to removing 'barriers to ... a more balanced location of industries' (1993: 92–3).

South Africa's Reconstruction and Development Programme Base Document (RDP BD) devoted a specific section to 'Southern African Regional Policy', highlighting the need to 'negotiate with neighbouring countries to forge an equitable and mutually beneficial programme of increasing cooperation, coordination and integration appropriate to the conditions of the region' and expressing support for the 'goals and ideals of African integration as laid out in the Lagos Plan of Action and the Abuja Declaration' (ANC 1994: 117). Like the MERG and Mandela papers, it emphasised the importance of the region for South Africa's manufactured exports while highlighting the unbalanced nature of trade relations and the consequent need 'to encourage and promote industrial development throughout the region', with 'the development of regional and industrial strategies for specific sub-sectors, such as mineral beneficiation, auto components and textiles' (1994: 117). Another element in common with the MERG paper was that 'minimum standards with regard to rights of workers to organise be established across the region as a whole' (1994: 118).

The RDP BD signalled South Africa's intent to join SADC, reform SACU and enhance joint capacity to engage with international trade and financial institutions (ANC 1994: 118). This was reinforced in the trade policy section of the RDP BD, which cautions that 'trade and industrial policy must respond to the demands of reconstruction and development', that the tariff is 'a strategic instrument for trade policy' and that trade policy must be 'sensitive to the interests of the Southern African region as a whole' (1994: 88–90). This suggests that a developmental regionalism approach was envisaged, while not explicitly stated as such.

By contrast, in the *White Paper on Reconstruction and Development*, gazetted in November 1994, there is no separate section on Southern African regional policy (Office of the President 1994). The *White Paper* acknowledges the link between trade and industrial policy when it states that 'trade policy must ensure a greater quantity of manufactured exports from South Africa, a process largely dependent upon the application of an effective industrial policy' (Para 3.7.2). However, the discourse of 'trade policy reform', absent in the original RDP, is evident in the *White Paper* (Para 3.7.1). Indeed, a 'firm commitment to gradual but steady trade liberalisation in all sectors of the economy' with 'use of socially responsible supply-side measures to assist sensitive industries in adapting' (Para 3.7.3) distinguishes the *White Paper* from the strategic thrust of the RDP BD. Furthermore, although the *White Paper* makes brief reference to the region in its intent to 'address uneven development within the regions of South Africa *and between the countries of southern Africa*' (with the latter phrase added to Para 3.2.1 in the *White Paper*, my emphasis), there is no mention of regional (Southern African) industrial development or strategy, let alone a sectoral approach, as in the RDP BD.

In their analysis of the more neoliberal orientation of the *White Paper* relative to the RDP BD, Adelzadeh and Padayachee (1994) criticise the momentum of trade liberalisation prior to the implementation of a comprehensive industrial policy. While the report of the Industrial Strategy Project (Joffe et al. 1995) was released in 1995, it focused on supply-side industrial policy and regional policy within South Africa, and did not address Southern African economic integration, despite the region's importance for South Africa's manufactured trade. In any event, from June 1996, the pace of trade liberalisation was intensified unilaterally by South Africa under the Growth, Employment and Redistribution (GEAR) strategy.

GEAR has little to say about regional (Southern African) industrial development and makes no mention of SACU. It notes, however, 'the expansion of market access through preferential trade arrangements with industrial countries and pursuit of regional economic integration' as a 'critical policy thrust' of the past few years (Department of Finance 1996: 13). In the first of only two other references to the region, GEAR's integrated strategy refers to 'an expansion of trade and investment flows in Southern Africa' (1996: 2) as part of improving market access for South African firms. Although the section on 'industrial support measures' for South African firms highlights 'the gradual integration of the economies of Southern Africa through the trade and investment protocols of SADC' (1996: 14), absent is any reference to the need to restructure relations with the region on a more equitable footing (in contrast to the MERG background paper [Davies et al. 1993], Mandela's 1993 article and the RDP). Nor, indeed, is the importance of the region for South Africa's manufactured exports highlighted, notwithstanding the imperative of an 'accelerated growth of non-gold exports' and the emphasis on an 'outward-oriented industrial economy' (1996: 2, 7).

In contrast to the RDP *White Paper*'s emphasis on 'gradual but steady trade liberalisation', GEAR stated repeatedly that accelerated tariff liberalisation would be implemented from mid-1996, in part to counteract the depreciation of the rand in the first few months of that year (Department of Finance 1996: 2, 4–6, 13, 21).[18] As shown by Bell (1997), South Africa's tariff phase-down schedule already incorporated considerable unilateral liberalisation that went beyond the country's negotiated General Agreement on Tariffs and Trade commitments. Bell explains that, even in the case of the textiles and clothing and auto sectors, for which special dispensations had been negotiated, the South African authorities decided on deeper and more rapid tariff cuts. Subsequent literature pointed to the damaging impact of rapid liberalisation on the country's industrial base, despite the introduction of supply-side industrial support measures.[19]

In his analysis of the transition period, Zarenda (1997) argues that despite the early statements of the ANC and the thrust of the RDP BD, the immediate post-apartheid period was characterised by 'relative inertia' on regional integration policy. While South Africa joined SADC and initiated the renegotiation of the apartheid-era SACU agreement, the country appeared to lack a coherent policy framework to address a programme of development integration. In Zarenda's view, this was the result of a focus on South Africa's trade liberalisation programme under its Uruguay Round offer and further unilateral liberalisation measures referred to above. The offer impacted significantly on the country's SACU partners because of the common external tariff and lack of consultation on the tariff phase-down. Furthermore, the implications of South Africa's trade negotiations with the EU for both its SACU partners and possible participation in a SADC FTA were of concern. Indeed, Zarenda (1997) argues that the liberalisation focus was indicative of a market rather than a development integration approach in this period, more in line with the recommendations of studies such as that of the World Bank (1991).

In the end, the new SACU agreement came into effect in 2002 with a brief and rather vague Article on 'Industrial Development Policy' recognising 'the importance of balanced industrial development of the Common Customs Area' and agreeing 'to develop common policies and strategies with respect to industrial development' (SACU 2002: Article 38). More concretely, Article 26 of the agreement allows BLNS (now including Namibia) to protect infant industries for up to eight years. Two decades later, numerous outstanding issues related to the agreement remain, particularly in respect of revenue-sharing, democratisation, lack of progress on developing common policies and lack of formalisation of planned institutional arrangements.

In the case of SADC, the move towards an FTA was gradual, from the signing of the SADC Trade Protocol in 1996 to the implementation of the FTA in 2008. The process involved asymmetric tariff reductions, with South Africa (effectively SACU) liberalising more rapidly. While Article 21 of the Trade Protocol included measures to allow infant industry protection, the evolution of an industrial strategy took longer, gaining momentum in the early 2010s. The SADC Industrialisation Strategy and Roadmap (SADC 2015a) was approved in 2015, together with a revised RISDP (2015–2020) (SADC 2015b) and later an Action Plan for the Industrialisation Strategy (2017) (SADC 2017). The revised RISDP differed significantly in character from the initial RISDP, 'frontloading' industrialisation and emphasising strategic interventions in key sectors. The programme rested on three pillars, industrialisation, competitiveness and regional integration, with a focus on the promotion of RVCs that would link back to domestic producers. The most recent RISDP (2020–2030) (SADC 2021) continues the industrialisation emphasis, with its pillars of industrial development and market integration, infrastructure, and social and human capital development.

In South Africa, the re-emergence of a development integration emphasis followed a post-2007 shift in the country's trade and industrial policy trajectory. This shift was exemplified by the 2007 National Industrial Policy Framework (NIPF) of the Department of Trade and Industry (DTI), which emphasised the need for coherence between trade and industrial policy, as well as other economic policy areas such as macroeconomic and investment policy. The use of the tariff as a strategic policy instrument, envisaged earlier in the RDP BD, was made explicit in the NIPF, against orthodox trade policy prescriptions. In 2010, the DTI released a Trade Policy and Strategy Framework aligned with the NIPF to facilitate coordination between trade and industrial policy. The heterodox approach embodied in the NIPF combined a strategic tariff policy with strategic global integration oriented towards participation in the world economy while preserving sufficient policy space to pursue domestic and regional development objectives.

On the regional integration front, the NIPF's goals included support for the development of productive sector capabilities across the continent. The NIPF's three-year rolling implementation plans (the Industrial Policy Action Plans) highlighted the development integration approach in 2012, and explicitly included regional integration as a transversal intervention from 2013 (DTI 2013). These more recent positions reiterate the importance of infrastructure, regional industrial policy, trade facilitation and the development of RVCs to build productive capabilities across the region (Davies 2019; Ismail 2018). For the trade pillar, the South African view is that trade integration to the level of an FTA is preferable to a customs union since, in an FTA, countries can still use their tariff as an industrial policy tool (Davies 2019).

The renewed emphasis on development integration in the post-2007 period emerged against the background of hopes for a more progressive economic policy trajectory from the late 2000s. A strategic trade and industrial policy approach with an emphasis on development integration was actively driven from 2009 onwards:

> Over the last four years South Africa has worked with partner countries in the region to advance a developmental regional integration agenda. This represents the beginning of a departure

from the narrow market integration approach, which focused primarily on the reduction and elimination of tariffs and neglected to address the most significant constraints to regional integration: primarily, underdeveloped productive capacity and inadequate infrastructure (DTI 2013: 54).

Conclusion

Regional integration policy in Africa appears to have evolved in accordance with Mkandawire's (2014) three phases of development planning, structural adjustment and a PWC phase of policy disarray or confusion characterised by 'paradigmatic incoherence' (Davies 2019: 8). In the development planning phase, a development integration approach was envisaged, with regional integration as an instrument of industrialisation, while in the structural adjustment period, a neoliberal-flavoured market integration view took hold. In the PWC period, it is not yet clear what regional integration seeks to be in the context of the AfCFTA – a tool for insertion into a global free trade system or an active instrument of industrialisation and development.

South Africa's position over the three phases can arguably be said to have evolved in a similar way up to the turn of the century, but in accordance with its own particular interests and circumstances. In the 'development planning phase', South Africa's interest in SACU was driven by the economic, political and security needs of the apartheid state. The country was able to use the SACU tariff in pursuit of its own industrial development, while it remained a revenue instrument for BLS. The common customs area provided a captive market for South Africa's manufactured exports, and it was able to extract migrant labour, energy and other services from the region despite its global pariah status. In the neoliberal era, the country's focus on its Uruguay Round offer, and unilateral liberalisation that intensified in the mid-1990s, was evidently accompanied by a period in which a developmental integration strategy was more muted. Indeed, some viewed the approach in this period as decidedly market-oriented.

In the post-2007 period, however, a shift in the country's trade and industrial policy trajectory was accompanied by the re-emergence of a strong development integration narrative on the part of South African trade and industry officials, which soon appeared to take hold more broadly in configurations such as the TFTA. South Africa's stance was actively driven during Rob Davies's tenure as trade and industry minister from 2009 to 2019, benefiting from his own long-standing articulation of the concept. However, industrial policy implementation in this period was frustrated by a series of domestic and external constraints. The NIPF was launched as the global financial crisis broke, while the turn of the decade saw the Covid-19 pandemic take hold. Internally, industrial policy was impacted by coordination problems and lack of coherence between industrial policy objectives, macroeconomic and other policy areas, industrial financing deficiencies, concentration of ownership and control, lack of investment in productive sectors, and key infrastructure constraints during the state capture era under the Jacob Zuma presidency.

Despite the disappointments of the past fifteen years in the economic policy arena in South Africa, the idea of a development integration approach appears to be taking root more broadly again on the continent. However, in the contemporary setting, there is a lack of focus on transnational actors, other interest groups and political economy factors, and how they impact on regional integration initiatives. An innovative approach is thus required in order for development integration to inform the evolution of the remaining AfCFTA negotiating processes. There are lessons to be learnt from early approaches to regional policy, such as the CACM's Central American Integration Bank and Regime for Integration Industries, and the Solidarity Fund of the early West African Customs Union. More is needed, however, including consultation with domestic stakeholders, negotiation with transnational actors, strong RVCs and collaboration on key issues such as intellectual property regimes, investment, competition and public procurement policy in trade negotiations with developed economies.

Notes

1. The TFTA Agreement was concluded in June 2015 between the three regional economic communities in Eastern and Southern Africa, namely the Common Market for Eastern and Southern Africa (COMESA), the East African Community and the Southern African Development Community (SADC). The intention was to consolidate existing trade arrangements and promote regional value chains (RVCs).
2. Each successive level of formal integration requires countries to cede progressively more policy space. The shallowest is a preferential trade area (PTA) in which tariffs are reduced on a limited range of products. By contrast, in an FTA all trade restrictions are removed between member states, but each retains its own

tariffs against non-members. A customs union is an FTA with a common external tariff, while a common market is a customs union with unrestricted flows of capital and labour. Finally, an economic union is a common market in which monetary and fiscal policies are also harmonised (Davies 2019).
3. Personal communication, African regional integration official, 1 July 2022.
4. Phase II of the negotiations is set to cover investment, competition policy and intellectual property rights, while Phase III will deal with e-commerce.
5. Another notable aspect of Vishnu Padayachee's scholarship is the contribution of the journal *Transformation: Critical Perspectives on Southern Africa*, of which he was an editor from 1987, to the transition debates on trade and industrial policy and regional integration.
6. See, for example, Padayachee (1998); Padayachee and Sender (2018).
7. This involved the use of various industrial cooperation instruments, as well as institutional arrangements to promote regional industrial development. In the CACM, a key institution was the Central American Integration Bank, which financed regional infrastructure projects and other productive sector activities.
8. For example, in the case of CACM's 'Regime for Integration Industries', designed to facilitate the regional distribution of new manufacturing activity, the US actively withheld external financial assistance for enterprises seeking to access regional incentives under the scheme (Wionczek 1968).
9. These were mainly the World Bank and the International Monetary Fund.
10. The report's proposals for African agriculture and cursory treatment of industry prompted strong critique in a special double issue of CODESRIA's journal Africa Development on the Berg report and the LPA. See, in particular, Amin (1982) and Mkandawire (1982).
11. The Frontline States were Angola, Botswana, Lesotho, Malawi, Mozambique, eSwatini, Tanzania, Zambia and Zimbabwe.
12. The marked contrast with SADC's subsequent RISDPs is highlighted further below.
13. Formed in 2002, the AU was the successor to the OAU.
14. The country studies in Johnson and Martin (1986) are a devastating testimony to the consequences of apartheid South Africa's regional destabilisation project.
15. See Padayachee and Sender (2018) for a detailed account.
16. See Note 2.
17. These may include regional development banks, targeted investment flows, asymmetric tariff reductions and compensatory payment mechanisms.
18. According to the South African Reserve Bank (SARB 1996: 1), the rand depreciation was 'based largely on unfounded rumours and speculative transactions'.
19. See, for example, Roberts (2000); Zalk (2014).

References

ADB (African Development Bank). 1993. *Economic Integration in Southern Africa, Volume 1*. Abidjan: African Development Bank.

Adebajo, A. 2014. 'Two Prophets of Regional Integration: Prebisch and Adedeji'. In: *International Development: Ideas*, edited by B. Currie-Alder, R. Kanbur, D.M. Malone and R. Medhora. Oxford: Oxford University Press.

Adedeji, A. 1970. 'Prospects of Regional Economic Co-operation in West Africa'. *Journal of Modern African Studies* 8 (2): 213–31.

———. 1983. 'The Evolution of the Monrovia Strategy and the Lagos Plan of Action: A Regional Approach to Economic Decolonization'. Lecture delivered in the Distinguished Lecture Series of the Nigerian Institute of Social and Economic Research, University of Ibadan, 24 March. https://repository.uneca.org/handle/10855/5726.

———. 2002. 'History and Prospects for Regional Integration in Africa'. Presentation at the Third Meeting of the African Development Forum, UNECA, Addis Ababa, 5 March. https://repository.uneca.org/handle/10855/47111.

Adelzadeh, A. and V. Padayachee. 1994. 'The RDP White Paper: Reconstruction of a Development Vision?' *Transformation* 25: 1–18.

Adi, H. and M. Sherwood. 2003. *Pan-African History: Political Figures from Africa and the Diaspora since 1787*. London: Routledge.

Amin, S. 1982. 'A Critique of the World Bank Report Entitled "Accelerated Development in Sub-Saharan Africa"'. *Africa Development* 7 (1–2): 23–30.

ANC (African National Congress). 1994. *The Reconstruction and Development Programme*. Johannesburg: Umanyano Publications.

Bell, T. 1997. 'Trade Policy'. In: *The Political Economy of South Africa's Transition: Policy Perspectives in the Late 1990s*, edited by J. Michie and V. Padayachee. London: Dryden Press.

Cattaneo, N. 1990. 'Piece of Paper or Paper of Peace: The Southern African Customs Union Agreement'. *International Affairs Bulletin* 14 (1): 44–58.

———. 1998. 'The Theoretical and Empirical Analysis of Trade Integration among Unequal Partners: Implications for the Southern African Development Community'. MSc dissertation, Rhodes University.

Davies, R. 1991. *Perspectives on Regional Cooperation from South Africa's Mass Democratic Movement*. Backgrounder 3. Cape Town: Centre for Southern African Studies, University of the Western Cape.

———. 1992. *Integration or Cooperation in a Post-apartheid Southern Africa: Some Reflections on an Emerging Debate*. Southern African Perspectives Working Paper 18. Cape Town: Centre for Southern African Studies, University of the Western Cape.

———. 1994. *The Southern African Customs Union (SACU): Background and Possible Negotiating Issues Facing a Democratic Government*. Southern African Perspectives Working Paper 33. Cape Town: Centre for Southern African Studies, University of the Western Cape.

———. 1996. 'Promoting Regional Integration in Southern Africa: An Analysis of Prospects and Problems from a South African Perspective'. *African Security Review* 5 (5): 27–38.

———. 2019. *The Politics of Trade in the Era of Hyperglobalisation*. Geneva: South Centre.

Davies, R., D. Keet and M. Nkuhlu. 1993. *Reconstructing Economic Relations with the Southern African Region: Issues and Options for a Democratic South Africa*. MERG Occasional Paper Series. Cape Town: Centre for Development Studies, University of the Western Cape.

Department of Commerce. 1969. *Customs Union Agreement between the Governments of the Republic of South Africa, the Republic of Botswana, the Kingdom of Lesotho and the Kingdom of Swaziland*. Government Notice No. R-3914, 12 December. https://www.tralac.org/documents/resources/sacu/1452-1969-sacu-agreement/file.html.

Department of Finance. 1996. *Growth, Employment and Redistribution: A Macroeconomic Strategy*. Pretoria: Department of Finance.

Deraniyagala, S. and B. Fine. 2006. 'Kicking Away the Logic: Free Trade Is Neither the Question Nor the Answer for Development'. In: *The New Development Economics: After the Washington Consensus*, edited by K.S. Jomo and B. Fine. New Delhi: Tulika Books.

DTI (Department of Trade and Industry). 2013. *Industrial Policy Action Plan 2013/14–2015/16*. Pretoria: Department of Trade and Industry.

Financial Times. 1992. 'South Africa Is Exporting Skills, Technology and Experience to Africa'. *Financial Times*, 17 November. https://archive.org/details/FinancialTimes1992UKEnglish/Nov%2017%201992%2C%20Financial%20Times%2C%20%23717%2C%20UK%20%28en%29/.

Fine, B. 1997. 'Industrial and Energy Policy'. In: *The Political Economy of South Africa's Transition: Policy Perspectives in the Late 1990s*, edited by J. Michie and V. Padayachee. London: Dryden Press.

Green, R.H. and A. Seidman, A. 1968. *Unity or Poverty? The Economics of Pan-Africanism*. Baltimore: Penguin.

Ismail, F. 2018. *A 'Developmental Regionalism' Approach to the African Continental Free Trade Area (AfCFTA)*. Trade and Industrial Policy Strategies Working Paper. Pretoria: Trade and Industrial Policy Strategies.

Joffe, A., D. Kaplan, R. Kaplinsky and D. Lewis. 1995. *Improving Manufacturing Performance in South Africa*. Cape Town: University of Cape Town Press.

Joffe, H. 1990. 'Business Looks North at the Once-forbidden Pastures of Africa'. *Weekly Mail*, 23 February–1 March.

Johnson, P. and D. Martin (eds). 1986. *Destructive Engagement: Southern Africa at War*. Harare: Zimbabwe Publishing House and Southern African Research and Documentation Centre.

Kamata, N. 2019. 'Julius Nyerere: From a Territorial Nationalist to a Pan African Nationalist'. *African Review* 46 (2): 309–32.

Kibble, S. and R. Bush. 1986. 'Reform of Apartheid and Continued Destabilisation in Southern Africa'. *Journal of Modern African Studies* 24 (2): 203–27.

Leistner, E. 1992. 'South Africa's Options for Future Relations with Southern Africa and the European Community'. Discussion document commissioned by the South African Chamber of Business. Mimeo.

Maasdorp, G. and A. Whiteside. 1993. *Rethinking Economic Cooperation in Southern Africa: Trade and Investment*. Occasional Paper Series, Konrad Adenauer Foundation, Johannesburg.

Mandela, N. 1993. 'South Africa's Future Foreign Policy'. *Foreign Affairs* 72 (5): 86–97.

Mazrui, A. 2005. 'Pan-Africanism and the Intellectuals: Rise, Decline and Revival'. In: *African Intellectuals: Rethinking Politics, Language, Gender and Development*, edited by T. Mkandawire. Dakar and London: Council for the Development of Social Science Research in Africa and Zed Books.

McCarthy, C.L. 1994. 'Revenue Distribution and Economic Development in the Southern African Customs Union'. *South African Journal of Economics* 62 (3): 167–87.

MERG (Macroeconomic Research Group). 1993. *Making Democracy Work: A Framework for Macroeconomic Policy in South Africa*. Cape Town: Centre for Development Studies, University of the Western Cape.

Michie, J. and V. Padayachee, V. (eds). 1997. *The Political Economy of South Africa's Transition: Policy Perspectives in the Late 1990s*. London: Dryden Press.

Mkandawire, T. 1982. 'The Lagos Plan of Action (LPA) and the World Bank on Food and Agriculture in Africa: A Comparison'. *Africa Development* 7 (1–2): 166–77.

———. 1985. 'Dependence and Economic Co-operation: The Case of SADCC'. *Zimbabwe Journal of Economics* 1 (2): 1–10.

———. 2005. 'African Intellectuals and Nationalism'. In: *African Intellectuals: Rethinking Politics, Language, Gender and Development*, edited by T. Mkandawire. Dakar and London: Council for the Development of Social Science Research in Africa and Zed Books.

———. 2014. 'The Spread of Economic Doctrines and Policymaking in Postcolonial Africa'. *African Studies Review* 57 (1): 171–98.

OAU (Organization of African Unity). 1980. *Lagos Plan of Action for the Economic Development of Africa*. https://www.merit.unu.edu/wp-content/uploads/2015/01/Lagos-Plan-of-Action.pdf.

———. 1991. *Treaty Establishing the African Economic Community*. https://au.int/sites/default/files/treaties/37636-treaty-0016_-_treaty_establishing_the_african_economic_community_e.pdf.

Office of the President. 1994. *White Paper on Reconstruction and Development*. Pretoria: Office of the President.

Padayachee, V. 1998. 'Progressive Academic Economists and the Challenge of Development in South Africa's Decade of Liberation'. *Review of African Political Economy* 25 (77): 431–50.

———. (ed.). 2006. *The Development Decade?* Cape Town: HSRC Press.

———. (ed.). 2010. *The Political Economy of Africa*. London: Routledge.

———. 2016. 'Ideas and Power: Academic Economists and the Making of Policy'. *New Agenda* 61: 24–9.

Padayachee, V. and J. Sender. 2018. 'Vella Pillay: Revolutionary Activism and Economic Policy Analysis'. *Journal of Southern African Studies* 44 (1): 149–65. https://doi.org/10.1080/03057070.2018.1405644.

Roberts, S. 2000. 'Understanding the Effects of Trade Policy Reform: The Case of South Africa'. *South African Journal of Economics* 68 (4): 607–38.

Rodrik, D. 2006. 'Goodbye Washington Consensus, Hello Washington Confusion? A Review of the World Bank's *Economic Growth in the 1990s: Learning from a Decade of Reform*'. *Journal of Economic Literature* 44 (4): 973–87.

SACU (Southern African Customs Union). 2002. *2002 Southern African Customs Union Agreement between the Governments of the Republic of Botswana, the Kingdom of Lesotho, the Republic of Namibia, the Republic of South Africa and the Kingdom of Swaziland*. https://www.sacu.int/uploads/documents/11ed59ad0efe7652a9f7ea25c343815919ed023c.pdf.

SADC (Southern African Development Community). 2003. *Regional Indicative Strategic Development Plan*. Gaborone: Southern African Development Community.

———. 2015a. *SADC Industrialization Strategy and Roadmap 2015–2063*. Gaborone: Southern African Development Community. https://www.sadc.int/document/sadc-industrialisation-strategy-and-roadmap-english.

———. 2015b. *Revised Regional Indicative Strategic Development Plan (RISDP) 2015–2020*. Gaborone: Southern African Development Community.

———. 2017. *Action Plan for SADC Industrialization Strategy and Roadmap*. Gaborone: Southern African Development Community. https://www.sadc.int/sites/default/files/2021-08/Action_Plan_for_SADC_Industrialization_Strategy_and_RoadmaP..pdf.

———. 2021. *Regional Indicative Strategic Development Plan (RISDP) 2020–2030*. Gaborone: Southern African Development Community. https://www.sadc.int/document/sadc-regional-indicative-strategic-development-plan-risdp-2020-2030-english.

SADCC (Southern African Development Coordination Conference). 1980. *Southern Africa: Towards Economic Liberation. A Declaration by the Governments of Independent States of Southern Africa Made at Lusaka on the 1st of April 1980*. Lusaka: Southern African Development Coordination Conference.

SARB (South African Reserve Bank). 1996. *Quarterly Bulletin* 200. Pretoria: South African Reserve Bank.

Secret Memorandum. n.d. 'Secret Memorandum of Understanding with reference to the Customs Union Agreement dated 11 Dec. 1969 between the Governments of South Africa, Botswana, Lesotho and Swaziland'. On file with the author.

Vaitsos, C. 1978. 'Crisis in Regional Economic Cooperation (Integration) among Developing Countries: A Survey'. *World Development* 6 (6): 719–69.

Walters, J. 1989. 'Renegotiating Dependency: The Case of the Southern African Customs Union'. *Journal of Common Market Studies* 28 (1): 29–52.

Wionczek, M.S. 1968. 'The Central American Common Market'. *Intereconomics: Review of European Economic Policy* 3 (8): 237–40.

World Bank. 1981. *Accelerated Development in Sub-Saharan Africa: An Agenda for Action*. Washington DC: World Bank.

———. 1991. *Intra-Regional Trade in Sub-Saharan Africa*. Economics and Finance Division Technical Department, Africa Region, Report 7685-AFR. Washington DC: World Bank.

Zalk, N. 2014. 'Industrial Policy in a Harsh Climate: The Case of South Africa'. In: *Transforming Economies: Making Industrial Policy Work for Growth, Jobs and Development*, edited by J. Salazar-Xirinachs, I. Nubler and R. Kozul-Wright. Geneva: UN Trade and Development and International Labour Organization.

Zarenda, H. 1997. 'Regional Integration Policies in Southern Africa'. In: *The Political Economy of South Africa's Transition: Policy Perspectives in the Late 1990s*, edited by J. Michie and V. Padayachee. London: Dryden Press.

16

The Engaged Intellectual, the State and Civil Society in the Post-Zuma Era
Lessons from the Eastern Cape

Janet Cherry

Now is not the time for cynicism. Nor is it the time for protest. Some argue that we have run out of time, facing the gravest challenge of the past two hundred years. It is a challenge to all of us, as engaged intellectuals, to which we must respond. At the same time that climate change is a grave threat, it necessitates a transition to a different society, a different economy. This is an opportunity to which we as engaged intellectuals can and must respond. We have the space and the position to explore alternatives, to put forward new models, to envision the future. How do we relate to the state in doing this? This is the central question of this chapter.

The utopian thinking of Rick Turner, the empirical scholarship of Ruth First, the counter-hegemonic organisation of Matthew Goniwe: these are the achievements of the engaged intellectuals who have inspired me to think through this question in the context of South Africa in the current conjuncture. Recently, an interaction with activists from Rojava, the ecofeminist autonomous communes in Syria, has provided an additional thought-provoking example of how to engage (or not) the state.[1]

On 6 September 2020, at a South African Students Congress (SASCO) anniversary conference, President Cyril Ramaphosa posed a challenge to SASCO students and to the entire university community in South Africa. Noting that it is the 'responsibility of young revolutionary intellectuals to shape the future of this country', he went on to stress that the national democratic revolution 'needs an educated society to build a sustainable and inclusive economy' and that 'universities have an immeasurable role to play in this regard'. He urged the university community to support the government and its programme of 'fundamental socio-economic transformation' through creating a 'conscientised and mobilised citizenry' (Ramaphosa 2020).

While the president was addressing himself to students, in particular the student body aligned to the ruling African National Congress (ANC), his speech challenges us as the broader university community to think of the role played by intellectuals, researchers and teachers in the current crisis in South African society, and in the long-term transformation of human society. Nelson Mandela University has as its slogan 'Change the World!', and a vision which clearly situates the role of the academy in a social and global context, with concomitant responsibilities.[2] The vision 'to be a dynamic African university, recognised for its leadership in generating cutting-edge knowledge for a sustainable future' provides the overall understanding within which our research into the transition from fossil fuels is situated. While this surely does not mean unconditional support for the programme of any political party in the national context, it does mean taking seriously the notion of 'engagement' and interrogating what this means for our pedagogy and our research practice.

In 2011, I argued that the development studies discipline was the ideal academic space in which to 'engage students in an exploration of new forms of social and economic organisation' and that 'ideally, we should engage our ... students in collaborative and applied research with government departments to explore new and innovative models for "transition societies"' (Cherry 2011: 78).

This proved easier said than done, however. The challenges of working across and between the academic space and state institutions and trying to explore alternatives, both at the level of ideas and in the implementation of pilot projects using participatory action research, were many. Here two accounts are presented of attempts made by the Department of Development Studies at Nelson Mandela University to bridge these divides in the course of the past decade.

In setting out these self-reflective accounts, let me take as a starting point two comments that were made by academic peers, which stood out as sharp but helpful criticisms of what I have been trying to do in the past decade. These criticisms, which are outlined below, essentially concerned the way in which we as academics related to the local state in the conduct of our research. Both criticisms can be analysed using the framework of 'modes of politics at a distance from the state' developed by Lucien van der Walt (2020) and related in turn to the very thorny question of the relationship of civil society to the state and, inevitably in the South African context, to the ANC as the ruling party during the decade of the research. The university works within this context, and academics who are activists and aligned to both civil society and the ruling party find ourselves straddling this three-way relationship with considerable – although not unmanageable – discomfort.

The politics of land and sustainability: The Sustainable Settlement Pilot Project

The Sustainable Settlement Pilot Project (SSPP) was a research project funded by the Eastern Cape Provincial Department of Human Settlements. Its objective was to find a solution to informal settlement development within the framework of the just transition. This involved identifying and testing alternative and local building materials, renewable energy systems, localised sanitation and water systems, as well as food production and other livelihood opportunities for residents. The concept of sustainable settlements was outlined (Cherry 2013) in *Human Settlements Review 01*, the first edition of a journal published by the Department of Human Settlements. As Zoleka Sokopo, then the chief director of Human Settlements Strategy noted in his foreword to the journal, 'a holistic understanding of human settlements is essential if we are to achieve sustainability – a fact that is underscored by Cherry's discussion of the need for settlements that enable the livelihoods of residents' (Sokopo 2013: 9).

The site selected for the pilot project was a small informal settlement called Zweledinga, on the western edge of the Nelson Mandela Metro, situated in a beautiful milkwood forest with views of the sea. The residents, understandably, did not want to be rehoused elsewhere. They had been living there for two decades in some cases, had access to some (although limited) work opportunities, and had created a community. They demanded (and were promised) housing and services *in situ*, but the presence of the protected milkwood forest meant that provision of bulk services and the conventional low-cost Reconstruction and Development Programme (RDP) subsidised housing model would not be possible. The Department of Development Studies at Nelson Mandela University was challenged by the municipality to come up with a sustainable solution. This was done through participatory action research with the residents of Zweledinga, who elected a Community Research Team which then conducted a baseline study that resulted in a proposal for settlement development (Cherry and Lemercier 2013a). This proposal was presented to, and welcomed by, both provincial and local government. In addition to the research, the team piloted sandbag housing construction, using locally available and sustainable building materials as an alternative to cement blocks, and community labour (Cherry and Lemercier 2013b). The idea was to access the RDP housing subsidy using the Enhanced People's Housing Process which allowed for community cooperatives to build the houses, as well as the Upgrading of Informal Settlements Programme and policies on alternative building materials. The proposal was never implemented, however.

This project ran from 2011 to 2013. The outcome was presented at a seminar at the International Institute of Social Studies in The Hague (Cherry 2015). The response from the international scholars of sustainable development present was one of puzzlement at why the project had failed (if failure is measured by whether the development had been implemented, and the residents had had their needs met; if it is measured by participation, empowerment, innovation, then perhaps it did not fail): was there no clear agreement with the government before the project started? they asked. Others queried why we had not obtained private or donor funding to realise the project. The answers to these questions are complex and go to the heart of the question of engaged scholarship, the state and civil society.

The initial response to the first question is simple: the reason the project was not implemented was because it was a pilot; it had not been undertaken before, and the state did not know how to proceed. The project did not fit neatly into any of the existing government policies and processes. It involved multiple departments at municipal level, and coordination between local and provincial government departments. Both provincial and local government lacked capacity to meet targets for delivery of housing and services within existing policy frameworks, let alone engage in implementing innovative solutions. Although the project report, the findings and the proposed solution were met with approval by both provincial and local government, they were unable to find a way of implementing our proposed 'sustainable settlement' model. More than a decade since the project began, the residents of Zweledinga are still living in the same conditions, and still regularly protesting about their lack of housing, sanitation and electricity.

While there are research projects testing alternative building technologies, renewable energy systems and self-build low-cost housing, the integration of these into one human settlement development initiative did not prove possible. We attempted to involve the national Department of Science and Technology, having been challenged by then Minister Derek Hanekom to find a solution, but unfortunately on the day officials from the department were due to visit the project, the frustrated residents engaged in a protest action once more. This settlement was then not considered stable enough for such an intervention to take place.

State capture, corruption and patronage all form part of the story, although they are not the focus, nor are they the primary cause of the failure of the SSPP. In the case of the SSPP, the intervention of government officials was decisive in undermining the project in the eyes of the community. As one community leader – one of the members of the Community Research Team – stated, this official explained to them that they were going to buy a 'big, big piece of land, where you can have everything you want, houses, electricity, proper toilets'; because of this, they (the residents) 'did not need to worry any longer about the university research project'.

One of my colleagues (cited in Cherry and Lemercier 2013a) noted that 'careless government entities on the electoral path and a naïve but frustrated community is quite an explosive mixture, wherein the SSPP has little chance to survive if these interferences are not rapidly dealt with'.

Indeed, the government did buy a piece of land from a private landowner. Without going into the details of the transaction and the assessment of the land – it turned out that it was not suitable for housing development – it was further established that the land had been purchased at an inflated price through a 'deal' which was investigated and resulted in a criminal charge of corruption.

As the university project leaders, we did not understand at the time that the project was being undermined by corruption. However, it was clear that the state was by no means speaking with one voice about this development. Our relationships with certain municipal officials were good, as were our relationships with the Provincial Department of Human Settlements, which had commissioned the research. We were optimistic that if the institutional or bureaucratic barriers could be overcome, the project could succeed. We were naïve in this optimism; we did not have a 'champion' in the state, and the project was not a state-led initiative, fitting neatly into an existing policy implementation framework.

To answer the second question – why did we not then secure private or donor funds to implement the project? – the answer was simply that we did not want this to be a community 'project' funded through foreign donor assistance. Indeed, there are good welfare projects in this community, supporting the crèche where we held many meetings and workshops. But the point of piloting an innovative model of housing and service provision was so that it could be mainstreamed as part of government policy. We did not want it to be a private initiative; this would have defeated the purpose of the research.

The politics of action research: The Transition Township project

The Transition Township project was initiated in 2015 by a former student of the Development Studies Department, a trade unionist and experienced organiser, an 'organic intellectual' from the working-class township of Kwazakhele. Also guided by the concept of a 'just transition' but situated in the context of a formal township rather than an informal settlement, the project's focus was on neighbourhood cooperatives becoming producers of (renewable) energy. Funding was obtained from the National Institute of Humanities and Social Sciences for a 'catalytic' research project and, using essentially the same methodology as the SSPP, a Community Research Team was recruited from among activists in four wards of Kwazakhele township. The baseline research and community mobilisation led to the piloting of a community-owned renewable energy facility, together with food production on a 'gap tap' (a public open space which in the 1960s and 1970s was used for a stand tap), run by a neighbourhood cooperative. The argument was essentially that a just transition from fossil fuels would involve changing relations of production – that working class neighbourhoods could be producers of energy as the means of energy production (through photovoltaic [PV] solar) could be decentralised. This electricity would then be sold to the municipality, and everyone would benefit. The intention was for this to be combined with vegetable and fish production in an integrated system with water capture and solar pumps – a system consistent with the concept of food sovereignty – together with the testing of circular economy principles through waste recycling to produce useful plastic products such as gutters, pipes and buckets.

Civil society initiatives were behind both the SSPP and the Transition Township project. The Nelson Mandela Bay Transition Network had been established before the Conference of the Parties (COP) 17 held in Durban in December 2011. This network involved mainly professionals who aligned themselves with the Transition Town movement in the Global North.[3] Some of the core Transition Township members are members of the Amandla Collective, aligned with the independent socialist and 'green left' in South Africa, which is also aligned with the Climate Justice network. The project was aligned with the South African Food Sovereignty Campaign and the Climate Justice Charter campaign, which gathered momentum as the Transition Township project was getting under way. In addition, the initiator of the Transition Township project was a National Union of Metalworkers of South Africa (NUMSA) organiser, committed to establishing worker cooperatives, and aligned with the One Million Climate Jobs Campaign that was launched by the Congress of South African Trade Unions at the COP 17 Civil Society Forum.

Despite these civil society alignments, the Transition Township project was not understood as an autonomous project, creating self-sufficiency in energy and food for a particular neighbourhood. Instead, from the beginning the university-based Transition Township team and the Kwazakhele-based Community Research Team worked together with the municipal electricity department and renewable energy experts from the German development agency Deutsche Gesellschaft für Internationale Zusammenarbeit, who were seconded to assist with municipal renewable energy (RE) projects. Together with RE industry experts, they advised on how Kwazakhele residents could 'feed into' the municipal grid. After extensive community consultations and public forums, the 'gap tap pilot' was mooted. The gap tap was selected precisely because it is municipal land and designated as public open space, de facto controlled by residents of the neighbourhood. This means that the facility can be communally owned; that it does not fall under another government department (as school or clinic vegetable gardens do); nor is it funded as a charity project by a church or an NGO. The residents of the designated gap tap were organised into the Saltuba cooperative, and a small PV solar array was set up together with two vegetable tunnels and a water capture system. A waste recycling centre and RE-based community and business centre were added in December 2022.

One of the reviewers of another essay written about this project (Cherry and Prevost 2023) provided a surprising critique, contrasting this project with Ruth First's work in Mozambique and implying that we were following an autonomist, even anarchist, approach:

> Ruth First's work with FRELIMO ... was about developing a guidance for FRELIMO as to how best to support people in context. This is very different to the action research approach that you adopted and is certainly very different to the almost anarchistic approach adopted by radicals in the Transitioning [*sic*] Townships frame.[4]

This critique stimulated some self-critical reflection on the project, together with an analysis of the relationship of such pilot projects with the state. It has also forced the project team to examine through dark-tinted spectacles the nasty political realities of attempting such development projects in a township such as Kwazakhele.

Kwazakhele was selected precisely because of its relative homogeneity and its long political history; in other words, it has a high level of social cohesion and political participation (Cherry 2000). This should bode well for attempts to implement something that requires good organisation and community cohesion. And indeed, the project was welcomed, and the organisation was good. At a political level, the project was presented to mayoral committees and standing committees of the council, as well as to the electricity department and the economic development department (which includes urban agriculture); and it was met with enthusiasm by all, both public representatives (the councillors in the ward and the ward cluster) and municipal officials.

As the implementation of the pilot began, there was little response from the municipal departments involved and the decision was made to proceed, nonetheless. The pilot was designed through a participatory co-design process and established with private funding; in addition to the research funding, a grant was obtained from a local business trust to buy the solar panels and erect water infrastructure and vegetable tunnels. With assistance from the electricity department, the PV solar array was connected to the municipal grid in December 2019; but the Saltuba cooperative was unable to obtain a formal 'offtake agreement', or to obtain a municipal account and a smart meter in order to receive payment for the electricity, or to 'wheel' it through a third party and sell it to private companies. Cooperative members could monitor the electricity they were producing and became frustrated with the lack of income; their expectations had been raised but the local state was not ready for the project. Despite public acclaim, and the municipal spokesperson promising that by mid-2021 the cooperative would be able to be paid (Rogers 2020), this was not realised (Rogers 2022), even after the passing of the Amendment to the Electricity Regulation Act (No. 4 of 2006) that came into effect in August 2021. At a seminar held in March 2022 to discuss the challenges and potential of such projects, the cooperative members expressed their dissatisfaction; and a National Energy Regulator of South Africa official made a sharp criticism of the project, stating that we should have had the agreement in place prior to implementing the PV solar array.[5] In September 2023 Saltuba finally obtained a municipal account, and the municipal electricity department committed to realising and expanding the pilot RE project.

In the course of the nearly fifteen years that these two projects have been running, starting in 2011, the Nelson Mandela Bay Municipality and the council have been confronted by severe challenges, both political and administrative. We presented the Transition Township project to three different mayoral committees, under different political party leaderships.[6] The administration of the municipality was caught, during the period of the first project, in a morass of corruption (Olver 2017). Subsequently, during the period of the second project, factionalism within the ANC and unstable coalitions with smaller parties have led to paralysis of the council (Cherry 2021; Ndletyana 2020). What impacted on the Transition Township project was at an even lower level, however. The politics of 'tenderpreneurship', and local turf battles for control over ward councillors and their allocation of resources, began to impact on the project.

As just one disturbing example, I received a telephone call one day in 2017 from a Mr 'Baba' Ningi, who requested a meeting with me at the offices of the Development Studies Department at the Missionvale Campus of Nelson Mandela University. He claimed to be the head of the Development Forum for Kwazakhele, and the director of the Black Business Caucus; and he presented himself as the 'gatekeeper' of all development projects in the township. He arrived at our offices with a group of about ten men, who crowded into our meeting room. We explained that the project was funded as a university research project and not a government project, after which he left us alone. In November 2019 he was gunned down at his Kwazakhele home, in what was later established to be connected to the 'drain cleaning tender' scandal in Nelson Mandela Bay (Ndletyana 2020; Wilson 2019).

More recently, in March 2022, the councillor for Ward 20, which is adjacent to Ward 22 where the Saltuba Gap Tap is located, was assassinated. It is widely believed that this was a political 'hit' related to factions within the ANC and access to resources through the ward councillor position (Prevost, Cherry and Brennan 2024). Karl von Holdt has characterised such violence as characteristic of a 'patronage-violence complex' whereby a new elite uses state institutions to accumulate wealth (Von Holdt 2022).

While the municipality had committed to the Saltuba project at its Economic Development Tourism and Agriculture Standing Committee meeting in May 2021, and promised substantial funding to realise the project and expand it to two additional gap taps, the local government elections in November 2021 together with the paralysis of the council meant that the funding has to date not been forthcoming. Despite these challenges and the element of fear produced by political assassinations in the metro, we have continued with the next stage of the project, the establishment of a waste recycling facility, with funding assistance through a Germany university partnership.

Inspirations
While Ruth First's work with the FRELIMO government during the socialist transition in Mozambique has been one inspiration for the Transition Township project, recently the Rojava experiment has provided another source of inspiration. Whereas First has been criticised for being 'too close to the state', the Rojava model of ecofeminism and localised democracy can be criticised as being 'too far from the state' and verging on anarchism (a criticism also directed at the Transition Township project). The Rojava activists we met explained that their model is 'democracy plus the state' – in other words they are not replacing the state completely but supplementing it with their local self-organised communes.

Going back to the 'modes of politics at a distance from the state' (Van der Walt 2020) referred to at the start of this chapter, I hesitantly apply this framework to development, and rephrase it as 'modes of development in relation to the state'. The 'developmental state' is of course one such model. Yet in the light of state failure at many levels, especially the local level, it is necessary to explore a different model. This is one where civil society takes the initiative; where citizens organise production, to meet their needs, at neighbourhood level. Production of energy and food, waste recycling and production of basic goods, building materials and water capture – much of this can be done by cooperatives that partner with the local state where necessary and with bigger business where necessary. The essence is the decentralisation, socialisation and localisation of productive assets. This is what makes it 'fundamental social change': it is concerned with changing the social relations of production, in a way that is consistent with the concept of a just transition, if the concern is with development in the context of climate change. It is also consistent with ecosocialist principles, if one wants to attach an ideological standpoint to it; or with the UN Sustainable Development Goals, if one wants to situate it in a global and politically correct framework; or with emancipatory human rights, if that is the goal.

The civil society networks involved in the climate justice space are almost invariably antagonistic to the state ('against the state', in Van der Walt's typology): either protesting against current policies or lobbying for alternatives; or establishing small, autonomous alternatives ('apart from the state'). Yet the premise of both the SSPP and the Transition Township is to explore alternatives 'with the state'.

What is the role of intellectuals in this process? To provide the evidence for the viability of such alternatives. This takes place at a number of levels: scientific experiment – for example, the development and testing of new technologies; action research – for example, piloting such new technologies in a community; and policy research and advocacy – convincing the state of the viability, and indeed the necessity, of such alternatives.

As academics in the transdisciplinary field of development studies, we should be constantly challenging ourselves to not accept the existing conventions of the various disciplines: economics, political science, sociology, and 'development' itself. This critical approach should not lead to paralysis in theory or in application to the real world. As First did, we should be sharply critical in our new context of the 'received wisdom', and attempt to test out new ideas, even when these are not in favour with society, the government or the academy.

Technology plus political economy: A tentative conclusion
One of the premises of our research is that science can provide solutions, but that these will only answer the questions we are asking – in other

words, respond to the challenges of the day – if the science is used by society to do so. In Marxist terminology, the advances in the forces of production – in other words technology – can be liberatory; but this depends on changes in the social relations of production. Enough food and energy can be produced to meet society's needs; enough can be produced without burning more fossil fuels. At the time of writing, the first green hydrogen-powered truck for platinum mining has come into use in South Africa. Anglo American is committed to mining – including mining of the platinum group metals used for hydrogen fuel cells and other batteries – using 'green' energy.

The way in which the research is carried out is also germane to whether it contributes to fundamental social change. We argue that our methodology, participatory action research (Rahman 1993), is able to change power relations in society. Research conducted by universities is often extractive of information from people, as the exploitation of gas and coal is extractive from the earth or the ocean. Through participatory action research and participatory rural appraisal methods, the 'subjects' of the research are themselves empowered to analyse their own reality and arrive at solutions (Chambers 1997).[7] The university can assist in the testing of such solutions.

Our concern here is with 'fundamental social change'; for us in the Transition Township project, this means changing the social relations of production. The underlying assumption is that new technology (in particular PV solar) combined with existing assets (land, infrastructure) can be used productively by residents. They are collective owners, as well as managers and workers, of their productive facilities. This is in clear distinction to the role of intellectuals as providers of strategic guidance to movements that are in opposition to the state, or are demanding certain things of the state. South African Communist Party leader Jeremy Cronin argues (2019: 18) that 'popular forces tend not to be mobilised as protagonists, as productive agents in building a new society. Rather they are mobilised as righteous beneficiaries of state delivery'. The Transition Township project is attempting to do precisely this: to use the resources of the university to mobilise working class communities as the protagonists of their own development. Professor Robert van Niekerk has similarly argued that a democratic social welfare state would prioritise and promote an inclusive concept of 'public good', in partnership with local community mobilisation into 'organs of people's power' such as street committees.[8]

The question may be asked: does not the mobilisation of residents for provision of goods and services result in a privatisation of what should be the function of a social-democratic state committed to realising the rights of its citizens? Cronin argues (2019: 18) that 'it is not a question of offloading the state's public responsibilities onto NGOs and communities, but rather how to build state-community mobilisation in which there is a co-production of a new society'. In a simpler formulation, but expressing the focus of the most recent economic policy document of the ruling ANC, National Executive Committee member Dakota Legoete (2022) stated that what is needed is to 'allow ordinary people to participate in the economy, expanding ownership'.[9] This is the 'outside but with the state' model, which entertains a mixed economy, an important role for the state as regulator and provider of certain infrastructure, and a decentralised economy in which the majority of citizens can participate as productive and creative beings. Our role as engaged intellectuals is to facilitate this co-production, to test the possibilities in complex societal contexts, and to assess through critical and rigorous research what does and does not work.

At another level, that of global justice and the existential threat posed by climate change, such projects as the SSPP and Transition Township prefigure a different society: one that is based on socialised production to meet the needs of people, using technology that enables sustainable use of the earth's resources and ensures that the earth is a habitat which can sustain life into the unimaginable future. Our role is thus also to engage, without cynicism, in utopian thinking.

Notes

1. The International Labour Research and Information Group facilitated a tour of Rojava activists to South Africa, which included a workshop at the Missionvale Campus of Nelson Mandela University on 21 May 2022.
2. See https://www.mandela.ac.za/About-us.
3. The Transition Town movement in the Global North promotes transition from fossil fuels as well as localised economies based on permaculture principles, as advanced by Rob Hopkins among others; see Transition Network (2016).
4. Peer review comments on Cherry and Prevost (2023).
5. 'Sustainable Energy for Local Economic Development' seminar held at Nelson Mandela University Missionvale Campus, 11 March 2022.
6. We started the project in 2015/16 when Zanuxolo Wayile was mayor, and Zukile Jodwana head of Economic Development. Both were aligned to NUMSA. The following ANC mayor, Danny Jordaan, supported the project; as did the Democratic

Alliance (DA) mayor Athol Trollip; he was succeeded by a fragile coalition council led by Mayor Bobani. At the time of the Vishnu Padayachee colloquium at Wits in July 2022, the ANC had the balance of power in a 'hung' council, with Mayor Eugene Johnson also coming from a NUMSA background, but power reverted to the DA-led coalition in September 2022.
7. My personal inspiration for using these methods over more than twenty years has been Robert Chambers of the Institute of Development Studies at Sussex University; see Chambers (1997), his influential book dealing with changing power relations through research which has been on the prescribed lists of my honours students in development studies.
8. Robert van Niekerk made this point at a seminar on 'Social Policy in South Africa' at Nelson Mandela University, as part of the master's course 'Advanced Development Policy', on 23 September 2020. See also Padayachee and Van Niekerk (2019).
9. On page 141 of the policy document the ANC states its commitment to 'interventions that seek to change the structure, systems, institutions and patterns of ownership, management and control of the economy' (ANC 2022).

References

ANC (African National Congress). 2022. 'Strengthening Economic Recovery and Reconstruction to Build an Inclusive Economy'. In: *Umrabulo Policy Conference 2022 Special Edition: Discussion Documents*. Johannesburg: African National Congress. https://docs.google.com/viewerng/viewer?url=https://www.anc1912.org.za/wp-content/uploads/2022/05/Umrabulo-Policy-Document-18th-May-2022.pdf.

Chambers, R. 1997. *Whose Reality Counts? Putting the Last First*. London: Intermediate Technology Publications.

Cherry, J. 2000. 'Hegemony, Democracy and Civil Society: Political Participation in Kwazakele Township, 1980–1990'. In: *From Comrades to Citizens: The South African Civics Movement and the Transition to Democracy*, edited by G. Adler and J. Steinberg. London: Palgrave.

———. 2011. 'Cutting Edge Social Science? Development Studies and the Transition to a Low-Carbon Future'. *Africanus: Journal of Development Studies* 41 (3): 73–9.

———. 2013. 'Jobs Versus Livelihoods: Sustainable Settlements within the Transition Paradigm'. *Human Settlements Review* 1: 43–64.

———. 2015. 'PAR and PRA in Development Practice: An Experiment'. Seminar presentation to the International Institute of Social Studies, The Hague, 29 April.

———. 2021. 'Democracy and Development in Nelson Mandela Bay: Reflections on Mcebisi Ndletyana's Analysis of the ANC in Power'. *Journal of Contemporary African Studies* 39 (3): 403–9.

Cherry, J. and P.L. Lemercier. 2013a. '"A big, big, big piece of land . . . " Land Acquisition on the Urban Edge: Seaview Continued'. Unpublished memo.

———. 2013b. 'Sustainable Settlement Pilot Project Seaview, Baseline Research'. https://www.academia.edu/9165790/Sustainable_Settlement_Pilot_Project_Seaview_Baseline_Research.

Cherry, J. and G. Prevost. 2023. 'Emancipatory Scholarship and Emancipatory Human Rights. The Transition Township Project: Lessons for University and Community Partnerships'. In: *Emancipatory Human Rights and the University: Promoting Social Justice in Higher Education*, edited by A. Keet and F. Tibbitts. London: Taylor and Francis.

Cronin, J. 2019 'Replacing "Delivery State, Passive Citizenry" with Active Citizens'. *New Agenda* 72: 13–18.

Legoete, D. 2022. 'Interview with Stephen Grootes'. *SAFM Morning Live*, 30 May.

Ndletyana, M. 2020. *Anatomy of the ANC in Power: Insights from Port Elizabeth, 1990–2019*. Cape Town: HSRC Press.

Olver, C. 2017. *How to Steal a City: The Battle for Nelson Mandela Bay, an Insider Account*. Johannesburg: Jonathan Ball.

Padayachee, V. and R. van Niekerk. 2019. *Shadow of Liberation: Contestation and Compromise in the Economic and Social Policy of the African National Congress, 1943–1996*. Johannesburg: Wits University Press.

Prevost, G., J. Cherry and P. Brennan. 2024. 'Battle for the Bay Revisited: The 2021 South African Local Elections in the Nelson Mandela Bay Municipality'. *Politeia* 43(1). https://doi.org/10.25159/2663-6689/15907.

Rahman, A. 1993. *People's Self Development: Perspectives on Participatory Action Research*. London: Zed Books.

Ramaphosa, C. 2020. 'ANC President Cyril Ramaphosa Addresses the 29th Anniversary of the South African Students Congress', *SABCNews*, 6 September. https://www.youtube.com/watch?time_continue=4&v=leTWAfKBkPc&feature=emb_title.

Rogers, G. 2020. 'Community Solar Project Should Start Reaping Rewards Next Year'. *The Herald*, 16 September. https://www.heraldlive.co.za/news/2020-09-18-community-solar-project-should-start-reaping-rewards-next-year/.

———. 2022. 'Saltuba Forges Ahead with New Smart Building'. *The Herald*, 12 December. https://www.heraldlive.co.za/news/2022-12-12-saltuba-forges-ahead-with-new-smart-building/.

Sokopo, Z. 2013. 'Foreword'. *Human Settlements Review* 1: 9.

Transition Network. 2016. *The Essential Guide to Doing Transition: Your Guide to Starting Transition in Your Street, Community, Town or Organisation*. https://transitionnetwork.org/resources-essential-guide-transition/.

Van der Walt, L. 2020. *Modes of Politics at a Distance from the State*. Pamphlet. Zabalaza Books, zabalazabooks.net. https://theanarchistlibrary.org/library/lucien-van-der-walt-modes-of-politics-at-a-distance-from-the-state.

Von Holdt, K. 2022. 'Rethinking the Categories of Sociology'. Inaugural lecture, University of the Witwatersrand, Johannesburg, 26 May.

Wilson, G. 2019. 'NMB Small-business Owner and Associate Gunned Down in Suspected "Hit"'. *TimesLive*, 12 November. https://www.timeslive.co.za/news/south-africa/2019-11-12-nmb-small-business-owner-and-associate-gunned-down-in-suspected-hit/.

17

'Exodus without a Map', 2
What Happened to the Durban Moment?

Edward Webster

Although I had known Vishnu Padayachee for nearly forty years, it was only in 2013 that I got to work with him. It was on a special edition of *Transformation* focusing on the 'varieties of capitalism' approach (Padayachee 2013). We became good friends when we both joined the new Southern Centre for Inequality Studies in 2018 and initiated a project on Alternative Forms of Ownership. The project's aim was to identify and analyse the alternatives to the traditional corporations emerging in the Global South. We wanted to examine in depth the forms these alternatives are taking. We wanted to find out whether there was a shift by enterprises towards greater responsiveness to societal issues, as well as towards workers and their communities. This is why we included a focus on cooperatives, co-determination and a stakeholder approach to the enterprise. The outcome of our first workshop in 2019 revealed a shift in some sectors in the opposite direction. There was a return, in the case of the platform economy, to the despotic rule of the 'robber barons' of late nineteenth-century American capitalism (see Michie and Padayachee 2021).

We – Vishnu, Robbie van Niekerk and I – were planning a follow-up workshop in late March 2020. But the severe lockdowns due to the Covid-19 pandemic scuppered all our plans. Sadly, Vishnu passed away three months later. The workshop was postponed indefinitely. In the notes for the opening speech he planned to give at the workshop, Vishnu wrote:

> My colleague Eddie Webster and I have engaged one another over the past two years in an on-going conversation over what a progressive pro-poor variety of capitalism that aims to reduce

inequality, promote economic growth, and strengthen social infrastructure may look like, and what it would have to offer South Africans.

The note continued:

> To be fair to Eddie, he had begun to probe these issues as far back as his piece with Karl von Holdt in 1992, in which he spoke of the possibilities and limits of radical social democracy. The notion of 'corporatism' and the term 'social accord' also emerged at the time as ideas for a middle, or third, way lying somewhere between conventional socialist and capitalist models (Padayachee 2020: n.p.).

As a tribute to Vishnu, I would like to take this conversation forward by revisiting his home city, Durban. I will explore the ways in which the 'politics of place' shaped a generation of left intellectuals, and the contemporary relevance of the ideas that emerged at that time.

The question I am posing is whether the embryonic political theory (Foster 1982; Turner 1972) that emerged in Durban was a missed opportunity for the development of a more pro-poor and egalitarian post-apartheid developmental path. I divide my argument into three parts. In the first part, I explore the resistance to apartheid that took a creative turn in Durban in the 1970s and early 1980s. In the second part, I examine the idea that, by failing to consolidate worker organisation, the Congress of South African Trade Unions (COSATU) missed an opportunity to shape an alternative path. In the third part, I conclude that COSATU's entering of the Tripartite Alliance, comprising COSATU, the South African Communist Party (SACP) and the African National Congress (ANC), in the 1980s and 1990s without a map – an overall strategy that integrated its different interventions – led to the federation's gradual marginalisation.

A creative turn: The Durban moment
I arrived in the city of Durban in late February 1973 – some forty-six years ago – to take up a post in the Department of Sociology at the then University of Natal (Durban [UND]). It was a dramatic moment, as South Africa was experiencing its first wave of worker unrest since the apartheid police massacred sixty-nine people at Sharpeville in 1960, the Durban strikes.

I was met at the airport by the head of department, a benign 'gentleman' in a safari suit. It was one of those hot, humid Durban afternoons before the days of air conditioning. I was taken to a hotel in the city centre. I felt I was entering the world of late colonialism.

I was woken the next morning by an emissary from the recently banned political science lecturer Rick Turner. He said Rick wanted to meet me. I readily agreed and spent the rest of the day with Rick and his wife Fozia Fisher at their rambling Bellair home. We discussed the organisational possibilities for change. Rick made it clear that he rejected armed struggle as unrealistic, and economic sanctions as counter-productive. He argued that there was only one sphere in which Africans had potential power, and in which their power potential was in fact growing. This, he said, was within the economy.

By the time sunset arrived, Rick had persuaded me to join the working committee of a planned workers college, the Institute of Industrial Education (IIE), and to join the board of the about-to-be-launched *South African Labour Bulletin*.

Soon after this encounter, I did what sociologists do. I undertook a survey of members of the embryonic trade unions that had been established in the wake of the 1973 Durban strikes. One of the questions I asked was: 'Why did you join the union?' I expected the union members to say 'wages' and 'benefits', because wages were low, and the apartheid system was built on cheap black labour. But as it is often said, surveys usually confirm common sense; however, they can also disturb common sense. Much to my surprise, it was neither to improve benefits nor to increase wages that workers gave as the dominant reasons for joining the union. It was for the sake of human dignity. 'I joined the union,' one worker said, 'because we are not treated like human beings' (cited in Webster 1979).

The first conclusion I drew from my survey was a challenge to the well-known conceptualisation of needs as hierarchical by Abraham Maslow (1943). His memorable pyramid depicts how individuals start with basic physiological motives, moving up through the hierarchy of needs to safety, belonging and love, esteem, and finally self-actualisation. But if my respondents saw recognition and dignity as more important than other concerns such as wages and benefits, even in the context of material adversity, this indicates that a critical component of inequality in South African society is inequality of recognition. Understanding the causes and consequences of recognition and of misrecognition is, writes Chris Desmond (2018), key to understanding how to combat inequality.

Interestingly, a young medical student at the Medical School, University of Natal, then called the Non-European section of UND, was addressing precisely this issue. Of course, I am referring to Steve Bantu Biko and his emerging philosophy of Black Consciousness. He and other young black radical intellectuals were focusing on how white racism dehumanised both white and black, and why 'in the long run the oppressed will have to free the oppressors who are unable (and unwilling) to free themselves' (cited in Webster 1974). This was a historic rupture with the mindset of apartheid. Black, Biko argued, is not a colour; if you are oppressed you are black.

Another question my research assistant, Judson Kuzwayo, asked the worker respondents was: 'Can you think of a leader, present or past, who can or could improve the position of African workers?' This is what they said:

Albert Luthuli	44%
Mangosuthu Gatsha Buthelezi	19%
Nelson Mandela	10%
Moses Mabhida	8%

Source: Webster (1979: 43).

When I presented the results of the research to the IIE in 1975, a member of the IIE Working Committee questioned their validity. 'Who,' he asked, 'is Moses Mabhida?' I said I did not know but that I trusted the interviewer. Subsequently, in 1977, I had time to read *Workers' Unity*, the newspaper from the 1950s of the South African Congress of Trade Unions (SACTU), the trade union arm of the Congress Alliance. Sitting in the banned materials section of the William Cullen Library of the University of the Witwatersrand, I soon 'discovered' that Moses Mabhida was a prominent leader of the SACP, ANC and SACTU in the province of Natal. The working class, I came to realise, was not some collective *tabula rasa* waiting for white intellectuals to tell it what to think. It had its own history and political traditions, one of which, the national political tradition, had deep roots in Durban and its surrounding areas.

Indeed, as Sakhela Buhlungu argues, the white full-time union officials in the black unions were mainly from middle class backgrounds.

They were never fully integrated into the movement with which they had pledged solidarity (Buhlungu 2006). Buhlungu applied Erik Olin Wright's notion of 'contradictory class location' to explain this incomplete integration. The social distance between white and black people in society existed also between white officials in the union on the one hand, and black workers and full-time officials on the other. Power relations between white officials and black unionists remained unequal and, Buhlungu goes on to argue, white officials performed expert functions while black unionists performed the more menial functions.

In his response to Buhlungu, Johann Maree does not dispute that there was a social distance between the white officials and black workers during the 1970s (Maree 2006). Instead, Maree argues, their strategy of building active democratic shop steward structures in the workplace helped build a democratic and powerful black trade union movement. Maree's argument is based on a historical overview of the two major black trade union federations that emerged in South Africa during the 1970s and 1980s. The Federation of South African Trade Unions was non-racial and accepted white intellectuals as officials. It eventually grew into COSATU, which played a major role in the mass democratic movement during South Africa's transition to democracy in the late 1980s and early 1990s. The other black trade union federation was Africanist, with some Black Consciousness orientations. It appointed only black officials and eventually grew into the National Council of Trade Unions (NACTU). NACTU, Maree argues, never matched COSATU in size, strength or strategic leadership. The non-racial federation grew much stronger than the Africanist federation by focusing on building active democratic shop steward structures in the workplace. This, Maree suggests, was part of a deliberate strategy by white intellectuals in the unions to put control of the unions into the hands of black workers, who gradually rose through the ranks into positions of leadership.

While this debate between Buhlungu and Maree on the role of white intellectuals in the post-1973 labour movement was important, it failed to identify the innovative aspect of what Tony Morphet called 'the Durban moment' (Morphet 1990: 92). Here, at the height of apartheid, two movements were to emerge, beginning a journey that was eventually to bring apartheid to its knees. In the words of veteran political scientist Mahmood Mamdani (2021: 164), 'the most important force for this change was not the armed struggle, nor exile politics, nor the international boycott movement'. The force that began to bring apartheid to its knees, Mamdani argues, 'was provided by student activists of all colours and by migrant and township labour' (2021: 164). He argues that together these two movements, the Black Consciousness Movement and the workers' trade union movement, dramatically shifted the locus of struggle from exiled professional revolutionaries to the communities of South Africa.

It could be argued that Mamdani overstates the significance of the Durban moment. But in bringing the struggle back home, a vision of a non-racial and egalitarian society re-emerged in the giant textile mills of Pinetown and the campuses of the University of Natal. Anti-apartheid resistance took a creative turn in the 1970s. For the first time, resistance did not reproduce the architecture of apartheid inside the resistance movement itself. Previously, resistance to apartheid was organised through separate organisations for different racial groups: the ANC for Africans, the South African Indian Congress for Indians, the Coloured People's Congress and the whites' Congress of Democrats. Resistance in the 1970s, Mamdani argues, 'broke through apartheid's cognitive order' (Mamdani 2021: 31). 'This epistemological revolution that would spur decolonisation,' he goes on, 'was characterised by a two-fold development: radical white students joined non-white migrant workers in a mobilisation that gave birth to South Africa's non-racial unions; and African, Indian and Coloured students, inspired by the Black Consciousness Movement, were reborn as black' (2021: 31).

What happened in South Africa was not, Mamdani concludes, a 'social revolution stalled but ... the most far-sighted transition to political independence in the colonial world' (Mamdani 2021: 189). However, for Mamdani, social justice was not attainable in 1994. Its attainment would, he argues, have required a revolution, but this was not practically possible, 'given the balance of forces. There was instead a stalemate between forces supporting and opposing apartheid, which was broken through a compromise agreement' (2021: 188). South Africa's achievement was a 'political revolution ... a radical attempt to imagine a postcolonial political community that is neither a return to the imagined precolonial nation nor a continuation of the colonial condition' (2021: 189).

I turn now to the idea of the Durban moment as a missed opportunity for a more pro-poor development path.

Was the Durban moment a missed opportunity?

I agree that a revolutionary rupture was not feasible at that time, but I disagree with Mamdani's false binary of either a revolution *or* a political compromise. I will argue, contra Mamdani, that what emerged in Durban in the 1970s and 1980s was the embryo of an alternative; an embryo that could be called a radical social democratic project which was stalled not through the unfavourable balance of power in South Africa but, as Alec Erwin (2017: 236) argues, through a failure to consolidate 'an embryonic political philosophy'. As Dikgang Moseneke, in his book, *My Own Liberator*, observes:

> The negotiators did not stare in the eye the historical and structural inequality in the economy, and the inequality rested and still rests in the disparity between those who own productive assets and management skills, on the one hand, and those who don't (Moseneke 2018: 5).

Erwin, a white academic and trade unionist at the time, argued that 'by failing to face the dangers of an unstructured relationship within the Alliance and paying insufficient attention to the need to find new ways of building worker-class organisation, the workerist leadership missed a major opportunity to build working-class power' (Erwin 2017: 251). What was needed, he said, was 'a second Joe Foster speech process after the formation of COSATU, and then again after the democratic transition' (2017: 250).[1]

At the centre of Erwin's argument is the significance of the Foster speech. This significance was twofold: first, it was not the product of one person but of a deep participatory process 'of some months of meetings, discussions and laborious drafts . . . by worker leaders . . . linked to factories as a result of the close proximity of the factories to the townships' (Erwin 2017: 237). Second, 'there was an "embryonic political theory" present in the Foster speech' (2017: 250).

What was articulated in the Foster speech, Erwin argued,

> was a well-disciplined worker organisation that had a national presence within the economy but that could also engage in local and regional matters and was conceived of as a working-class movement that would be so significant that the Alliance

would have little option but to accommodate it and pay heed to working class needs (2017: 250).

Erwin's argument as to why this second process did not happen is that 'there was an overestimation of how far towards worker organisation the Alliance could be cajoled, and there was an overestimation of the resilience of the worker leadership structures that had been built up within COSATU' (2017: 251). The result was that there was no platform where 'a longer term reflection on how the relationship between worker organisation and the Alliance should be structured' could take place (2017: 251). Erwin concluded: 'For worker power to be built, it has to be built from the bottom again. It should be worker leaders who deal with the local issues of service delivery, and they should then use their national power to ensure that delivery is provided' (2017: 252).

Erwin raised a fascinating counter-factual. But to answer it more fully, we need to revisit the debates in the early 1990s on the relationship between unions and political parties – I offer some preliminary thoughts.

In the wake of the 1973 strikes in Durban, a non-racial trade union movement emerged after some decades of repression by the apartheid state (Maree 1985). These unions were not entirely new, but they presented a challenge not only to the apartheid state and employers but also to the dominant national democratic tradition in South Africa. These embryonic unions placed strong emphasis on building a cadre of shop stewards with deep roots in their workplaces, and on industry-wide bargaining and organisation. Their critics in the national democratic tradition labelled these unions as syndicalist in orientation or, later in the 1980s, as 'workerist' (Erwin 2017).

The formation of COSATU in December 1985 brought together unions from these different traditions into an uneasy strategic compromise: the well-organised industrial unions drawn from the shop floor tradition, and the general unions drawn from the national democratic tradition, as well as the National Union of Mineworkers, which had recently broken from the Black Consciousness tradition.

With the imminent establishment of the ANC as a dominant ruling partner in the first Government of National Unity (1994–97), an intense debate took place in the early 1990s inside COSATU, and within its largest affiliate, the National Union of Metalworkers of South Africa (NUMSA), in particular. The debate focused on how they would relate to their Alliance partner, the ANC, once it came into power. The 1991 NUMSA congress resolution stated that 'the trade unions must remain independent of political parties. The development of party political groupings in NUMSA will lead to party political domination of the union and disunity among workers' (Forrest 2011: 476). But instead of remaining independent of political parties, ironically, the ANC's electoral victory in May 1994, polling a nearly two-thirds majority (62.5% of the vote), precipitated an exodus of COSATU and NUMSA officials into government. How did this come about?

At a special COSATU congress in August 1991, delegates decided to release twenty COSATU leaders to stand as parliamentary candidates on the ANC list. These included some of the trade unions' most senior office bearers and strategists. In late 1995, a much larger number of leaders were similarly released to stand on local government lists. The guiding idea was that such individuals would strengthen the capacity of the ANC and simultaneously shape its direction towards labour's goals. These aims proved elusive. While perhaps some ex-COSATU leaders gained influence, especially those who became cabinet ministers and chairpersons of parliamentary committees, COSATU itself did not. Instead, it suffered a 'brain drain' in which many of its leading figures, especially at regional and local levels, left the organisation (Buhlungu 1994).[2]

Once in parliament, these trade union movement individuals found themselves detached from any accountability to their old federation. Simultaneously, they became relatively isolated from the centres of power in the ANC. Within the ANC and the SACP the labour leaders seldom had the same seniority and credibility as those who had earned their status as ex-Robben Islanders, or through leadership in exile, especially in the ANC's armed wing, Umhkonto we Sizwe. Furthermore, these ex-unionists were subject to party discipline. Indeed, in the early years, a clause in the interim constitution compelled members of parliament to resign their seats if they disagreed with ANC party policy. In the memorable words of the general secretary of NUMSA at the time, Enoch Godongwana, the decision to go to parliament could best be described as an 'exodus without a map' (cited in Webster and Adler 2001: 12).

'Exodus without a map'

For a moment in the 1970s and early 1980s it appeared that an alternative working class politics was emerging in Durban. It involved a new generation, influenced by the European New Left, and committed to translating participatory democracy into a strong shop floor movement. But the 'hidden voices' of the national political tradition were an essential part of the early 1970s, and their determination to embed working class interests within the Alliance was eventually rewarded with the launch of COSATU in 1985. It seemed for a moment as if the vexed 'labour question' had been resolved through an equal partnership between COSATU and the ANC.

But this was not to be. Instead, COSATU sent its leading officials to parliament without a 'map' to ensure its goals. I am not suggesting that COSATU should not have joined the Alliance; their constituency demanded it. For example, in a survey of COSATU members on the eve of the first democratic elections, 70 per cent of members said they would vote for the ANC in the next elections, even if the government failed to deliver (Ginsburg et al. 1995). The members' views did not contradict their assertion that COSATU would best represent their interests in the transition. Rather, they saw COSATU as best representing them within the Alliance, where they believed they could influence government policy (Ginsburg et al. 1995).

But it was a strategy that contained contradictory imperatives. The one imperative stressed participation within government while the other stressed autonomy and opposition to capital and independence from the state. Could these contradictions have been resolved through an overall strategy – a map – that integrated the different interventions made by COSATU? Such a map would have required two elements: the maintenance of a strong shop floor structure, and a macroeconomic programme that provided a realistic alternative to neoliberalism. Neither element was to be achieved in the decades that followed. The authors of a recent study describe a 'democratic rupture' in COSATU (Bezuidenhout and Tshoaedi 2017); and Padayachee and Van Niekerk (2019) describe the marginalisation of the left Keynesian economic and social policy think tank, the Macroeconomic Research Group, which the ANC initiated and later disowned.

Much has changed in the world of work and politics since those heady days of the Durban moment, when black and white South Africans crafted a vision that transcended the narrow roles the architects of apartheid had assigned to each. I hope, by revisiting Durban and this vision, I have laid the foundations for a deeper understanding of the life and work of our friend and colleague Vishnu Padayachee. I hope, too, that this brief essay will contribute to our conversation on what happened to the 'embryonic political theory' that emerged in those exciting years.

Notes

1. In 1982, Joe Foster, the general secretary of the Federation of South African Trade Unions (FOSATU), made a landmark speech, 'The Workers Struggle – Where Does FOSATU Stand?' to the 2nd National Congress of FOSATU warning of the dangers of democratic, worker-controlled trade unions being subsumed into the mobilisations of community-based organisations, organisations which did not have a democratic mandate nor were accountable to workers in the trade union. See https://www.scienceopen.com/hosted-document?doi=10.1080/03056248208703502.
2. Buhlungu (1994) estimated that eighty key leaders had left the trade union movement by the time of the national elections in 1994. And a lot more left after the local government elections in 1995.

References

Bezuidenhout, A. and M. Tshoaedi (eds). 2017. *Labour Beyond COSATU: Mapping the Rupture in South Africa's Labour Landscape*. Johannesburg: Wits University Press.

Buhlungu, S. 1994. 'The Big Brain Drain: Union Officials in the 1990s'. *South African Labour Bulletin* 18 (3): 25–32.

Buhlungu, S. 2006. 'Rebels Without a Cause of Their Own? The Contradictory Location of White Officials in Black Unions, 1973–94'. *Current Sociology* 54 (3): 427–51.

Desmond, C. 2018. 'How We Shape Each Other: Balance, Denial and Corrosion'. Presentation at the inaugural conference of the Southern Centre for Inequality Studies, University of the Witwatersrand, 5–6 September.

Erwin, A. 2017. 'Workerists and the National Question'. In: *The Unresolved National Question: Left Thought under Apartheid*, edited by E. Webster and K. Pampallis, 235–53. Johannesburg: Wits University Press.

Forrest, K. 2011. *Metal That Will Not Bend: National Union of Metalworkers of South Africa 1980–1995*. Johannesburg: Wits University Press.

Foster, J. 1982. 'The Workers' Struggle: Where Does FOSATU Stand?' *South African Labour Bulletin* 7 (8): 99–114.

Ginsburg D., E. Webster, R. Southall and G. Wood. 1995. *Taking Democracy Seriously: Worker Expectations and Parliamentary Democracy in South Africa*. Durban: Indicator Press.

Mamdani, M. 2021. *Neither Settler nor Native: The Making and Unmaking of Permanent Minorities*. Johannesburg: Wits University Press.

Maree, J. 1985. 'The Emergence, Struggles and Achievements of Black Trade Unions in South Africa from 1973 to 1984'. *Labour, Capital and Society / Travail, capital et société* 18 (2), Numéro thématique sur L'Afrique du Sud / Special Issue on South Africa: 278–303.

———. 2006. 'Rebels with Causes: White Officials in Black Trade Unions in South Africa, 1973–1994: A Response to Sakhela Buhlungu'. *Current Sociology* 54 (3): 453–67.

Maslow, A.H. 1943. 'A Theory of Human Motivation'. *Psychological Review* 50 (4): 370–96.

Michie, J. and V. Padayachee. 2021. *Ownership and Governance of Companies: Essays from South Africa and the Global South.* London: Routledge.

Morphet, T. 1990. '"Brushing History Against the Grain": Oppositional Discourse in South Africa'. *Theoria* 76: 89–99.

Moseneke, D. 2018. *My Own Liberator.* Johannesburg: Picador.

Padayachee, V. (ed.). 2013. 'Capitalism of a Special Type? South African Capitalism Before and After 1994'. *Transformation* 81–2, Special issue.

———. 2020. Planned opening address to the Southern Centre for Inequality Studies Workshop on 'Alternative Forms of Ownership', Johannesburg, 25 March'. Published posthumously as Chapter 1 of this volume.

Padayachee, V. and R. van Niekerk. 2019. *Shadow of Liberation: Contestation and Compromise in the Economic and Social Policy of the African National Congress, 1943–1996.* Johannesburg: Wits University Press.

Turner, R. 1972. *The Eye of the Needle: An Essay in Participatory Democracy.* Johannesburg: Ravan Press.

Webster, E. 1974. 'Black Consciousness and the White Left'. *Dissent* March–April: 1–4.

———. 1979. 'A Profile of Unregistered Union Members in Durban'. *South African Labour Bulletin* 4 (8): 43–74.

Webster, E. and G. Adler. 2001. 'Exodus Without a Map? The Labour Movement in a Liberalising South Africa'. In: *Labour Regimes and Liberalization: The Restructuring of State-Society Relations in Africa*, edited by B. Beckman and L. Sachikonye. Harare: University of Zimbabwe Publications.

18

Race and Identity
The Revival of the Natal Indian Congress, 1971–74

Goolam Vahed

I was confronted by the debate over the revival of the Natal Indian Congress (NIC) while doing research for two co-authored studies on Monty Naicker and the NIC (Desai and Vahed 2010, 2021a, respectively). The intense debates in local newspapers in the period from 1971 to 1973 between young Black Consciousness Movement (BCM) members and supporters of the NIC about the revival of the organisation provide a fascinating insight into how these political groupings attempted to confront the issue of race.[1] There are important studies on the NIC (Bhana 1997; Dhupelia-Mesthrie 2006; Vahed and Desai 2014) that allude to this debate, but not in any substantial way. The article by Ratnamala Singh and Shahid Vawda is an exception (Singh and Vawda 1988).

While Singh and Vawda (1988) are critical of the retention of the 'I' in the NIC, this chapter relies on contemporary newspaper reporting and interviews conducted by the historian Julie Frederikse and the University of KwaZulu-Natal's Voices of Resistance Project with NIC and BCM activists and ideologues to understand the NIC's rationale for reviving an organisation with a racial identity, and the BCM's opposition to that.[2]

Steve Biko, who studied at the Natal Medical School (now the Nelson R. Mandela School of Medicine), espoused the idea of Black Consciousness (BC) in the late 1960s. Adherents to the movement included Indian tertiary students in Durban. Though some of Biko's African colleagues, such as Aubrey Mokoape, criticised him for including Indians in his definition of 'black', he was determined to achieve a broad black unity (Ramphele 1995). BCM activism brought life to anti-apartheid activism after a decade of relative quiescence resulting from the banning of the African National Congress (ANC) and the Pan Africanist Congress (PAC) in 1960. These congresses became invisible in the country, as their resistance was confined to guerrilla warfare waged from their bases in neighbouring countries.

In a 1999 interview, Docrat reflected on political activism in Durban in the 1960s:

> After the protesting in the 1950s, the 1960s saw the Nats really entrenched. They closed down on everything. You didn't know what was happening in Pondoland, but you knew there was an awful lot of suppression going on. But as you got to the end of the 60s and young men like Steve Biko were being educated at the Medical School here [in Natal], various other lights seemed to arise. It galvanised the people who were people on the move, and that's what the Nationalists can't cope with. They could suppress but they couldn't delete the will, the forward march (of the people) (Docrat 1999: 4).

It was in this context that Mewa Ramgobin, who was married to Mohandas K. Gandhi's granddaughter Ela, and was the organising secretary of the Mahatma Gandhi Centenary Celebrations in 1969, decided to revive the NIC. He established a 'Committee of Clemency' in February 1971 to campaign for the release of political prisoners and, in June 1971, formed an ad hoc committee to canvas public opinion about reviving the NIC. He presented a document titled, 'The Case for the Revival of the Natal Indian Congress' at a meeting at the Bolton Hall in Durban on 25 July 1971. According to the document, South Africa was 'a multi-racial society' and the NIC 'reject[s] racial discrimination on any level'. The organisation was being revived to 'unhesitatingly remind [the government] that a people can be pushed thus far and no further'. In doing so, 'we will be performing our duties to be identified with the vast mass of blacks in southern Africa' (Edwards 2015: 206). The NIC was officially relaunched at a convention at the Phoenix Settlement on 2 October 1971.

The Black Consciousness Movement's response
BCM supporters spoke out against the revival of an 'Indian' Congress. Strini Moodley, whose father was a member of the Communist Party before its banning, a trade union organiser and a schoolteacher, enrolled at the University College for Indians on Salisbury Island. Young BCM activists included the likes of Saths Cooper, Sam Moodley, Kogs Reddy,

Dennis Pather, Ben David, Kriba Pillay, Nash Naina, Asha Rambally, Vino Reddy and Archie Augustine.

Strini Moodley's political activism led to his expulsion from the university in 1967. In an interview in 2002, he recounted how BC had emerged at a time when apartheid ideology was taking root at all levels of society. The only people speaking out were white liberals like the parliamentarian Helen Suzman and author and former Liberal Party member Alan Paton. Moodley felt that black people could not 'sit and watch what is happening in this country when they were the victims. They had to take their future into their own hands and fight for their own liberation'. It was their view that 'the world has been designed and coordinated by White people who made the assumption that they were superior, that they were civilised, that they exploited the labour of Black people, that their riches, their wealth, their privilege was all built on the sweat, blood and tears of Black people'. To liberate themselves, black people had to take pride in their blackness, become self-reliant, and 'unite, stand up and overthrow regimes that oppressed and exploited us' (Moodley 2002: 13–14).

Saths Cooper, who matriculated from Sastri College in Durban in 1967, also attended the University College for Indians, where he was a member of the Debating Society, started a Speech and Drama Society, and was involved in 'underground activity' with the likes of Steve Biko, Barney Pityana and Moodley. They formed the South African Students Organisation (SASO) in 1968, after Biko led a walkout from the white liberal university student body, the National Union of South African Students (NUSAS), accusing it of token gestures, since black delegates to its meetings were forced to eat and sleep separately from white delegates. For Cooper, BC ideology meant 'not using white as a point of reference and describ[ing] everything else in the negative using white as your point of departure'. The descriptor 'non-white' was 'pejorative, was diminutive of people, was really interiorising a whole group of people'. BC, in contrast, 'stood for the affirmation of people who were disenfranchised and disadvantaged by an apartheid system, which completely excluded from all power and privilege anybody who was not classified white'. Equally importantly, BCM members aimed to 'rise above any narrow ethnic or tribal definition' because the apartheid state, through its policies of Group Areas and Bantustans, was dividing people residentially by race and ethnicity and entrenching racial, ethnic and tribal identities (Cooper 2003: 22).

The BCM rejected apartheid-created institutions such as the homelands (or Bantustans), as well as representative bodies for Indians and coloureds such as Local Affairs Committees, the Coloured Representative Council and the South African Indian Council, which was still in the making. Biko warned against participation in these structures:

> Ever since word was let loose that the Indian Council will at some near future be elected, a number of intelligent people are thinking of reviving the Indian Congress and letting it form some kind of opposition within the system. This is dangerous retrogressive thinking which should be given no breathing space. These apartheid institutions are swallowing too many good people who would be useful in a meaningful programme of emancipation of the black people (Biko 2017: 40).

BCM members attended the early meetings convened by Ramgobin to advocate a single organisation of the oppressed (Indian, coloured and African). Moodley recounted that 'these ethnic organisations were terrified of us, primarily because we didn't bring Indians, Africans and Coloureds together, we brought "Black" people together'. He further observed that it was a lost opportunity: 'The atmosphere throughout the country, because of the work of the Black Consciousness Movement, was that White people were getting very scared' (Moodley 2002: 10).

The Congress riposte
Singh and Vawda (1988: 7) argue that 'the NIC did not provide a clear response to the critique of BC directed to the revival of an ethnically based political organisation'. The danger for them was that 'discourses which jumble together intra-community concerns and trans-community commitments may produce the effect that the "Indian" as an ethnically constituted political subject remains intact'. But the ideologues of the NIC justified its revival by arguing that such criticism failed to take into account the consequences of the long history of racial division in South Africa. They further insisted that the 'I' in the NIC did not make it a racial organisation because they supported non-racial majority rule and the ideals of the Freedom Charter, while the BC ideology was inherently racist (Desai and Vahed 2021a).

NIC ideologues saw the revival of the NIC as a tactical response to the prevailing material conditions in South Africa. Vishnu Padayachee wrote in 1999 that 'at one level, this community [Indians] has always been complexly stratified'. He said that the formative generation included 'mainly Tamil and Hindi-speaking [Hindu] indentured workers ... internationally-connected merchants and smaller traders, who were in the main Urdu or Gujarati-speaking Muslims and Gujarati-speaking Hindus ... [and] a small middle-class of clerks, teachers and nurses, predominantly Christian'. But, as Padayachee observed,

> all these people, despite differences in language, roots, religion and class, came to be legislatively defined or described themselves as part of 'The Indian Community'. Until recently, many of these different strata existed alongside one another in segregated districts in relative harmony (Padayachee 1999: 393).

George Sewpersadh, who became the first president of the NIC due to the banning order imposed on Ramgobin, while not directly replying to BC critique, stated in 1972 that the revival of the NIC was 'practical and realistic'. Apartheid had separated South Africans according to race, he wrote, and an 'organisation representing all the races ... is unlikely to get massive support from the different races'. The task of the NIC was to

> drive home to Indians that their problems cannot be divorced from the problems of other oppressed races. Constant cooperation with people of other races will no doubt pave the way for the creation of a democratic organisation consisting of human beings and not a particular racial group (Sewpersadh 1972: 13).

The formation of racial identity was acknowledged by Vishu's 'mentor' and bridge partner, A.K.M. Docrat. Docrat had a stellar resistance resumé.[3] He was a member of the Communist Party, a trade unionist, and part of Monty Naicker's 'radical' NIC. He had volunteered in the Defiance Campaign of 1952, was detained during the 1960 State of Emergency, and was banned in 1962 for two years; his banning order was extended each time it expired until it was finally lifted in 1978. Docrat was subject to house arrest for twenty-two hours per day and from Friday evening to Monday morning for most of this period. He was heavily involved in trade unions and political activism in the 1940s, when thousands of Indian workers were unionised and participated in NIC rallies in support of the passive resistance campaign against residential segregation from 1946 to 1948 and the Defiance Campaign of 1952. These union activities and political protests drew thousands of Indians into the struggle against race and class oppression.

Did this signify the emergence and entrenchment of non-racial working-class consciousness among sections of South African Indian society?

According to Docrat (1999: 5), the Indian working class 'were still feeling their way around' in the urban areas. The radicalisation of the NIC was due to the efforts of a small core of activists who mobilised workers to attend rallies and mass meetings. It was not the workers (via their unions) who gave impetus to the radicalisation of the NIC. This explains why, from the 1950s onwards, Indian workers became conservative and protected their niche position in the local economy (Padayachee, Vawda and Tichman 1985). Docrat (1999) argued that Indian workers were drawn into the struggle to address bread-and-butter issues that affected their daily lives.

Thus, Padayachee, Vawda and Paul Tichman posit that to credit workers with a 'consciousness that supposedly led them to spearhead the "radicalisation" (whatever this might imply) of Indian politics in Natal in the 1940s is to engage in an ex-post-facto romanticisation of their role' (Padayachee, Vawda and Tichman 1985: 155). Padayachee and Vawda (1999) conclude that the possibility of non-racial industrial, and by extension political, action was lost when the state, police and employers clamped down on the unions and striking workers, while the involvement of political bodies diluted workers' organisations.

Billy Nair, an NIC member, trade unionist, member of the SACP, Umkhonto we Sizwe activist and ANC member of parliament in the post-apartheid period, underscored the point that industrial work and unions failed to nurture a non-racial identity:

> Workers have their prejudices. [Do you] actually suggest that the moment the worker leaves the factory floor level, he maintains his non-racial attitudes? No, far from it, because the worker goes back into his particular community ... You have a tentative non-racial thing for eight hours a day, but this is mitigated by the fact that you are in a wider racial set-up, so unless you actually smash

the wider prison in which the workers are engulfed, you are not going to have real non-racialism (Nair 1985: 5).

Relations between Indians and Africans, Keith Hart and Vishnu Padayachee observe (2000: 690), were 'uneasy. These tensions occasionally erupted into violence, most notably in the 1949 Durban riots in which eighty-seven people were killed.'

The ANC Youth League put forward the idea of four nations in 1948, with the stipulation that three of them (white, coloured and Indian) were minorities, and three suffered from national oppression (African, coloured and Indian). By the time of the formulation of the Freedom Charter in 1955, the Congress Alliance was speaking of a 'multiracial' society. According to historian Jon Soske, the term multiracial, which recognised the maintenance of racial groups, was eventually replaced by the term 'non-racial', which 'was frequently employed in the international, English-language press to refer to racially integrated spaces and institutions' (Soske 2015: 19).

This is not to adopt a 'race relations' perspective that assumes the existence of biological and coherent 'race' groups. As Soske points out,

> segregationist policies, African and Indian political organizations, and everyday social practices continuously reproduced an 'African/Indian divide' despite both the enormous heterogeneity of each group and the quotidian intimacies of urban life ...This division shaped the development of the anti-apartheid struggle in Natal (Soske 2009: i).

Under these circumstances what was the most efficacious way to organise anti-apartheid resistance? Should activists organise resistance along racial lines to ensure maximum participation, or would this further separate the masses?

M.D. Naidoo, a prominent activist from the 1940s who represented the South African Indian case at the UN and was imprisoned on Robben Island in the 1960s, told historian Julie Frederikse in a 1987 interview that 'you couldn't grow up in South Africa and not be infected by racism in some way, so there was that sensitivity awareness [among activists]'. Naidoo argued further that in a society which is riven by racial prejudice, trying to bring people together who were already being infected by racial prejudice would not be the best way to unite them. In the interests of building a mass political organisation it was still necessary to operate, irrespective of how close the leadership of these organisations may be to each other, on the basis of the historical conditions in which they grew up ... Segregation in South Africa and, later, Apartheid, built a whole structure of laws for each race group. Different policies applied to Blacks, Asians, and Coloureds ... (Naidoo 1987: 11).

Ramgobin, who revived the NIC in 1971, supported the views expressed by Naidoo and Nair. Due to the restrictions imposed by the Group Areas Act (No. 41 of 1950), he said,

[it was] virtually impossible for me to have the courage to go into Soweto and organise people there because I do not understand the needs of the people. I do not suffer as they suffer and vice versa. I cannot for the life of me see a person from Soweto going out to Lenasia and organising people towards the creation of a non-racial democratic society, only because the Government has succeeded in putting us into ghettos, so that the dynamics of each area are characterised, unfortunately in South Africa, by race, but if we are thrown together, or if we are left to live as we wish to live, then naturally our emphasis on non-racialism would have been in our everyday activity (Ramgobin 1986: 4).

NIC activists rejected the notion that the establishment of racially based political organisations amounted to racism. According to M.D. Naidoo,

if a particular people get together because they find it more convenient to mobilise themselves, but the objectives for which they are working are identical with a similar group of a different kind – that's not racism. We needed an Indian organisation to reach the people who were politically less developed, even the conservative elements. To reach them, you had to find an organisation which, on the basis of tradition, on the basis of history, would be meaningful to them, and the NIC fulfilled that role ... (Naidoo 1987: 15).

Billy Nair emphasised that the racially separate political organisations had a common goal:

> The [political] organisations were divided on racial and ethnic lines but it did not follow that they were divided politically... Notwithstanding that it was racial, the key factor was what the organisation [NIC] actually stood for. It stood for a non-racial democracy and for convenience, because we were resident in [racially] grouped areas, it was convenient for Congress to operate under the banner of the Indian, though it stood for a broad non-racial democratic South Africa. Congress was the vehicle which mobilised the vast masses of the Indian people under its wing, across class lines (Nair 1985: 7).

Those critical of the NIC position should consider the difficulties from another perspective. Steve Biko faced opposition to coloureds and Indians being included under the rubric 'black'. His then comrade and partner, Mamphele Ramphele, recounted that

> Aubrey Mokoape used to engage Steve in serious all-night discussions... Aubrey argued from his Africanist perspective against the inclusion of 'Coloureds' and 'Indians' in the Black Consciousness Movement... He would argue that Indians should be reminded that there was a ship leaving Durban harbour every Thursday for India which they should be encouraged to make use of... A number of African students shared this view ... Langa Dube, a final year student in 1969 would occasionally stagger into Steve's room... and express his dismay at the company Steve was keeping: 'Biko, you are going down my friend. Your room is full of curry! You are going down my friend!'... The rise of Idi Amin as the leader of Uganda and his expulsion of Asians simply fuelled the fires of hatred and mistrust. Strini Moodley, the SASO Director of Publications at the time, devoted an entire address to warn[ing] Indian students that they would face the same fate unless they dedicated themselves to the struggle for liberation and justice for all (Ramphele 1995: 60).

While Biko's stance was to challenge the apartheid divide by developing a united black subject, Ramphele underscores the antipathy towards the equal involvement of Indians among some Africans in the BCM. Moodley's drawing on the Ugandan example to jolt Indians into joining Africans in the anti-apartheid struggle to safeguard their futures suggests that NIC activists were probably not too far off in their analysis that they should initially attempt to organise Indians as Indians, while at the same time committing to a non-racial South Africa.

The ANC itself dismissed racial parity in the liberation movements. At its 1969 Morogoro Conference, the ANC's 'Tactics and Strategy' document stated that in any political alliance, the inclusion of 'non-Africans' (coloureds, Indians and whites) in the 'national front does not mean a mechanical parity between the various national groups ... This has never been so and will never be so' (ANC 1969). Neville Alexander argued that this perspective saw Africans as 'constitut[ing] the nation of South Africa and the other three "nationalities" constitut[ing] "national minorities"' (Alexander 1986: 75). It was only at the 1985 National Consultative Conference of the ANC in Kabwe, Zambia, that a decision was taken to formally adopt non-racialism at all levels of the organisation, from the grassroots to the National Executive Committee (Desai and Vahed 2021a).

Attempts at cooperation

Though they opposed the revival of the NIC, Cooper and Moodley initially joined the NIC executive on the understanding that it would 'investigate' the option of becoming non-racial (Khoape 1973: 7). At the launch of the NIC on 2 October 1971, the Durban Central Branch, which was heavily influenced by BCM activists like Cooper, Moodley and Ashwin Trikamjee, submitted a memorandum motivating for the NIC's name to be changed to 'The People's Congress'. The provincial congress voted to retain the name NIC by a narrow majority of thirty-two votes to thirty (Dhillon 1999).

The Durban Central Branch organised a symposium on BC on 31 December 1971, at which the divisions within the NIC became clear. Led by Jerry Coovadia, who had presented a paper arguing that at its core BC was racist, some members persuaded the majority to reject the ideology. This resulted in the executive rejecting BC because of its 'racial exclusiveness' (Khoape 1973: 7) – while somewhat ironically refusing to drop 'Indian' from the NIC's name.

BCM activists convened several meetings in an attempt to form a national front of black organisations opposed to apartheid. A Black People's Convention (BPC) was formed in Bloemfontein in April 1971; another meeting was held in Pietermaritzburg in mid-August 1971 and a third in Lenasia on 23 January 1972. NIC executive members Coovadia, D.M. Naidoo and Sewpersadh attended the Lenasia meeting as 'observers' only. They did not join the BPC, but stated that the NIC would cooperate with other organisations where its principles were not compromised (Graphic 1972).

Moodley explained that BCM activists had wanted to 'work with the NIC primarily because we wanted to change how they were thinking'. However, it eventually became apparent that most NIC executive members would not be swayed into a name change. More annoying for Moodley and other BC ideologues was that the NIC executive failed to understand the message and meaning of BC and compared its ideology with that of the PAC, labelling BCM members 'as nothing more than the PAC' (Moodley 2002: 25).

This charge was made, for example, by NIC secretary Ramlal Ramesar. The NIC refused a demand from SASO to retract the statement, and instead Sewpersadh reiterated the charge (Bhana 1997). Moodley, in recounting this incident in 2002, argued that both the ANC and the PAC had shortcomings that the BCM was hoping to overcome:

> For us, the Freedom Charter was too accommodating. We had to take it a step further. We felt that the PAC also was brought down by too narrow Africanism. In the sense that in its conscientisation programme, it narrowed the concept of Pan Africanism. That the BCM, as we had formed it, truly represented the notion of Pan Africanism as had been interpreted by Kwame Nkrumah, by Frantz Fanon and by numerous other Pan Africanists, Aimé Césaire. But that also in Pan Africanism, they needed to embrace the notion of socialism. And that, therefore what we were were going to do was beyond the ANC and beyond the PAC. While they might have a little more history behind them, they were certainly, in their intellectual definitions, still living in the past (2002: 17).

Moodley insisted that there were similarities but also significant differences between the BCM and the PAC. One of these differences was that Indians and coloureds were considered black in the BC definition, whereas 'system' Africans were not. Being black, in other words, was about consciousness as much as it was about pigmentation. The accusation that there was no difference between them and the PAC was the last straw for BCM activists, who realised that it was pointless trying to change the NIC's thinking from within, and 'a large number of us who were in the Indian Congress, pulled out, resigned en bloc' (Moodley 2002: 26). It was also a charge that could be seen as playing into the hands of the repressive apparatus of the state. The PAC was a banned organisation, and if the BPC was seen as a front for it, it could also come under the hammer of the state.

Farouk Meer, an executive member of the NIC, conceded that

> perhaps we might have misunderstood the BC philosophy, at the time . . . Although I heard Biko speak, I didn't have one-on-one interaction. The one-on-one interaction was through people like Saths Cooper and Strini Moodley. And the way they were promoting BC, it came across as a racist ideology – no whites should be in the organization . . . even if he's a person who believes in non-racialism. We saw it as catering exclusively for so-called Blacks as opposed to the Congress philosophy which was an all-embracing philosophy, which says look, believe in non-racialism (Meer 2002: 12).

At the time and since then, however, most NIC members have repeated the mantra of the BCM as having a racial underpinning. Sewpersadh, for example, stated in 2002:

> Well, the BCM was an influential movement; it had an effect . . . but we never really agreed with the ideology fully, although we recognised their contribution. The ANC contribution was always non-racial, we didn't have the Black Consciousness idea as part of our policy. And so we used to, we carried on with the non-racial policy of the ANC, which I think in the end proved to be the correct policy politically because that's the only solution to the South African problems (Sewpersadh 2002: 26).

Ramgobin saw the positive dimension of BC, but also pointed to its limits in a 1986 interview:

> The BC movement was undoubtedly a very good dimension in the black man's history at a given time in our history. It was a psychological reassertion of a personality that was being trampled all over all the time ... but does it become an end in itself? If it is blackness per se then it will be nothing more and nothing less than a majority of black South Africans saying to the people of South Africa: OK, here are the rules; here's the game we play; here are the laws of the land; here's the kind of society we want (Ramgobin 1986: 4).

Despite the intensity of these differences and debates there was also mutual respect, and Meer, for example, then a vice president of the NIC, spoke at the funeral of Biko in King William's Town in September 1977.

The Lenasia meeting of the BPC was followed by the two-day first annual conference of the revived NIC in Durban on 28–29 April 1972. Members from thirty-one branches attended the meeting. It was here that the NIC was officially reconstituted. According to one report,

> regarding the possibility of going nonracial, attitudes were extremely divided within the NIC. A number of people felt that the 'all-Indian' stance of the NIC was contradictory to the whole philosophy to which the NIC had committed itself by joining the Congress Alliance and accepting the Freedom Charter. On the other hand some advocates of a 'go-slow' approach were convinced that there was still a place in South African politics for the NIC as presently constituted. Some people argued that it would be arrogant of an all-Indian organisation to perfect its machinery first and then declare itself open to other groups. In the end a compromise agreement was reached through a resolution mandating the Executive to 'investigate' the possibility of the organisation becoming both nonracial and national (Khoape 1973: 6).

The significance of the NIC's relaunch is that it was the only black political organisation operating in the country outside of government structures. Cooper resigned from the NIC executive in June 1972 in protest against the decision to retain 'Indian' in its name (Bhana 1997). The existence of the BPC forced activists to make a choice, as they could not keep a foot in each organisation. It was reported in July 1972 that NIC members attending a BPC conference in Pietermaritzburg were made to feel 'unwelcome' and left the conference (Khoape 1973: 8).

In March 1973, amidst this debate, eight BCM members, including Cooper, Moodley, Biko and Pityana, who were heavily involved in the debate, were banned, and BC influence within the NIC subsided (Khoape 1973: 4).

At the July 1973 NIC provincial conference, A.S. Chetty and R. Paparam of Pietermaritzburg proposed changing the name to the South African People's Conference. Their motion read that '[a] purely Indian body, political in character, and operating outside the system of apartheid, is an anachronism' (Bissetty 1973).[4] Delegates were divided on the issue. Rabi Bugwandeen asked: 'What right have Indians to take a unilateral decision to become nonracial? Without first consulting other race groups, how can we presume to foist Indian leadership on the other races?' Coovadia described non-racialism as 'a brilliant idea' but one that would get Congress nowhere if it lost the support of Indians'. Chetty withdrew the motion after the two-hour-long debate, with the forty-five members 'bitterly divided' (Bissetty 1973).

There was a concession in 1974, though, when at its annual conference in September the NIC passed a resolution that 'with the changing events in Africa, it could no longer remain an Indian-only organisation' (Daily News Reporter 1974). By agreeing to open its membership 'to all groups', the NIC 'effectively broke a longstanding tradition of exclusiveness on the part of the NIC in their membership' (Mbanjwa 1975: 116). Though the 'Indian' was retained in the name Natal Indian Congress, membership was no longer exclusively Indian. NIC president M.J. Naidoo told the *Black Review*, a BPC publication, that he would facilitate cooperation with the BPC, though a merger was unlikely. The difficulty was that while 'the Congress was completely nonracial', the BPC had closed its doors to all whites, even democratic ones who were sincere in opposing apartheid. He said that 'the Congress was completely nonracial' (Mbanjwa 1975: 116).

According to Moodley (2002: 26), differences between Congress and BCM members intensified when 'ANC-supporting people called a Black Renaissance Convention [at Hammanskraal from 13 to 16 December 1974] in which they wanted the BCM to redefine itself' and commit itself to the Congress movement and the Freedom Charter. Within the BCM, however, some saw themselves as an alternative to the ANC and wanted to use the BCM as a forum to unite the ANC, PAC and other liberation movements. The BCM therefore rejected these overtures from the Black Renaissance Convention (Karis and Gerhart 1997).

Conclusion

BCM activists held that the revival of the NIC aimed to undermine their attempts to mitigate the apartheid regime's policy of rooting racial divides in society by building a movement that included Africans, coloureds and Indians. Despite vocal opposition, however, the 'I' was retained in the NIC. NIC ideologues justified this on several grounds. They argued that the revival of the NIC was strategic. As Coovadia (2002) pointed out, the NIC 'was the only game in town' and was vital to mobilising the Indian masses (UKZN). Sewpersadh argued that the revival of the NIC was significant at several levels. It was essential to the broader anti-apartheid movement since 'it fulfils a need that has existed for some eight years in the political structure of South Africa' following the banning of the ANC, Congress of Democrats and Coloured People's Congress (Sewpersadh 1972: 12). The NIC, he said, was a critical counter to the establishment of government structures; it provided a forum for Indians to express alternative views to those of system politicians.

The link to history was important. The NIC had been started by Gandhi, an iconic anticolonial resistance fighter, and had had a presence in the community since the 1890s. There was a fear that this connection would be lost with a name change. The NIC executive also argued that it was the only organisation that spoke to the Congress tradition of the 1950s and helped to draw people into a progressive anti-apartheid fold. In practice, however, the NIC generally kept within a tradition that saw the country as divided into national, racial groups that would organise separately and converge in an alliance led by the ANC to achieve majority rule.

Other NIC leaders stated that while they agreed in principle that they had to organise on a non-racial basis, this was not practical in light of the prevailing conditions. They insisted that the NIC was a non-racial organisation because it was not fighting exclusively for Indian rights; non-racialism was entrenched in the NIC's 1972 constitution. They argued that segregation and apartheid had created deep social and cultural divisions along racial lines, a barrier to a united anti-apartheid organisation. Group Areas divisions and Bantustans exacerbated this problem by making it difficult to go into 'other' areas to mobilise. The state's divide-and-rule ideology might have been an imposition from above, but it had impulses from below that divided people according to a particular racially circumscribed categorisation. As long as racially bounded areas existed, they said, Indians, many of whom feared black majority rule and enjoyed material conditions that were relatively better than those of Africans, had to be organised separately to ensure that they bought into the anti-apartheid project and did not give their support to system politicians and bodies. It was never explained at what point Indians and Africans would be able to meet on common political terrain.

The NIC regarded itself as 'non-racial' and BC as racist; conversely, BCM activists argued that the NIC, as a racial organisation, was cementing racial identity. The NIC defended its assertion of being non-racial by referring to its commitment to a non-racial South Africa. Presumably it assigned itself the task of bringing a non-racial consciousness to the mass of Indians. Many leaders of the NIC were in exile, in prison, underground, or banned during the 1980s, and therefore unable to actively organise in Indian townships. This haunted the NIC when non-racial democracy was looming, and they did not have a presence in the former Indian areas.

While the NIC soldiered on in the 1980s, the BCM, whose leadership faced the full might of apartheid repression, failed to mobilise effectively among Indians in the 1980s. This is understandable. Cooper and Moodley were part of the SASO/BPC leadership arrested in October 1974 for organising a Viva Frelimo Rally in Durban; they were charged with terrorism and jailed on Robben Island. Other BCM activists like Sam Moodley and Asha Ramabali were banned. The leading organisations of the BCM were also banned. The inspirational Biko died in September 1977 from injuries suffered when he was severely beaten in police custody.

The NIC, by contrast, mobilised large numbers of Indians in the first half of the 1980s around issues of education, housing, unemployment and service delivery. Yet, when the country's first democratic election was held in April 1994, as Padayachee pointed out,

> the NIC largely failed in its principal objective and *raison d'être* of winning support for the ANC at the first democratic elections ... I would surmise that the ANC overall only received about 30–35 per cent of the total Indian vote. Clearly, neither the NIC nor the ANC were able totally to allay fears over cultural, religious,

language, and property rights [which appeared to have been the main concerns of many Indian voters] in 1994 (Padayachee 1999: 395).

Unfortunately, as Padayachee wrote in 1999, the post-apartheid period was witness to 'new fears and vulnerabilities [among Indians] around issues such as affirmative action, job security, crime and, most significantly, about the quality of schooling for their children' (1999: 395).

Was the NIC right that many Indians feared majority rule and therefore had to be organised separately in the hope of changing their political behaviour, or would the NIC have been more effective in doing so had it abandoned this racial/ethnic organisation in favour of a unified black or non-racial political body?

Does what didn't happen matter, or should we accept, as British historian Richard Evans said, that '"What If" is a waste of time' (Evans 2014)?

Notes

1. This chapter accepts that race has no biological basis. However, race was a social and legal fact in South Africa during the apartheid era, when the racial categories, which changed over time, were white, coloured, Indian and African. In the post-apartheid period, racial categories continue to have legal consequences and social meaning, with the official census categories being Black African, Coloured, White and Asian/Indian.
2. Some of the issues discussed in this chapter are covered in Desai and Vahed (2021a: 29–46) and Desai and Vahed (2021b).
3. In an email to me on 1 September 2022, Robert van Niekerk, one of the editors of this volume, recounted that in an interview he had conducted with Enver Motala, the latter 'regaled us with stories of their bridge playing, among other things and the fascinating character of A.K.M. Docrat, a major mentor of Vishnu's of course, alongside Ike Mayet and Enver himself'.
4. Newspaper cuttings cited in this chapter are housed in a file titled 'Natal Indian Congress, Box 16, NIC Press Cuttings 1970s', in the Gandhi-Luthuli Centre, University of KwaZulu-Natal.

References

ANC (African National Congress). 1969. 'Strategy and Tactics of the ANC'. Document adopted by the Morogoro Conference of the ANC, Morogoro, Tanzania, 25 April–1 May 1969. https://www.marxists.org/subject/africa/anc/1969/strategy-tactics.htm.

Alexander, N. 1986. 'Approaches to the National Question in South Africa'. *Transformation* 1: 63–95.

Bhana, S. 1997. *Gandhi's Legacy: The Natal Indian Congress 1894–1994*. Pietermaritzburg: University of Natal Press.

Biko, S. 2017. *I Write What I Like*. 40th anniversary edition. Johannesburg: Picador Africa.

Bissetty, N. 1973. 'Surprise Move May Rock NIC'. *Natal Mercury* 21 July.

Cooper, S. 2003. 'Saths Cooper: Interview by Musa Ntsodi, 14 April 2003'. *Voices of Resistance Collection*. Gandhi-Luthuli Documentation Centre, University of KwaZulu-Natal.

Coovadia, J. 2002. 'Jerry Coovadia: Interview by Mwelela Cele, 25 July'. *Voices of Resistance Collection*. Gandhi-Luthuli Centre, University of KwaZulu-Natal.

Daily News Reporter. 1974. 'Natal Indian Congress to Admit All Race Groups'. *The Daily News*, 23 September.

Desai, A. and G. Vahed. 2010. *Monty Naicker: Between Reason and Treason*. Pietermaritzburg: Shuter and Shooter.

———. 2021a. *Colour, Class and Community: The Natal Indian Congress, 1971–1994*. Johannesburg: Wits University Press.

———. 2021b. 'A Fool's Errand? Black Consciousness and the 1970s Debate over the "Indian" in the Natal Indian Congress'. *New Contree* 86. https://journals.co.za/doi/full/10.10520/ejc-newcontree_v2021_n86_a2.

Dhillon, D.S. 1999. 'The Indians of Natal: Resistance to Apartheid, 1970–1985'. BA (Hons) thesis, National University of Singapore.

Dhupelia-Mesthrie, U. 2006. 'The Revival of the Natal Indian Congress'. In: *The Road to Democracy in South Africa: Volume 2 1970–1980*, edited by the South African Democracy Education Trust. Pretoria: UNISA Press.

Docrat, A.K.M. 1999. 'A.K.M. Docrat: Interview Conducted by Ruth Lundie, Jewel Koopman, and Jabulani Sithole', 22 October. Alan Paton Centre and Archives, University of KwaZulu-Natal, Pietermaritzburg.

Edwards, I. 2015. *Faith and Courage: The Political Papers of Mewa Ramgobin*. Johannesburg: Iain Edwards.

Evans, R.J. 2014. '"What If" Is a Waste of Time'. *The Guardian*, 13 May. https://www.theguardian.com/books/2014/mar/13/counterfactual-history-what-if-waste-of-time.

Graphic. 1972. 'Indian Congress Shock'. *Graphic*, 4 February.

Hart, K. and V. Padayachee. 2000. 'Indian Business in South Africa after Apartheid: New and Old Trajectories'. *Comparative Studies in Society and History* 42 (4): 683–712.

Karis, T.G. and G.M. Gerhart. 1997. *From Protest to Challenge: A Documentary History of African Politics in South Africa, 1882–1990. Volume 5: Nadir and Resurgence, 1964–1979*. Bloomington: Indiana University Press.

Khoape, B.A. (ed.). 1973. *Black Review 1972*. Durban: Black Community Programmes.

Mbanjwa, T. (ed.). 1975. *Black Review 1974/75*. Durban: Black Community Programmes.

Meer, F. 2002. 'Fatima Meer: Interview by Musa Ntsodi, 10 October'. *Voices of Resistance Collection*. Gandhi-Luthuli Documentation Centre, University of KwaZulu-Natal.

Moodley, S. 2002. 'Strini Moodley: Interview by D. Shongwe, 24 July'. *Voices of Resistance Collection*. Gandhi-Luthuli Documentation Centre, University of KwaZulu-Natal.

Naidoo, M.D. 1987. 'M.D. Naidoo: Interview by Julie Frederikse'. *The Julie Frederikse Collection, South African History Archive*, AL2460. A14.02. https://www.saha.org.za/collections/AL2460/a14021.htm.

Nair, B. 1985. 'Billy Nair: Interview by Julie Frederikse'. *The Julie Frederikse Collection, South African History Archive*, AL2460. A14.06. https://www.saha.org.za/collections/AL2460/a14061.htm.

Padayachee, V. 1999. 'Struggle, Collaboration and Democracy. The "Indian Community" in South Africa, 1860–1999'. *Economic and Political Weekly* 34 (7): 393–5. http://www.jstor.org/stable/4407648.

Padayachee, V. and S. Vawda. 1999. 'Indian Workers and Worker Action in Durban, 1935–1945'. *South African Historical Journal* 40 (1): 154–78. https://doi.org/10.1080/02582479908671353.

Padayachee, V., S. Vawda and P. Tichman. 1985. *Indian Workers and Trades Unions in Durban, 1930–1950*. Durban: Institute for Social and Economic Research, University of Durban-Westville.

Ramgobin, M.T. 1986. 'Mewa Ramgobin: Interview by Julie Frederikse'. *The Julie Frederikse Collection, South African History Archive*, AL2460. A18.04. https://www.saha.org.za/collections/AL2460/a184.htm.

Ramphele, M. 1995. *A Life*. Cape Town: David Philip.

Sewpersadh, C. (George). 1972. 'George Sewpersadh: Natal Indian Congress: The Significance of Its Revival'. *Reality* (May): 12–13.

———. 2002. 'Interview by Mwelela Cele, 11 August'. *Voices of Resistance Collection*. Gandhi-Luthuli Documentation Centre, University of KwaZulu-Natal.

Singh, R. and S. Vawda. 1988. 'What's in a Name: Some Reflections on the Natal Indian Congress'. *Transformation* 6: 1–21.

Soske, J. 2009. 'Wash Me Black Again: African Nationalism, the Indian Diaspora and Kwa-Zulu Natal, 1944–1960'. PhD thesis, University of Toronto.

———. 2015. 'The Impossible Concept: Settler Liberalism, Pan-Africanism, and the Language of Non-Racialism'. *African Historical Review* 47 (2): 1–36.

Vahed, G. and A. Desai. 2014. 'An Instance of "Strategic Ethnicity"? The Natal Indian Congress in the 1970s'. *African Historical Review* 46 (1): 22–47.

19

The University of Durban-Westville
Transition to an Open University and Merger with the University of Natal (1990–2003)

Jairam Reddy

Despite the conclusion in 1953 of the Holloway Commission on Separate Training Facilities for Non-Europeans at Universities that segregated universities would not be economically viable, the National Party government introduced the Separate University Education Bill in March 1957, which became law in June 1959 as the Extension of University Education Act (No. 45 of 1959). This Act, which legitimated the structuring of university education in South Africa along racial lines, was met with strong opposition in South Africa and abroad. In particular, the decision to close the white residential universities to African, coloured and Indian students was rejected by the open universities (the universities of the Witwatersrand, Cape Town and Natal), and by student formations in these universities.

The policy of apartheid had been rejected at the UN as contradictory to the Universal Declaration of Human Rights (UN 1948). The Separate University Education Bill was described as 'shameful and unjustifiable racial discrimination' (Oosthuizen et al. 1981: 33). The Bill was attacked world-wide on the grounds of morality and expediency. An article in *Graphic* in February 1959 stated that

> it is pathetic and inexplicable that the University, the highest pedestal of learning where good sense and understanding should be the guiding factors, should be riddled with discrimination on grounds of colour. It is the negation of the very principles for which a university is constituted (Graphic 1959).

Despite the widespread objections, the University College, Durban, established for Indian students in November 1960 in terms of the Extension of University Education Act, was placed under the aegis and tutelage of the University of South Africa (UNISA), following its syllabus, writing its examinations and being awarded its degrees. The university began its operations on Salisbury Island, utilising naval barracks which had previously been used to house Hungarian refugees. Lectures commenced on 1 March 1961. Professor S.P. Olivier, the dean of the Faculty of Education at the University of Cape Town, was appointed the first rector of the University College. The nine-member council comprising only white appointees was chaired by Professor A.J.H. van der Walt of UNISA. The first degrees offered were those of UNISA. In 1968 the institution was granted autonomy, and it became the fully fledged University of Durban-Westville (UDW). The new campus of UDW was established on a 200-hectare site in Westville. The campus was originally planned to accommodate 2 500 students, but by 1981 1981, student numbers stood at 5 000, with 35 per cent being female.

The university awarded its first nine degrees in May 1964. By 1981 three doctoral degrees had been awarded, one each in the faculties of education, science and arts. Distinguished students of this time included Ramachandran Govender, who became a Rhodes Scholar, doing a BA (Hons) degree in mathematics at Balliol College, Oxford, and Professor K. Bharuthram, who obtained a DPhil in physics at Oxford

On Professor Olivier's retirement in 1980 Professor J.J.C Greyling was appointed rector of the university. In the late 1980s the political terrain in South Africa was beginning to change quite dramatically, with the National Party government coming under intense local and international pressure to make meaningful political changes in the country. At the time, Professor Greyling was also under increasing pressure to resign as rector of the university, and he did so in the middle of 1989.

My appointment as rector and vice chancellor
The decision to appoint the rector is made by the University Council, as is the case with other universities in the country and across the world. The University Council is usually an autonomous body appointed by a range of constituencies such as the Senate, the Students' Representative Council (SRC) and civil society, with a few members appointed by the Department of Higher Education of the government of the day. In the

case of the apartheid universities such as UDW, the council members were all appointed by the National Party government. It came as somewhat of a surprise to the university community when I was appointed rector and vice chancellor, following interviews of three candidates for the position. There was jubilation across the university, especially among the students and progressive staff, and hopes were high that there would be significant changes at the institution.

> The appointment in July 1990 of the University's first non-nationalist Vice-Chancellor and Rector, Professor Jairam Reddy, coincided with the momentous political events which led to the dismantling of the apartheid state. In this milieu a new style of management was needed and curricula and research activities would need to be restructured; student admissions and staff appointment to be reconsidered. Improving the public image of the former apartheid institution and addressing community needs were to be its important priorities (Linscott 2012: 127).

Shortly after my election as vice chancellor and rector of UDW, the African National Congress (ANC) held its first national congress as an open and lawful organisation on the campus of the university. In opening the congress and welcoming the delegates, I expressed my pleasure at the enormous and unanticipated publicity it had generated, both locally and overseas. The fact that the congress was peaceful, democratic and very successful was a big bonus for the university. It was not the council's practice to allow political organisations to hold meetings or conferences at the university facilities. The fact that the council allowed the ANC to use the UDW sports hall was an indication of the changing times. In his opening address Nelson Mandela thanked me and all members of the UDW community for making the university available for this historic gathering, saying that

> we have no words to express our gratitude, but trust that the results will help reinforce the work in which you yourselves are engaged, of transforming the centre of learning and the educational system as a whole in keeping with our common aspiration to create a just society (*Varsity Voice* 1991: 5).

In my installation address on 21 June 1991, I spelt out my vision of the university and the direction it should take:

> Mr Chancellor, I have advanced some thoughts on a transformational vision of universities, as well as some options for the future of tertiary education in the context of a changing South Africa. It is a vision that has been informed and textured by study, travel, repression and conflict. In the ultimate analysis it is a vision informed by an intensely personal history and development – one that might have been very different if I were perhaps a privileged son, having gone to Hilton College or Durban High School and then UCT [the University of Cape Town]; or if I were the son of a township resident with all the pain, trauma, disadvantages, frustration and radicalism that may imply. Instead, you have heard tonight something of the vision of a son whose father, an indentured labourer, eked out a living on the sugar fields on Natal and subsequently raised a family on the tilling fields of Westville – only to have this land snatched away by the Group Areas Act. A son who was denied university education in the country of his birth due to his colour and who had endured the frustration of working under a higher paid, less qualified white counterpart. Finally, a son who suffered the daily humiliation of living in a society deeply stratified by race, prejudice and intolerance. From the dust and ashes of apartheid, at this seminal period in our history, South Africa has the space and opportunity to create, not only for its citizens, but for Africa and mankind, a constitutional model, a Bill of Rights, an economic system and an educational dispensation that are imaginative and innovative, and will protect its citizens from tyranny from any quarter, once and for all. These exhilarating tasks must occupy our minds in the years to come. Mr Chancellor, ladies and gentlemen, we must pay tribute to those who have brought us to this turning point; let us be grateful to be living in these auspicious times; and let us resolve, with all the vigour and courage we can muster, to make the most of the opportunities presented to us to build the new South Africa.

Under the new leadership, a mission statement was crafted through a consultative process to signal a new direction for the university:

The University of Durban-Westville, recognising the need to respond to socio-economic political changes and to meet the increasing demand for tertiary education, commits itself to achieving a number of specific goals. These will enable the University to develop its activities for the maximum benefit of the constituencies it serves. In pursuing these goals and tasks, the University will seek to be guided by respect for the principles of university autonomy and academic freedom and the rejection of racism, sexism, sectarianism and political intimidation.

A changing student profile
Under the new leadership, there was a distinct change in the profile of students at UDW, including admission of an increasing number of black students, who hitherto had been prohibited from attending the university. The student body of 7 642 students registered in 1990 comprised 58 per cent classified Indian, 35 per cent classified African and 7 per cent classified either coloured or white. By 1996, the demographic undergraduate profile was as follows: Africans 4 441 (50 per cent), Indians 4 104 (46 per cent), coloureds 123 (1 per cent) and whites 223 (3 per cent); 53 per cent of the student population were women. The diversification of the student body was not without controversy. Some of these students were under-prepared for university education, as a result of having attended poorly funded and under-resourced schools under the policy of Bantu Education. Failure rates were rising, and academic support programmes had to be provided at additional cost to the university. This trend has continued across the South African universities, with high failure rates especially in the first year, and some students taking seven to eight years to complete a three- to four-year degree programme.

Staff changes
The appointment in 1993 of Advocate Hassan Mall, an acting judge and anti-apartheid activist, as UDW's new chancellor was a significant milestone in the history of the university. A respected member of the council for the previous six years, Advocate Mall was well known for his integrity and his impartial intervention during debates.

Following a selection process, the council appointed Dr Marcus Balintulo as vice rector (Academic and Support Services), Professor John Butler-Adam as vice rector (Academic Affairs and Human Resource

Development), Professor Robin Jacobsen as registrar of the university, Professor Michael Sutcliffe as the director of Public Affairs, Dr Jeya Wilson as the deputy director of Public Affairs and Sibusiso Ndebele as the head of residences. Professor Irina Filatova of Moscow State University was welcomed to UDW as its new head of the Department of History.

Professor Christine Lucia, the head of the Department of Music, recruited Deepak Ram as a junior lecturer in Indian performance, Melvin Peters as a lecturer in musicology and Musa Xulu as a specialist in African music, especially Zulu wedding songs and modern syncretic styles. On Saturday 7 September 1991, internationally acclaimed virtuoso concert organist Dr Gillian Weir officially inaugurated the newly installed baroque organ in the Music Department's Recital Studio, which was designed specifically to enhance the organ's sound and appearance.

Graduation ceremonies and awards of honorary doctorates
Fatima Meer, a well-known academic and political activist, was the guest speaker at the UDW graduation ceremony on Friday evening 17 May 1991. The former director of the UN Centre Against Apartheid, Enuga Reddy, gave a public lecture at the university on 18 September 1991. A UDW delegation, which included Dr Michael Sutcliffe and myself, accompanied him on a visit to the Luthuli family in Groutville and the Phoenix Settlement, the site of Mahatma Gandhi's printing press. Before he departed, Enuga Reddy presented UDW's Documentation Centre with valuable archival material, including a copy of the recording of Albert Luthuli's Nobel Peace Prize acceptance speech. A copy of the recording was also presented to Nokukhanya Luthuli, the wife of Albert Luthuli, at her home in Groutville.

The graduation ceremony on Saturday 18 May 1992 was addressed by guest speaker Kader Asmal, a professor of law at the University of the Western Cape and an anti-apartheid stalwart. In his address he said that

> we want a non-racial, non-sexist, democratic and peaceful South Africa where there is economic justice and the doors of learning and culture are open. The basis of non-racialism this country seeks to establish is historically, morally and conceptually to be found in the unity of the oppressed. There rests, therefore, particular heavy responsibility on African and Indian students to show that non-racialism is realisable in the practice of our everyday living.

The progressive vision of the university was exemplified by the awarding of honorary doctorates. During the period 1990–94 honorary doctorates were awarded to Dr Beyers Naudé, the theologian and anti-apartheid activist; Chris Mann, a poet, playwright and director of the community-based Valley Trust development project; Professor Phillip Tobias, a prominent South African scholar and world-renowned palaeoanthropologist; Professor Y.K. Seedat, a professor of medicine at the University of Natal School of Medicine; Father Trevor Huddleston, who was renowned for his opposition to the apartheid regime; A.M. Rosholt and A.S. Vahed, entrepreneurs; Vella Pillay, an economist; E.S. Reddy, the head of the UN Anti-Apartheid Secretariat; and John Kani, the illustrious South African actor.

New initiatives on the campus of UDW

The African Centre for the Constructive Resolution of Disputes (ACCORD) is a conflict management, NGO headquartered in Durban, that works throughout Africa to bring creative African solutions to the challenges posed by conflict on the continent. ACCORD was established in 1992 at UDW as an educational trust associated with the five historically disadvantaged universities – the universities of the Western Cape, Transkei, Fort Hare, the North and UDW – to provide a mechanism to deal with conflict arising out of South Africa's transition from apartheid to democracy. For the past thirty years the institution has been building the capacity of Africa's leaders to resolve conflict and to address the underlying political barriers to growth and stability.

UDW's Faculty of Dentistry is based on the UDW campus, where basic science education is undertaken, and at the clinical facility where patients are treated on the premises of King George Hospital in Sydenham. The first intake of students training in oral hygiene and dental therapy was in 1980. In the mid-1980s the Department of Dentistry became a faculty, and in 1987 a dean was appointed to develop a School of Dentistry to train in addition dentists and postgraduates, and to undertake research. The Oral and Dental Training Hospital underwent a major refurbishment in 1996 at a cost of R1.58 million. The hospital employs both teaching and service staff because of its dual functions, namely providing a dental service to the public while also educating and training students. There were 70 students in 1996. About 30 000 patients are treated annually at the hospital, which has a complement of 12 full-time academic staff and a support staff of 75.

The Inter-Disciplinary Health Information Group was established in 1990 as an interest group in the Faculty of Health Sciences; it represents ten core departments at UDW and operates across five faculties. Director Anil Bhagwanjee explained that the group 'was born from the realisation that health personnel education, at both undergraduate and postgraduate levels, often fails to equip graduates with the skills to meet local health needs. This is reflected in the bias towards urban curative services at the expense of preventative health care.'

The Education Policy Unit was established in the Faculty of Education out of a concern for the development of national policies in education, in the context of alternative strategies for economic reconstruction in post-apartheid South Africa. It received two grants, one from the Ford Foundation of $50 000 and another from the Swiss government of R100 000.

The emerging research profile at UDW

Professor Jeff McCarthy, the director of the Institute for Social and Economic Research (ISER) at UDW, said that in a typical year researchers produced three books, twenty articles and fifty research reports. At any one time the institute ran about forty research projects, with six full-time and three contract researchers. Ninety per cent of the work was applied and increasingly policy-oriented. ISER's work was, and continues to be, clustered around four niche fields of urban reconstruction, rural development, environmental management and economic policy. It began contributing to university teaching, and currently its staff are supervising twelve postgraduate students and are working on a master's programme in social policy.

By 1996 the Faculty of Science was expanding its already considerable research capacity. The Foundation for Research Development (FRD, now called the National Research Foundation) deemed a number of its focused research areas worthy of its support. The faculty had 27 rated scientists among its staff complement of 109. Many of its academic staff members were actively engaged in community-based programmes including the Inanda Development Project, the Chatsworth Community Outreach Programme and the Palmiet Nature Reserve Management Committee. Faculty links with industry and international institutions were strengthened, with GENCOR providing R80 000 towards purchasing computers, and DAAD, the German Academic Exchange Service, awarding a similar sum for the purchase of research equipment.

Research output, publications and conference attendance were reported to have grown. One index of the increase in research was the steady expansion in numbers of publications ('units') in peer-reviewed journals accepted by the Department of National Education. The number of units rose from 21.7 in 1984 to 70.51 in 1989. UDW Research Committee awards for attendance at local conferences grew from 66 in 1986 to 94 in 1990, and for attendance at overseas conferences from 16 in 1988 to 29 in 1990.

The FRD was supportive of new projects in the science, health sciences and engineering faculties. A major aim of the FRD's University Development Programme was to intensify efforts to train engineers, scientists and technical experts among the disadvantaged students. Dr Ahmed Bawa of the Physics Department enjoyed P-status at the FRD; he was one of a number of UDW science researchers with high-level research ratings. As a young researcher with a doctorate held for less than five years and who had demonstrated exceptional potential in his published work, he was likely to become a leader in the field. In 1990, he won the prestigious FRD President's Award, which included a grant of R500 000.

Student and staff conflicts
The formation of the Combined Staff Association (COMSA) in the early 1990s was welcomed as representing all staff; it purported to play a constructive role in academic affairs specifically and in the transformative trajectory of the university more generally. Initially it did achieve these objectives, in particular in championing the rights of the workers and students. However, in time it became a conflictual and divisive organisation and took a confrontational stance with respect to the rector and management. This stance can be seen in a statement by Dr Ashwin Desai, the chairperson of COMSA, in a *Sunday Times Extra* report in 1994, when he claimed that 'after the euphoria over the rector Professor Jairam Reddy's appointment, the old days of nepotism, favouritism, and political "narrowists" seem to be rearing their ugly head again'. He also claimed that I had not spoken to a gathering of staff in the past year and that I was always away from the campus. In his rebuttal, the director of Public Affairs of UDW, Dr Michael Sutcliffe, replied as follows:

> The varsity denies Dr Desai's allegations of nepotism, favouritism, and political narrowists ... Prof Reddy has an open policy, visits

departments as time permits; and is accessible to his senior managers and staff. Only this week Dr Desai met the Rector almost daily, dealing with matters other than the overtime issue. Dr Desai's assertion that the Rector is always away from campus is without substance ... the appointment of senior members is vested in UDW's Council which now has representatives from all sectors, including staff and students (*Sunday Times Extra* 1994).

Edwin Naidu reported in the *Herald* in October 1994 that the executive of COMSA resigned after widespread criticism of its leadership:

The association has been accused of displaying 'bully-boy' tactics, operating undemocratically, ignoring the interests of academics on campus and doing little to promote academic excellence ... COMSA was also accused of pursuing a unionist role instead of supporting academics and research programmes. The new Chairman, Professor Dhiru Soni elected in fresh elections said COMSA would strive to promote reconciliation and healing on campus while not ignoring the interests of workers. Professor John Daniel, the newly elected publicity officer said that COMSA should continue as an umbrella body under which all constituencies on campus would have 'one loud voice'.

In another instance of conflict on the campus, angry students wreaked havoc in the rector's reception office and the Public Affairs Department during a protest by the (ANC-leaning) South African Students Congress against the launch of the South African Democratic Students Movement (SADESMO), an Inkatha Freedom Party (IFP)-aligned student organisation. About one hundred and fifty toyi-toying students smashed windows, destroyed a photostat machine and damaged desks and computer equipment. Following the protest, the university was closed for the rest of the day to protect life and property. Security personnel were posted at all main gates to prevent any unauthorised person from entering the campus. A very serious clash was avoided when Inkatha and SADESMO were persuaded to call off a meeting that was to be addressed by Chief Mangosuthu Buthelezi in the Joosub Hall. Mo Shaik (a lecturer in optometry at UDW and a member of the ANC) and Vishnu Padayachee (the special assistant to the vice chancellor) were able to reason with Faith

Gaza of the IFP and persuade her to call off the meeting. Fortunately, by this time Chief Buthelezi had not yet arrived for the meeting. After extensive discussions members of the rectorate, the administration, SENEX, the University Senate, COMSA, the SRC and some sixteen clubs and societies reaffirmed their commitment to freedom and democracy, as well as to the core values contained in the UDW mission statement.

University finances
Prior to attaining autonomy in 1984, the university was granted an annual budget and all its unspent budgetary allocation had to be returned to the responsible government department at the end of each financial year. Student fees collected were paid over to the department. Thus, the university could not use any surplus funds, or retain donations it received, to establish reserves. It was granted autonomy in 1984 on the following conditions: that the state would fund all capital projects; and that it would grant *ex gratia* payment to the university equivalent to one-quarter of the funding based on the South African Post Secondary Education formula in terms of which all autonomous universities were allocated funding for the year. In addition, the state would cover all liabilities related to leave payments and study benefits for children of employees enrolled at other tertiary institutions in South Africa for a period of five years (amounting to approximately R2.5 million).

After 1994, the university ensured that it operated on a very strict budget by not overspending its annual income received from government grants, student fees, revenue-generating activities and unencumbered donations. The university undertook a major restructuring of its academic sector and administrative/support/services sector to reduce personnel costs during the early 1990s. This was done by offering severance packages to surplus staff. This resulted in a substantial reduction of the personnel costs by approximately 15 per cent annually. The university also solicited external funding for specific research projects and developmental activities from overseas philanthropic organisations such as the Ford Foundation, W.K. Kellogg Foundation and Wellcome Trust. The W.K. Kellogg Foundation awarded UDW a seven-year grant of $615 000 towards meeting tuition, accommodation and related expenses of disadvantaged students in the education, commerce and health science faculties. UDW went into the merger with the University of Natal in 2004 in a very strong financial position, with available reserves of more than R300 million. The excellent management by the finance department of UDW, headed by Malcolm Stewart, his deputy Selva Govindsamy and their staff, must be fully acknowledged.

Changing leadership at UDW and the merger with the University of Natal

The ANC, which won the first democratic election in April 1994, installed Nelson Mandela as the first president of the Republic of South Africa. Shortly afterwards, the new government put in place a series of measures to fundamentally transform South African society into a progressive, non-racial, democratic order. One aspect of this transformation was the dismantling of the racially segregated system of universities, to be replaced by a modern, responsive, unified higher education system. To this end, the government appointed a National Commission on Higher Education comprising thirteen commissioners. It was a rare honour for UDW when I was asked by the first minister of higher education in the new government, Sibusiso Bhengu, to chair the commission. As a result, I tendered my resignation as rector and vice chancellor of UDW at the beginning of my second term and took up the post of chairperson.

After my departure, difficulties associated with the conduct of COMSA persisted under Professor Balintulo, now the acting rector and vice chancellor. The findings of the Butler-Adam report were released to the press on 23 May 1996 and at an off-campus meeting more than two hundred 'concerned academics' discussed the possibility of forming an alternative staff association that would be independent of COMSA. These and associated events led to the appointment of the Gautschi Commission of Inquiry into Management and Transformation Difficulties Experienced at the University in Durban-Westville on 21 May 1996. The Gautschi Commission found that the teaching and learning activities at the university were hampered by governance problems that were complex in nature. Despite this, the commission concluded that the institution had the potential for progress in the areas of academic development and curriculum changes. The problems identified by the commission were profound, and put the management, staff and students under considerable stress. However, it asserted that there were many positive aspects to be celebrated during the fifteen years prior to the merger.

In October 1997, Professor Mapule Ramashala was appointed rector and vice chancellor; she was the first woman to lead UDW. In her inaugural address she indicated the need to develop a culture of learning, respect and accountability and pledged to provide the university with informed and decisive leadership. In her first annual report she noted that the broad stability that characterised the university environment enabled it to focus on its core business, namely its academic activities. The strategic plan developed by the university management, staff and students envisaged the reduction of faculties from seven to four and the design of new academic structures with an emphasis on interdisciplinary programmes. The university's research and academic achievements continued throughout Professor Ramashala's term in office.

She was succeeded in January 2002 by Dr Saths Cooper, who was in office as the rector and vice chancellor for one year before a merger of UDW with the University of Natal took place in January 2004. The merger was the subject of considerable debate in all the faculties. In this regard, a memorandum of understanding was signed with the chairperson of the Council of the University of Natal on 30 May 2003. This provided for a framework to facilitate the merger, with a commitment to full disclosure of the relevant information. A Joint Academic Task Team was established to harmonise the integration of academic functions across the universities. A Merger Office was also established.

Regrettably at this crucial juncture, as merger talks were under way with the University of Natal, serious governance and management problems arose at UDW. This compelled the minister of education, Kader Asmal, to appoint an independent assessor in terms of the Higher Education Act (No. 101 of 1997) to investigate the reasons for the breakdown of governance by the university council and other structures on campus, and to suggest remedial measures. The assessor recommended that the UDW Council should be dissolved and that the minister should appoint an administrator to take charge and carry out the governance and executive/management responsibilities of the institution (Independent Assessor 2003). The merger was to proceed as planned and would take effect on 1 January 2004.

Conclusion

What was the status of 'transformation' at UDW during the post-National Party period 1990–2003? The term has become an intrinsic part of the post-apartheid discourse but has a spectrum of often contradictory meanings. Some use it as a goal, while others lay emphasis on it as a process. It may be characterised as providing the space for an alternative political and social order to emerge with values, principles and practices that would lead to a just and equitable society in post-apartheid South Africa. In practice, it would involve deep-rooted restructuring rather than piecemeal tinkering, accountability mechanisms and the reorganisation of power relations (Singh 1992).

At the broad level of governance and management as evidenced by the regular meetings of the University Council, University Management Committee and SENEX, UDW had indeed made measurable progress. The robust debates at the levels of faculty boards and senates were reinvigorated and resulted in the strengthening of academic freedom. The broad representation of university constituencies at these levels ensured democratic participation and accountability. As Ahmed Bawa et al. indicated,

> important gains have been registered in the fields of wage increases, gender advancement, and working conditions. Concessions have also been granted to lower echelons within the academic hierarchy with the election of six non-professorial staff members to Senate, the highest academic decision-making body within the university. These developments have been accompanied by the university shedding its authoritarian, ethnic public image, in favour of a more democratic, non-racial one (Bawa et al. 1992: 13).

Some two decades after the merger of UDW and the University of Natal into the University of KwaZulu-Natal, questions continue to arise about the wisdom of the decision to merge the two institutions. Excellence in a number of programmes and departments at UDW – in mathematics, physics, engineering, accounting, music, research at ISER and a number of others – was lost. Unique programmes in Indian philosophy, Indian languages, Hindu and Islamic studies and music came to an abrupt end. UDW's developing historic mission to cater for disadvantaged students and address the development needs of poor and impoverished communities, and its unique cultural niche in the area of Indian studies, have been halted. The size of the university's student body – some ten to twelve thousand students – ensured a degree of closeness, intimacy and personal attention, all concentrated on a single campus, that were enabling factors for a quality student experience. In contrast, the merged University of KwaZulu-Natal, with some forty thousand students dispersed across five campuses in Durban, Pinetown and Pietermaritzburg, has certainly resulted in the loss of this closeness and cohesiveness. Have there been decisive benefits from the merger? This is an open question.

This concluding chapter in the history of UDW was well captured by Professor Dasarath Chetty at the Alumni Reunion at the Beachwood Country Club in 2004 when he said:

> The University of Durban-Westville has had a proud history of struggle against all forms of authoritarianism, both at the University and [in] society generally. Numerous student activists had cut their teeth in student politics and community issues at the Westville campus in the 1980s when both the University, because of its undemocratic administration, and our country, because of its oppressive regime, were being systematically opposed. The reunion of alumni at the Beachwood Country Club served to rekindle pride in our history and it was a celebration also for those who have become the captains of commerce and various structures of government to recommit themselves to supporting the University of KwaZulu-Natal (Linscott 2012: 134).

References

Bawa, A., A. Desai, A. Habib and V. Padayachee. 1992. *The University of Durban-Westville and the Question of Transformation*. Macro-Education Policy Unit Occasional Publication. Durban: University of Durban-Westville.

Graphic. 1959. 'University Is Constituted'. *Graphic*, 6 February.

Independent Assessor. 2003. 'Independent Assessor's Report on the University of Durban-Westville, October 2003'. Durban: University of Durban-Westville.

Linscott, G. (ed.). 2012. *University of KwaZulu-Natal: 100 years of Academic Excellence in the Province (1910–2010)*. Durban: University of KwaZulu-Natal.

Oosthuizen, G.C., A.A. Clifford-Vaughan, A.L. Behr and G.A. Rauche. 1981. *Challenge to a South African University: The University of Durban-Westville*. Cape Town: Oxford University Press.

Naidu, E. 1994. 'UDW's New COMSA Executive to Address Academic Concerns'. *Herald*, 9 October.

Singh, M. 1992. *Transformation Time*. Macro-Education Policy Unit Occasional Publication. Durban: University of Durban-Westville.

Sunday Times Extra. 1994. 'UDW – Official Response to Criticism of Rector'. *Sunday Times Extra*, 6 February.

UN (United Nations). 1948. *Universal Declaration of Human Rights Proclaimed by the United Nations General Assembly in Paris on 10 December 1948*. https://www.un.org/en/about-us/universal-declaration-of-human-rights.

Varsity Voice. 1991. 'Mandela Thanking the University'. *Varsity Voice*, September.

20

Graduate and Research Outputs and Efficiency in South African Universities

Pundy Pillay

Given the expected decline in government revenue in the short to medium term as a consequence mainly of low economic growth, it is quite likely that public resources for universities will fall significantly in the short to medium term, that is, for at least the next three to five years. The budget presented by the minister of finance in February 2023 provided a clear indication that, for the first time since the advent of democracy, there will be a decline in real terms (namely, after adjustment for inflation) in both the basic education and higher education budgets. Given gloomy economic growth predictions, it is quite likely that higher education funding from the state will continue to decline for some time. This situation will be quite challenging for university leaders given increasing numbers of students.

In such a climate, it may be opportune to assess how institutional resources are being utilised. In particular, it may be prudent to examine the issue of 'efficiency' in higher education. In this regard, the issue explored here relates to what universities are achieving with respect to the utilisation of the funds they receive from the government, students, donors and other sources.

This chapter is based on a report commissioned by the Council on Higher Education (CHE), and it examines the relationship between university funding, enrolments and graduate outputs for the period 2017–19. The report also examines the trend in research outputs for this period, as well as reflecting on the relationship between enrolments and graduation.

Ideally an exercise such as this should involve all universities in the country. However, given constraints induced by Covid-19, the chapter analyses the issue of financial efficiency only for a sample of universities in Gauteng and Limpopo, namely, the University of Johannesburg (UJ), University of the Witwatersrand (Wits), Tshwane University of Technology (TUT), University of Pretoria (UP) and University of Limpopo (UL).

Given Covid-19-induced circumstances, the methodology used was limited to an analysis of university reports and other information provided by the institutions, and of data from the CHE, the Department of Higher Education and Training (DHET) and Statistics South Africa.[1]

The quality and depth of the analysis presented here is therefore dependent on the nature of the information provided by the institutions. This information varied significantly across institutions in terms of both depth and quality.

Three interrelated issues are examined in this chapter in the context of concern for institutional efficiency, namely, total expenditure and expenditure per student by institution, research outputs, and linking student expenditure to graduation rates (GRs).

Expenditure by institution

In terms of total expenditure and expenditure per student, there are huge and significant variations across the five institutions in the sample. For example, total expenditure in 2019 for the five institutions was as follows: R1.87 billion (UL), R4.8 billion (UJ), R4.2 billion (TUT), R6 billion (UP) and R4.2 billion (Wits). Several factors account for this variation in funding, and therefore in expenditure – for example, the DHET funding formula, which takes into account, inter alia, student enrolment by level of study, research activities, and huge institutional differences with respect to donor funding.

Table 20.1 provides a summary of per capita student expenditure by institution. The figures in Table 20.1 show the huge variance in expenditure per student across the five institutions; in 2019, for instance, the respective per capita figures were R50 500 (UJ), R87 110 (UL), R62 063 (TUT), ~ R135 000 (UP) and R102 715 (Wits).

Where the data were available, the indications are that there are large discrepancies within institutions between faculty expenditure per student

Table 20.1. Per capita student expenditure by university, 2017–19 (rands)

University	2017	2018	2019
UJ	–	50 708	50 500
UP	–	120 481	~ 135 000
Wits	90 490	109 712	102 715
UL	73 612	64 169	87 110
TUT	56 241	57 645	62 063

Sources: DHET (2019, 2020, 2021b).

and total institutional expenditure per student. For example, in 2019, at TUT the respective figures were R46 664 and R62 063; and at UP the corresponding figures were R49 940 and R120 481.

Several factors might explain the huge institutional discrepancies in per capita student expenditure (for example, research versus teaching universities, higher salaries). For instance, it is to be expected that research and other infrastructure costs will be higher in the research universities. Moreover, UP and Wits, the 'historical research universities' in this sample, have considerably more non-DHET sources of revenue in the form of tuition fees and third-stream (donor) income.[2]

However, the fact that in relation to the figure for UJ, per capita expenditure in 2019 was 2.7 times greater at UP, 2 times greater at Wits and 1.7 times greater at UL should be a matter of concern with regard to institutional efficiency. All of the additional expenditure in the latter institutions can scarcely be attributed to 'research'.

Research outputs

Even though there is an unofficial classification of South African universities as either 'research' or 'teaching' institutions, all universities undertake research to varying degrees. This section provides an analysis of the quantity and type of research publications of the sample of five universities for the period 2019.

Table 20.2 shows total book units for the five universities examined in this report, as well as the total for all 23 South African universities in 2019 (a book unit refers to a chapter in a book that was submitted to DHET for a subsidy claim).

Graduate and Research Outputs and Efficiency 331

Table 20.2. Book units by institution and in total, 2019

University	Ranking	No. of book units	% of total
UJ	1	359.0	14.05
UP	4	296.0	11.58
Wits	5	272.4	10.66
UL	16	13.1	0.51
TUT	18	8.2	0.32
All South African universities		2 554.7	

Source: DHET (2021a).

Table 20.3 shows total conference proceedings units for the five universities examined in this chapter, as well as the total for all South African universities in 2019.

Table 20.3. Conference proceedings units by institution and in total, 2019

University	Ranking	No. of units	% of total
UJ	1	294.8	23.2
UP	4	82.2	6.5
Wits	7	68.5	5.4
UL	15	25.9	2.0
TUT	9	58.4	4.6
All South African universities		1 270.8	

Source: DHET (2021a).

Similarly to the production of book units, for the three-year period under consideration UJ was consistently the highest producer of conference proceedings units in the sample of institutions, also by a significant margin. UJ averaged between 2.5 and 3.5 times higher than the next institution (UP) in the sample for the three-year period. Moreover, for the three-year period, UJ recorded the highest number of conference proceedings units in the country, as it did for book units in 2017 and 2019.

Finally, Table 20.4 shows the number of 'journal units' by institution for 2019.

Table 20.4. Journal units by institution and in total, 2019

University	Ranking	No. of units	% of total
UJ	4	1 622.6	9.4
UP	2	1 682.4	9.8
Wits	6	1 577.8	9.2
UL	14	348.7	2.0
TUT	16	294.8	1.7
All South African universities		17 194.2	

Source: DHET (2021a).

The numbers of journal units produced by UP, Wits and UJ were significantly higher than those of UL and TUT. This is to be expected, given the fact that Wits and UP are considered as research universities and UJ is moving rapidly in that direction. The former group produced 28–9 per cent of all journal units nationally during each year of the period 2017–19, while the corresponding figures for UL and TUT were 3.5 and 3.7 per cent respectively.

With respect to research outputs, it is therefore evident that UP, Wits and UJ are better endowed in terms of research capacity and funding, and this is reflected in their significantly higher research production both in comparison to UL and TUT and as a percentage of the national total. In this regard, special mention should be made of UJ, which receives significantly lower levels of state funding than UP and Wits but is faring exceptionally well in terms of research outputs in some areas; for example, with regard to book units it has consistently been the highest performer nationally.

Graduation rates (1)

In this section an attempt is made to link expenditure to graduation rates (GRs). The indicator of efficiency used in this section is the GR.

The GR for 2017, for example, is calculated as the number of graduates in 2017 divided by the headcount enrolment in 2017 and is expressed as a percentage. This is strictly speaking not the correct way to measure the GR, as one should measure the proportion of graduates in relation to the year in which they enrolled. However, the data available across the institutions do not enable this type of analysis, so the institutions (and the DHET – see below) use a 'proxy' GR as defined above. This chapter shows that there is a close correlation between the calculations presented here and those of the DHET with respect to the GRs.

An attempt was made to link expenditure to GRs in the quest to examine efficiency. The data show that GRs, particularly at the undergraduate (UG) level, are exceptionally low across the five institutions. The GRs are quite similar by level and field of study.

UG GRs are low by institution, varying from 19 per cent at Wits to 25 per cent at UJ. Postgraduate (PG) rates are understandably higher, with the average in the mid-30 per cents. The GRs in the master's (low 20s) and doctoral (14 per cent) degrees are exceptionally low, and quite costly both to the individual and to society as a whole (DHET 2019, 2020, 2021b). Furthermore, the GRs in the science, engineering and technology disciplines are usually far below the average rates for both UGs and PGs.

These results suggest that education policy-makers in South Africa need to focus urgently on how GRs can be raised, particularly in a context where the number of young people wanting to access universities is constantly increasing but the financial resources to accommodate such increases are clearly lacking. In particular, much more attention needs to be paid to improving the quality of mathematics and science education in schools – this is not a new finding but is worth repeating because of the human and financial wastage implicit in the findings of this analysis.

Greater attention needs to be paid also, by both policy-makers and institutional leaders, to determining whether limited financial resources are being put to their best possible use in South African universities. The huge gap between expenditure at the faculty level and at the university as a whole hints at a bloated bureaucracy and/or inefficiencies across institutions in several instances. Such inefficiencies need to be addressed as a matter of urgency so that the best possible use can be made of limited (and possibly declining) resources in the university sector.

In spite of the data limitations – for example, it was not possible to track students from enrolment to graduation – and hence the need to calculate GRs in a less-than-ideal manner, the analysis presented here does provide some useful information about systemic efficiency in terms of graduate outputs by institution, by level of study (UG versus PG) and discipline (for example, social versus natural sciences).

Graduation rates (2)
This section uses data from the DHET (DHET 2019, 2020, 2021b) to compare GRs by qualification type and institution, and GRs by field of study and institution.

The purpose of providing these data is to illustrate that, while the definitions of efficiency and the GR used in the analysis up to this point are not perfect, they correlate fairly well with the calculations by the DHET in this regard.

Table 20.5 shows the 2019 GRs for the five institutions evaluated in this chapter, by qualification. The GRs are based on DHET enrolment and graduate data.

Table 20.5. GRs by qualification type and institution, 2019

University	UG certificates & diplomas	UG degrees	PG below master's level	Master's	Doctoral
UJ	25.9	24.7	56.3	25.1	15.9
UP	39.1	18.4	60.4	32.2	16.8
Wits	n.a.	19.5	65.4	22.4	12.5
UL	n.a.	19.5	70.7	14.9	12.0
TUT	21.3	33.9	51.3	14.1	13.6
National average	20.8	17.1	45.4	21.7	14.1

Sources: DHET (2019, 2020, 2021b).

Note: The average given in the table is for the whole South African university system, and is relatively low because of the much longer completion rate of University of South Africa (UNISA) students.

For UG certificates and diplomas, the average national GR for 2019 was 20.8 per cent. For UG degrees, the national average was around 17 per cent, a worryingly low number. The range for the sample of universities in this study (for UG studies) was between 19.5 per cent (UL) and 33.9 per cent (TUT).

For PG studies lower than a master's degree, the GR was 45.4 per cent in 2019, with the ratios varying from 51.3 per cent (TUT) to 70.7 per cent (UL). At the master's level, the average national GR was unacceptably low, at 21.7 per cent in 2019, ranging from 14.1 per cent (TUT) to 32.2 per cent (UP) at the sample of institutions. The GRs at the doctoral level are a source of major concern across all institutions. The average rate for all institutions in the country was 14.1 per cent in 2019. Such low rates are indicative of a huge wastage of financial resources on the part of institutions as well as individuals.

Table 20.6 shows GRs by field of study for 2019 using the same DHET data set as for Table 20.5.

Table 20.6. GRs by field of study and institution, 2019

Field of study	UJ	UP	Wits	UL	TUT	Average
SET	26.6	21.7	20.4	17.0	20.2	21.2
BM	27.9	35.9	30.1	28.1	21.8	28.8
Education	24.6	30.8	26.9	23.2	16.8	24.5
AHSS	27.4	27.6	24.7	27.4	23.5	26.1
All HE institutons	27.0	26.4	23.9	22.7	21.0	24.2

Sources: DHET (2019, 2020, 2021b).
Note: SET = science, engineering and technology; BM = business and management; AHSS = all other humanities and social sciences.

The following conclusions can be drawn from the analysis above:

The average GR for all institutions in the country in 2019 was low at 24.2 per cent. For the sample of institutions in this study, the average ranged from a high of 28.8 per cent for business and management courses to a low of 21.2 per cent for science, engineering and technology courses.

Analysis by faculty shows that the GR for science, engineering and technology ranged between 17.0 per cent (UL) and 26.6 per cent (UJ). For business and management, the highest GR was at UP (35.9 per cent), and the lowest was at TUT (21.8 per cent). In education, the average GR ranged between 16.8 per cent (TUT) and 30.8 per cent (UP). In the category 'all other social sciences and humanities', the average GR ranged between 23.5 per cent (TUT) and 27.6 per cent (UP).

Conclusion

Three interrelated issues were examined in the analysis presented in this chapter, in the context of concern for institutional efficiency, namely, expenditure per student by institution, research outputs and linking expenditure to GRs.

In terms of total expenditure and expenditure per student, there are huge and significant variations across the five institutions in the sample. For example, total expenditure in 2019 for the five institutions was as follows: R1.87 billion (UL), R4.8 billion (UJ), R4.2 billion (TUT), R6 billion (UP) and R4.2 billion (Wits).

Expenditure per student also varied significantly in 2019: R50 500 (UJ), R87 110 (UL), R62 063 (TUT), ~ R135 000 (UP) and R102 715 (Wits).

Several factors might explain the huge institutional discrepancies in per capita student expenditure (for example, research versus teaching universities, higher salaries). However, the fact that in relation to UJ, per capita expenditure was 2.4 times greater at UP, 2 times greater at Wits and 1.7 times greater at UL should be a matter of concern with regard to institutional efficiency. All of the additional expenditure in the latter institutions can scarcely be attributed to a greater focus on research.

On the issue of research outputs, UP, Wits and UJ lead the way with respect to capacity and funding – this is reflected in their consistently higher research outputs compared to those of UL and TUT. They also rank highly in the comparative national picture in this regard. What should also be noted is the rapid progress made by UJ with regard to outputs (such as book units) even though it receives relatively lower funding.

The data show that GRs, particularly at the UG level, are exceptionally low across the five institutions. The GRs are quite similar by level and field of study.

UG GRs are low by institution, varying from 19.5 per cent at Wits to 24.7 per cent at UJ. PG rates are understandably higher, with the average in the mid-30 per cents. The GRs in the master's (low 20s) and doctoral (14 per cent) degrees are exceptionally low, and quite costly both to the individual and to society as a whole (DHET 2019, 2020, 2021b). Furthermore, the GRs in the science, engineering and technology disciplines are usually far below the average rates for both UGs and PGs.

The data from the DHET comparing GRs by qualification type and institution, and GRs by field of study and institution, show that the methodology used in the analysis in the chapter is grounded in reality.

The findings presented here suggest that education policy-makers in South Africa need to focus urgently on how GRs can be raised, particularly in a context where the number of young people wanting to access universities is constantly increasing but the financial resources to accommodate such increases are clearly lacking. In particular, much more attention needs to be paid to improving the quality of mathematics and science education in schools – this is not a new finding, but it is worth repeating because of the human and financial wastage implicit in the findings of this analysis.

Given these findings, it is imperative that policy-makers and university leaders pay greater attention to ensuring more efficient and effective use of limited financial resources. The analysis in this chapter suggests the possibility of inefficiencies due to bloated bureaucracies in several instances. In an environment where the state's higher education budget is constantly under threat, the need to demonstrate 'internal efficiency' with regard to resource utilisation is of paramount importance.

In spite of the data limitations – as indicated earlier in the chapter, it was not possible to track students from enrolment to graduation – and hence the need to calculate GRs in a less-than-ideal manner, the chapter does provide some useful information about systemic efficiency in terms of graduate outputs by institution, by level of study (UG versus PG), and by discipline (for example, social versus natural sciences).

The study does suffer from some methodological shortcomings, primarily because of the limitations imposed by the spread of the Covid-19 pandemic. For instance, the research would have benefited immensely from interviews with a sample of administrators and academics from each of the universities examined here. The study was also limited to five institutions, four in Gauteng and one in Limpopo, so it would be inappropriate to extrapolate the findings nationally.

The major findings of the study showing the relatively low levels of efficiency across institutions and faculties within institutions suggest, inter alia, that a study of this nature should be replicated nationally so that policy-makers can be better informed about the nature and depth of the efficiency challenge across both urban and non-urban institutions. Given the poor efficiency rates, it is clearly imperative that DHET policy-makers should work together with universities and other stakeholders to address this question of low efficiency, particularly in the context of limited financial resources, which will be the case especially in the short and medium terms as the prospects of high economic growth are seemingly not very promising.

It would be useful also to combine higher education efficiency studies that describe and analyse the relationship between financial resources and graduate outputs with 'cost effectiveness' studies that measure both the extent to which university graduates obtain employment in the formal sector of the economy and, importantly, whether such employment is in line with their education and training. The limited information available on graduate employment suggests that it is relatively high, both in absolute terms and in comparison with individuals who do not have a university degree. However, less is known about the extent to which graduates are actually in occupations for which they were trained. It may well be that while graduate unemployment is indeed low, graduate 'under-employment' might be relatively high.

Various forms of cost analysis are possible in education, and more specifically in higher education. These include, inter alia, cost-effectiveness analysis, cost-benefit analysis, cost utility analysis and cost-feasibility analysis (see, for example, Levin and McEwan 2000). The nature and depth of any one of these evaluations is dependent on both the quantity and quality of data available, for example in the higher education sector.

In developing countries more generally, and in South Africa specifically, both the quality and quantity of data vary substantially across systems and institutions. This has historically limited the types of analysis that could and should have been undertaken in higher education to inform policy-makers and to ensure more efficient and effective use of very limited financial resources.

In this study an attempt is made to measure efficiency in the utilisation of financial resources in a sample of South African universities, by linking GRs to institutional expenditure. Ideally, this study should be linked to a study on effectiveness that examines graduate placement in the labour market with respect to employment and, importantly, the type of employment in relation to university qualifications.

Notes

1. These data sources included CHE (2017); Ministry of Higher Education and Training (2018); Statistics South Africa (2019, 2020); TUT (2017, 2018, 2019); UJ (2017, 2018, 2019, 2020); UL (2017, 2018, 2019); UP (2019); Wits (2019, 2020, 2021); and financial and enrolment data provided by the staff of UJ, UL, UP, TUT and Wits.
2. 'Historical research universities' are characterised as such because they have undertaken more research and produced more research outputs than the 'teaching universities'. The former group also coincides with what were known as historically white universities and the latter group with the historically black universities.

References

CHE (Council on Higher Education). 2017. *Vital Stats – Public Higher Education 2015*. Pretoria: Council on Higher Education.

DHET (Department of Higher Education and Training). 2019. *Statistics on Post-School Education and Training in South Africa: 2017*. Pretoria: Department of Higher Education and Training.

———. 2020. *Statistics on Post-School Education and Training in South Africa: 2018*. Pretoria: Department of Higher Education and Training.

———. 2021a. *Report on the Evaluation of the 2019 Universities' Research Output*. Pretoria: Department of Higher Education and Training.

———. 2021b. *Statistics on Post-School Education and Training in South Africa: 2019*. Pretoria: Department of Higher Education and Training.

Levin, H.M. and P.J. McEwan. 2000. *Cost-Effectiveness Analysis: Methods and Applications*. 2nd edition. London: Sage.

Ministry of Higher Education and Training. 2018. *Ministerial Statement on University Funding: 2019/20 and 2020/21*. Pretoria: Ministry of Higher Education and Training.

Statistics South Africa. 2019. *Higher Education and Skills in South Africa 2017*. Report 92-01-05. Pretoria: Statistics South Africa.

———. 2020. *Education and Labour Market Outcomes in South Africa 2018*. Report 92-01-06. Pretoria: Statistics South Africa.

Tshwane University of Technology. 2017. *Annual Report and Financial Statements 2017*. Pretoria: Tshwane University of Technology.

———. 2018. *Annual Report and Financial Statements 2018*. Pretoria: Tshwane University of Technology.

———. 2019. *Annual Report and Financial Statements 2019*. Pretoria: Tshwane University of Technology.

University of Johannesburg. 2017. *Annual Report 2017*. Johannesburg: University of Johannesburg.

———. 2018. *Annual Report 2018*. Johannesburg: University of Johannesburg.

———. 2019. *Annual Report 2019*. Johannesburg: University of Johannesburg.

———. 2020. *Annual Report 2020*. Johannesburg: University of Johannesburg.

University of Limpopo. *Annual Report 2017*. Polokwane: University of Limpopo.
———. 2018. *Annual Report 2018*. Polokwane: University of Limpopo.
———. 2019. *Annual Report 2019*. Polokwane: University of Limpopo.
University of Pretoria. 2019. *Annual Report 2019*. Pretoria: University of Pretoria.
University of the Witwatersrand. 2019. *Annual Report 2019*. Johannesburg: University of the Witwatersrand.
———. 2020. *Facts and Figures 2020*. Johannesburg: University of the Witwatersrand.
———. 2021. *Facts and Figures 2020/21*. Analytics and Institutional Research Unit, Business Intelligence Sources. Johannesburg: University of the Witwatersrand.

21

Books, Bannings and Activism
Excerpts from an Interview with Omar Badsha

Rajend Mesthrie and Robert van Niekerk

Around 1983, still early in his lecturing and research career, Vishnu Padayachee became actively involved in resistance politics. He often cited Ike Mayet (the eponymous owner of Ike's Books), A.K.M. Docrat ('Doc') and Enver Motala as mentors at this time in regard to books and politics. Omar Badsha is an acclaimed photographer, artist and political activist, and was part of an active group in Durban mentored by Docrat from the 1960s onwards. Omar was later detained and harassed by the security police and prevented from travelling overseas. In 1982 he co-founded Afrapix, a pioneering initiative to promote documentary photography. Omar is also the co-founder of *South African History Online*, founded in 1999, which remains the country's largest and most important online historical resource.

In our interview with Omar at his home in Woodstock, Cape Town on 15 March 2023, we encouraged him to give us an insider's account of what it was like to be part of the resistance movement. In this chapter we reproduce – in a lightly edited form – the first part of the interview, which stresses the artistic and literary concerns of the group as part of the building of a resistance culture and movement.[1]

RM and RVN: Could you tell us about your early associations with Ike and Doc?

Omar: After Sharpeville there was a state of emergency, with people like Doc and so many others being detained. And when they came out, they were banned. That was, in my recollection, Doc's second or third banning. And so, there was a huge shift in his life, including having his close friends and comrades also banned. So, he would come to our house on Friday evenings, sit down, have a meal, or he would bring something. Ike Mayet stayed around the corner from us in Lutchman Avenue, off Wills Road. Now Ike and my father (Ebrahim Badsha) were friends from the time they were young. And so, these three guys would meet, and I would be included, sitting around listening to them – this was in 1963-64, when I was just around seventeen years old. But it was the most fascinating getting together every Friday and hearing them discuss the politics of the day. They would start by telling a joke; they would collect jokes and tell them, and everybody would have a good laugh. There was one that I remember well. Doc would say 'What's the difference between Verwoerd and Seretse Kama?' We would all mill around, and then he said, 'One was ruthless and the other had ruth' (referring to Ruth Williams, whose marriage to Sir Seretse Khama of Botswana had caused major political controversies).[2] These guys would start the evenings with their humour and playing chess; this became a routine, and a couple of years later more people joined the group, including Enver Motala and Mafika Gwala. Discussions would revolve around what they had read or were currently reading. Ike Mayet was a boilermaker, a big guy with a gammy leg. If you looked at him, you'd think he could have come out of the Transvaal Afrikaner farming community – he was big-built like a farmer and had had no education. When he was a child, he developed a problem with his leg which put him in hospital for years.

And Ike's son Rafique tells me the story about when he was in St Aidan's Hospital.[3] Mrs Gandhi, the young Indira Gandhi, came visiting the hospital in the 1940s.[4] She saw this youngster of about seven or eight years old sitting and reading a Greek classic. Being absolutely taken aback by this, she took time to talk to him. Ike was in fact self-taught, yet I've never come across anyone who was as incredibly well read. He was this working-class man, a hard, tough guy, who proudly considered himself black. He could have passed as a white man, he even had the right to vote, but he never took it up. His father was a Gujarati Muslim, his mother was German. The white buses wouldn't accept him, so he would not take the white bus when he went to work. The green mambas wouldn't take him on board because they took him for a white man.[5] It was only the Indian buses that would take him. But that meant he had to walk a long way with his gammy leg before he could catch a bus. The idea of blackness, race and culture, was one of the themes in our group. They would talk about Doc and my father growing up in India and their family backgrounds there. And Ike was born in Leopold Street (Durban). As I've said, his father was a Gujarati Muslim, while his mother was German. And they had married and had a number of children. Some parts of the family could pass as white, and did. Whereas Ike, and I think his sister and others, didn't want to be considered white. So, there was all this issue of identity and history, which the group would talk about, in addition to discussing literature and playing chess.

For me there was always something new to learn at meetings. When I started out with the group – after failing my matric – I was in a bad state. My father gave me some art material and said, 'Go and draw'. And that was like a lifeline for me because I was very depressed. He also got me jobs with his friends, but I didn't last more than three or four months – one was on a building site, one was in a printing press, and another at a big departmental store for a couple of months. The reason for this frequent changing was that after I'd start a job, the security police would come and say to the bosses that you should not employ this chap. So I would lose my job, and not realising why – only being told much later in life what had happened. Anyway, when I started working on drawing and doing woodcuts, I brought my first woodcut (or virtually the first one) to the meeting one evening and said to the guys, 'Have a look'. They looked at it and Ike said, 'Why don't you submit it to the *Art South Africa Today* exhibition?' So, I submitted it, and it won a prize, which gave me a huge boost. But when I came back after the prize-giving the next Friday, they sat me down and said, 'Now Omar, why do you think they gave you a prize? Is it that they wanted more black faces? Or is it that your work was good? Just remember this – there are always underlying issues with black and white prizes and awards. Don't get too carried away'. So that was a big lesson, you know, which made me sit up and think about things. Every week, there was something new to learn.

And then when Doc got banned again [in 1966], I had already been drawn into a group that comprised him, Phyllis Naidoo and others, which was like an ANC network. Every day Doc collected newspapers from around the country, some of which came in a day or two after publication, especially the *Rand Daily Mail*, because of having to be posted or transported from Joburg. And he had his network in the Grey Street area of shopkeepers, who were all friends of his. And they would send out a parcel once a week to London to M.P. Naicker, who was the editor of *Sechaba*.[6] And then within these parcels there would be other materials and notes and things, all in secret writing. So, I was now part of that network, because after Doc and Phyllis were banned I became the one who would carry messages – mainly to people who lived in the townships, old comrades. And I used to walk from one end of Grey Street to the women's hostel at the other end. In each building there were women who were banned – stalwarts of the movement – and I would get reports from them. I would start at Lodson House, go down to Dr Padayachee's surgery in Short Street, then to Gladys Manzi at the Women's Hostel, and then on to Dr Naicker's surgery. I would also meet Poomani Moodley, who was a nurse and an activist, and still others. These were all comrades and stalwarts of the movement. I then became part of a network that was in touch with political prisoners on Robben Island: we kept in touch with or looked after their families and received prisoners released from the Island. Through that process I came to know an enormous number of people: people from the Transkei, from Pondoland and all along the coast and the interior. When Jacob Zuma came out of prison in 1973, I was one of those who met him and assisted in other ways, including finding him a job at a pet shop in Durban.

At one of the Friday night meetings Doc comes in and says, 'Dr Khorshed Ginwala is very concerned about the library, the Gandhi library in Durban'. The books were very old and valuable but were being attacked by bookworms and all of that. And Dr Ginwala wanted to find somebody who could help restore the books. And we racked our brains, but couldn't think of anyone appropriate to undertake this recovery. So, Ike said, 'Leave it to me, let me think about this'. Now Ike worked with his hands as a boilermaker and engineer. By the time of the next meeting, he had built a wooden press and had taken a book apart and put it back together. And he said to Doc, 'I think I can do it'. Doc went to Ginwala and said, 'I think we found a way around this issue, and it won't cost you a lot'. Ike got to work. He lived in a tiny flat with one main bedroom and a space with a dining room table – not quite a lounge. And there was a small room at the side, where the children (Rafique and his sister) slept. We would meet there, especially when things got a bit hectic on my side. Ike then turned a little room at the back of the building into a workshop. And he became good enough at bookbinding and restoring for Adams Bookstore to give him work. Doc knew Adams's manager, Ernest Rabjohn, and took that first book to him. After that Adams started sending their customers who had collectible books needing binding or restoring to Ike, who eventually gave up boilermaking for bookbinding.

RM and RVN: The group had other art-related interests too?

Omar: Our Friday and Saturday night meetings drew in young artists and writers like Mafika Gwala. There were always animated discussions on many issues. And one very, very interesting time was when Dumile Feni came, and stayed with us – for months. And the discussion was on revolutionary art and politics and their relationship. The production of 'samizdat' or radical literature in Russia, circulated secretly in underground political activist circles in eastern bloc countries during the Cold War era, led us to a whole discussion about more freedom for artists. One of the artists that was discussed was Picasso, because while he was a member of the Communist Party, he didn't draw in the social realist mode. He was his own man. We discussed his most famous painting, *Guernica*, and the Spanish Civil War and so forth. This led to a number of new works by us, but in particular by Dumile Feni, who started the sketches which later became his massive drawing, *The African Guernica*. It is an iconic piece of artwork – charcoal on newsprint – that has become justifiably famous and remains in South Africa, despite Dumile's exile in 1968.

I also was sent to the International Debating Society, which met in the basement of the City Hall. The City Hall had a pretty big basement, where a whole group of white liberals would meet and run this debating society. So Doc said, 'You guys need to learn to speak and debate publicly, so go and join them'. And I did. Later, when Rick Turner came to Durban, I got him to join. He was banned at the time, and one of the organisations he was banned from joining was in fact the International Debating Society. But we proceeded, nevertheless. We also joined the Durban Film Society. I in particular was given a lot of tasks to carry out, including having to read up on labour matters. I was introduced to old comrades who were in the trade union movement. I would talk to them and read whatever material they had. Also, Doc had an incredible library, which came in handy. So, I was drawn in and moulded politically and out of that discussion group, while Ike became a bookbinder.

Then Doc got banned and put under house arrest. He and Helen Joseph were house-arrested for twenty-four hours a day – i.e., a permanent detention. But Doc then made an application to the magistrate and the minister saying 'please, I have to go to mosque every day at lunchtime'. (A devout communist!) So, they gave him two hours' grace. Now Doc's business was selling books. He would collect books, and he would sell books. And he had a whole network of the black intelligentsia in the Grey Street area, the lawyers, doctors and activists. And knowing what each one would like to read, he would find those books, carry them along and sell to them. That was one way of making a living, but more importantly it gave him two hours to go around, and also do his political work.

Books were an ever-important part of this group's life. We studied first editions like Peter Abrahams's first collection of poetry, which was produced in Durban and dedicated to I.C. Meer, because when he came here from Dundee in northern Natal he was adopted by the Communist Party group in Durban. Doc, I.C. Meer, M.P. Naicker, Cassim Amrah and others were part of the Liberal Study Group, which would meet once a week with speakers from all over. And that became the Ginger group that started mobilising against A.I. Kajee's wing of the Natal Indian Congress. I was one of the few people who had access to Doc's library, as he wouldn't allow anyone else to touch his books. I would read stuff that was published in the 1940s that came from India or from the Caribbean. There were original copies, small mimeograph copies of poetry and literature and political tracts – an incredible library. And there was Ike, who was now making a living from bookbinding.

We would collect books and distribute them in our reading groups – in the 1960s, from around '64 to '65. We set up semi-clandestine reading groups, which were also political discussion groups. We had our reliable contacts in one or two of the bookshops who would bring in banned books, and other books by leftist writers and theorists – Deutscher, Trotsky, Lenin and so forth. There was Fischer's Bookshop, a small bookshop in an arcade linking West Street and Commercial Road. It was run by its Jewish owner, Mr Fischer. And once he worked out our interests, he would pick up a book and ask, 'Would you be interested in this?' And it was often something that was banned. And the word got around in our network, 'you can go to Mr Fischer, just give him my name, or of one or two others or Doc's name, and he will keep stuff for you'. So, he knew he had this market via us. Somehow or other he was able to bring in the books.

In those days, all book parcels would come to a depot for international post. It was a small place in a little lane off Smith Street – Mona Road. And you had to go in there to pick up the parcel. They would open it in most cases, especially if you were a black person, check the book against their lists and either give it to you or confiscate it. It was something that I dreaded. You would walk in there without knowing who's sending you stuff, and you don't know what stuff it is. And we used to also get a lot of stuff from Peking. One of my father's artist friends had left the country and became a PAC member. He made sure that we were on this postal list and so we used to get weekly reviews and other publications. We would face police raids at home. The security police would come, and we'd say, 'I don't read the damn thing; it comes in the post. If you want it take it'.

And then the Group Areas Act came in and we were all kicked out of the Greyville area. Ike went to Chapel Street, Overport; my father and family to Spencer Road, Clare Estate; and in fact, a number of other families from the same street (Lutchman Avenue) all went there. So they continued their own little network after they transported themselves there. So Ike went to Chapel Street and by chance Enver Motala was round the corner from there at Silver Palm Road. And Phyllis Naidoo was nearby. My wife, Nasima, and I went to live in the flat next to Phyllis. And down the road on the other side was Harold Strachan. And when Harold came out of prison, this group met and planned how to get some work for him to make a living. And it was about the time when Westville was being built, and wealthy Indians were moving in. And my father then said to some of them, 'Hey, guys, you need some nice artwork in your new home'. So, he got Harold to do some mosaics for the entrances to some of the houses. And we also entered one of Harold's paintings surreptitiously in the *Art South Africa Today* exhibition. And nobody knew or made any fuss about it. There were now all these layers, connections with art and books.

Then Kulsum Motala decided that she was going to set up a studio, a ceramic workshop where her friends and other women from the area could come and learn pottery. And the front part of this old shop was given to Ike, with the window, entrance and one section that was partitioned off. And that was Ike's bookshop, and was also his workshop, for restoring books. So now pottery was added to our world of art, books and making a living.

I have to recount one book-related memory from after the move to Chapel Street. That part of Overport was declared white under Group Areas, but the side parts of some of the roads had Indian homes. I would walk past some of the houses and the park and noted an old colonial house with beautiful grounds, a large veranda and a couple of massive trees. One Saturday I was walking past the house, and I saw books lying there in the veranda – piles of books, so I gingerly walked into the yard to take a look. Wow! They were all from an Africana collection of early Natal and South African writings. I then ran to Ike and I said, 'There's an abandoned house and nobody living there, but all these books are in a huge pile.' And we got some helpers, brought a car and loaded the stuff, absolutely priceless collector's items all abandoned. There we were with books in boxes and under our armpits and running up through the park and into Chapel Street. Ike restored the books and sold them at a very good price to Adams Bookstore. This was a rare windfall for the group.

Ike was running the little bookshop and making a living in Chapel Street. After that he moved the shop from that little kiosk to the Overport City shopping centre in Ridge Road. And one of the new people in the broad network was Vishnu, introduced via Enver Motala. We became friends and we moved our discussions to my place or Vishnu's flat in Silverpalm Road.

RM and RVN: What were your impressions of Vishnu at this time?

Omar: Vishnu was always very quiet, very well-spoken and very well-read. He dressed differently, he was always smartly dressed, unlike us ruffians. And he was lecturing at UDW [the University of Durban Westville] then. And so, he wasn't totally part of us, he was more with Enver, you know. And through Enver he met Ike, and from that acquaintance he would go and speak to Doc at his flat – they became very friendly. Again, a case of books holding people together in politically turbulent times.

To go back a bit to the time after Sharpeville and after Doc's banning – there was a hiatus and there was a lot of uncertainty in thinking through what the next step should be. How do we now move forward and start building a new movement? And again, during a Friday night discussion, Doc said something that was quite profound. He said, if you are hiding from the police, you are also hiding from the people. This insight came out of his own experience in India, under British rule, and their reading on Algeria and the French and the role of the intellectuals, literature and all of that: if you hide from the police, you also hide from the people. We shouldn't become so clandestine that we do nothing. So, you now had to learn to get to the people in a way that doesn't expose you too much: you had to try to find ways of organising people. I became interested in the labour movement. One or two of us in the group began organising young workers. We also started a couple of reading groups and cells in Chatsworth, the apartheid township for Indians which was still being built in the 1960s. Tales of those activities and trade unions must be related another time.

Notes
1. The second half of the interview, in the editors' possession, has yet to be transcribed.
2. While acknowledging that sexism is a feature of this anecdote, we have chosen to keep it in, rather than act as censors.
3. Rafique Mayet (known as Rafs), born in 1955, the son of Ike and Khateja Mayet, is an acclaimed photographer known for his documentary work on the Warwick Avenue complex (the Casbah) and the jazz scene in Durban–Pinetown.
4. In 1941 a young Indira Gandhi – then a student in England – visited Durban en route to India.
5. 'Green mamba' is a colloquial term for the green buses run by the Durban Corporation.
6. *Sechaba* was a journal established in 1967 as the 'official organ' of the banned ANC in exile.

22

An Intellectual in a Time of Struggle

A Tribute to Vishnu Padayachee

Alec Erwin

Vishnu Padayachee was an intellectual, and a fine one at that. He matured in a time of struggle and lived to play a role in the establishment of a democratic state. In itself this is something worth reflecting on. In recent times two events have caused many of us to reflect on those times of struggle – a symposium in honour of Vishnu, 'Scholarship, the Intellectual and Fundamental Social Change', held at the University of the Witwatersrand on 20–22 July 2022, and the fifty-year commemoration of the 1973 Durban Strikes. These events have been important in trying to construct – with the benefit of hindsight – what those times meant: how they have shaped the present and whether we are missing critical lessons that they pointed to. Such reflection is no easy task, as hindsight often clouds as much as it elucidates.

However, it is a rewarding task to reflect on Vishnu's role, since the path he walked highlights some of the enduring challenges facing the intelligentsia in any time of social and economic change. The term 'struggle' is widely used to refer to the pre-1994 times. Given the stark and violent contest between an apartheid regime and the resistance to such segregation and oppression by the vast majority of South Africa's people, the term seems very appropriate and self-evident. However, the actual content of the struggle was far from self-evident. It was a very complex set of events, involving choices to be made and organisational capacity to be built. It was a maelstrom of events, depictions of reality, many paths to be walked, and a constant lurking threat of possible harm to one's person and family. Vishnu chose one of those paths.

In the symposium referred to above we got some interesting insights into Vishnu's road to the Faculty of Economics at the University of Durban-Westville. Once there, he, like many other academics, could restrict his work to the halls of academia – not an unimportant task by any means – or he could take on an additional burden of forming supportive links with the organisations of internal resistance from the early 1970s that were rapidly re-forming. These ranged from adult education institutions to trade unions (and their education structures), groups linked to the churches, and later many research institutes on campuses that were later to play very important roles in policy development. Many also developed direct links with the African National Congress (ANC) underground structures, while others went into the legal profession after being banned and continued to play a key role.

Vishnu formed links with the trade union movement and was active in forming some of the research institutes just mentioned. I came into contact with him through our wonderful mutual friend Enver Motala, who was the head of the South African Committee on Higher Education (SACHED) branch in Durban. Enver's offices were a good place to discuss strategy and tactics, since on the floor above A.K.M. Docrat could be consulted when we needed to obtain some wise counsel.[1]

In the early 1970s the embryonic trade unions, working from Bolton Hall in Gale Street in Durban, had formed the Institute of Industrial Education (IIE), whose first chancellor was Chief Mangosuthu Buthelezi. This latter fact in itself says something about the complexity of political change at the time, since it has to be seen in the context of the fact that the main inspiration behind the IIE was the brilliant Marxist intellectual Richard Turner. Rick was a politics lecturer at the University of Natal before being banned. Many an IIE book appeared under names other than that of their real author. His assassination in 1978 was a tragic loss of a great mind.

I mention these brief anecdotes in the context of the choices that Vishnu himself made, because they point to a very important component of those times – often referred to as the 'Durban moment'. There was a vibrant interaction between academia, organic intellectuals of the struggle who were being released from prison in the 'University of Robben Island', some of whom were banned on their release, student activists, and a shop stewards' movement emerging in the unions. Intensive union education was a key component of the building of this emerging movement. Many of the shop stewards obtained master's degrees after 1992 and then occupied senior positions at all levels of government in the new democratic dispensation.

Our experience of the fertility and efficacy of this learning process stayed with Vishnu, and he always attempted to contribute to it. Engagement, discourse and problem-solving trumped dogma and didactics. Praxis was paramount, but it had to have rigour – 'pessimism of the intellect but optimism of the will', to paraphrase Antonio Gramsci. This is not only an effective learning mode but an effective form of political leadership development, because it involves listening, engaging, and then taking action on the basis of analysis and organisation. This approach was often referred at the time as 'workerist', since it gave priority to effective power emanating from worker organisations; the dynamism came from such worker organisations rather than only from the structures and strictures of the ANC. The resultant tension was almost inevitable once worker organisation became a more and more effective force. For the ANC to retain its own formidable mobilising power from exile and through underground structures required discipline, and for many of its activists on the ground the 'workerist' tendencies seemed tantamount to ill-discipline and even anti-ANC activity.

Added to this was the fact that divisions within the Left between those critical of what they saw to be dogmatic communist parties and those, like the New Unity Movement, who were closer to Trotskyist traditions, tried to play themselves out within the increasingly significant union movement. These varying left-leaning groupings within South Africa and fraternal international organisations quickly understood the importance for the Left of the rising power of the trade unions and tried to align themselves with that emerging power. This could have fuelled factionalism.

However, these tensions were never able to become too serious or to break the growing union unity. I think three factors contributed to this ability to retain unity. The first was that senior leaders in the ANC understood that these tensions would emerge and realised that they should not be allowed to fragment the emerging unions. This leadership, both in exile and among senior comrades who had come off the Island, listened to the new union leadership and understood their arguments. An important factor here was the need to avoid division in Natal between Inkatha and ANC supporters.

The second factor was that the vibrant internal debates among the Left allowed them to assist in charting a way forward for the emerging unions. However, there is little doubt that the most important factor was the organisational form taken by the new unions, with their stress on shop stewards, worker control and participatory decision-making.

So, while the debates were often intense, even vitriolic at times, they remained debates, and the unions unified rather than divided. This provided massive opportunities for intellectuals to immerse themselves in praxis, hence sharpening both theory and practice. Sadly, one of the most pernicious failures of the recent democratic period is that these lessons have been forgotten and politics has fragmented the union movement, greatly to the cost of its organisational power. There will always be contending political paradigms, and this is a very necessary process. However, a union movement is only as strong as its ability to subordinate such debates to a greater, collectively determined discipline.

Maintaining such coherence is no easy task. Some of the choices confronting the unions illustrate this complexity well. The call for sanctions is a very good example. Such a call made perfect sense from the perspective of the ANC in exile and was indeed one of their most effective organisational achievements. However, from the perspective of the internal unions this presented some acute problems, for some obvious reasons.

A key part of the organisational strength of the emerging unions was their success in achieving plant-based bargaining, despite the fact that the industrial relations law was heavily oriented towards industry-level bargaining. The unions did this by structuring their organisational strength around the plant-based shop stewards and using the legal space available to obtain enforceable legal agreements. The state inadvertently assisted them by banning some extremely capable people, who then studied to become lawyers and provided a powerful cadre of legal support to the unions. This development of legal capacity would also allow the union movement to have a major influence on the development of democratic South Africa's labour law dispensation.

However, at the outset multinational companies were key to this strategy, as it was possible to combine internal organisation with solidarity support from unions abroad. The conundrum was manifest. Demanding that companies that had just conceded to plant-based agreements, thereby creating valuable organisational capacity, should now withdraw their investment seemed very unwise from an organisational perspective.

Furthermore, it is never easy for unions to demand action that will lose workers their jobs. However, for the unions to speak out against the sanctions call would only take pressure off the apartheid regime. It took lots of explaining and dialogue with the ANC leadership and our fraternal unions abroad to address this manifest complexity. However, an effective modus vivendi had evolved to ensure that we retained the organisational base but kept up the external pressure on the regime.

Two lessons were learnt from this experience. The first was the importance of having organisational structures that can analyse and grapple with the complexity that will always arise in any process of societal development, be it in the normal course of development or in situations of social struggle and contestation. Good political formations are those that can fulfil this immensely complex function.

The second lesson, which we acted on immediately, was the realisation that any effective union movement needed to have a clear conception of what form of political economy it wanted in the best interests of workers. It was not enough to merely proclaim support for socialism. The Congress of South African Trade Unions (COSATU) then started a number of major research and training programmes that drew on the various research groups mentioned earlier. Study tours and special courses were arranged for shop stewards and organisers. When COSATU linked up with the ANC's Economic Transformation Committee in 1993 a fairly systematic programme of training was embarked upon.

COSATU pushed for the formation of the National Economic Forum, now the National Economic Development and Labour Council (NEDLAC). We were, of course, fortunate that Minister Derek Keys was a brilliant and far-sighted finance minister. Important work was done towards creating new forms of collective bargaining, especially in the automotive sector. The formation of the Sector Education and Training Authorities was primarily driven by the union movement. In short, important foundations were laid.

I cite these examples to try and illustrate the extent of constant engagement with and interaction between the union movement and universities and training structures. This arose from both the organisational structure adopted by the unions and the widespread commitment of intellectuals like Vishnu to being involved in such interaction.

One of the more elaborate programmes that COSATU gave leadership to was the development of the Reconstruction and Development

Programme (RDP). From the perspective of COSATU this programme was designed to set an agenda for engagement with big business and the apartheid regime. The Ready to Govern conference convened by the ANC in 1992 had made it clear that a new democratic government had much work to do, and that pre-election engagements with business and the government were also crucial. The RDP was intended to be the COSATU platform for engagement. Such engagement was important and led to many areas of agreement emerging between COSATU, the ANC and business leaders.

The process certainly gave rise to new tensions within the Left. In the view of some, we were abandoning our socialist commitment by cooperating so actively with the ANC and being prepared to engage with big business and the apartheid regime. However, the COSATU leadership was able to move with confidence, since these issues would be debated at seminars and conferences and in courses. Debates were held with the ANC in places such as Harare and London.

These processes led to some important structural decisions. One example of this is also one of the few examples where we differed with Vishnu. This was the issue of what was known as macro-balance. Stated simply, this is whether to follow an expansive monetary policy or to attempt to attain a defined balance between key prices through a more conservative monetary policy. The natural inclination of the unions and the broad left was towards the former and constituted our starting point. The latter was seen as merely a component of the so-called 'Washington Consensus', which was designed to protect the interests of the global multinationals.

This is a pretty simplified statement of one of the more complex policy choices facing governments, and during the past few years we have seen massive use of expansionary monetary policy in the US and EU. So, the question has usually to be answered in the context of specific conjunctures. By the early 1990s, COSATU and the ANC's Economic Transformation Committee had come to the conclusion that the macro-balance approach was more appropriate for the conjuncture we were in. We had the benefit of much global advice and long discussions with the Workers' Party in Brazil. Later we were to tighten the approach further through the Growth, Employment and Redistribution (GEAR) policy. This further angered members of the Tripartite Alliance and was now seen as a retreat to neoliberalism. Who was right and who was wrong will be debated for a long, long time. In all political economies this matter is usually a key potential divide. Analysis of the conjuncture and of the state's capacity to effectively spend resources, rather than dogma, is probably the best approach.

On a visit to London, before 1994, Nelson Mandela asked a group of economists who had long had ties with the ANC and had worked with many of the COSATU projects mentioned above, to make proposals on economic policy. This led to the formation of the Macroeconomic Research Group (MERG). Vishnu was asked to be a key contributor from South Africa. Understandably, MERG felt that its proposals were designed to be the basis for policy. The Economic Transformation Committee did engage with it many times, but from the Economic Transformation Committee's perspective MERG was an input into the unfolding RDP process, where certain policy issues had been decided.

This led to some tension, and Vishnu felt that MERG had been let down. Each side has its views on this, and I only mention it because it was one of the few times where we disagreed with him. However, this disagreement never influenced the respect we had for his advice. A few years into our democracy the same people that he had argued with pushed for him to be brought into the South African Reserve Bank, because we knew he held the views he did about monetary policy and we felt that that stance should always be kept in the frame of consideration, precisely because of the inevitable changes in the conjuncture.

One of the dangers of being an intellectual in the struggle is that political organisations can ignore your advice. This is the tough part of being an activist, but it seldom outweighs the benefits of being an activist. I am sure that Vishnu was listened to many more times than he was ignored.

Reflecting on the life of Vishnu Padayachee allows us to recall the dynamic and active environment that brought intellectuals, experienced political leaders and organised workers into a mass movement that proved to be very effective. There are surely lessons to be learnt from this experience, as our political economy once again faces serious challenges that must be addressed, if we are indeed to provide the 'better life for all' that we aspired to. We need to revive the ability to work as disciplined collectives capable of dealing with complexity and managing debate and difference.

Vishnu, you served your people well, and we will miss that sharp intellect as we grapple with challenges to the stability of our political economy and the democratic order that must hold our society together.

We are doing this in a rapidly changing context of global geopolitics. Once again intellectuals may opt to stay in the good sphere of academia, or they may choose to forge links with and assist forces of change. What we are learning is that the struggle to provide humans with a better life never ends, and the contours of those struggles change. Apartheid is replaced by poverty and inequality, threats of climate change and a changing global economic order. As we chanted many times, *a luta continua*!

Note
1. Aspects of A.K.M. Docrat's life and contribution to the anti-apartheid struggle are documented in the interview with Omar Badsha in Chapter 21.

23

Vishnu Padayachee
An Economist's Tribute

Imraan Valodia

Vishnu Padayachee passed away in the early hours of 29 May 2021, following a series of health challenges during the previous two years. Over the almost forty years that I knew Vishnu he was my teacher, my mentor, my head of department, my colleague, my collaborator and among my closest friends.[1]

I first met Vishnu when he walked into my Economics 101 class in 1983 at the University of Durban-Westville (UDW) to lecture on introductory microeconomics. He immediately made a lasting impression on me. As he began his lecture, I was immediately mesmerised by this handsome, urbane, genial, exceptionally articulate lecturer, his mannerisms more akin to those of an English upper-class gentleman, who made Economics 101 not only interesting but also tinged with radical economic ideas. For a young student growing up in apartheid South Africa, and studying at a university where many of the lecturers were members of the Broederbond and economics was taught in the most unimaginative way, this was truly extraordinary stuff. At the time, I was only doing economics because it was a requirement of the accountancy qualification that I was then pursuing. Vishnu's inspirational teaching of economics changed my academic trajectory.

I made regular visits to Vishnu's office when he moved to the Institute for Social and Economic Research (ISER) at UDW, and he 'fed' my curiosity about South Africa. He introduced me to the work of, among others, Harold Wolpe, Martin Legassick and Rick Turner, and to the famous speech by Federation of South African Trade Unions (FOSATU) general secretary Joe Foster at the FOSATU congress, which outlined the federation's views on the relationship between the struggle for workers' rights through trades unions and the struggle for political freedom in South Africa (Foster 1982). Most of the literature he shared with me at the time was classified as banned in terms of the apartheid state's Publications Act (No. 42 of 1974). None of it was, of course, part of the economics curriculum. In those days, people went to jail for distributing this kind of material. Suddenly, economics was exciting and I began to understand the world around me. These early years shaped my academic trajectory forever. Over the years, Vishnu's influence had the effect of steering me towards a better understanding of the world, linking up with exciting new research ideas, striving for academic excellence, and enjoying books and leisurely lunches. Remarkably, he had the same effect on many, many others.

Vishnu was born on the south coast of (then) Natal in the town of Umkomaas on 31 May 1952. His father was a teacher and school principal. In those days, the life of an Indian school principal involved having to move from one little Natal town to the next. Vishnu's parents lived this life. As a result of this Vishnu was brought up by his relatives in Umkomaas, a well-off and globally connected family with connections in, among other places, Germany. I think this upbringing was instrumental in cultivating Vishnu's love for the good things in life – good food, sporty cars, good wine and the best whisky – notwithstanding his lifelong work for a democratic and egalitarian society.

Vishnu studied at UDW, at the time the only place where Indians were able to study, completing a BComm, BComm (Hons) and MComm in economics in 1973, 1975 and 1979 respectively. He began working as a junior lecturer in the Economics Department at UDW in 1977, while completing his master's degree. He completed his PhD under the supervision of Bill Freund at the University of Natal in 1989. He went on to have a stellar academic career, publishing ten books and some hundred and ten journals articles, supervising some seventy master's and doctoral students, and achieving recognition across the globe, with appointments at Oxford, Cambridge and Johns Hopkins universities, among others. In 2018 Rhodes University recognised his outstanding contributions and awarded him an honorary doctorate for his 'exceptionally distinguished contribution to the post-apartheid transformation of economic policy'.

His academic career was influenced by a number of colleagues in those early years while he was at UDW. One of his early research papers, co-authored with Shaheed Vawda and Paul Tichman, was an economic history study of Indian workers and trade unions in the period 1930–50

(Padayachee, Tichman and Vawda 1985), and in some ways this reflected the scholar that he would become – an economist, with a keen interest in the history of the downtrodden. In these early years, some key collaborations shaped him. He lived in a flat in a small three-storey block in Overport, Durban. The flat above his was occupied by Enver and Kulsum Motala. Enver was at the time the director of the South African Committee on Higher Education (SACHED) office in Durban and was steeped in worker education. Vishnu taught a number of courses on economics to workers and activists through the SACHED programme. Kulsum was a keen collector of all things old. Shireen Hassim, at the time a young political science lecturer, was a regularly visitor, as were many other young academics and activists.

In this network was Ike Mayet, an artisan who was also a bookbinder and book collector. A.K.M. Docrat, the Communist Party of South Africa stalwart who was repeatedly banned from the 1960s until 1990, was an important figure in this world. He made a living from buying and selling books. In later years while we were colleagues at Natal University in Durban, Vishnu often went off to see 'old man Doc'.

For all of his life, Vishnu remained a close friend of Rajend Mesthrie, the famous South African linguist, who also hailed from the little town of Umkomaas. All of these influences were to shape him in profound ways.

In 1985 and 1986, Vishnu was invited to lecture on the African studies programme at Johns Hopkins University in Washington DC, where he taught a course on the political economy of South Africa under apartheid. For a young economist, until then having experienced academic life only at UDW, these two years at Johns Hopkins were intensely significant in this formative stage of his academic career. They opened his eyes to a much larger academic world and were probably a key marker for his lifelong pursuit of academic excellence, and for promoting the idea of collaboration with international academic institutions.

Moving from the Economics Department at UDW to a full-time research position in ISER, Vishnu began working more closely with the economist Trevor Bell, and shifted his gaze to South Africa's international economic relations, especially its relations with the International Monetary Fund.

Around this time, Bill Freund joined the Economic History Department at the University of Natal (Durban [UND]), and so started a life-long friendship between the two. Two more unlikely bedfellows you could not find. Vishnu, meticulous and organised to a fault, and Bill, somewhat unkempt and totally disorganised, formed, on the face of it, a most unlikely collaboration and companionship. But theirs was a deep and very special friendship, and I don't think anyone had a bigger influence on Vishnu. Bill supervised his PhD on South Africa's international economic relations in the period 1960–89, and their collaboration, which included work on economic development in cities, lasted until Bill's untimely death in 2020.

Vishnu completed his doctorate, and politically exciting years followed in the early 1990s. Under the leadership of Jairam Reddy, UDW became a hotbed of exciting intellectual activity as the democratic transition unfolded. Vishnu moved into Reddy's office as special assistant to the vice chancellor and took up the cudgels to build a new progressive university. During this period, Bill Freund, Gerry Maré and Mike Morris started the journal *Transformation*, and Vishnu joined them as an editor. He remained a part of *Transformation* in one way or another pretty much until his death. His most recent article in *Transformation* was published a few days before he died (Padayachee and Rossouw 2021). When Vishnu decided to leave the editorial team at *Transformation* in 1999 and the other editors decided they needed an economist on the team, I had the great honour of following in Vishnu's footsteps and joining the editorial board. Later, we managed to convince him to rejoin the board, and we worked together on building *Transformation*'s role as a key outlet for debates on South Africa's economic policy during the first two decades of democracy.

On the economic policy front, having been involved in the Economic Trends Projects (which advised the Congress of South African Trade Unions on economic policy matters), Vishnu took up a leadership position in the Macroeconomic Research Group (MERG), the economic think tank of the African National Congress (ANC), to design post-apartheid economic policy. In MERG, Vishnu worked closely with Vella Pillay and other members of the ANC's (then) Department of Economic Planning (DEP), a host of local and international economists who assisted the DEP at the time, including Ben Fine, John Sender and Chris Cramer of SOAS. In MERG, he became involved in dealing with some of the key economic questions during the transition, including questions about the importance of the South African Reserve Bank's mandate and its accountability. He was part of the team that drafted the final MERG report (MERG 1993). Vella, who became a sort of father figure to Vishnu, and the SOAS economists remained lifelong collaborators with him.

Sadly for Vishnu, the ANC had pretty much ditched the MERG report even before it was finalised. On the issue of the Reserve Bank, the government opted for an independent monetary policy authority and an inflation-targeting regime. This became a focus of much of his later work, as he searched for documents and logical arguments for why the ANC, a supposedly left party, had opted for what was, in his view, a neoliberal economic policy. Vishnu explored these themes with a number of collaborators around the world, including Jonathan Michie, who collaborated with him extensively over many years and was the co-editor of what was to be Vishnu's last book (Michie and Padayachee 2021). Other collaborators included Asghar Adelzadah, Adam Habib, Keith Hart and, most recently, Robert van Niekerk (see Padayachee and Van Niekerk 2019).

As MERG's recommendations were ditched, so was the exciting project of university transformation at UDW unravelling. Having worked more or less full-time for MERG for much of 1993 and 1994, Vishnu returned to UDW, which by 1995 was a shadow of the vibrant early years of the Jairam Reddy administration. It was now something of an alien place for Vishnu. Bill Freund rescued him from this world and offered him some solace by arranging an office for him in the Economic History Department at the University of Natal.

I had joined the School of Development Studies (SDS) at UND, then under the leadership of Mike Morris, in 1996. Vishnu joined us in 1997 as a research professor. Bizarrely, a few months before he took up the professorship at SDS, the Economics Department at UND had opted not to appoint him.

He took up the headship of the SDS for two spells during the period 2002–11. For many of us in the SDS, and especially for Vishnu, these were intellectually exciting times. The school grew to have a talented group of academics, a highly successful academic programme, large amounts of research funding, research and teaching collaborations across the world, and a highly impressive research output. The academic programme attracted the smartest students from all parts of the globe – our intake in any one year would have included students from, among other countries, South Africa, Zimbabwe, Zambia, Mozambique, Uganda, Japan, Canada, France, Sweden, Norway, the UK and the US. As the senior academic in this milieu, Vishnu led much of the initiative, built what was considered by many to be among the world's most innovative and productive development studies programmes, created a truly collegial community (something almost impossible in the cut and thrust of academic life), and encouraged younger members of staff by being a generous leader.

These were the heady days of policy experimentation in post-apartheid South Africa, with many of the school's staff leading important policy initiatives in government. For much of this time, Vishnu remained involved in economic policy issues.

He was fortunate to inherit an excellent administration team, which he enhanced and which, in turn, pampered him. A key unwritten rule in the school, which Vishnu and his predecessors enforced, was a communal teatime at 10 a.m., when all the staff gathered for tea and a convivial chat. Samoosas, cakes and bake-offs were very much the order of the day. For all his years at SDS, Vishnu loved lording over the teatime chat, and the seat in the middle of the room was unofficially his. Notwithstanding his administrative responsibilities, this was a period when he was highly productive, supervising a number of master's and doctoral students, and publishing books on Durban's economy (with Bill Freund [Freund and Padayachee 2002]), cricket (with Ashwin Desai, Krish Reddy and Goolam Vahed [Desai et al. 2002]), and numerous journal articles on economic policy in South Africa, macroeconomics, investment, inflation-targeting, social policy and central banking, among others – many of these in collaboration with colleagues in the school.

While the school remained an exciting space, by then the University of KwaZulu-Natal (UKZN) had entered a period of turmoil, with some of Vishnu's closest colleagues, among them Robert Morrell, being forced to leave the university.[2] In 2013, the UKZN management decided to dissolve the SDS into a larger structure that merged development studies with a set of built environment disciplines. The model apparently worked at the University of Manchester and, so argued the management, what was good for Manchester had to be good for Durban. Deeply angered and distraught at the destruction of the institution that he had done so much to build, Vishnu withdrew and found a new inspiring space at Rhodes University, where Robert van Niekerk and others had created an environment in which Vishnu thrived.

The economics programme at the University of the Witwatersrand (Wits) benefited greatly when Vishnu decided to take up an appointment as distinguished professor and Derek Schrier and Cecily Cameron Chair in Economics there in 2014. At Wits, he played an instrumental role in developing the Applied Development Economics postgraduate programme and contributed hugely to the conceptualisation and consolidation of the Southern Centre for Inequality Studies. Notwithstanding ill health, this last period of his life was also highly productive. He completed work on *Shadow of Liberation* (Padayachee and Van Niekerk 2019) and another book, *Ownership and Governance of Firms* (Michie and Padayachee 2021), and he authored thirty-five journal articles on topics including economic policy in South Africa, Reserve Bank independence, inflation, inequality, Keynesian economics and business in South Africa.

Given the volume and scope of Vishnu's academic work, it is impossible to capture all aspects of it. Five threads really stand out for me. The first was his work on economic policy in South Africa, beginning with his early work on South Africa's international economic relations and the more voluminous work on MERG, the Growth, Employment and Redistribution (GEAR) policy, and post-apartheid economic policy, which is unparalleled and without doubt his most important contribution. The second was his passion for economic history, much of it in collaboration with Bill Freund, but including also important works with Robert Morrell on Indian Merchants and Dukawallahs in Natal (Padayachee and Morrell 1991), with Shahid Vawda and Paul Tichman on Indian workers (Padayachee, Tichman and Vawda 1985), and more recent work on central banking. The third was his interest in corporations and the varieties of capitalism, a thread that runs through much of his academic work. The fourth, based on his doctoral studies, was his work on South Africa's international economic relations. And the fifth thread was the broad range of his work with a political economy approach – from economics, central banking and politics to cricket.

Vishnu was the most organised, meticulous and systematic person I have ever known. He and I shared a preference for an early start to the day. Vishnu was usually at work at 6 a.m., and by the time I arrived at 6.45 a.m. he had cleared his email from the previous day and begun writing for a paper that he would be working on. We shared a coffee before 7 a.m., caught up on the gossip, and then he wrote uninterrupted until about 9 a.m., when the others arrived. From then on, Vishnu's door was always open and there was a steady stream of staff members and students knocking on the door. He gave generously of his time. Remarkably, even if you arrived unannounced you left feeling that he had been waiting to talk to you. He loved having an elaborate and leisurely lunch, and most days he combined lunch at a Durban restaurant with a work engagement or discussion. Late afternoon was most often spent at Ike's Books. This was his routine pretty much for all of the time that we worked together in Durban.

Everything he did was meticulous. He updated his CV immediately after a new paper was accepted for publication. Every book in his office had a specific place on his bookshelf, and every one of the books was perfectly ordered.

His work output was remarkably efficient. In all the years I knew him, I cannot recall him ever missing a deadline, or not being adequately prepared for a meeting.

Outside of his academic work, Vishnu's contribution to books was second to none. For much of the late 1980s, he spent many hours with Ike Mayet at Ike's Books in Chapel Street, Overport. From these humble beginnings, Vishnu, later with Joanne Rushby and Julian May, established Ike's Books and Collectables in Florida Avenue. It quickly became the intellectual hub of Durban – not only for the book launches but for all sorts of other events and discussions. The typical stream of visitors to Ike's on any given day included visiting academics seeking Vishnu's counsel on research matters, colleagues popping in for a chat and students seeking advice, a book hunter looking for an out-of-print book . . . It was an unending stream and Vishnu was always at the heart of it. He was himself a great book collector, with pride of place on his shelf being a complete set of J.M. Coetzee's novels – all first editions and signed. He collected art, too, and introduced me to some of South Africa's best art; we shared a small collection of Mithila art, which David Szanton had introduced him to.

Although he did have his fair share of academic fallouts (which academic has not?), Vishnu had an extraordinary ability to engage across ideological boundaries. Though firmly in the left, post-Keynesian economic camp, he was able to supervise students more firmly to his right and engage with academic disciplines from accountancy to politics. He never imposed his ideological views but was always clear on where he stood on important matters of ideology.

He had his shortcomings, too. For one, he supported Tottenham Hotspur, and somehow came to terms with their promise of potential success with little, if anything, to show for it. Though a highly successful collaborative worker, he did sometimes bail out of collaborations that he had committed to. Almost everyone who worked closely with him will, I think, attest to having received an email from him, meticulously constructed and written in the early hours of the morning, with news that he had decided to withdraw from a project. It happened to me on more than one occasion, but we were able to move on. I put this down to his high academic standards and the need to be fully in control of his academic commitments.

Though we wrote a lot together, most of the time he and I spent together was spent talking over morning coffee in one of our respective offices, which for many years were adjacent to each other, in the bookshop, or over lunch. Our conversations were mainly about academic matters – universities, the latest paper, anger at the ANC – but often drifted into sport. He loved cricket and, more than anyone else I know, understood the intricacies of how the *doosra* was bowled, or the technical adjustments that Hashim Amla had made to his batting.

We spoke a lot about his personal life, a source of great joy – he unconditionally loved his daughter Sonali – but also great pain as his relationships entered challenging and complicated realms.

Due to his poor health, I saw less of Vishnu during his last two years. But we continued to have conversations over the telephone, and on occasion when I was in Durban I made a point of seeing him over lunch. Three issues dominated our most recent conversations. The first was his concern with the state of our universities. It bothered him no end that our universities were being distracted from the core concern with academic and research excellence, and that increasing pressure on them – from students' demanding free higher education to political interference – was undermining our ability to retain South Africa's place in the international scientific community. He implored me, as a university manager, to focus on the core issue of academic excellence. The second issue was the state of our economy and politics in South Africa. That the party he had so strongly supported in the 1990s and worked tirelessly for in the heady days of the transition, and the movement that was a part of for all of his life, had chosen a set of economic and political strategies that resulted in such outlandish corruption, poverty and unemployment, depressed him. He urged me to use the spaces at Wits to shift our economic policy towards addressing poverty and inequality in our society. Finally, he wanted to ensure that the autobiography of our friend Bill Freund just published by Wits University Press, *Autobiography: An Historian's Passage to Africa* (Freund 2021), should be given the recognition it deserved. A few days before he died, Vishnu called, uneasy, incensed and concerned that unless we made sure it happened, the launch of Bill's book would not be given the prominence that it should. 'We owe Bill so much, because he made it possible for us to be what we are,' he said.

Though he had a taste of being seated at the table of power, with appointments to the board of the Reserve Bank and various other formal and informal relationships to political power, Vishnu was unflinching in maintaining his independence, and remained critical of the ANC's policy choices.

Vishnu's contribution to economics in South Africa is unmatched, as is his contribution to so much more. Go well, Mahavishnu Srinivasan Padayachee (his full name, which is what I often called him – being the contrarian he was, he responded by shortening my name to 'Ims'). You have made an indelible and deep contribution to making this world a better place.

Notes

1. This tribute draws extensively from an obituary that I wrote for Vishnu which was published by the journal *Transformation* (Valodia 2023).
2. In 2004, the University of KwaZulu-Natal was formed as a result of a merger between the University of Natal (its Durban and Pietermaritzburg campuses), and the University of Durban-Westville.

References

Desai, A., V. Padayachee, K. Reddy and G. Vahed. 2002. *Blacks in Whites: A Century of Cricket Struggles in KwaZulu-Natal*. Pietermaritzburg: University of Natal Press.

Foster, J. 1982. *The Workers Struggle: Where Does FOSATU Stand?* Occasional Publication 5. FOSATU Printing Unit, Durban. https://files.libcom.org/files/Foster.pdf.

Freund, B. 2021. *An Historian's Passage to Africa: An Autobiography*. Johannesburg: Wits University Press.

Freund, B. and V. Padayachee (eds). 2002. *(D)urban Vortex: South African City in Transition*. Pietermaritzburg: University of Natal Press.

MERG (Macroeconomic Research Group). 1993. *Making Democracy Work: A Framework for Macroeconomic Policy in South Africa*. Cape Town: Centre for Development Studies, University of the Western Cape.

Michie, J. and V. Padayachee. 2021. *Ownership and Governance of Companies: Essays from South Africa and the Global South*. London: Routledge.

Padayachee, V. and R. Morrell. 1991. 'Indian Merchants and Dukawallahs in the Natal Economy, c. 1875–1914'. *Journal of Southern African Studies* 17 (1): 71–102.

Padayachee, V. and J. Rossouw. 2021. 'The Political Economy of South Africa's Constitutional Road to Central Bank Independence'. *Transformation* 105: 74–97.

Padayachee, V., P. Tichman and S. Vawda. 1985. *Indian Workers and Trades Unions in Durban 1930–50*. Durban: Institute for Social and Economic Research, University of Durban-Westville.

Padayachee, V. and R. van Niekerk. 2019. *Shadow of Liberation: Contestation and Compromise in the Economic and Social Policy of the African National Congress, 1943–1996*. Johannesburg: Wits University Press.

Valodia, I. 2023. 'Vishnu Padayachee: 1952 to 2021'. *Transformation* 106: 1–9.

24

The Most Special of Special Assistants
A Tribute to Vishnu Padayachee

Jairam Reddy

Vishnu Padayachee, a senior researcher in the Institute for Social and Economic Research (ISER) at the University of Durban-Westville (UDW), was seconded to the rector's office as special adviser in 1993, for a period of three years. The desired transformative changes at UDW were daunting and formidable. The non-racialisation of the university, one meant predominantly for Indian students, the increasing admission of disadvantaged students with provision of financial and academic support for them, staff changes and promotion, and improvements in the university's infrastructure were among the challenges facing the new administration at UDW from 1990 onwards. In this atmosphere anger, frustration, impatience and conflict were easily aroused, and the office of the rector was the target of demands for instant relief, if not miraculous solutions.

Vishnu's calm and sober judgement, his disarming style, his deep knowledge of the context of the university and its environs, together with the fact that he was a young and rising star in academia, provided enormous strength to the office of the rector. His structured approach, meticulous note-keeping and quiet sense of confidence were invaluable in dealing with the intractable issues and what may be termed wicked problems in the leadership discourse at the time.

Vishnu stood shoulder to shoulder with the rectorate in dealing with critical, conflictual and volatile matters on campus. Several tense clashes exemplify his mediation and conflict management skills, which he used in interventions to avoid a major conflict on campus when the Inkatha-leaning South African Democratic Students Movement invited Chief

Mangosuthu Buthelezi to speak on campus and was opposed by the ANC-leaning South African Students Congress; when the Pan Africanist Congress-aligned student body prevented Frederik van Zyl Slabbert from addressing staff and students; and in dealing with the Combined Staff Association, which in my view wanted to either govern or co-govern the institution.

Notwithstanding these conflicts, it was during this period that UDW became a hotbed of intellectual activity and democratic transition. High-calibre academics were attracted to the university, research activity intensified, and debates at the level of the university senate and faculty boards about academic issues and the place of UDW in the transition became open, vigorous and contested. Vishnu's contribution in stabilising and enriching the office of the rector in this milieu was invaluable.

In the changing university milieu, it became necessary to democratise the university council, changing its membership from the existing one that was dominated by state-appointed individuals. Vishnu produced a carefully researched (unpublished) paper that provided a blueprint for a council consisting of twenty-six members representing all sectors of the university. In 1990 the council appointed a representative committee to change the composition of the membership, and a new twenty-seven-member representative council was agreed to. These changes were submitted to Parliament, and the University of Durban-Westville Act (No. 49 of 1969) was amended accordingly. Vishnu's paper provided a useful model for the committee's work.

After leaving the rector's office, Vishnu's academic journey during the next twenty-five years was rich and highly productive. It is a truism that the quality of master's and PhD supervision at universities leaves a lot to be desired, both here and abroad. Vishnu was a model supervisor. His students would testify to his demanding, rigorous scholarship and a disciplined approach that ensured each dissertation was completed in the allotted time. His capacity to listen and his compassion and caring attitude were deeply appreciated by students – especially those who had emerged from disadvantaged schooling and social backgrounds.

The citation by Rhodes University when he was awarded an honorary doctorate in economics in 2018 exemplifies Vishnu's scholarship, especially in the field of developmental economics. It stated: 'Prof Padayachee has made an exceptionally distinguished contribution to the post-apartheid transformation of the South African economic policy in ways that serve the economic and social needs of all South Africans and marginalised black South Africans, in particular' (Rhodes University 2018).

Vishnu also had an abiding concern for the state of our universities, from the early days we spent together at UDW in the late 1980s. In this regard his contribution to postgraduate studies and research stands out as a beacon of unparalleled excellence.

Sadly, in 2021 Vishnu took seriously ill and had to be nursed in intensive care for a period of more than a month. During his period of recuperation, in between doing household chores and picking up his daughter from Westville Girls' High School, Vishnu made Maynard Govender's law practice, located between his home and Westville Girls High School, his second home.[1] There he found time to relax, engage in animated conversation and enjoy his favourite whisky or wine. Personal circumstances led him to relocate from his home in Westville to a flat in Currie Road. This appeared to give him a new lease of life. It was a lovely flat in one of the older buildings with a lot of character, and with stunning views of Greyville Racecourse and the city of Durban extending to the Indian Ocean. The magnificent yellowwood dining table and the walnut bookcase accommodated the fine things that Vishnu loved – his books, paintings and sculptures. His many friends would join him in this congenial flat for lunch, tea or a drink.

One day, as I was having lunch with Vishnu and interviewing him about our days at UDW for my memoir, the caretaker of the building entered with a box of books. Vishnu explained that these books were put out for sale once a month at the Sunday antique market in La Lucia Mall. Vishnu's deep love of books took him to this mall on a Sunday, despite his fragile state of health. As we conversed, he mentioned that when he interviewed candidates for academic positions, his stock question 'What you been reading recently?' would tell him much about the candidate.

As I live in an apartment in Musgrave Road, my early morning walks took me past Vishnu's flat in Currie Road. One day I was delighted to see him walking along Currie Road at about 6 a.m.– the winter mornings can be fresh and exhilarating in Durban. On another occasion I saw him in animated conversation with the security guard across the road from his flat. Two weeks later, rather inexplicably, he again had to be admitted to intensive care. He was in a critical condition for just over a week, and then was weaned off oxygen, becoming stronger and ready to return to his flat. It came as a shock to his family and friends when he succumbed to his illness on 29 May 2021 at the age of 69 years.

Mahavishnu Padayachee was a man of human decency and humility, with values of ethics and integrity, compassion and caring, and the capacity to listen to people and engage in animated conversation, whether it was with the security guard across the road, his housekeeper, his students, or a professor. He will be sorely missed by his family, friends and academic colleagues, but there is much to celebrate and be thankful for: in his rich and productive life he contributed immensely to research and scholarship in economics and cognate fields.

Note

1. Maynard Govender was an administrator at the University of Durban-Westville, who later went into legal practice, running a progressive law firm in Durban, which Vishnu often spoke glowingly of as embodying the spirit of the freedom struggle and development.

Reference

Rhodes University. 2018. 'Rhodes Confers Honorary Doctorate to Prof Vishnu Padayachee'. https://www.ru.ac.za/latestnews/archives/2018/rhodesconfers honorarydoctoratetoprofvishnupadayachee.html.

25

Four Slips and a Gulley
Reflections on Cricket in Vishnu Padayachee's Life

Suresh Naidoo

The first memory I have of meeting my cousin Vishnu goes back to 1967. My Uncle Nad, referred to by my mother by his full name, Nadaraj, brought Vishnu to our house to attend a test match between South Africa and Australia. We lived a moderate walk away from Kingsmead cricket ground in what was called the Grey Street Casbah. I suspect that my mother ferried him to the game in her blue Vauxhall Velox. If I recall correctly, he stayed overnight. He arrived with his cricket cap and bat; children played on the outfield during breaks at the cricket matches and Vishnu, who was fifteen at the time, must have played a few shots in the break. I knew little about cricket at the age of six. In that test match, which took place between 20 and 25 January 1967, South Africa beat Australia by eight wickets. South Africa had the Pollock brothers, Goddard and Barlow. I don't have such a perfect memory, but I Googled all the test matches from 1967 to 1969 in Durban to get a precise date.

Umkomaas, where Vishnu grew up, was a long way from Durban in 1967. I remember my mother's delight upon seeing her brother and nephew after quite some time. In the Grey Street Casbah area, we played cricket on the pavements. When I had grown older, the streets were used on a Sunday when there was no traffic. My love for the game grew as we visited Umkomaas more often. We would spend many holidays at my maternal grandmother's home in Umkomaas. That home included the homes of my three uncles: Nadaraj, as my Amah (mother) would call him, Satchie (aka Mayor) and Vasu. These three uncles lived on the same property as my grandparents. In between my grandparents' home and The Divine Life Society ashram built by my grandfather was a patch of land that provided a narrow but lovely cricket ground. Vishnu would get

373

all his cousins, uncles, neighbours and friends to come and play cricket. It was test match cricket because it lasted days. The players might have changed, but during the holidays it was a test match. No short version T20 like today. Vishnu was the catalyst for this. Each one of us had the name of a famous cricketer as a nickname.

It must be remembered that cricket was hardly played in Umkomaas. There was no cricket ground – even at the school. Vishnu was the first to initiate playing the game, even casually in Umkomaas. All of us developed a love for the game from Vishnu. It must also be noted that South Africa was banned from test cricket in 1970, yet we spent hours with Vishnu selecting a national team and debating who should and shouldn't be in this team that never played. Quite a pointless but highly entertaining pastime. Sadly, I still do it alone, to this day.

I would always beg Vishnu to take us to the cricket matches because sitting next to him at a game gave me insight and a deeper understanding of the game. Today, the broadcasts on TV give you the most amazing stats graphically. We never knew the speed of a ball or the number of good, short or Yorker-length balls bowled. We still loved the game, and had our very own analyst, Vishnu, who would give us the in-depth background. He could speak for hours on the game and would have us all in awe.

I have stayed involved in cricket up to today. I serve as chairman of the finance committee and a member of the management committee of the KwaZulu-Natal Cricket Union and was a member of the Cricket South Africa remuneration committee.

To discuss cricket only will not do justice to Vishnu's immense range of sporting interests. He introduced us to other sports that were lesser-known to our community in the 1970s. He introduced me to rugby, a game I still watch every Saturday. When the All Blacks visited in 1977, Vishnu had magazines and newspaper clippings of the tour and drummed up excitement in all of us.

I thanked Vishnu a few years ago for introducing me to rugby, and we had a chat on the status of the game. It was, before 1990, a game known as a game of the white man, yet Vishnu was *au fait* with the game and its very complex rules. He also introduced us to Formula 1 racing, another sport unknown to people of colour. Vishnu was way ahead of his time.

Both cricket and rugby have a lot of space for analysis, and Vishnu loved this, especially about cricket. Vishnu taught his younger cousins all the fielding positions, silly mid-on, short leg, cover, extra cover, third man and so on. All very amusing to us youngsters. His love for the game and his social consciousness were welded together. The book *Blacks in Whites: A Century of Cricket Struggles in KwaZulu-Natal,* which he co-authored with Goolam Vahed, Krish Reddy and Ashwin Desai, takes an in-depth look at the history and development of non-racial cricket in KwaZulu-Natal, and chronicles the courage, trials and tribulations of truly non-racial sports personalities determined to knock the bails out of apartheid sport (Desai et al. 2002). Vishnu also wrote or co-wrote a number of essays and articles on the topic of transformation in cricket, some of which are listed at the end of this essay (Padayachee 2005; Vahed, Padayachee and Desai 2006, 2010).

With so many years having passed since South Africa's readmittance to international sport, we would expect that the transformation of cricket is not as thorny an issue as it remains. The fact that we still need to have a social justice and nation-building project, or an inquiry into cricket, reflects the lack of change in the game. The fact that we have arguments about taking the knee for the 'Black Lives Matter' movement speaks volumes for the lack of transformation in the game. If you had asked me about which of cricket or rugby would transform more quickly or with less painful readmission, I would have emphatically answered cricket. Today, I will easily say that rugby is ahead. Rassie Erasmus won the 2019 Rugby World Cup with no fewer than six black players, including the captain, in his starting line-up. You cannot win a World Cup with six 'quota' players. The documentary 'Chasing the Sun' about the 2019 win (Lomas 2020) shows very clearly that the team management had full confidence in the black players in the team – this isn't necessarily the case in cricket.

Some fundamental errors were made at the outset in cricket administration after readmission. The appointment of apartheid administrators like Ali Bacher, who was the architect of the Rebel Tours, to the position of the first CEO of the United Cricket Board still reflects in the current conflicts. The fact that it was a huge problem to implement the Nicholson recommendations to have an objective board with more non-cricket members overseeing the affairs of Cricket South Africa (Nicholson 2012) speaks volumes for the lack of transformational thinking in cricket. The West Indian cricketers who toured South Africa as rebels during the apartheid era are still ostracised by the people of their countries to this day – yet, we opened our arms to the architect of the rebel tours, Ali Bacher, and asked him to guide the transition to 'normal' cricket. The documentary on the West Indian rebel tour, *Fire in Babylon* (Riley 2010), is highly recommended for those seeking further perspective.

It would be remiss of me not to say a few personal things about Vishnu, and particularly about his relationship with my late mother in her twilight years. There were many years in which he hardly met with my mother, but in the last few years of her life he would be a regular visitor at my home to see her. Surprisingly, we discovered that both he and my mother enjoyed Swedish crime fiction. He would bring books for her to read every few weeks. My mother appreciated her nephew's visits, and they grew closer. There is so much to be said about Vishnu, not just about cricket. There are many things I discovered about him from the many eulogies published. Things that he and I sadly never got around to talking about. Many of his achievements and work only came to light to some of us in his family after he passed. His memory will be cherished by his family.

References

Desai, A., V. Padayachee, K. Reddy and G. Vahed. 2002. *Blacks in Whites: A Century of Cricket Struggles in KwaZulu-Natal*. Pietermaritzburg: University of Natal Press.

Lomas, G. 2020. 'Chasing the Sun: A 5-Part Rugby Story'. *MNet Television/Mzanzi Magic, Supersport*. https://www.youtube.com/watch?v=eW6dI78-3R0.

Nicholson, C. 2012. *Report of the Ministerial Committee into Cricket*. https://www.gov.za/sites/default/files/gcis_document/201409/cricket-final-report-2012-1.pdf.

Padayachee, V. 2005. 'Living in Cloud Cuckoo-Land: Politics and Cricket in White South Africa'. *Transformation* 59: 109–21.

Riley, S. 2010. *Fire in Babylon*. Cowboy Films, E & G Productions, ECN Motion Pictures. https://www.dailymotion.com/video/x3iyqne.

Vahed, G., V. Padayachee and A. Desai. 2006. 'Beyond Apartheid: Race, Transformation and Governance in KwaZulu-Natal Cricket'. *Transformation* 61: 63–88.

———. 2010. 'Between Black and White: A Case Study of the KwaZulu-Natal Cricket Union'. In: *The Race to Transform Sport in Post-Apartheid South Africa*, edited by A. Desai. Cape Town: HSRC Press.

26

Vishnu Padayachee at Ike's
A BMW Life (Books, Meanders and Wine)

Joanne Rushby

There is a photograph that I look at every day. Vishnu on the floor of Ike's. Books splattered all around, his nose deep between the covers. Child-like. Who would guess that here was a scholar who reached the heights of academia, a fellow of Johns Hopkins University and the Royal Society? A key figure in the unfolding of economic policy in post-1990 South Africa and board member of the South African Reserve Bank.

I had known Vishnu as a postgraduate student at the School of Development Studies. Economics was not my beat, but his lectures dazzled, always running over the allotted hour. None of us complained. Through the grapevine, I had heard that he and Julian May were looking for assistance in their bookshop. Although I had worked in bookshops in Charing Cross Road, I arrived at Ike's Books, which had moved to Florida Road in 2000, as an apprentice. Julian and Vishnu knew their books. They knew their food and wine even better. It was the beginning of an adventure and a world of wonder. Book lovers who had first gone to Ike's original headquarters in Chapel Street in the early 1990s, made a turn, younger readers hunted for Homer and famous authors launched their books and signed the wall. There are memories embedded in every book and corner; laughter, tears, joy, conversation as the bookshop grew into so much more: a meeting place for debate, art exhibitions, wine tasting; an institution so fluid that it spilled onto the balcony, down the stairs and into Mama Luciano's, the Italian restaurant below the bookshop.

Vishnu and I shared a mutual love for foraging in bookshops as well as for cricket and English football, and so, every month, we would drive inland, to Pietermaritzburg, the Midlands. Dusty shops, houses, barns, collections belonging to old Natal families and retired academics – the search never ended. Vishnu went cucumber sandwiches to Harris tweed with the best of them. They spoke cricket, he knew more than them. They went to Michaelhouse, he had just spoken at Cambridge University. They showed off their wine cellars, he pulled a rare pinotage from the boot of his beloved BMW. Lunch was always in competition with book-hunting, and as late afternoon fell over the Dargle Valley, people were always ready to offload their first edition *Biggles* to this man who came out of nowhere but had been everywhere.

As we turned onto the N3, there was a hint of a smile at a bargain wrought, or too much paid to a biddy who thought she had a rare signed copy of Enid Blyton. In a few weeks, we would be down on the South Coast. Taking a turn past his hometown of Umkomaas. This most learned and cultured man taught me so much. So it was. Will never be again. We took a different turn for the past few years. But then, in 2021, and thanks to his incredible friend Maynard Govender, we spoke again. It was as if we were still on the road. We laughed, talked of books and life, of his recent finds, and once more I was the apprentice and he the craftsman.

Vishnu thought about the politics of South Africa all the time. How could he not, occupying a vantage point to observe the economic policies chosen in the early 1990s? He thought there were paths not taken, that the choices the ANC made were a dead end. He would express these views quietly but with candour. He too would make his choices. He joined the board of the Reserve Bank but never offered details of what really went on in this institution. I always wondered at this strange juxtaposition: a man who agonised over whether we should offer R10 or R20 for a book, could never really make up his mind about what to eat at a restaurant, but drafted policies that would affect millions of people. I expect that is what *makes a life* in a country going through major changes, while much remains the same. It is true, too, that for all the articles and books on economics, Vishnu was incredibly proud of his co-authored book on cricket, *Blacks in Whites* (Desai et al. 2002). I helped with the editing, and was there when the book was launched at Kingsmead in the midst of the 2003 World Cup. Vishnu was in his element in the longroom. And then later, Rahul Dravid and Dennis Brutus came to an incredible night at Ike's. Dennis the Robben Islander, the poet of *Letters to Martha* (Brutus 1968), and Dravid, shy, charming, a far cry from the man known as The Wall. Vishnu stuck between the two, wine glass in hand, refusing to let them go. I saw him out of the corner of my eye and he looked like a man who had just scored a hundred at Lords.

Cricket, I think, was the spine that kept Vishnu's many lives together. J.M. Coetzee was invited to Ike's. Vishnu was on edge for a week before the event. Reading aloud from Coetzee. Berating me for not having read *Waiting for the Barbarians* (Coetzee 1987). And then he told me how much he identified with *Boyhood*, when Coetzee relates setting up a contraption to bowl and bat by himself. Vishnu, the only child, bowled for hours against a wall in Umkomaas. He marked a line of *Boyhood* that I still have: 'With this he was satisfied: he bowled and batted all by himself, he has triumphed, nothing is impossible' (Coetzee 1997: 30).

Vishnu lives at Ike's. On the bookshelves, on the walls, and on the floor. Surrounded by books is how I remember him. I have no doubt he is up there in the sky, combing the stars for first editions and vintage wines. The world of books and literature in Durban owes a debt of gratitude to Vishnu. And, so do I.

I think Vishnu would be extremely proud and pleased to see where Ike's is today: there is lively debate, chance meetings, and friendships born and reborn. It is a place of laughter and life, continuing the journey of books, meandering and wine.

References

Brutus, D. 1968. *Letters to Martha and other Poems from a South African Prison*. London: Heinemann.

Coetzee, J.M. 1987. *Waiting for the Barbarians*. Harmondsworth: Penguin.

———. 1997. *Boyhood: Scenes from a Provincial Life*. London: Secker & Warburg.

Desai, A., V. Padayachee, K. Reddy and G. Vahed. 2002. *Blacks in Whites: A Century of Cricket Struggles in KwaZulu-Natal*. Pietermaritzburg: University of Natal Press.

Notes on Contributors

Omar Badsha is a photographer, artist, historian and political activist. He was part of an activist group in Durban mentored by A.K. Docrat from the 1960s onwards. He was later detained and harassed by the security police and prevented from travelling overseas. In 1982 he co-founded Afrapix, a pioneering initiative to promote documentary photography. He is also a co-founder of *South African History Online*, founded in 1999, which remains the country's largest and most important online historical resource. Among his published books of photographs and essays are *Imijondolo*, *Letters to Farzana*, *Imperial Ghetto* and *Seedtimes*.

Bradley Bordiss holds a PhD in economics and economic history awarded by the University of the Witwatersrand in 2021, for which he was supervised by Professor Vishnu Padayachee. He was also supervised by Professor Padayachee in his MComm in economics, awarded by Rhodes University in 2014. He taught the history of economic thought, a third-year undergraduate course, at the University of Cape Town from 2013 until 2022. He is the author or joint author of nine academic journal articles, mostly co-authored with Vishnu Padayachee. He also runs a property management business with his wife Odile that manages retail properties throughout South Africa.

Keith Breckenridge is a professor of history based at the Wits Institute for Social and Economic Research, where he holds the Standard Bank Chair in African Trust Infrastructures. He writes about the economic and intellectual history of South Africa, and particularly about the country's distinctive preoccupation with fingerprinting as a tool of government. His 2014 book, *Biometric State*, won the inaugural Academy of Science of South Africa humanities book prize. He has published many articles on specific aspects of biometric governance on the African continent, including a piece on the South African Net1 catastrophe, 'The Global Ambitions of the Biometric Antibank', in the 2019 special issue assembled by Vishnu Padayachee for the *International Review of Applied Economics*.

Nicolette Cattaneo holds an MSc in economics from Rhodes University in Makhanda. She is a senior lecturer in the Department of Economics and Economic History at Rhodes University, where she has taught since 1990. Prior to that, she was a researcher at Rhodes University's Institute for Social and Economic Research. She teaches postgraduate courses in trade and industrial policy and econometrics, and she is the co-course director of the African Programme on Rethinking Development Economics, a high-level training programme that aims to build capacity in economics and economic policy-making, with a focus on alternatives to mainstream economic thinking. Her research areas are trade and industrial policy, regional integration, and the impact of trade agreements on development policy space.

Janet Cherry is a professor of development studies at the Nelson Mandela University in Gqeberha. She has a PhD in political sociology from Rhodes University. Her main areas of research are sustainable development, political economy of development, democratic participation and social and political history. She has published two books as well as a number of articles and chapters in books on South African history, labour, women's and social movements, transitional justice and sustainable development. Her recent publications include the chapter 'At the CORE of the Democratic Energy Transition: A Township Based Renewable Energy Project' in *South Africa's Contested Transition to Energy Democracy* (2021).

Alec Erwin was a lecturer in economics at the University of KwaZulu-Natal, a unionist in the emerging trade union movement, and then an education officer of the Congress of South African Trade Unions. He was the deputy minister of finance and minister of trade and industry in President Nelson Mandela's Cabinet. He was subsequently the minister of trade and industry and minister of public enterprises in the Cabinet of President Thabo Mbeki. He has served in positions in UN Trade and Development and the World Trade Organization. He is now a director of Ubu Investment Holdings and works on various projects in South Africa and elsewhere in Africa relating to work done by the African Association of Automotive Manufacturers with many governments and the African Continental Free Trade Area.

Ben Fine is emeritus professor of economics at the School of Oriental and African Studies (SOAS), University of London, and a visiting professor at the Wits School of Governance, University of the Witwatersrand. He has published three hundred articles and thirty books, winning both the Deutscher and the Myrdal book prizes. He has worked on the South African economy for forty years, coining the expression 'minerals-energy complex'. He has been the chair of the International Initiative for Promoting Political Economy. The third in his series of volumes of edited articles on the critical reconstructions of political economy, *Cliometrics as Economics Imperialism: Across the Watershed*, was published in 2024.

Gillian Hart is professor emerita in geography at the University of California, Berkeley, and a distinguished professor at the University of the Witwatersrand. Her books include *Rethinking the South African Crisis: Nationalism, Populism, Hegemony* (2014) and a co-edited volume, *Gramsci: Space, Nature, Politics* (2013). She is currently working on a book provisionally titled *Warring Tendencies: Populist/Liberal Battles in a Global Frame*. Her article 'Modalities of Conjunctural Analysis' appeared in *Antipode* 56 (1) in 2024.

John Keith Hart's intellectual home is the North Atlantic quadrilateral – Western Europe, West Africa, the United States and the Caribbean – which was formed by the slave trade and made the modern world. He is a writer with homes in Paris and Durban, who has worked in twenty-four countries in the belief that engaged intellectuals should try to understand and shape emergent world society. His work focuses on economy, money, the internet and Africa. His most recent book is *Self in the World: Connecting Life's Extremes* (2022).

Gavin Keeton is an associate professor emeritus in the Department of Economics and Economic History at Rhodes University. He was in the economics office of Anglo American Corporation from 1990 to 2008 and was responsible for advising the group on developments in the South African and global economies and their implications for the mining industry. For many years he wrote a fortnightly macroeconomic policy column in *Business Day*.

Rajend Mesthrie is emeritus professor and senior research scholar in linguistics at the University of Cape Town. He was head of the Linguistics Section at the university from 1998 to 2009, and concurrently held an NRF Research Chair in Migration, Language and Social Change. He was also president of the Linguistics Society of Southern Africa (2002–2009) and president of the International Congress of Linguists (2013–2018). He is a past co-editor of *English Today* (2008–2012). Among his recent published books are *Youth Language Practices and Urban Language Contact in Africa* (edited with Ellen Hurst-Harosh and Heather Brookes, 2021), *Sociolinguistics Around the World* (edited with Martin Ball and Chiara Meluzzi, 2023) and *Language in the Indian Diaspora* (edited with Sonal Kulkarni-Joshi, 2024).

Seeraj Mohamed is the deputy director for economics in the South African Parliamentary Budget Office. He was an associate professor in the Department of Economics at the University of the Western Cape and the director of the Corporate Strategy and Industrial Development Research Programme at the University of the Witwatersrand. He has worked on economic and industrial development issues since the early 1990s, including as a research trainee in the Macroeconomic Research Group in 1993. He has published in international economics journals and has held senior appointments in the public sector and academia. His PhD in economics is from the University of Massachusetts, Amherst.

Robert Morrell is a senior research scholar at the University of Cape Town. He began his academic career as a lecturer in history at the University of Transkei in 1982, and subsequently worked at the University of Durban-Westville, University of Natal (Durban), the University of KwaZulu-Natal and the University of Cape Town. From the early 1990s, he studied gender issues in South Africa with a specific focus on masculinities. He guest-edited a special issue of the *Journal of Southern African Studies* (1998) and edited *Changing Men in Southern Africa* (2001). He wrote *From Boys to Gentlemen: Settler Masculinity in Colonial Natal* (2001) and subsequently researched schooling, HIV and violence. In 2019, he co-authored *Knowledge and Global Power: Making New Sciences in the South* together with Fran Collyer, Raewyn Connell and Joao Maia.

Suresh Naidoo holds a CA from the University of South Africa. He is a director of Accensis, a firm of chartered accountants. He is a member of the management committee and chairperson of the finance committee of the KwaZulu-Natal Cricket Union.

Pundy Pillay is a visiting professor and former professor of economics and public finance in the School of Governance at the University of the Witwatersrand. He has also been a visiting professor at the Berlin School of Economics and the universities of Johannesburg, Oslo and the Western Cape. His previous positions include senior economist at RTI International, head of the Policy Unit in the Office of the President and director of the South African Financial and Fiscal Commission. He has also worked in Bangladesh, Egypt, Kenya, Iran, Lesotho, Namibia, Nigeria, Pakistan, Rwanda, Uganda and Zambia.

Dorrit (Dori) Posel holds the Helen Suzman Chair in Political Economy and is a distinguished professor in the School of Economics and Finance at the University of the Witwatersrand. Prior to that, she held the NRF/DST Research Chair in Economic Development in the School of Development Studies at the University of KwaZulu-Natal. She specialises in applied microeconomic research and has published widely on issues relating to labour force participation, unemployment, labour migration, the gender division of labour, marriage and psycho-social well-being.

Jairam Reddy was the vice-chancellor of the University of Durban-Westville from 1990 to 1994. He is the recipient of honorary doctorates from the University of the Western Cape, Birmingham University and the Open University in England. He was appointed to chair the National Commission on Higher Education of South Africa in 1995, on whose report much of the *White Paper on Higher Education* and the Higher Education Act (No. 101 of 1997) are based. He also chaired the Task Team on Leadership, Governance and Management for the Twenty-year Review of Higher Education of the Council on Higher Education in 2013–14. He was appointed by the secretary general of the UN to serve on the Council of the UN University in Tokyo from 1998 to 2004. He was the director of the UN University International Leadership Institute in Amman from 2004 to 2008, and he was hired as a consultant by UNESCO and the World Bank to work on the restructuring of the higher education systems in Afghanistan (2009–2012) and Liberia (2011).

Jannie Rossouw is a visiting professor at Wits Business School at the University of the Witwatersrand, after a period of service as its interim head. He retired as a deputy general manager (Level 2) of the South African Reserve Bank (Head: Currency Management) in 2012. He is a political economist and consults on several economic issues and challenges in South Africa. He often comments in the print media and on radio and TV on economic matters and political developments. His recent publications include a chapter with Vishnu Padayachee on the independence of the South African Reserve Bank in *The Political Economy of Central Banking in Emerging Economies* (2021).

Joanne Rushby graduated from the University of Leeds with a BA (Hons) in modern Slavonic studies, and then started travelling the world, teaching English in Bulgaria and North Yemen for a number of years, before furthering her studies at the University of KwaZulu-Natal with an MSc in urban and regional development planning. Her real passion, however, is books, and having worked in bookshops and libraries in the UK, she has found her natural home at Ike's Books, managing the shop since 2000 and becoming the owner in 2014.

John Sender was the director of research for the Macroeconomic Research Group, which was based at the University of the Witwatersrand in 1992–93. He is now emeritus professor of economics at the School of Oriental and African Studies (SOAS), University of London. His earlier appointments include director of the African Studies Centre at the University of Cambridge and senior research fellow at the African Studies Centre, Leiden. He has been a consultant to the Office of the President in South Africa and Ethiopia, as well as consulting for the UN Food and Agriculture Organization and International Fund for Agricultural Development (Rome), the UN Research Institute for Social Development and International Labour Organization (Geneva), the UN Industrial Development Organization (Vienna) and the UN Development Programme (Vietnam).

Goolam Vahed teaches in the Department of History at the University of KwaZulu-Natal. He received his PhD from Indiana University. His research interests include identity formation, citizenship, migration and transnationalism among Indian South Africans, and the role of sport and culture in South African society. He has published numerous peer-reviewed journal articles, book chapters and books. His most recent work, co-authored with Ashwin Desai, is *Durban's Casbah: Bunny Chows, Bolsheviks and Bioscopes* (2023).

Imraan Valodia is a professor of economics, the pro vice chancellor for Climate, Sustainability and Inequality, and the director of the Southern Centre for Inequality Studies at the University of the Witwatersrand. He is a member of the Presidential Economic Advisory Panel, and he co-edited the acclaimed *Oxford Handbook of the South African Economy* (2022).

Robert van Niekerk is the professor and chair of public governance at the Wits School of Governance, University of the Witwatersrand. He has undertaken research, publication and teaching in the area of redistributive social policy with specific reference to the history of universalisation of public goods, in particular health and emancipatory thought and black intellectuals as this relates to social democracy, social citizenship and health care reform in South Africa. He is a co-author of *Shadow of Liberation: Contestation and Compromise in the Economic and Social Policy of the African National Congress* (with Vishnu Padayachee, 2019).

Edward Webster was professor emeritus in the School of Social Sciences and a research associate in the Southern Centre for Inequality Studies at the University of the Witwatersrand. His research centred on the world of work, labour movements and social inequality. In 2009, his book co-authored with Rob Lambert and Andries Bezuidenhout, *Grounding Globalisation: Labour in the Age of Insecurity*, was awarded the prestigious American Sociological Association award for the best scholarly monograph published on labour. His most recent work was *Recasting Workers' Power: Work and Inequality in the Shadow of the Digital Age* (2023).

Index

Abrahams, Peter 346
Abuja Treaty (1991) 244, 253
Academic Staff Association (UDW) 3, 47
Adams Bookshop 344-5, 348
Adelzadeh, Asghar 362
Afrapix 341
Africa
  development 170-1
  economic policy 240
  population 178
  regional integration 241, 242–3, 244, 245-6, 258, 259
African Centre for the Constructive Resolution of Disputes (ACCORD) 318
African Claims (1943) 191
African Common Market 243
African Continental Free Trade Area (AfCFTA) 238, 239, 246, 258, 259
African Development Bank (ADB) 243, 251
African Economic Community (AEC) 244, 245
African National Congress (ANC) 8, 18, 19, 20, 23, 110, 130-1, 145, 146, 147, 153, 157, 171, 172, 178, 185, 186, 189, 191, 199, 205, 207, 210, 220, 250, 255, 268, 279n.9, 289, 293-4, 302, 306-7, 313, 352, 354
African Union (AU) 172
Afrikanerdom 201

Agricultural Research Council 224
Aliwal Shoal (KZN) 27
Amahlongwa (KZN) 26
Amin, Samir 88-9
Amrah, Cassim 346
Anglo American Corporation 11, 125-7, 128, 131, 277
anti-apartheid resistance 285-7, 289-90, 299, 343-4, 348-9, 350, 351
antiretrovirals (ARVs) 220, 221, 222-3
apartheid 119, 120-1, 208, 312
Aristotle 76, 78
Asmal, Kader 317, 324
Aspenovax (drug) 227
Atlantic Charter (1941) 189
Attlee, Clement 182, 183
Augustine, Archie 295
autocracy 176

Bacher, Ali 374-5
Badsha, Ebrahim 342, 343, 347
Badsha, Nasima 347
Badsha, Omar 6, 341, 343, 344, 345, 346, 347-9, 380
Balintulo, Marcus 315, 323
banned literature 16-17, 346-7, 359
Bannon, Stephen 116
Bantu Education 190
bantustans 185, 186, 187, 191
Bawa, Ahmed 320
Baykedagn, Gebrehiwot 83, 86
Bell, Trevor 360
beneficiation *see* industrialisation

389

Bentham, Jeremy 78
Berg report (1981) 243-4, 260n.10
Berlin, Isaiah 92-3
Bhagwanjee, Anil 319
Bhana, Kasturi 47
Bhana, Surendra 47, 49
Bharuthram, K. 313
Bhengu, Sibusiso 323
Biko, Steve Bantu 91-2, 284, 293, 295, 296, 301-2, 305, 306, 308
Black, Anthony 51
Black Consciousness (BC) 7, 23, 91-2, 93, 284, 286, 293, 294-5, 301-2, 303-5, 306-7, 308
black economic empowerment 203
Black People's Convention (BPC) 303, 304, 305-6
Black Renaissance Convention 306, 307
Bodin, Jean 81, 83
Böhmke, Heinrich 19-20
Bond, Patrick 147
Botero, Giovanni 83, 85
Boyd, Leslie 129
Brain, Joy 49
Bretton Woods Agreement (1944) 60, 68, 69, 71, 201
Brimer, Alan 47
Broederbond 119
Brutus, Dennis 378
Bruwer, Andries Johannes 78-9, 95n.1
Buchanan, Patrick 113, 115
Bugwandeen, Rabi 306
Buthelezi, Mangosuthu 321, 322, 351, 369-70
Butler-Adam, John 42, 47, 48, 51, 316-17, 323
Buys, Jim 126

Callinicos, Alex 18
capitalism 85, 173, 174-5, 176, 198, 208
Carey, H.C. 86

Central American Common Market (CACM) 241-2, 259, 260n.7, 260n.8
central banks 70-1, 135, 138, 142, 149
Chamber of Mines 220
Cheadle, Halton 18
Chemical and Industrial Workers Union 45
Chetty, A.S. 306
Chetty, Dasarath 47
civil service 187, 188
civil society 22, 171, 172, 230-1, 268, 272, 275-6
Clansthal (KZN) 26-7
climate change 278
coalition politics 195
Coastal Group 169
Coetzee, J.M. 7, 14, 379
Colbert, Jean-Baptiste 84
Cold War 110, 112, 113, 114, 115, 120, 121, 176, 345
Coloured Representative Council 296
Combined Staff Association (COMSA, UDW) 3, 47, 48, 320, 321, 322, 323, 370
Common Market for Eastern and Southern Africa (COMESA) 245, 246, 259n.1
Common Monetary Area (CMA) 135, 138-9, 140-1, 142, 246
community participation 278
conflict resources 61-2
Congress Alliance 299
Congress of South African Trade Unions (COSATU) 19, 51, 130, 282, 285, 287, 288, 289, 290, 291n.2, 354-5
Constellation of Southern African States (CONSAS) 245, 248
Convention for a Democratic South Africa (CODESA) 185-6, 194
Cooper, Saths 294, 295, 302, 304, 305, 306, 308, 324
cooperatives 271, 272, 276

Coovadia, Jerry 302, 303, 306, 307
corruption 64, 158, 270, 274-5
Couzens, Tim 39
Covid-19 155-6, 158-9, 219, 222, 224, 225-8, 231n.7, 329
Cramer, Chris 361
Cresswell, Christopher 52
cricket 14, 53, 374-6
Cronin, Jeremy 277

Daniel, John 321
data quality 12, 100-1, 105, 329
David, Ben 295
Davies, Rob 18, 258-9
De Kock, G.P.C. 137
De Kock, Mike 136
De Santis, Marc Antonio 84-5
De Villiers, Henri 249
democracy 176, 177-8
Desai, Ashwin 19-20, 167, 320-1
destabilisation, Southern Africa 248
development studies 276
Dhlomo, H.I.E. 39
disengagement and disempowerment 213
Divine Life Society 30-1, 373
Docrat, A.K.M. 6, 18, 297-8, 309n.3, 341-3, 344, 345-6, 347-8, 351, 360
dollar (US) 69-70
Dravid, Rahul 378
Dube, Langa 301
Durban
  anti-apartheid resistance 6, 7
  moment 7, 18, 43, 54, 282-3, 285-7, 289-91, 351
  research on 51-2
  riots (1949) 299

East African Community 241, 242, 245, 259n.1
Eastern Cape 187, 191, 268-71
Economic Community for Central African States 243

Economic Community of West African States (ECOWAS) 243
economic integration 238-9, 259n.2
economic liberalism 85-6, 87
Economic Trends Group (ET) 19-20, 51, 209
education *see* social policy
engaged intellectuals 266-7, 276, 278
Enlightenment 86-7, 88, 89, 92, 93-4
Erwin, Alec 5, 18, 209, 218, 287-8, 381-2
Eskom 231n.11
European Union (EU) 238, 246, 256
exchange controls 127, 129
Extension of University Education Act (1959) 312, 313

Fallism 23, 42, 43
Federation of South African Trade Unions (FOSATU) 285, 287-8, 358-9
Femi, Dumile 345
Filatova, Irina 317
financial institutions 59, 70
financialisation 202-3
Fine, Ben 8, 205-6, 361, 382
First, Ruth 17, 23, 266, 273, 275, 276
fiscal policy 147, 149, 153, 155, 158, 159-60
Fischer's Bookshop (Durban) 346
Fisher, Fozia 283
food sovereignty 271
Foster, Joe 287-8, 291n.1, 358
Fourie, Louis 17
Freedom Charter 125, 183, 194, 296, 299, 303, 306
Freund, Bill 4, 48, 51, 52, 88, 359, 360-1, 362, 364, 366-7
Friedman, Steven 222
Fukuyama, Francis 89
fundamentalist religion 121-2

Gandhi, Indira 342, 349n.4
Gandhi, Mohandas 90, 91, 92, 307

Gandhi library (Durban) 344
Garvey, Marcus 90
Gautschi Commission of Inquiry into Management and Transformation Difficulties Experienced at the University of Durban-Westville (1996) 323
Gaza, Faith 321-2
Gelb, Steven 48, 51, 209
gender 110
Ghana 63-4, 65, 68
Gibbon, Trish 47, 48
Gilbertson, Brian 129
Ginwala, Korshed 344
Glaser, Daryl 19
globalisation 168, 175-6
Gluckman Commission on a National Health Service (1944) 192-3
Godongwana, Enoch 289
Goedhals, Mandy 49-50
gold 12, 59-60, 68-9, 70-1
gold mining 60-1, 62-7, 68
Goldman Sachs 177
Goniwe, Matthew 266
Govender, Maynard 371, 372n.1, 378
Govender, Nundgopaul (Ronnie) 40
Govender, Ramachandran 313
Govindsamy, Selva 323
Gramsci, Antonio 91, 111, 118, 352
Grey Street Casbah (Durban) 373
Greyling, J.J.C. (Jaap) 47, 313
Group Areas 300, 307-8, 347
Growth, Employment and Redistribution (GEAR) 9, 131, 146-8, 155, 156-7, 158, 188, 204, 208, 210, 254-5, 355
Gwala, Mafika 342, 345

Habib, Adam 167, 362
Hamann, Johann Georg 92-3
Hanekom, Derek 270
Hart, John Keith 362, 382
Hassim, Shireen 49

health sector, private 228-30, *see also* social policy
Herder, Johann Gottfried 92, 93
heterodox economics 123, 148, 151, 207-8, 210, 211, 212
Hindson, Doug 48, 51
Hindutva 112, 116, 119, 121
Hirsch, Alan 218
history, radical scholarship 49, 50
HIV/AIDS 19, 218-21
Hofmeyr, Jan 190
Holloway, John Edward (Jack) 77-8, 95n.1
Holloway Commission on Separate Training Facilities for Non-Europeans at Universities (1953) 312
Horn, Pat 45
Huddleston, Trevor 318
human commons 176
humanism 87

Ike's Books 6-7, 14, 365, 377, 378, 379
immunisation 226-7, 331n.10
Imperial (logistics firm) 227-8
imperialism and colonialism 84-5, 89-90
import-substituting industrialisation (ISI) 201-2, 224
Indian community 29-31, 33-4, 35-7, 38, 168-9, 297-9
Industrial Strategy Project (ISP) 208-10
industrialisation 83, 239, 241, 242, 243, 247-8, 253, 254, 256-7, 259
inflation 134-5, 137
informal sector 103
informal settlements 268-9
Inkatha Freedom Party 321, 352
Institute for Economic Justice (IEJ) 211
Institute for Social and Economic Research (ISER, UDW) 3, 51

Institute of Industrial Education (IIE, Durban) 283, 284, 351
intellectual life 5, 19-23
International Debating Society 345
International Monetary Fund (IMF) 77

Jacobsen, Robin 317
job creation 103
Johannesburg Stock Exchange (JSE) 127
Joshi, Ravi 18

Kajee, A.I. 346
Kani, John 318
Kaplinsky, Raphie 209
Kedourie, Elie 89-90, 91, 92
Kemmerer, Edwin 77
Kerdachi, Neville 167
Keynesian economics 12, 59, 69, 70, 76, 84, 92, 93-5, 172
Keys, Derek 354
King, Martin Luther 121
Krugerrands 63
Kunene, Masizi 26
Kuyper, Abraham 117, 119
Kuzwayo, Judson 284
Kwazakhele (Eastern Cape) 271, 272, 273, 274

labour regulations 129, 130
Lagos Plan of Action (LPA, 1980) 243, 244, 245, 253
Legassick, Martin 49, 50, 358
Lenin, Vladimir 85, 89
Liberal Study Group 346
Local Affairs Committees 296
Lucia, Christine 317
Luthuli, Nokukhanya 317

Maasdorp, Gavin 45
Mabhida, Moses 284
Macozoma, Saki 129
Macroeconomic Research Group (MERG) 8-9, 10, 12, 145-6, 148-50, 151-2, 153, 154, 156, 157, 187-8, 204, 205-6, 208, 210, 213, 218, 219, 222, 228, 230, 249, 250, 252, 253, 290, 356, 361-2
Makgoba, Malegapuru 54
Makoape, Aubrey 301
Mall, Hassan 316
Mandela, Nelson 125, 126, 129, 130, 145, 153, 178, 189, 199, 205, 206, 220, 252-3, 284, 314, 356
Mann, Chris 318
Manuel, Trevor 8, 102, 130, 131, 146, 147, 152, 153, 218
Manzi, Gladys 344
Maré, Gerry 361
Marxism 175
Maseko, Milos 44
Maslow, Abraham 283
maternity services 229
May, Julian 51, 166, 167, 365, 377
Mayet, Ike 6, 18, 166, 341, 342, 343, 344-5, 346, 347, 348, 360
Mayet, Rafique 344, 349n.3
Mbeki, Thabo 19, 102, 130, 131, 145, 172, 199, 205, 209, 220-1
Mboweni, Tito 127, 130, 153
McCarthy, Jeff 319
McGrath, Mike 45
Meer, Farouk 304, 305
Meer, Fatima 317
Meer, I.C. 346
Mehta, Harish 169, 170
mercentalism 76-7, 80-5, 86, 87-8
Mesthrie, Rajend 360, 383
Michie, Jonathan 362
minerals-energy complex 200, 201, 202, 209, 210, 211
Modi, Narendra 112
Mokaba, Peter 220
Mokoape, Aubrey 293
monetary policy 77, 355-6
Monetary Policy Committee (MPC) 137, 139, 142
Moodley, Perisamy (Perry) 40

Moodley, Poomani 344
Moodley, Priscilla 36
Moodley, Sam 294, 308
Moodley, Strini 294, 295, 296, 301, 302, 303-4, 306, 308
Morrell, Robert 47, 50-1, 364, 365, 383
Morris, Mike 48, 51, 52, 361, 362
Motala, Enver 6, 18, 46, 341, 342, 347, 348, 351, 360
Motala, Kulsum 18, 347, 360
multinationals 223
Mun, Thomas 81-2, 83-4, 85
Murray, Robin 209
Musk, Elon 177
Mxenge, Victoria 47

Naicker, Monty (Gangathura Mohamby) 39, 45
Naicker, M.P. (Marimuthu Pragalathan) 343-4, 346
Naidoo, C.S. 33, 36, 38
Naidoo, Dayanand 39, 45
Naidoo, D.M. 303
Naidoo, Jay 231n.5
Naidoo, M.D. 299-300
Naidoo, M.J. 306
Naidoo, Parvathy 36
Naidoo, Phyllis 343, 344, 347
Naidoo, Prem 47
Naidoo, R.C. 29-30, 33-4, 36, 38
Naidoo, Tej 39
Naidoo Memorial Primary School (Umkomaas) 33-4, 35-6, 55n.2
Naidu, Ambigay 36
Naina, Nash 295
Nair, Billy 298-9, 300, 301
Natal (colony) 50
Natal Indian Congress (NIC) 7, 46, 76, 293, 294, 296-7, 298, 300-1, 302, 303, 304, 305-6, 307-9, 346
national capitalism 10, 168, 171, 177

National Commission on Higher Education 323
National Council of Trade Unions (NACTU) 285
National Development Plan 210
National Economic Development and Labour Council (NEDLAC) 354
National Health Insurance (NHI) 11, 183, 192, 229
National Industrial Policy Framework (NIPF) 257, 259
national liberation *see* anti-apartheid resistance
national minimum wage 211
National Population Register (NPR) 225
National Union of Metalworkers of South Africa (NUMSA) 19, 288-9
National Union of Mineworkers 288
National Union of South African Students (NUSAS) 295
nationalism 12, 13, 19, 79-81, 89, 90-1, 92, 111-13, 117-19, 120, *see also* mercantilism
Naudé, Beyers 318
Ndebele, Sibusiso 317
Nelson Mandela Bay 274-5
Nelson Mandela Bay Transition Network 272
Nelson Mandela University 267-9
neoliberalism 8, 9, 10, 20, 110-11, 113-14, 116, 147, 149, 150-1, 152, 153, 155, 157-8, 160, 172, 173-4, 198-9, 200, 202, 203-4, 205, 207, 210, 211-12, 243-4
New Partnership for Africa's Development (NEPAD) 172-3
New Unity Movement 352
Ningi, 'Baba' 274-5
Nkrumah, Kwame 241, 242
non-racism 304, 306, 317
Nyerere, Julius 241, 242
Nzo, Alfred 249-50

Index 395

offshore listing 127-8, 130, 131
Old Mutual 128, 130, 131, 218
Olivier, S.P. 313
Oppenheimer, Ernest 126
Oppenheimer, Harry 126
Organization of African Unity (OAU) 242, 243, 249

Padayachee, Mahalutchmee (Leila, née Moodley) 30, 36
Padayachee, Mahavishnu Srinivasan (Vishnu)
Background
appearance and character 38, 182, 213, 218, 364, 365, 372
childhood 31-2, 33, 359
family 30-1
health 366, 371
at high school 34-5, 44
poetry and music 32, 38
and Tamil language 31
and Umkomaas 2, 3
Academia
degrees and awards 359
as historian 9, 13, 50, 58, 167, 364
and imperialism 76, 100
at ISER (UDW) 42, 48, 51, 359, 360
at Johns Hopkins University 17-18, 46, 48, 360
and Keynes 95
as lecturer and special adviser at UDW 3, 16-17, 45, 47-8, 321, 351, 358-9, 361, 369-70
and Marxism 76
as political economist 7-8, 9, 12-13, 16-17, 48-9, 54, 58, 109-10, 122, 123, 130, 135, 142, 145-6, 147-8, 150, 151-2, 154, 155, 157-8, 160, 164, 170, 183, 212, 239, 240, 355, 356, 359-60, 361, 364, 370-1, 378
research 48-9, 52, 53, 54, 364, 365-6

and Rhodes University 363, 370-1
at School of Development Studies (UND/UKZN) 4-5, 51, 53, 54, 106n.1, 164, 166, 167, 212, 362-3
as student 2-3, 39-40, 359
as supervisor 5, 370
and *Transformation* 260n.5, 281, 361
and universities 43, 366
and Wits 212, 281, 363-4
Politics
and ANC 52-3, 54, 55, 366, 367
and anti-apartheid politics 341, 348
and civil society 178-9, 195
world view 46
General
as a collector and at Ike's 6-7, 14, 164, 165, 166, 167, 364-5, 371, 376, 377, 378, 379
and Durban 10, 51-2, 164, 165-6, 363
intellectual life 1-2, 6, 19, 20, 212-13, 214, 350, 352, 356-7
and the SARB 53, 134-5, 167, 212, 213, 356, 367, 378
and sport 4, 34-5, 37-8, 53, 166, 363, 365, 366, 373-5, 378-9
and trade unions 45-6, 76, 351, 354
Padayachee, R.N. (Nadaraj) 30, 36, 373
Padayachee, R.S. (Satchie, 'Mayor') 36-7, 373
Padayachee, R.V. (Vasu) 37, 373
Padayachee, Sonali 366, 371
Padayachee, Srinivasan Ramsamy 30-1, 36
Pahad, Essop 18
Pan Africanist Congress (PAC) 293-4, 303-4, 307, 370
Pan-Africanism 171, 172, 174, 241
Paparam, Raj 306
Parekh, Angina 48
Pather, Dennis 295

Paton, Alan 295
Peters, Melvin 317
Petty, William 84, 85
Pillay, Kriba 295
Pillay, Rajen 169, 170
Pillay, Vella 8, 146, 152, 204, 206, 214n.7, 218, 318, 361
Pityana, Barney 295, 306
Plato 76, 78
Polanyi, Karl 77, 96n.2
population growth 178
populism 12, 111, 112-13
post-modernism 88-9
poverty and inequality 103-5, 128-9, 150, 283, 287
Prebisch, Raúl 241

Quinlan, Tim 51

Rabjohn, Ernest 344
Ram, Deepak 317
Ramabali, Asha 308
Ramaphosa, Cyril 199, 211, 220
Ramashala, Mapule 323-4
Rambachan, B.C. 29
Rambally, Asha 295
Ramesar, Ramlal 303
Ramgobin, Mewa 294, 296, 297, 300, 304-5
Ramphele, Mamphela 128, 301-2
Rappa gold refinery 63
Ready to Govern conference (1992) 355
reason 87, 88, 94
Reconstruction and Development Programme (RDP) 153-5, 160, 188, 204, 253-4, 255, 257, 269, 354-5, 356
Reddy, Enuga 317, 318
Reddy, Jairam 4, 47, 314-15, 317, 320-1, 323, 361, 384
Reddy, Kogs 294
Reddy, Vino 295

regional integration, Southern Africa 238-40, 249-52, 253, 254, 255-6, 257-8
regional value chains (RVCs) 238, 256, 257, 259
Relly, Gavin 125, 126
renewable energy 271, 272, 273-4, 277
research
  participatory action 267-8, 273, 276, 277
  progressive 6, 52, 53, 54
Rethinking Economics for Africa 211
Ricardo, David 78-9
Rojava (Syria) 266, 275
Rosholt, A.M. 318
rugby 374, 375
Rushby, Joanne 167, 365, 377, 378, 385

Sachs, Jeffrey 127
Saltuba cooperative (Kwazakhele) 272, 273-4, 275
SASOL 200
Saul, John 51
School of Development Studies (SDS, UN/UKZN) 4-5, 362-3
School of Oriental and African Studies (SOAS, London) 210
Sechaba 344, 349n.6
Seedat, Y.K. 318
seigniorage 135-6, 138, 139-41, 142
Sender, John 8, 361, 385
Sewpersadh, George 297, 303, 304, 307
Shaik, Mo 321
Shepstone, Theophilus 27
Simons, Jack 17
Simons, Ray 17
Singh, Mala 47, 48
Singh, Narend 36, 40
Slabbert, Frederik van Zyl 370
Smit, Dan 48

Smith, Adam 78, 82, 84
Smuts, Jan 189, 192, 193
social policy 184-7, 188-94
Soni, Dhiru 321
South Africa
  competitiveness 168
  doctoral graduates 224
  elections 308-9
  foreign policy 252-3
  mortality rate 218-20, 224-6, 231n.2
  post-apartheid scenarios and economy 110, 125-6, 127, 128-30, 131-2, 208
  provinces 185-7, 191, 192-3
South Africa Foundation 129, 130
South African Committee on Higher Education (SACHED) 360
South African Communist Party (SACP) 178-9, 204, 289
South African Democratic Students Movement (SADESMO) 321, 369-70
South African History Online 341
South African Indian Council 296
South African Industrial Cellular Corporation (SAICCOR) 26, 43-4
South African Labour Bulletin 283
South African Pulp and Paper Industries (SAPPI) 26
South African Reserve Bank (SARB) 13, 77, 134, 135, 136-7, 138, 139, 141, 142, 147, 153, 204, 361, 362
South African Students Congress (SASCO) 266-7, 321, 370
South African Students Organisation (SASO) 295, 303
Southern African Customs Union (SACU) 246, 247-8, 249, 253, 254, 255, 256, 258
Southern African Development Community (SADC) 172, 241, 245, 246, 248, 249, 250, 252, 254, 255, 256-7, 259n.1
Southern Centre for Inequality Studies (Wits) 364
Spicer, Michael 126, 127, 128, 130
Stals, Chris 250
state institutions 83-4
Stewart, Malcolm 323
Strachan, Harold 347
struggle *see* anti-apartheid resistance
sugar industry 27, 28, 29
Sunter, Clem 126
Sustainable Settlement Pilot Project (SSPP) 268-71, 272, 276, 278
Sutcliffe, Michael 317, 320-1
Suttner, Raymond 19
Suzman, Helen 295
Szanton, David 365

tariffs 202, 255, 256, 257
technology 276-7
Terreblanche, Sampie 147
thymos 89
Tichman, Paul 46, 359, 364
Tobias, Phillip 318
Trade Policy and Strategy Framework 257
trade unions 18, 22, 282, 284-5, 286, 287-9, 351-4
traditional medicine 221-2, 226
Trahar, Tony 130
Transformation 52, 361
Transition Township project 271, 272-4, 275, 276, 277, 278
Trikamjee, Ashwin 302
Tripartite Alliance 129-30, 199, 204-5, 282, 289, 290
Tripartite Free Trade Area (TFTA) 238, 246, 258, 259n.1
Trumpism 112, 113, 114-17, 119-20, 122
Turner, Rick 18, 23, 54, 266, 283, 345, 351, 358
Tutu, Desmond 91

Umkhonto we Sizwe (MK) 289
Umkomaas
  history 25-6, 27-8, 43-4
  Indian community 29-31, 33-4, 35-7, 38
  Italian community 26, 43, 44
  name 27, 40n.2
  race relations 44
  Zulu community 26, 33
unemployment 101-3, 105, 106n.2, 150, 151, 152
Union of Democratic Staff Associations 48
United Democratic Front (UDF) 42, 46
United Nations Economic Commission for Africa (UNECA) 241, 242, 243, 249
Universal Printing 169-70
universities
  councils 313-14
  culture of 53-4
  financial efficiency 328, 329-30, 336-8
  graduation rates 5, 332-5
  legislation 312
  and progressive intellectuals 20-1, 22
  research 330-2, 339n.2
University College (Salisbury Island, Durban) 313
University of Durban-Westville (UDW)
  council 324, 370
  departments and institutes 49-50, 318, 319, 325
  finance 322-3
  history 3-4, 16, 313-26
  research 320
  staff 47-8, 316
  students 46-7, 316, 321, 325
  transformation 324-5, 369, 370
University of KwaZulu-Natal (formerly Natal) 54, 167, 312, 322-3, 324, 325, 326, 363

University of South Africa (UNISA) 313
University of the Witwatersrand (Wits) 312

Vahed, A.S. 318
Validation Clearance Bureau 167
Valodia, Imraan 17, 51, 386
Van der Walt, A.J.H. 313
Van Niekerk, Robert 362, 386
varieties of capitalism (VoC) 109-10, 122-3, 281-2
Vaughan, Anne 51
Vawda, Shahid 46, 50, 359, 364
Venketas, Chundra 35, 40
Venter, Rina 193

Webster, Eddie 19, 281, 282-3, 284, 386
Weir, Gillian 317
Wilson, Jeya 317
Wilson, Woodrow 86
Wolpe, Harold 18, 23, 49, 50, 214n.3, 358
workerism 352
World Bank 150, 153, 210, 243-4, 249, 251, 256
World Trade Organization 238

Xulu, Musa 317
Xuma, Alfred Bitini 189, 191

*zama zama*s 60, 61, 62, 65, 66
Zartman, William 17
Zuma, Jacob 19, 112, 183, 199, 194, 259, 344
Zweledinga (Eastern Cape) 268-70

Printed and bound by CPI Group (UK) Ltd, Croydon, CR0 4YY
22/04/2026

14866399-0001